CLOUDLESS MIND

Volume 2

CLOUDLESS MIND

Conversations on Buddhahood

with

Daniel P. Brown, PhD

SENTIENT PUBLICATIONS

First Sentient Publications edition 2025

Transcribed and edited by: Susan Pottish and Scott V. Anderson MD

A paperback original
Book design and cover design by Laura Waltje

Library of Congress Control Number: 2024952907
Publisher's Cataloging-in-Publication Data

Names: Brown, Daniel P., 1948-2022, author.

Title: Cloudless mind : conversations on Buddhahood , volume 2 / with Daniel P. Brown, PhD.

Description: Includes bibliographical references. | Boulder, CO: Sentient Publications, LLC, 2025.

Identifiers: LCCN: 2024952907 | ISBN: 9781591813545 (vol. 1) | 9781591813569 (vol. 2) | 9781591813583 (vol. 3)
Subjects: LCSH Buddha (The concept) | Buddhahood. | Buddhism. | Meditation--Buddhism. | Spiritual life--Buddhism. | BISAC RELIGION / Buddhism / Tibetan | BODY, MIND & SPIRIT / Mindfulness & Meditation | PSYCHOLOGY / Psychotherapy / Spiritually Integrated
Classification: LCC BQ7612 .B76 2025 v. 2 | DDC 294.3/923--dc23

Printed in the United States of America
10 9 8 7 6 5 4 3 2 1

Sentient Publications
A Limited Liability Company
PO Box 1851
Boulder, CO 80306
www.sentientpublications.com

Contents

May the knowledge, guidance, and wisdom shared by Dan Brown in this collection be helpful to all in understanding their path to wellbeing and freedom in this life.

Editor's Foreword

Daniel P. Brown, PhD was known professionally as Doctor Brown, but in his interactions with students and colleagues, as in the question-and-answer sessions making up this book, he was always addressed simply as Dan. He spent forty-six years as a clinical psychologist, and researcher; he was also an expert witness on trauma and the veracity of children's memories and testified in courts across the U.S. as well as at War Crimes Tribunals in eastern Europe. This deep expertise gave him a unique perspective on and a depth of knowledge of human potential—both positive and negative. His forty-five years as an authorized teacher of Buddhist practices to Westerners gave him an opportunity to integrate his psychological knowledge with the wisdom of the Buddhist path to spiritual awakening. The ultimate principle guiding him, in all areas in which he worked, was to enhance the wellbeing of others.[1]

In 2008 Dan began inviting students, friends, and associates to join him at a meeting room in a small two-story building in Newton Center, Massachusetts, to explore spiritual and psychological understandings of healing, positive growth potential, and flourishing for human beings, including the path to spiritual awakening and enlightenment as presented in Tibetan Buddhism and as Dan had been teaching for decades by then. The recordings of these sessions by students began in 2012.

---

1 For a fuller picture of Dan's work over the years, please see his biography and C.V. at the end of the book.

There were no guidelines given for questions. People were invited to ask questions about "whatever." Thus, neither Dan nor anyone else knew what the topics would be on any given night, and yet Dan often gave his answers to the myriad subjects raised in rather astonishing detail.

The pointing-out style of teaching that Dan developed was not something he did on his own. First, at the direction of H. H. the Dalai Lama, Dan hiked to a remote area of Tibet and sat with a yogi practitioner who demonstrated "rainbow body" (physically dissolving into light and then reappearing) to Dan, while describing in words what he was doing at each stage of the way. The yogi also told him specifically never to practice or teach what he saw. The question in Dan's mind remained, "Why did His Holiness send me there? What was I supposed to learn?" After nearly two years, he understood that the benefit of that encounter was to have the experience of learning from a teacher who was teaching him by "pointing out" each stage of a practice. After that, and after fifteen years of teaching meditation in the traditional manner with Denma Locho Rinpoche, a high lama in the Gelugpa lineage (assigned to teach with Dan by H. H. the Dalai Lama), Dan proposed an innovative method using "pointing out" instructions when they taught together to increase efficacy in learning by students. The increased efficacy was demonstrated so well to Denma Locho Rinpoche that he gave Dan permission to continue teaching in that pointing out way on his own. (Dan published *Pointing Out the Great Way: The Stages of Meditation in the Mahāmudrā Tradition* in 2006 as an homage to his teachers.)

In 2009 Dan partnered with his longtime spiritual friend, Rahob Tulku Rinpoche, and they agreed that Dan would prepare students for the higher transmissions to be given by Rinpoche. Rahob Tulku was viewed by H.H. the Dalai Lama as an emanation of Guru Padmasambhava for our time. Although living quietly at a small center in Petersburg, New York, Rinpoche became well-known and beloved by many of Dan's students as he met them individually to give them guidance in their practice either in retreats with Dan or at his small center in upstate New York. When Dan mentions "Rinpoche" in the Wednesday Night talks, it is Rahob Tulku Rinpoche to whom he is referring.

Also, Dan made it clear that he would never teach alone, meaning he was always overseen and held accountable by a lineage master. While he often had to be the sole teacher at his retreats, he preferred to have a co-teacher whenever possible. There were multiple reasons for this, including the understanding that teaching by oneself could easily lead to a sense of "self-importance," which, in

Dan's view, was a disastrous failing.[2] Thus he taught his wife, Gretchen Nelson (a physical therapist and yoga teacher), to teach his pointing-out way, and they taught together internationally for nearly thirteen years.

His commitment to being accountable and overseen expanded later when Dan discovered and began studying and practicing teachings from the Bon tradition that preceded Buddhism in Tibet. At that time, Dan became a heart-student of H.H. the 33rd Menri Trizin, whom Dan recognized as his Root Lama in 2014 and who encouraged Dan both to teach and to translate texts never translated before into English. This he did in collaboration with Geshe Sonam Gurang, a Bon Geshe also accountable to H.H. Menri Trizin.

Because Wednesday Night sessions rarely focused on a single topic, the titles given to each chapter in this collection consist simply of the date each took place and a subheading of "themes," attempting to capture something of the range of that evening's questions and answers. Also, as the talks often included conversation, the conversational style has been preserved throughout, with no attempt to edit Dan or questioners into something like "written" material. On occasion, if it seemed like Dan left out a word accidentally or because a word was inaudible on the tape, the most likely missing word has been put in brackets [like this] or indicating a group response like [Laughter]. Also, because the names of people asking questions were mostly inaudible or unknown, the people who asked questions are identified simply as Student 1, Student 2, etc.

When Dan does mention someone's name, it has been changed to honor their privacy.

On another slightly technical note, Dan often used Tibetan words in his responses to people, particularly when explicating the Tibetan Buddhist interpretation of a given topic. Instead of using a formal glossary that gives Wylie transliterations (which does not convey pronunciation), the approach chosen here was to give the best phonetic rendering of the words Dan spoke as heard on the recordings, just as he said them.

---

2 He cited the declaration by one of the early Christian Desert Fathers that self-importance, or pride, was "the eighth deadly sin." Nevertheless, several of Dan's students, both in the U.S. and abroad, have chosen to teach on their own. Dan would not have approved of this, giving his wife, Gretchen Nelson, sole authority to train and approve new teachers. For information on approved teachers, please contact admin@pointingoutthegreatway.com.

Another aspect of Dan's later work included pioneering neuroscientific research using EEG measures in relation to levels of mind. His goal was not to show that the brain was the cause or the source of mind nor of its awakening, but rather to show that as awakening progresses there are also detectable changes in the brain's activity. Some thirty of his students were assessed by Dan and an assistant teacher for their capacity to shift into and out of a number of what he called the "basis of operation," or well-established and continuous states of mind, including "awakened awareness," and then, in a laboratory environment, participants underwent brainwave evaluation while making those shifts.

This research was sponsored by the Fetzer Foundation and performed in the neuroscience lab of Judson Brewer, MD PhD in Boston at UMass Medical School. (See the Wednesday night talk #65 of July 19, 2017 for a basic description of the study.) The results reported by Dan were "stellar" because they showed uniquely high levels of activation of specific centers in the brain when the subject shifted through levels of mind they had learned from Dan, and most especially when shifting to the level of awakened awareness.

To our knowledge, this kind of research had never been done before. In a meeting to review the results of the study, a representative of the Fetzer Foundation and a representative of the National Academy of Sciences found the outcomes to be highly valuable and worthy of further research funding. Unfortunately, that additional research didn't happen because the lab was closed during the Covid pandemic, and Dan passed away in April of 2022.

It has recently come to our attention that there are several new initiatives in contemplative neuroscience (CN) to investigate deeper levels of practice than have been the focus (of CN) previously. Among these initiatives are the Harvard Meditation Research Project,[3] and the initiatives reported in a recent article in *Scientific American*—"Advanced Meditation Alters Consciousness and our Basic Sense of Self"[4]—that provides a link to Dan's innovative study.

In the Wednesday night conversations, Dan describes steps, stages, levels, and ranges of spiritual development. He describes the spiritual path according

---

3 Mass General Meditation Research. "Research." Massachusetts General Hospital. https://meditation.mgh.harvard.edu/research/.

4 Zanes, Anna. "Advanced Meditation Alters Consciousness and Our Basic Sense of Self." Scientific American, Joe 24, 2024. https://www.scientificamerican.com/article/advanced-meditation-alters-consciousness-and-our-basic-sense-of-self/.

to three progressive maps, with explicit instructions along the way, and also warning practitioners against trying to jump ahead. He made it clear that just because the map is there, if a particular location is not where you are, it's better that you don't focus on that location. Why? Because if you're not there yet, you will be thinking about it, using ideas, images, or concepts; and such thinking about it, he says, actually hardens the mind and makes it more difficult to experience awakening. So, even though Dan discusses the full range of experiences, it is not to encourage people to imagine them, but rather to know that there is a path that leads to their natural and spontaneous appearance.

Finally, at the start of each Wednesday night meeting, Dan would routinely ask for people attending for the first time to identify themselves and speak a bit about how and why they came to the meeting. Sometimes those conversations went on for quite a while. Then, at the end of the introductions, Dan would clarify for everyone the purpose and structure of the meeting, which was, first, to create a completely open forum for questions that anyone might have about literally anything; and second, once the question and answer period was over, there would be a bathroom break and people would reassemble for a guided meditation—what Dan called "meditation improv"—in which he created on the spot a novel guided meditation to give people some direct experience of what had been spoken about earlier in the evening. (Those meditations were not transcribed and thus are not part of this collection.)

Because the opening conversations were often personal, and also repetitive, rather than repeat the introductory descriptions by Dan for each Wednesday Night meeting, one very simple version has been included at the beginning of each talk, namely, "Welcome everybody. You have a question?"

The reason there is no introduction for the first talk presented in this text is that on that particular occasion Dan did something unusual, introducing the topic for the night without asking for questions, and then offering a summary of the Buddhist path to enlightenment. While not planned by anyone, of course, it does seem to be a wonderful introduction in this publication to the scope and depth that Dan presents throughout the Wednesday Night talks, and thus also seems a perfect opening. We hope you will delight in the experientially derived scope and depth of Dan's unique integration of Eastern Wisdom traditions and Western psychology.

Susan Pottish & Scott V. Anderson, M.D.

December 10, 2014

Themes: Empathy and Compassion; Common Humanity Practice

Dan

Welcome everyone. You have a question?

Student 1

Just a question about the distinction between how the teachings and the practice deal with the difference between empathy and compassion.

Dan

Oh, okay. There's a Western and an Eastern answer to that. So, I'll give you each. Empathy has to do with perspective-taking. And, when we are being empathic, we try to feel our way into the other's experience, as if that were our own experience. We take the perspective as if that happened to us, what would we be experiencing? And you feel your way into it. And, that will evoke, hopefully, a set of feelings that resonate with what that person experiences, if we're accurate in our empathy. Specifically, it has to do also with [how] when we are being empathic, it will also evoke similar or comparable experiences within ourselves.

So, if something happens to you where you feel hurt in a certain way by someone, and you were talking to me about it, I could take the perspective as if that happened to me. And probably I could scan my entire data base of experiences, and I could probably find some experience that was like that, similar enough to it that it evokes comparable feelings within me. At that point I would be empathic, and I would be resonating with your experience based on some similar experience within myself.

Now, the neurobiology of perspective taking is that this is part of the right [inferior] parietal system, the lower part of the parietal system of the brain. There's a number of functions that go on there. And, in primates, the parietal system has to do with anticipating potential location and movement in space at high speeds. So, if I were using a tachistoscope and flashing little blips on the screen at different locations, in thousandths of a second, your capacity to recognize where it might come up on the screen next, that would activate that right inferior parietal system, the lower part of it.

That part of it, the inferior parietal system, is well developed in primates. That's why a monkey can grab a banana out of the air jumping from one tree to another tree at a high speed. And a baseball player who's trying to locate the ninety-five miles per hour fastball that's coming across the plate in four hundred milliseconds, that's why he can do that. Because if he activates that area of the brain, it will allow him to locate that event with awareness, not with thought, at very high speeds, the same way the monkey grabs the banana off the tree branch while he's jumping through the air.

Humans have that, not as well developed as primates, but it's there. Only on top of that, humans have other aspects of the parietal system. One aspect has to do with self-agency. So, when you feel like an effective agent in doing things in the world, and when you feel like you are getting others to continually respond to what you're doing—in other words if you feel like you're shaping somebody else's behavior—you're activating another part of the parietal system that has to do with the sense of perceived agency that we have in the world and the world of others.

Another aspect of the parietal system has to do with perspective-taking. So, when you shift in meditation from the mind perspective to the event perspective, when you shift from one perspective to the other, as you learned in the retreat, you're using the perspective part of the parietal system. When you are being empathic about somebody else's experience and you're taking a perspective that something like that might have happened to you so you can resonate with it, you're activating the same part of the parietal system, involved in switching from mind to event perspective. That's the perspective part.

And another aspect of the parietal system, which is really interesting, has to do with span of apprehension, or how much we take in of the world. So, dissociative, traumatized dissociative patients who have non-epileptic seizures—where there's nothing wrong with the brain but they have seizure-like activity, and they're sort of out of it for five to ten minutes—the part of their parietal system that has to do with awareness of the surroundings is temporarily shut off. So, they're literally out of it and nonresponsive. Even though there's nothing wrong with that part of the brain.

And there's right next door, there's another part of the parietal system that has to do with shifting from local to globalized awareness and vice versa. So, when you shift out of individual consciousness to awakened awareness, you activate that part of the parietal system. And it's not an accident that when you set up your instructions for awakening, it has to do with taking a perspective about the nature of space and the vastness of space, and then orients you toward that space, because all of that is built upon this foundation of spatializing. They're all interconnected.

Except humans can do things that primates can't do—they can become awakened. They can be empathic. So, that's empathy. You activate something in your own experience and take the perspective of what the other's experience is, like what you went through, so you can resonate emotionally with that empathic behavior.

In Western terms, in psychotherapy, we use the word "compassion" for situations in which you can't be empathic because you can't activate something from your own experience. I spent the first ten years of my professional clinical life doing psychotherapy with psychotic patients. I've never been schizophrenic, although some of you might think I am. [Laughter] And maybe some days I think I am. But I don't think that's the case. So, when I sat with the schizophrenic patients and they would talk in ways where their thinking was disordered, sometimes very difficult to follow, or they would hear voices, or they would, with great fear, have some delusion that somebody was following them—the CIA was following them, which may be true. [Laughter] So, when they had psychotic-like symptoms, I can't empathize with that, because there's nothing I can find in my experience like that. I've never heard voices, except my dog. [Laughter] Okay, I've never heard voices, I've never had delusions of being followed by anyone, I've just had actual experiences … [Loud laughter]

And since during the Bobby Kennedy assassination stuff, it's turned out to be true—they aren't delusions. And I've never had disordered thinking. So, you see, when I sit with a psychotic patient, I can't find—I can't evoke anything in my regular experience that resonates with that in a way that I can empathically feel into that.

So, that requires something beyond empathy. And it was best described by the Western philosopher Paul Ricoeur, a French philosopher, who, as a hermeneutic philosopher, did extensive studies of psychoanalysis. And he called it "adopting the second naïveté." And what he meant by that is when you sit with somebody who's had those experiences you cannot be empathic about because you can't find anything in your own field of experience like that, then you have to put the mental work into trying to act as if that were your field of experience and feel your way into it. It's much harder to do. It means a kind of listening that goes beyond just trying to conjure something up in your own experience that matches, because match isn't going to work.

So, you really have to work at getting into what phenomenologists used to call "the structure of the mind of the other." And then allowing yourself the mental work of imagining what it might be like to experience a delusion that someone is following you and how terrifying that would be, if that were the case. Or what it would be like to hear a voice, and what the experience of that might be. Or to watch your mind get disorganized and not know what's happening.

And then, in just the same way that you reflectively listen with empathy, you can do that with a compassionate response. You can say out loud to the psychotic patient, "This is what I think it might be like for you—help me to understand it more." And you make a rough attempt, even though you can never resonate with it, to match.

So, in our daily life in the West, when people have experiences beyond what we have, we can only make a rough attempt to match. Mostly that means that you try, and the person thinks that you're there; they perceive you as trying to be there along with them. And that's a good enough response. It's not perfect, but the more you're working at it, the more they're going to take that as compassionate.

And it's not limited to psychosis. If you're sitting with somebody who has some extreme trauma, if they're a victim of domestic violence or a victim of rape, and that's not something that you've ever experienced, you have to feel along with them what that might be like. And imagine it as much as you possibly can and invite them to tell you what it's like. And somewhere, in between the two of you, if you really work hard, with that second naïveté, you say, "I'll act as if I could figure this out, even though it's beyond my experience;" with that work, and doing that together, somewhere in that "between space," as Winnicott used to call it, you find a match that's good enough. But it's not empathic, you follow me?

Student 1

Yes.

Dan

And both of those perspectives on empathy and compassion in the West are very strongly relationally based. It has to do with the nature of the here and now relationship.

Now in the East, at least in Buddhism—they're different in different traditions—it means two things: There's a generic term, and there's a specific term. Generally, compassion is a category or a generic category for the broad things that we do in response to other beings. And under that, there's two types of compassion. One is called compassion, and what it means is a response to suffering. And it's very specific. And the Tibetan, or generally Buddhist, Indo-Tibetan Buddhist use of compassion—and all Theravādin use of compassion is very similar—is that when you're being compassionate, you are being responsive to, specifically, the suffering of another. It's all about suffering.

Now, in Buddhism that version of compassion is part of a larger set of practices called the Four Immeasurables. And it was first a practice that came up in the older Theravādin Buddhism. And the first … there's a sequence to it. And the practices are loving-kindness, compassion for the suffering of others, sympathetic joy, and equanimity.

And loving-kindness means the generation of the impulse to be kind towards others—"random acts of kindness." You generate kindness towards all others because it's a good thing to do.

Second is compassion, which specifically means compassion of not just being kind but being resonant, responsive to their suffering. Compassion is always about suffering, very specifically.

The third is sympathetic joy. And sympathetic joy, we don't have a term for it in the West; I like it a lot. And it's actively cultivating a joy towards others' gain. It's the positive opposite of competition and jealously. So, if you're sitting in your meditation retreat and people are talking and sharing their experience and you're sitting there and everyone's getting it on, and you're the only one that's not going to get anywhere, and you're feeling angry and jealous of all the people because their meditations obviously are far superior to yours, and you're the only one lagging behind, that's not sympathetic joy. [Laughter]

And even if you're lagging behind, at that point you say, "Hey, you know what, I'm really happy that that person's getting it. I wish I could do it too, but you know, maybe I can learn something from their getting it. And even if I don't, I'm really happy that they're getting it. Because if more people get it, then it's good for all of us." That's sympathetic joy.

Now, equanimity means being impartial towards all beings, and nonreactive. And what's interesting is, the original list, the Theravādin, the old lists, where the Four Immeasurables were developed, shortly after the time of Shakyamuni, equanimity is last on the list. After you go through all of those, you try to do it impartially towards all beings. But, when the Mahāyāna took over the Four Immeasurables, they put equanimity first on the list. Why do you think they changed the order?

Student 2

Universality.

Dan

Because you can't really do this from a self-perspective. What you find in the Mahāyāna that's unique to the Mahāyāna is emptiness of self. If you try and be kind, and you do it in selective ways that feed the needs of the self, it's just self-reinforcement. It's not selfless love. If you try and be compassionate but you do it to make yourself feel good about yourself, that's not ultimate compassion. We've destroyed entire cultures in the same way, in the name of compassion. We call it "missionary behavior." And the arrogance that thinks that other cultures need what we have, and ours is better, and it's okay to destroy dying cultures over that, that all comes from self and self-importance.

But, if you are practicing compassion from the selfless perspective, then it's impartial. We say that ultimate compassion is like the sun. When you practice ultimate compassion, because it never comes from self, it spreads impartially towards all beings. The sun doesn't decide where to shine its rays; it shines its rays towards everyone equally. When you practice ultimate compassion without self, we say that it's—that compassion is "inexhaustible." There's no self to have compassion fatigue. You don't get caught up in it, there's no reactivity. So, it just is, which is the ultimate expression of realization.

So, what the Mahāyānas did is they took the Four Immeasurable and basically changed the order so that equanimity came first. So, that all the other three Immeasurables are practiced from the perspective of emptiness of self. And it's never about self. It's cleaner.

Now, the other practice in Mahāyāna Buddhism, the second kind of compassion, is called "compassion with respect to common humanity." And there you take the perspective that all beings have the same basic set of concerns, wishes, wants, desires out of life, motivations. We all want to be happy; we all want happiness for ourselves, our family, and our friends. We all want to be healthy. We want our family and friends to be healthy. Even our worst enemies want the same things in life. We want a better life. As Westerners being targeted by terrorists, terrorists want a better life. Their fundamental needs are no different from our own. We just disagree on how to go about it.

But there's no difference. So, we have to remember the common humanity that we all share. If you were trapped in a prison cell for months, with little food, you would suffer greatly from that. But we forget what it must have been like for Saddam Hussein to live underground for six months, hiding, with almost no food, and no place to go to the bathroom. His final months were not very pleasant, I'm sure. But because he's an "evil person" in our eyes, it's hard to step back and look at what he might have wanted as the same thing we all want which is basic comfort in life, and not that enormous suffering. That doesn't excuse his actions. But if you take a wider perspective, we all want the same things; there are no differences.

And as the Dalai Lama says, "When we practice common humanity, common humanity means that every person is deserving of the same dignity and respect just by virtue of being human." And when you practice common humanity, the most important part of that is to practice a kind of presence—that everybody in your interpersonal field is acknowledged. The traditional practice of that, as you know from the Level 1 course, is *manam*, the Mother of All Beings. In Tibetan practice, the epitome of selfless, giving human love is a mother's love towards her child. The mother gives everything of herself. She gives her body, she gives her sleep, she gives all of her time to raise this little being.

There's very few other instances in life that require that kind of self-sacrifice, to raise a young child.

And they see that as the epitome of selfless human love that cherishes another being. So, the visualization practice of common humanity is, you imagine your mother's experience, your mother's selfless love towards you and all that you got from that, until you familiarize yourself with that state. Then you imagine giving that same kind of selfless love to a child, in a similar way. Then you imagine giving that same kind of—generating that state, and bringing that same kind of selfless, nurturing mother love to relationships that you're close with, and to relationships where you have difficulty. Watch how it changes it. And then you imagine what it's like to bring that into relationship with all the people you don't know that come into your personal view.

The epitome of the practice of *manam*, common humanity, is to carry about a continuous presence all day long, that you acknowledge in your awareness all the people that go through your interpersonal field that normally go unnoticed, and you put the intention into try and develop your awareness towards all the forgotten people that pass unnoticed.

Some people do that naturally. And some people cultivate that as a practice. I once asked my first Root Lama, Geshe Wangyal, towards the end of his life, I said, "What's the hardest practice you ever did?" And without any hesitation he said, "Treating every person impartially. Liking everybody the same." Because we don't do that. Social psychologists tell us that we decide within three seconds of meeting a person whether we dislike them, like them, or are neutral about them; and we rarely change after that.

And it's based on nothing about the interaction. So, we're sort of a flawed species that way. We make these snap judgments, and we stay by them. How many people did we decide we're neutral towards or dislike that we would never take in to really know, that might be really interesting beings in our life?

Now, if you practiced *manam*, or Mother of All Beings, you'd go about with the view that everybody you come in contact with at some time in your life—in these many millions of lifetimes we go through—everybody that you come in contact with at some time was your mother and you were their mother. And you take the view that you are their nurturing selfless mother. So, you are charged with the duty of the growth and development of all beings. That's the lofty goal of the Mahāyāna view.

And those who do that well, their spontaneous behavior is different from other people. Because what it shows is that they notice others better. So, not this time that the Dalai Lama was just here, but sometime ago in the early 2000s, I don't remember exactly when it was, I forget the date, but there was a three-day Mind & Life science conference here on neuroscience and the brain, the mind and the brain—a Buddhist dialogue with the Dalai Lama and neurobiology.

The Dalai Lama was staying at the Charles Hotel, and he got up in the morning to go to this talk and he opened his door, and outside the door was a woman with a cart, a cleaning lady. And he went over to her and said, "Where are you from?" And in broken English she talked about where she came from, I forget where that was, and he said, "Well, that's interesting, I've never been there before. Tell me what it was like to grow up there." And he spent some time and care showing genuine interest. Why? Because she was in his interpersonal field, and therefore she deserved the dignity and respect that he would give to anybody in this shared view of common humanity. And the next morning he got up to go to his talk again and he opened the door and all the cleaning ladies [Laughter] for the entire Charles hotel were there, and he stopped and talked with all of them. Because they were in his interpersonal field.

And he was here a couple of weeks ago and some of us went to [his event]. He takes a long time to get up to the stage because everybody who's standing there, including all the Tibetans who never have any contact with him, he stops and acknowledges each one of them, because they're in his interpersonal field, and they deserve dignity and respect. So, it matters. So, that's common humanity.

Now, in Buddhism, so far as I understand, and maybe I'm wrong about this, but I can't immediately identify anything comparable to the Western idea of empathy. It's not how they think about this. There's nothing in Buddhist writings about how you can resonate with something in your own experience like the other person's experience. Because it's not a content-of-the-mind based tradition; it's about awareness.

So, in the sense of feeling into the compassion of all beings, whether you resonate with that or not, compassion becomes a kind of general term that supersedes all the more specific stuff that we do in one of our relationships, and in therapy relationships. It's just not how it is. I'm not saying it doesn't exist. It's superseded by compassion.

So, why do we practice compassion? Because it makes us better people; it makes the world better. When Howard Cutler, a Western psychiatrist, did a series of interviews with the Dalai Lama about the theme of compassion, the Dalai Lama said, "The reason why I practice compassion is because it leads to my own happiness, as well as what it does for others." If you get out of yourself and you're compassionate, then it generates positive emotions within yourself. You feel better. You're more positive about everything.

There was an interesting experiment. Richie Davidson is an old student of meditation for years. He did his graduate work at Harvard many years ago, and we worked at the same lab in Maimonides Medical Center in the '70s. Now he's a big neuroimager, a professor at the University of Wisconsin. And Richie did a neuroimaging scan of a Western lama who spent a number of decades practicing compassion. And that's, some of you know, Matthieu Ricard.

Matthieu Ricard was a French molecular biologist who, in his twenties, dropped molecular biology, became a Tibetan Buddhist monk, and a translator of His Holiness, and has done decades and decades of compassion practice. So, Richie Davidson scanned Matthieu's brain before and during practice of compassion. And what he found was that the medial orbital prefrontal cortex was substantially, significantly activated during the compassion practice. And, that the volume of his medial orbital prefrontal cortex was significantly higher than what we usually see in that area of the brain when compared to norms.

So, what does that tell us? The medial orbital prefrontal cortex does three things. It assigns salience to emotions, what emotions are given salience. Secondly, it's the center of positive emotions in the brain—all that good positivity stuff. And thirdly, it's the prosocial part of the brain, when we act kindly and prosocially towards other beings. All that's from the same area. In neurocircuitry, positive emotions and pro-social behavior are all connected. I suppose you could oversimplify it and say that's the compassion part of the brain.

So, autistic kids who grow up to be Asperger's adults, they show anomalies in the medial orbital prefrontal cortex. It doesn't seem to work right, which is why they often don't feel a lot. They're very smart. They're very smart little robots who don't feel a lot, and they don't really understand social rules and conventions and they are sort of socially awkward. And they can oftentimes be very brilliant. But that part of the brain doesn't seem to work very well.

Well, in this age of neuroplasticity, we know that areas of the brain ... that the brain isn't a constant structure. It changes size and structure depending on use. So, for example, the part of the brain that has to do with spatial memory, the hippocampus, they took people who were just learning to drive taxis in London. And taxi driving is a noble profession in London. You have to spend two years memorizing all the streets. So, they scanned at the beginning and six months later after cramming all these streets' names for six months. And they found about an 8 percent increase in the overall volume of the hippocampus at that time. If you use it, it grows. On the other hand, some traumatized people, who can't access memories of their traumatic experience show a significant decrease in the hippocampal volume. But not just volume changes, also structural changes.

When you do our good old Elephant Path of concentration, the anterior cingulate cortex lights up, gets activated as you focus effortfully on one thing and tune everything else out. That's the same area of the brain that's underactive in children and adults who have attention deficit disorder. So, the ACC, the anterior cingulate cortex, usually gets activated in concentration meditation. It also gets activated in athletes when they get into the flow and they're super concentrated when they're doing their peak performance. It also gets activated during hypnotic induction.

But what we know is when people activate the ACC through concentration training, if they continue to train concentration, after three or four months there's a significant increase in the size of the ACC—it gets bigger. And there's an increase both in white matter and gray matter associated with the ACC and its connectivity. So, if you keep concentrating, it's a lot of work, but after a while, you don't lose the effects anymore when you stop concentrating because you actually changed the size of the structure.

So, the brain is like a muscle: if you use the tissue it grows; if you don't use it, it shrinks and you lose structure. So, we can say the same thing: compassion is something you have to practice, like Matthieu Ricard doing it for years and years. So, he's fundamentally altered brain volume and structure and connectivity. So, he's a permanently compassionate being, based on that. And any one of you could develop that.

The social anthropologist, Paul Gilbert, says that somewhere along the line of evolution we figured out that cooperation and collaboration work better than competition. And primates were the first to start figuring it out. Basically, if they shared food, and they didn't fight as much, they survived better. But humans did something that went beyond what primates can do. They developed a capacity for cooperating towards shared interests and goals; and to develop the capacity for mutual collaboration. It's wired into the species.

Infants younger than a year old naturally have the impulse to give something to their mother or to another child. It's when they have something that interrupts attachment that that natural prosocial behavior is interrupted. It's hardwired into the species to be prosocial. Which means all the stuff we're doing to each other is unnatural from an evolutionary point of view.

Most of Gilbert's work was about how as a species, we are inherently co-operative and collaborative. And the culmination of that was, mostly he does compassion training to teach people how to do what we're losing as a species. I spent the last eight days in Los Angles teambuilding for this project on CEOs. They were trying to take the most influential multinational CEOs and people in the banking and securities industry who've created this culture of greed—Wall Street being the stereotype of that—and steep them in all the best of human growth and spirituality; and see if they can change them to get them out of their selfish power and behavior to thinking of the greater social good, by immersing them for a week or so in these intensive programs—because if we don't, we're not going to survive.

Right now, as of today, 1.5 percent of the people on the planet own 95 percent of the wealth. That doesn't work. Unless we reach that population and change it, the discrepancy is so huge that we probably can't survive. We have to change the culture of greed to a more compassionate view of the world where we share resources and give freely, which is our ecological, our evolutionary nature as a species. Cooperation, collaboration, works better for the individual and the species than competition with power orientation. Somehow, we're losing sight of our basic humanity. And if we don't change it, we won't survive. I'm saying that with a certain urgency.

So, good question.

January 14, 2015

Themes: Ethics; the Need for Moral Development and Conduct

Dan

Welcome everyone. You have a question?

Student 1

This is a follow on to a prior question, but the events of the recent week have brought it into relief. And the exercise of compassion that you talked about before where you're concerned about someone else's welfare; but if you think about the people who have exercised compassion to the point of putting themselves at risk—and you had spoken at the film the other night about the importance of human life, the value that's placed on it. And the question is, at what point—I hope that none of us ever get to this, where we would be in this situation—but just to think about the people who put themselves at risk like, we talked a little bit about the occupation of Europe during the Second World War, just the whole issue of basically heroic culture. How does that work for someone who puts themselves at risk?

Dan

Wow. I'll answer that in Western terms and also in Buddhist terms, because the answers are a little different. The general domain of that, within social psychology in the West, is: what are the conditions that generate prosocial behavior, where you do good things for other people? Generally, when people are happier and they have more life satisfaction and wellbeing, they tend to be more prosocial. That's number one.

Number two, prosocial behavior is enhanced in people when people act kindly to them. There was, particularly in the '80s, a genre of social psychology experiments that got known as the "random acts of kindness experiments." One experiment [included leaving] quarters in some phone booths and some not. We don't have phone booths anymore, but in those days, of course, we did. So, in one case, if you went to the phone booth you might discover there was a quarter in the phone booth—in some phone booths they would have left these quarters, and in other phone booths, they wouldn't leave quarters. And then in either case, as the person stepped out of the phone booth, the confederate[1] for the research experiment would be walking by them and would drop papers all over the ground. And what they found was that if the person discovered a random act of kindness, like getting a quarter in their phone booth, and somebody dropped all of their papers right after that, they were significantly more likely to stop and help the person to pick them up if they got their quarter than if they didn't.

When people are recipients of prosocial behavior, they're more likely to act prosocial. In that sense, that has profound implications. If people were to act more kindly towards others then they would spread it around. It has a contagion effect. That makes other people more kind. Not everybody, but there are ... generally speaking, that's the case. For people who have low self-esteem, people who are narcissistically vulnerable, they don't help people very much, and you can be kind to them, and they still don't help people very much. So, people who are esteem vulnerable tend not to be very kind under those circumstances, even if they are recipients of random acts of kindness.

On the other hand, you're talking about something very different. That is the studies on altruistic behavior, and it's not just helping somebody pick up

---

1 A "confederate" in a research experiment is part of the experiment's team.

papers they dropped. You're talking about altruistic behavior in extreme circumstances. Like, which would mean, putting your life at risk for a stranger. So, that's an unusual and extreme situation. Therefore, there were a number of studies done after World War II on people who hid Jewish families during the Nazi occupation, particularly in France and the Netherlands and other areas. And, knowing that if they got caught, they would be killed and maybe their whole family would be killed. So, there were detailed post hoc interviews of people who acted with extraordinary altruism, putting their life at risk for people that they didn't know.

What's interesting about the altruist studies, as we call them, is that pretty much if you interview lots of people who did that, they all say the same thing. They didn't think about the risk. They didn't think about the actions they were doing. You just did it because it was the right thing to do. So, people who tend to be altruistic and rise to the occasion and risk situations, it represents their level of moral development. It's not compromisable. They just do it because it's what you do. They don't think about the actions. They don't think about the people who do it, whether they know the people or not. They don't think about the consequences. They don't think about the risks. It's just what you do. And you don't think about it, and that's clearly an exception because most people don't do that.

In fact, there are studies that show almost the opposite for most people. There are FBI statistics where they did studies of the likelihood that bank tellers would embezzle. And the stats weren't very good. Basically, they found that two people [out of ten] would do it if they knew they could absolutely get away with it. Another six, if the circumstances were just right and they were convinced they wouldn't get caught, would consider it. And only two people would never consider it under any circumstances whatsoever. That's not a very good statistic.

Situations create sociopaths in some sense. It's a bell curve. On one tail there are usually people who won't do anti-social acts under any circumstances because it's not their values, and at the other end, they'll do it most of the time, and then the largest group would do it under certain situations if they knew that they could get away with it. This bigger group is the [middle of the] bell curve.

It's like that also with people who do extraordinary acts of altruism. It's the bell curve. Only a small percent of that tail end of people would do it under any circumstances no matter what the risk. They just do it. But, most people don't. So, we don't live in a world where we think prosocially.

I remember some years ago (now this is a personal story) and I went to a movie theater in Harvard Square—it still exists—with my first wife. This was some, maybe twenty years ago. And we were watching the movie, and she had put her pocketbook under her seat, and she put down the pocketbook and there didn't seem to be any issue. But then she looked around and there was a big guy who had clearly reached under the seat and pulled it out and she saw that and said, "Hey, that's my bag," and he quickly ran out of the theater before the lights went on, and we got a good look at him. And he dropped the bag, so that was the end of the incident. He was about 6'6," a Black guy.

Then we went back to that theater about six months later, and sure enough we're sitting there in the middle of a movie and here's the same guy and this time he walks in front of us and we watch him go sit behind a couple and reach under the seat and start to pull the bag out and I look and say, "We've got to do something here," and as soon as I looked at my then wife, and said, "We've got to do something here," the wife of the couple caught him and said, "Hey, you're stealing my bag," and then the people from the theater came in and turned the lights on. So, here's this guy standing there in front of ... standing up, he's like a towering Black guy, about 6'6"; he's got the bag in his hand, caught red handed, and the lights go on and everybody's looking at him and she says, "You have to stop him." And nobody does anything whatsoever. And he runs out and the only people that chase after him were the husband of that couple and myself.

And the security guard gets out of the way and doesn't chase him. He doesn't want to get involved. So, we chase him, and this was in Harvard Square, so we chase him into this building, and we called the police, and the police surrounded the building and they caught him. But then I'm thinking, who's the criminal here? This guy is a petty thief and obviously this was where he goes because he could get some money from this. That's how he made his living. He was a poor street guy.

But what was more interesting to me, in terms of what we define as criminal behavior, was the fact that the movie theater knew that he was there every day, and they didn't say anything about it because they didn't want to get a bad reputation. So, they intentionally let him do that and shut it up, for a couple of years, just so they wouldn't lose business. So, who's stealing from whom here? And then nobody would get involved. So, where's the prosocial behavior? You need help, and the woman asked for help, and nobody responds. That's a pretty good paradigm of our Western modern society.

No one wants to get involved. It's somebody else's problem—until it happens to you. Unless you're in that minority of people for whom, under any circumstances, you've got to respond because that's just your make up. But that's not the case. Most people don't. I went to the trial and testified, and I said that I thought he was a petty thief, and the main problem was the real thievery of the theater and their deception of letting that happen to so many people. Not good. Because they knew it and let it happen anyway.

What kind of duty do we owe each other? To protect each other? Is it broken down that much that it's only about selfishness and making more money? At other people's inconvenience? So, that kind of selfish preoccupation doesn't work. But most people are not going to come out of that selfish thing unless they evolve. And, you know, if people engage in spiritual practices, the hope is that through the nature of their realizations, they evolve to higher levels of spiritual development. And then, in the course of that, maybe they become more prosocial.

I teach more in Switzerland than any place else and almost all my students are Swiss bankers and national bankers. I do that on purpose. Because now some of my students, as a function of their realizations, they're talking about sharing resources and international collaborative banking, rather than what they used to do, which was basically set up private accounts to launder money and to tax shelter the wealthy so they don't have to pay anything, and so make more and more wealth at the expense of everybody else. That's a good thing, even if it's only one person who changes. It contributes something.

We have to evolve to a higher level of moral development so it's not the rare moral exemplar who is altruistic and puts themselves at risk in any position, in any situation.

But, now from a Buddhist perspective, it's complicated. You see, in Mahāyāna Buddhism you open up a level of mind where everything and everyone is interconnected. And if you operate out of that experience, then it changes your ethics. Because everything we do affects everyone else in the field. You can't escape from living in an interpersonal world where we're all connected and, therefore, how we act towards each other matters. That's where *bodhisattva* activity, selfless activity for the sake of all beings, comes out of that realization. It's not an abstract concept. It comes out of the direct experience of interconnectedness.

But, what's complicated about it is, as is true also in Western ethics, you often have competing ethical concerns. We face that in legal ethics all the time, as you know. And Buddhism is no different from that. You've got competing ethical standards. Because one standard is, you always put aside your own needs for the sake of all beings. But the other competing ethical standard is that human life is precious. You don't throw it away. And sometimes those things clash; and we saw that in a movie the other day. Somebody came and gave us a preview of a movie with three generations of Tibetan women and how they adjust to coming to the West. At the end of the movie, they had some self-immolation scenes. Tibetans don't have a country, they'll never have a country again, and the movie ended with a political statement, at least this version of it. I think she's going to change it, but it had Tibetans giving up their life by lighting themselves on fire so the Tibetan cause isn't forgotten. That's a grim way of ending the movie.

But, as Westerners, we think that that's a healthy protest for their political cause so they can have their country back, but it's not as simple as all that. It's been fifty years and eighty-seven percent of the people in Tibet are now Chinese. It's a dwindling minority. The country's changed in a half a century. One of my Tibetan friends calls and says that for us as Americans to think that China should give Tibet back to the Tibetans is hypocritical. It's like asking us to give Texas back to Mexico. It's just not going to happen. Too much time has passed. It's not going to happen, although some of us would like Texas to be given back to Mexico. [Laughter] But anyhow, you know what I'm saying, it's complex. It's not as simple as that.

But, what's more complex about it is that this idea that in the millions of lifetimes and rebirths that you have within this larger view of Tibetan Buddhism, it's very rare that you get a precious human birth. And why is that important? Because everybody has the seed of awakened awareness. Everybody has buddha nature, from a human down to the smallest insect. Mosquitoes have buddha nature—what do you think of that? But the difference between animals and humans is that we have metacognitive capacity. So we're the only beings that can actually recognize our own true nature and awaken to that. So you can only become awakened in the human birth—in a human body. And you could only reach buddhahood in human form. So, that's why, for the purpose of supporting realizations, having a human body is useful.

As the Tibetans say, the odds that you get a precious human body in this lifetime, and the odds that you landed in an area for this lifetime that actually has teachings, and get exposed to those teachings, is not very high. Lots of people who get reborn as human don't live in times of history where there are any teachings. There are dark ages. Or they live in places that they don't have access to the teachings. Or they live in war-torn countries where it's too chaotic to learn anything or do any spiritual practice. Think of the odds of getting this right. You get born in a human body and being born at a time in history when teachings are flourishing, and being born in the area where you have access to them in a reasonably stable culture; that's a lot of things to get right.

The Tibetans liken that to turtle hunting. Because in Tibet, they have these big lakes and they have sea turtles, and they go out in round boats made out of yak hide, called coracles, and of course they are off the Tibetan tundras that are very windy so that the round boats just bounce up and down, and the turtle hunters stand out in the boats with a lasso waiting for the turtle to poke it's head up; and the odds that you're going to have a turtle poke its head up next to the boat, and with the bouncing of the boat that you're going to be able to lasso this thing—as you can imagine, they don't catch very many turtles. [Laughter]

And they say catching a human birth with all the conditions right to support the teachings is about the same odds as catching a turtle. And we don't catch many turtles. If you get all the conditions right and you practice, and as a statement of that practice you decide to light yourself on fire for political protest, just throwing away all the conditions that were right and precious—so, you see, the Tibetans think that's a strange anomaly. I'm not saying it doesn't happen. But that's what's unusual here, because you think of self-immolations much more in Theravādin Buddhist culture in South Asia, like you saw that a lot in Cambodia or in Burma, because the Theravādin Buddhism doesn't have this notion of *daljuwa*, precious human life, and how it's the support of all your realizations.

So, you see, for Tibetans it's much more complex. They want to protest the fact that they don't have a country and probably will never have it again, but it's a violation of another principle to light yourself on fire and kill yourself out of protest for that. Because it goes against all that preciousness of what's possible, what you can do with this life.

And, you know, it makes a statement, but is it a lasting statement? We don't hold in our minds very much news beyond the day it happened. So, all those sorrowful folks who lit themselves on fire and killed themselves lost the chance of developing that life in a way that might have contributed something—more than that statement. So that's the predominant Tibetan view. Even when

Tibetans sometimes self-immolate. So, it's complex, you see, because you've got two competing ethical concerns: The duty to develop this human birth to the best that you can bring and develop this spiritual practice to full buddhahood, and the duty to serve the benefit of others. And mostly, most Tibetans—because at least in Mahāyāna, it's much more positive, it's not all about suffering. It's about enhancing and developing all of the positive states of the mind. At least in the Essence traditions, like Dzogchen and Mahāmudrā, where the emphasis is so much more positive that they would see any kind of self-destructive act for the sake of other people—like lighting yourself on fire, or stories of the *bodhisattva* feeding his body to the tiger because the tiger was hungry—they're not so keen on those stories. Because it's a violation of your own body-mind continuum and the duty to develop that to its fullest.

Also, because from a wider perspective, the more you evolve your spiritual practice, you have *wang*, and *wang* means influence. If we're all interconnected, the evolution of your own spiritual practice has influence on all of those around you. You create a field of positive influence. Evolved spiritual beings leave a wake of positivity behind them. That's much more important an influence than the single self-destructive act where you light yourself on fire or feed yourself to the tiger, because from a wider perspective, if you evolve yourself, you've got to help many more beings with your evolution than that single instant where you fed yourself to the tiger.

Those things are destructive, and truthfully, self-destructive. It's not what this tradition is for the most part. Even when some people do that. But I think that, in that sense, Tibetan Buddhism and Western Christian practices aren't terribly different. It's not about Christian practices or Buddhist practices, it's about monasticism. Because what you find in monasticism is a kind of self-effacing-ness around the body. You find a self-effacing-ness, that the body is somehow bad. The most popular book in Indo-Tibetan Buddhism is *Entering the Path of Enlightenment: The Bodhicaryavatara of the Buddhist Poet Santideva* by Shantideva.

Every Mahāyāna Buddhist reads that book. It's their most favorite book. And even our precious [Rahob] Rinpoche is writing his own Tibetan commentary on that, which he'll give to his people as his last testament. But from my point of view, that book has a lot of positive things in it. It's got a clear chapter on concentration, a clear chapter on wisdom—those are the best chapters. It's got six perfections in it. But the stuff about the body is just disturbing to me, because it's so negative and it's self-effacing and self-aggressive. But that's not about spiritual realization. That's about monasticism. That's the problem.

Shantideva weighed about three hundred pounds. He was a binge eater. He was called before the abbot because the other monks thought he was lazy and not practicing. And he had to show some proof that he was making use of his time at the monastery or otherwise they were going to throw him out. So, he went into meditation and connected with that place where everything is interconnected and came out and wrote it down, just like channeling. He wrote all twelve chapters in Rime, Sanskrit verse—pretty hard to do without any editing. Unedited, he handed it to the abbot, and nobody made any more comments about it. He stayed at the monastery.

But, his attitudes about his body were screwed up in Western clinical terms. [Laughter] They're screwed up because you could see that in his writings. The part about the body is really screwed up in that text. I couldn't use his emptiness and body meditations without modifying them so they're not in this kind of remarkably self-effacing, self-judgmental way. And his attitudes about women are pretty bad. Because what you're getting there is not realization, you're getting monastic culture. It's no different from the Flagellants in the Middle Ages in Western mysticism in Germany. They sit there and beat themselves with whips as if that was a good thing to do.

Maybe no one stopped to ask. Maybe there's something aberrant about how practice is here, because the basic assumptions are wrong. So, you see it's not an accident that most of that self-immolation comes up from people in the monastic culture. The real culture of Indo-Tibetan Buddhism is not the monasteries. The real culture is the cave and hermitage yogis. They network. Everybody knows where the caves are, and everybody knows where their hermitages are. And they all go there. And they spend, you know, some years, meditating. Not necessarily in isolation. There's a number of caves that are close to each other in hermitages, and they get together and they talk about their practices and share that.

They are the real yogis, because they meditate all the time. They're not sitting there doing prayers and all this other kind of stuff they do in monasteries other than meditate. They work at it all the time. It's their life. It's not monastic. And there's nothing in the cave yogi culture that's self-effacing. It's deeply positive. You ever hear of a cave yogi lighting himself on fire? It just won't happen. Think of somebody like Milarepa. All of his teaching was through spontaneous song and dance. That's pretty deeply happy.

So, I think that if you evolve your own practice, then that's where you can make the best contribution. Because you see, unlike our Western stereotype, if you evolve your practice, the highest levels of realization are always measured by conduct. Conduct spontaneously arises from awakened *dharmakāya* space. All conduct spontaneously arises from awakened *dharmakāya* space as the best fit to the situation at hand. So, you measure the degree of realization by how a person lives their life. And the only authentic test of the truth of any individual's realization is how they act, and how they live their life. Because if you can't live it, it's all bullshit.

But it has to come from the realization, every moment. It's not like a persona that you try and act like a spiritual being. That's garbage. We've seen how much a lot of Western Christianity is deteriorating into that form. You have to act a certain way. But it's the intention to put on a certain behavior. It doesn't arise spontaneously every moment from the realization. So it's all conceptual. It doesn't represent the spontaneous nature of the realized mind.

We've all seen the discrepancies that come up with that kind of spiritual persona. Teachers who, in any tradition—Christianity or Buddhism—who talk the nature of their beliefs and realization and engage in exploitation of their students, or sexual misconduct, or collecting power and money all in the name of spirituality. That kind of conduct is totally incongruous with realization. Not possible. Because, going back to what we said earlier, that the studies that were done in the West on people who sheltered Jews during the Nazi occupation, any one of them said, "I didn't think about it. I didn't think about the risk." It was just what you did. That's how you treat people.

And people who have genuine spiritual realization rather than a spiritual persona, it's the same thing. You don't think about it. You just act that way because that's who you are. You never think about, "I have to act a certain way," to put on a certain front. It doesn't come like that. It's just your being.

I'm not very good at that, but I've learned something. And that is that this culture is so morally deprived, they have a reasonably good life, and people gravitate towards that because they want so much for someone to serve as a moral exemplar. And it breaks my heart. Because the culture needs it so much because it's so absent. So even being that a little bit goes a long way. Do you understand what I'm saying?

The influence that I have for you is not in the nature of the teachings or the clarity of that. It's how I am being with you that you trust—because it's so absent here. And that's what I've learned. But it's not a role. It's just a way of being that is a natural expression of the nature of the realizations. That's very different from it being a persona. You see, I don't have any choice. But I'm not saying that as a limit or even as a burden or responsibility. It's just the way I experience things and the nature of how I see it. I don't have any choice. It's just who I am. And when you understand that, you're free. We can all do that, just by the way we are with each other. It matters what you do with your practice and the nature of your realizations.

How you develop your practice, each and every one of you, and the positive influence that that has—each of you is important. And that matters. It matters deeply because if we don't do this, we're not going to survive because the selfish greed and preoccupation with power and wealth with smaller and smaller numbers of individuals doesn't work anymore.

There's an interesting debate in Switzerland. There's identification of 130,000 people who have most of the wealth in the world, who have private bank accounts where they've mostly sheltered money in order to not pay taxes in any countries or launder money. And the people would like that to be fully transparent. What happens if all of that stuff of laundering money and not paying any taxes is transparent to the rest of the world? That's an interesting debate because the whole game changes, because it can't be done anymore without deception. And even the thought that that would open up changes everything.

What if we started to think about sharing resources? Let's take it the other way. Suppose we don't. Smaller and smaller numbers of people accumulate more and more. We don't have a middle class anymore in this country. We've sold this country. Let's keep going with that. There's a lot of shopping centers out there. Who's going to have any money to use them anymore? Eventually, at some point, it's coming back to bite all the people who basically got and accumulated too much. Who's going to buy the stuff? There are no resources left. But that's the direction we're going.

It's like that very prophetic line in the movie *Network* of the 1970s. There are no countries anymore. It's just the ebb and flow of capital between powerful interest groups. That's what we've created. The rest of it's an illusion. We all participated and let it happen. So, unless we turn around the selfishness and greed, the *samsāra* that we created becomes more hellish than it already is at a rapidly accelerated rate.

So, that's where the practice matters. I think. But not in a self-effacing way. I'm getting old. It's hard to travel as much as I do. I get tired for the first time after ten days of teaching. I didn't used to ever get tired. But, you know, I'm not self-effacing. I try and take care of my body, because if I don't do that, I don't have anything to teach you, because I won't be able to.

So, Buddhism has these pockets of all this monastic baggage, like Shantideva, that there's no place for. Rinpoche says, "You're in your body for a short time in this life," he says, "body is like a hotel. Better to have a good hotel. [Laughter] You're just guests, but have a good hotel. Then, after you die, you're like the homeless," he said. [Laughter]

But, in situations that involve some risk, would you do it? You just don't think about it. You just do it because it's the right thing to do; the rest of it plays itself out—whatever that may be. So, it was a good question. It's got some depth to it. I appreciate that, thank you.

January 21, 2015

Themes: Mindfulness; Awareness; Metacognition; Neurocircuitry

Dan

Welcome everyone.

I thought I would share with you something, it's sort of interesting. Some of you are also doing that, but yesterday I spent the day in UMass Medical School, as some of you other students have participated in their study of the brain and meditation. So, it was really interesting. They have 128 channels EEG, which gives them not exactly the same closeness resolution as fMRI, but close enough that you can identify circuitry and regions of interest better in some ways because you can do something close to real time. So, maybe I'll talk a little bit about meditation in terms of neuroimaging.

There are two broad categories of meditation. In the traditional literature, what we might call concentration meditation and pure awareness meditation. So, the ordinary mind is considered dysfunctional. And when you're training meditation, you are training whatever the dysfunction of the ordinary mind is. The ordinary mind is like a wild elephant that goes out of control. So, one way of training a wild elephant is to tie the elephant [with] a chain around the elephant's neck [or leg] and put a stake in the ground, and every time the elephant wanders off, it feels the pull at the chain, so it can't go very far and keeps being pulled back. And hundreds and hundreds of times later, it figures out that it can't go anywhere. It learns to just stay put. That's a metaphor for concentration training.

We say if you tie the rope of concentration onto a concentration object, like say the rising and falling of the breath, and whenever it chases after an interesting thought or sense experience, you pull it back to the concentration object until it learns to stay put. So, either you're focused on the concentration object, or you are distracted elsewhere. So, continuously directing the mind back to the concentration object is one of the fundamental skills in concentration; and another is what we call intensifying, directing the mind towards the object, say the rising and falling of the breath, and then putting the effort to looking in such a very carefully refined way that you stay so close, close on the concentration object, the mind is too busily engaged with the concentration object that it doesn't go anywhere else. So, directing the mind, we call that *semtong* in Tibetan, like a steering wheel. And intensifying is like stepping on the accelerator. You don't have any problem understanding that when you're driving a car and learning for the first time that the use of a steering wheel and accelerator are different skills. Likewise with concentration, you're learning to see that steering your mind back to the object and [how] it intensifies, and you stay closely, are separate skills that you learn.

And there are degrees of refinement on how much you stay on the object. So, in the Buddhist tradition of Asanga's stages—it's called the Semnegu in Tibetan, the Nine Stages of Staying—there are nine gradations of staying more closely engaged with a meditation object that you can train. So, when you concentrate, you focus on one thing, and everything else is a distraction, So, you're either on the object, or you're distracted in a given moment.

Now, another skill, at least in the Indo-Tibetan tradition is that you don't just sit and try and concentrate. You try and train your metacognitive awareness of the quality of the concentration. So, that means training your metacognition to quickly be aware of when the mind goes off, so you can catch that point that it goes off more and more immediately, not after the fact that you're caught in a daydream, and thirty minutes into that daydream, "Oh yeah, I was meditating."

You try and catch that thought immediately as it goes off track. And that requires what we call metacognitive awareness, *shezjhi* in Tibetan. So, you don't just sit quietly, you have to use a skill of metacognitive awareness, or metacognitive intelligence, to refine the quality of your meditation so you keep improving it. If you just sit quietly, you'll make lots of subtle and not so subtle bad habits of the mind. And it goes off track. You don't even know it's off track, so you stay, the meditation bottoms out and sometimes for years, because you don't even know you're making bad habits. There's a Sufi tale that says, "A log sits very quietly in a wood pile for years. It's very still and quiet, but logs never realize God. So don't sit like a log, sit intelligently." Use your metacognitive capacity to see the quality of your sitting.

So, what does that look like in terms of neuroimaging? There's a part of the anterior cingulate cortex, part of the prefrontal system called the ACC or the anterior, the front part of the cingulate cortex. And that's traditionally associated with how the brain resolves competing attention demands. So, the way we study that in Western psychology is with a Stroop test. You show people a card with, say, a printed text with the word "green," but the color of the letters is red. And most people do a double take, "Do I respond to the text, or do I respond to the color?" So, it requires some effortful attention to focus on the colors as opposed to the text, or the text as opposed to the color. And in terms of functional MRI, the ACC, the anterior cingulate cortex lights up and gets turned on, gets activated when you are effortfully focusing on one thing and tuning everything else out. So, when you're fighting with your partner, you're trying to tune out what they say and activate the ACC. [Laughter]

So, the ACC is that area of neurocircuitry that is underactive, basically deactivated in children and adults who have attention deficit disorder [ADD or ADHD]. The ACC is selectively activated by Ritalin and Adderall. That's why it's used in the treatment of ADHD in kids. The ACC is activated when someone gets hypnotized, and they go into a hypnotic trance. The ACC is activated in concentration meditation. When an athlete gets into a peak performance state and they're in the flow, sort of like the Patriots[2] were last week ... [Dan and group laugh a lot.] So, when athletes are in their peak performance mode, they activate the ACC.

So, what's common about all of this? That part of the neurocircuitry that gets you to attend to one thing at the expense of everything else gets activated. And now in this age of "neuroplasticity,"[3] we know that the brain circuitry changes

2 Dan was a longtime fan of the New England Patriots, a professional American football team based in Boston.

3 That the brain can change and adapt in adulthood was only widely accepted in neuroscience in the latter half of the twentieth century.

size and structure depending on usage. So, the brain isn't a constant organ. It's changing in size and structure, depending on how we use it. So, for example, there's a famous taxi study in London. Taxiing is a noble profession in London. So, taxi people, when they first start, they spend two years memorizing all the streets in London. And the hippocampus is that part of the brain that's associated with spatial memory. So, they scanned the hippocampus with people the first day on the job, and then after cramming street spatial awareness and spatial memory for six months, they rescanned the hippocampus, and they found that the taxi drivers showed about an eight to ten percent increase in the volume of the hippocampus. And there was an increase in white matter connectivity associated with the hippocampus. So, change in volume and structure.

Likewise, people who were advanced concentrating meditators, as opposed to beginning concentrating meditators, over twelve weeks of concentration training, showed an increased volume—increase in the size of the ACC, the anterior cingulate cortex. They showed greater conductivity in the white matter, which is the connective part of the neural circuitry. And also, increase in gray matter, which basically means an increase in neuronal content.

What does that mean? It means that it takes a lot of work to concentrate, but at a certain point, there's a skill level where you just have it. You just do it at will, because you've actually improved brain structure and content to be able to do the task easily. The brain is sort of an equal opportunity employer. It doesn't care whether you use drugs like Adderall or Ritalin or mind/body techniques like hypnosis or concentration meditation. They all do pretty much the same thing. They put the ACC back online. And of course, that has major implications for people who are poor concentrators, like those who have ADHD, because you can retrain it. There's nothing wrong with it, it just never developed fully to what it's capable of doing.

So, that's concentration meditation. Now some systems of concentration meditation, in the way that they're taught, like the Asanga Elephant Path that we teach, emphasize training metacognitive capacity so you're aware quickly when you go off track. You try and catch it more quickly before you get lost in it. Because when you're lost in a daydream for five minutes and say, "Oops, I think I was meditating," what's happened there is you had a lapse in metacognitive monitoring. You can't step back and be aware of the fact that you lapsed. You get totally lost in it. And of course, it's easy to get lost in thought. If you train the metacognitive capacity, you pick up the thought at the head rather than the tail. You catch it more quickly, in other words. And you can use your metacognitive intelligence to judge the quality of the meditation, so you're always keeping it a good quality and not letting it get sloppy.

So, the metacognitive center of the executive control frontal system is the right dorsolateral prefrontal cortex, this piece up here [Dan gestures to his right forehead just above the hairline]. And there are now studies that show that advanced meditators ... when they looked at beginning concentrators and advanced concentrators, the difference was that both groups activated the ACC, the anterior cingulate cortex, but only the advanced meditators, in addition to that, activated the right dorsolateral prefrontal cortex when they were meditating. So, you put that metacognition back online in a sharpened way until you're constantly improving the quality of meditation.

In fact, that's one of the things that's fundamentally different between hypnosis and concentration meditation. Because in hypnosis, you deactivate the dorsolateral prefrontal cortex—you take metacognition offline, so you have uncritical acceptance of whatever is suggested to you, a heightened suggestibility in hypnosis. So, in that sense, in terms of metacognitive capacity, it's the exact opposite. But they both share the common feature of being concentration skills. The difference is that in hypnosis, somebody is reminding you what to keep the focus on, so it's a little bit easier to keep on track without getting distracted. And when you concentrate, you typically have to do it yourself unless you do something like a guided meditation, which we do here. Then it's easier to keep on track. But they're both similar in different states in that sense. You follow me—is that clear enough?

Now the other main type of meditation is a pure awareness meditation. The goal for concentration is to stay for extended periods of duration on whatever you're absorbed in, concentrated on. You can stay for an hour, four hours, just staying on one thing, and your mind doesn't go anywhere else—there's no distracting thought. In pure awareness meditation, the goal is not about staying on the object. The goal is reducing the lapses in our awareness. In our ordinary, everyday life, awareness is not a continuous thing. We have chunks missing. We have periods of forgetfulness, lapses in our awareness. And the extreme of that would be a dissociative condition, so major chunks of your awareness missing.

So, the goal of mindfulness is to train for continuous awareness in contrast to the discontinuities or interruptions of awareness. So, the Zen student goes for his interview with the Zen master thinking he's gotten somewhere with his practice, very proud of his accomplishments of quieting the mind. And the Zen master says, "And when you were waiting outside, tell me, where did you put your shoes?" And the student didn't remember. So, where is the great realization here, when you can't have continuous awareness of even the basic things in life? So, pure awareness meditations are where you try and approximate the ideal of continuous uninterrupted awareness through every moment and whatever is going on in your field of experience.

Using our wild elephant metaphor, the other way of training the elephant is you don't tie it up, you simply track it. No matter what the elephant is doing, wherever it's wandering, you never take your eyes off the elephant. You continuously track it uninterruptedly. So, no matter what comes into your consciousness, you track every moment, by moment, by moment, by moment no matter what it is. Examples of pure awareness meditation would be Krishnamurti's "choiceless awareness." Every moment you just be aware, without any preferences, without any reactivity; you just be aware. Or Shikentaza's "just sitting" style of Zen. You see there's no object of concentration, whatever comes up next is the next thing you're aware of. There's no concept of distraction, whatever comes up is the next thing you're aware of.

Now, the Burmese mindfulness that got popular in the West; it's a little bit more complicated than these two pure types, because the kind of Burmese mindfulness that got popular here originated from Mahāsī Sayādaw. And he thought, not incorrectly, that counting on most people to just be aware of everything at every moment is just too hard. So, he thought if people concentrated somewhat first, and you quieted the mind, that would make it easier to then switch to pure awareness meditation.

And secondly, he thought that if people used labels, the labels would help them approximate continuous awareness. So, you concentrate on the rising and falling of the breath to quiet all that background noise of thought. And when it starts to get a little quiet and still in there, you use labels. If a thought is occurring, you say, "thinking." You don't think about the content of the thought, just at that given moment, thinking is occurring. If you hear a sound, "hearing." If you're looking at something, "looking." It's not what you're looking at, just the fact that looking is happening. Sensing, feeling, thinking, hearing, looking, smelling. And using those labels, you approximate a continuous, uninterrupted awareness of everything every moment.

The trouble with that system is it's a hybrid system. It has some degree of concentration, but not to the same intensity and precision; that system doesn't have the tool of intensification, or there isn't much emphasis on training metacognitive awareness; it's just pure mindfulness. But that's the one that became popular here in the West. So, we don't know about pure awareness meditations except [to the degree] the Krishnamurti stuff is popular here.

For those of you who are ongoing students of mine and have been to the retreats, you know pure awareness meditation, which begins at the stage of practice when you do automatic emptiness. Everything comes up spontaneously every moment, and as soon as it expresses itself, it's already empty. So, you don't have to do anything. Everything is immediately empty upon arising, and there's no grab, there's no reactivity, it just goes by itself. And after a while, since everything is another momentary expression of emptiness-liveliness, things lose discrimination and preference, which is where whatever comes up next is the next thing that comes up.

So, where the neuroimaging work is going is the other half of the cingulate system, the posterior cingulate cortex, the PCC. And the PCC is traditionally the error-monitoring part of the brain. So, when you are trying to distinguish a remote memory, whether it's something that you actually experienced, or something that you read about or something that somebody told you, then it was called a "source monitoring mistake." People who are prone to confuse those things and have memory distortions, at those points, they're deactivating the PCC, putting it offline.

When schizophrenics hear voices, what they're really doing is they're taking inner speech—we all talk to ourselves—and they're misperceiving that as an external voice. When they make that category error, [at] that point in time that they're having the voice, they've deactivated the PCC. When you try and carefully discriminate some aspect of your experience, is this a memory or real experience? Or is it something you imagined? When you're distinguishing between real memory and imagination, you're activating the PCC.

So, it's used to distinguish between different categories of consciousness, conscious experiences. And it also is used to distinguish how, or what preferences that you make about different experiences. So, if you think about that, it's really interesting because the current scanning that is being done on mindfulness meditation, even the Burmese kind, shows deactivation of the PCC. And what you get is a kind of pure awareness. And in that pure, nonreactive awareness mode, you're just aware of whatever comes up. And there's a tendency to just be aware of it without reacting to it, and without preferring one thing over another. So, that's what the neuroimaging of mindfulness looks like, but as I said, it's a hybrid.

And what was interesting is—I went to play with the machinery yesterday. And Mike went and some of the other students went, and what you all were doing is automatic emptiness, when you were subjects there. And I did the same thing. And what was clear is a couple of things. One was there's a lot of other things happening, but they set up the machine when we played this—just look at their hypothesis, which was PCC deactivation. So, that's what came up on the screen. But for myself and the other subjects within our group, when you're doing automatic emptiness or non-meditation meditation … essentially it was PCC deactivation. No preferences, just pure awareness with no preferences and no reactivity.

The difference, however, was really interesting because from what they told me, from what they have from preliminary data, the cleanness of the data set is just pure PCC deactivation, so you're not all over the map, you're not going back to thought mode; and just staying in that mode was much stronger for the students that we see from our group than the mindfulness group. And at least, when I did it, the magnitude of the PCC deactivation, the amplitude, was much stronger than usual.

So, what you're getting in non-meditation meditation, in Mahāmudrā, is a kind of a pure putting of the PCC offline; and everything comes up with equal awareness. And it's that state of not just nonreactivity, but no preferences that become the precursor for the foundation of the crossing-over instructions for awakening. Or, as the Third Chinese Patriarch[4] reportedly says, "The Great Way [which is the way to awakening] is not difficult for those who have no preferences. But make the slightest distinction between this and that, then heaven and earth are set infinitely apart." That's a crossing over instruction. It's not an instruction about everyday likes and dislikes. It's about setting up the natural state of the mind, a state of no preferences and equal continuous awareness. So, that was really interesting, I thought.

The other thing is that in some ways, what was more interesting that sort of surprised me—you know, I've done this for forty-three years now; that's a long time. So, one of the things you develop in meditation is what they call "mental pliancy," *shinshong* [in Tibetan]. And it's a kind of flexibility or pliancy of mind, so whatever the mind intends, whatever awareness intends, it just does that

4 The reference here is to the Third Patriarch of Chan/Zen, Xinxin Ming ca. 600-700 AD.

and only that. So, if you have strong pliancy, like a laser beam, intention has directionality, and it just goes to that with no interference as long as you want; so you can put your mind on an object and stay there for two hours without any distraction if you want. It just goes to that with lightning speed, the laser speed of thought.

So, when I was playing on the screen, I promised myself that if I wanted to get them a good baseline, I had to crowd up my mind. So, I intentionally didn't do anything with meditation. And I'm working on writing my attachment book. So, it's nice and filled with thought. And as a baseline, I just allowed myself to continue to compose writing my book in my mind. And during that baseline, it was all secondary association cortex activity. Basically, I was totally in thought mode. No awareness whatsoever, just pure thought mode.

And then, when they asked me to switch, what I did was automatic emptiness and then shifting immediately to non-meditation meditation in the natural state, free of conceptualizing. For that period, which was about ten minutes, there wasn't even a single shred of thought activity. It was pure PCC deactivation the whole time and nothing else. And everything just goes right through.

So, that was pretty clear; and later they gave me a biofeedback thing, and it actually interfered. Because I'd switched to awake awareness and stayed in awakened awareness; but every time they'd ask me look at the feedback on the screen it would cause me to particularize in such a way that the particularizing would—at that moment it would blip me out of awakening. And then I would drop back into it. So, I stopped looking at the screen. I said, "Look, I don't need the screen feedback to stay in the state, it's easier without it." So, it was interesting.

But what was most clear to me is the definition of mind that comes with meditation. So, for example, if you work for the first time with a set of new exercises on a Pilates machine, you don't isolate out the muscle groups that are needed for that exercise, you recruit surrounding muscles. But when you get really good at that exercise, you just use the muscles for that exercise and you don't recruit all the surrounding stuff anymore; it's just noise.

And the same thing happens with the brain. So, when I was in thought mode, it was just pure thought parts of brain activity, nothing else. And then when I was in pure non-meditation meditation, pure awareness mode, it was just PCC deactivation, no thought, nothing else. And no matter what I was doing was just like that. And the time to make those transitions was less than a second, but that's all they could measure—"speed of light." So, it's sort of interesting. It shows you that you can actually define and shape and recruit just the neurocircuitry that's relevant to the task at hand without a lot of noise in it. Just like you could do the same thing with the striate musculature, you can do the same thing with the neurocircuitries of the brain. So, skilled meditators have flexibility, and you could see on the response what pliancy and flexibility of the mind means. Whatever you put the mind on, it does just that and nothing else.

Now what I don't know is [something else.] I went through and I did automatic emptiness, nonduality, awakened awareness, awakened awareness plus the appearance aspect of awakened awareness, which is continuous liveliness as whatever came up. And when I did the awakening simultaneous to thought and perception, which is liveliness, all the thought activity came back, but there was nothing on the PCC; it was not activated. So, it's clear that awakening is a different neurocircuitry than PCC deactivation. It's something else.

So, I went through several rounds of that, and they have to go back now—I marked for them linguistically what the shifts in state were, and they've got to go back and look and see if they can figure out some markers for awakening. They're going to try and put together a study to look at the neurocircuitry of awakening.

And I said, "You know, stop studying this little mindfulness stuff; let's focus on awakening, let's focus on all-at-onceness, let's focus on buddhahood. And then look at what the brain's doing at those points." And they got excited about that. So, I think we'll try and do that. They didn't think they could have the subjects before. Now it's local; they think that we can supply them with the subjects, and some of you who participated that we sent there are doing different things than what they're used to, so now they're getting interested.

And from my point of view as a teacher, the neurocircuitry is a kind of useful metaphor, because the Western science shows us more precisely the type of skills we need to develop in meditation. Concentration meditation needs the foundation of concentration. You don't really build that from mindfulness training. It's a separate skill. It's a much more foundational skill for everything else. The problem is that mindfulness is so popular here that no one's learning basic concentration practice. And that's not the best system to train concentration, in my opinion.

The Asanga Elephant Path in the Buddhist tradition, which is what we do in the Level 1 course, or in the Hindu system Patanjali's Yoga Sutras, are the great systems of concentration training and they have many more elaborated tools than you find in Burmese mindfulness for concentration. But it's also very clear, at least from the neuroimaging studies, that it's not enough to just sit there and meditate and be totally oblivious to the meditation. You have to evaluate the quality of the meditation.

There are two ways of doing that. One is what we call "episodic disengagement." From time to time, you disengage momentarily from the object, check the quality of the meditation, make the correction, and go right back to what you're doing with the object. Or, for advanced practitioners, Denma Locho used to say, "Reserve a small part of the mind to continuously monitor." In every moment you're checking and improving it. But don't do that unless you're an advanced meditator because otherwise you're going to train partial staying because you're splitting, you're dividing your attention. If you're not very concentrated, then you're basically multi-tasking. And that's not a good thing to do unless you move beyond the multi-tasking part of this. So, if you are more deeply concentrated and you're moving beyond what we call "partial staying," then you can do that, and it works.

So, that's as far as we got. But it also shows you that pure awareness meditation is a different skill and is not just trying to be mindful and nonreactive. In the Mahāmudrā sense of non-meditation meditation and then what's called *trekchö*, "cutting-through instructions" in Dzogchen, it's the foundational state for awakening. So, training that state, it matters, and training it correctly matters.

Student 1

I have a question.

Dan

Please … he participated; he was one of the subjects.

Student 1

During the playing around part, one of the meditations I practiced was compassion, just lovely thoughts toward people and all beings. And the graph just went shooting up off the charts during that part of it, and then it came down when I did something else. I wonder, what does that reflect?

Dan

Well, I did the same thing, and I asked them about that, but when I did the compassion thing, I was moved. It brought tears to me. So, they were saying that a lot of that is a muscle artifact, from the crying.

Student 1

I wasn't crying, though.

Dan

But still, you might have been moved. I don't know. But there is a neurocircuitry of compassion. And the best study done on that was out of Richie Davidson's lab at the University of Wisconsin. Richie is an old, old-time meditator, old-time friend of mine. Now he's become one of the best, most prolific neuroimagers in this country. And he's particularly interested in the neuroimaging of emotion and neuroimaging of meditation.

So, on one of the many studies, they brought Matthieu Ricard in. And Matthieu is an interesting character. He's from France. He was a molecular biologist, very brilliant. And then in his twenties, he dropped out of molecular biology and became a Tibetan monk—I think in the Gelugpa tradition.[5] And he's been an ordained Tibetan monk for the last thirty years. And as a Gelugpa, that means they do a lot of compassion meditations. Mostly Chenrezig, Avalokiteśvara. His Holiness the Dalai Lama is the emanation of Avalokiteśvara for this generation. He *is* Avalokiteśvara. That's why he's so dogged in his nonviolent negotiation and compassion for even those who harmed his people and his country.

So, Matthieu has practiced Chenrezig as his main visualization practice for three decades. And when they scanned him in his compassion and visualization mode, he showed significant activation in the medial orbital prefrontal cortex,

---

5 Matthieu lived for nearly twelve years with the Nyingma and Rime master Dilgo Kyentse Rinpoche who, although not formally a Gelugpa, was universally respected by all Tibetan traditions and, since the passing of Kyentse Rinpoche in 1991, has taught extensively around the world, including Gelugpa monasteries.

right in the center here in the front. And the medial orbital prefrontal cortex [OFC] is that part of the brain that does, at least so far as we know so far, three things. One is it assigns emotional salience to things; in other words, what gives the amplitude to a feeling state. Second, it's the positive emotion center of the brain. When you activate a positive emotion like love or compassion or joy or happiness or inspiration, all that set of positive emotions comes from OFC activation. And thirdly, the OFC is the social connectivity center of the brain. Your awareness of sensitivity to the people in your environment is OFC activation. So, it's both positive emotions and social connection.

And that area of the brain is interesting clinically because children who are autistic and who then grow up to be Asperger's adults show aberrations in OFC structure and volume, but mostly structure, which means it doesn't grow right. So, we don't know how it happens, but people who are adolescents and adults who have Asperger's, they are oftentimes in one area absolutely brilliant, like idiot savants. But what they can't do is that they are remarkably socially unskilled. They just don't get basic social cues, so they're sort of awkward and out of it around people and don't do the social world very well. And so, think of *Rain Man*, Dustin Hoffman's portrayal of Rain Man; that's a good portrayal of an Asperger's adult—brilliant in certain areas, but socially not able to pick up the basics of social consciousness.

And the other clinical group is the people who have complex trauma with a social identity disorder, what used to be called multiple personality. They show significant … it's not damaged, unlike autism and Asperger's, but the OFC is basically deactivated; it stays offline. Just like the ACC, the anterior cingulate cortex, stays offline with people with adult attention deficit disorder. The OFC is basically offline in the dissociative identity disorder, which basically means that they are out of it socially. They have profound emotional numbing; they just don't feel much, except every now and then they switch into trauma and then they feel too much. But mostly, they just are emotionally numb and socially not connected very well.

And now the opposite of that is somebody like Matthieu Ricard because when he did his compassion meditation, not only did they find that he had unusually high activation of the OFC, but if you take a single subject, you compare value … we have norms of what brain activity should look like for regions of interest. So, his activation level of the OFC was significantly higher than the norms. And the volume was significantly greater than the norms.

So, it shows you that if you spend decades practicing compassion, you actually, from a neuroplasticity point of view, you change your neurocircuitry and you become more compassionate. You activate the compassion part of the brain, and that becomes a learned skill that you operate out of and don't lose. And since the OFC is not only the socially connecting compassion center of the brain, but also the positive emotion center of the brain, you're activating all that at once and that helps us understand something that his Holiness the Dalai Lama once said—because psychiatrist Howard Cutler did a series of interviews with him about compassion, and one of the things he says in that book that they wrote together was, "When I practice compassion, it makes me happy. I feel better about myself." And you can see why that is. If you practice the compassion, you activate the social center, which is the OFC. But that also, concurrently, activates all the positive emotions. So, being loving, kind, and compassionate does make us happy in addition to making the people around us happy. It's got a kind of contagion effect. So, that's what I would say about the neurocircuitry.

A couple of years ago, I played with a sixteen channel EEG with a friend of mine. And what I tried to do was set up the view of the Lion's Gaze for awakening, and then shift to awakening and let him try and mark it. But the resolution wasn't very good. But we were particularly looking at the parietal system, which is back here. [Dan taps the back of his head.] And there's an area of the parietal system, where the processing system is least understood and most complex, where you shift from a localized to global awareness and vice versa. And when I was setting up the view of the Lion's Gaze, that part of the parietal system on the left side was activated, which is the more cognitive part of that. And then when I shifted into awakening and stayed there, the same system on the right side of the parietal was activated.

So, when I went out yesterday [to UMass, an hour East of where Dan was speaking], I suggested they ought to look at that region of interest to see if they can get a marker with that. Because it looks like what's happening is when, you know, you shift out of the seeming localization [of] your little individual consciousness and information processing system and you become the unbounded wholeness of awakened awareness-love, that's a shift from localized to global in the big sense. We shift out of ordinary mind in its localization. And that's one of the ways you recognize awakening; it is what we call the pathway of nonlocalization. At some point you may recognize that you're no longer operating out of the constraints of individual consciousness, but operating on being that unbounded wholeness—a place that is no place, has no location, and has no reference points.

So, I think that that probably is one of the understudied systems and probably within a year or so we'll end up getting some markers for what's happening with awakening. And then eventually, hopefully, we'll be able to look at markers of buddhahood. But you have to become buddhas first, if you move along in your practice. And become Western buddhas.

Student 2

There's going to be a contest, I hope. [Laughter]

Dan

The first to arrive at buddhahood contest. We'll put little charts on the board … [more laughter]

Student 2

Thank God he has no ego.

Dan

What's that?

Student 3

Thank God you have no ego.

Dan

[Grinning.] That's true, none of that stuff.

Student 4

With no preferences, how are we going to be incentivized? [Group laughter]

Student 2

Your teacher is allowed to have preferences.

Dan

[Grinning] Oh, don't worry about it. Spiritual pride is alive and well. We'll all find ways of rediscovering that in ourselves over time. [Laughter]

Student 3

Dan?

Dan

Yeah.

Student 3

I'm curious about how as Western science starts to study this stuff, it changes the conversation in a way that you've emphasized, and I think most traditions, too. We don't talk about this stuff. We don't talk about this stuff except when speaking to a teacher. Or, we don't talk about realizations, except maybe in a space like this. But it changes the conversation in a way. So, I'm just curious, like how would you …

Dan

That's a good point. If you get a precious secret instruction that will help you to shift from ordinary mind to awakened mind, and it works for you, then you have *damchik*, you have a spiritual duty, or *samaya* in Sanskrit, *damchik* in Tibetan. And every time, if you read Padmasambhava, and he gives you some precious secret instruction that's going to open up a whole other level of mind for you, the text always ends with, in Tibetan, or in Sanskrit, "*samaya*." Remember your spiritual duty.

Or the Tibetan version of that, which you see a lot, particularly with Padmasambhava, who's sitting over there; [Dan is referring to a *thanka* of

Padmasambhava in the room] that's Padmasambhava, you don't want to mess with him because at the end of every text he'll say, "*Gya, gya, gya*," "Seal, seal, seal." And what it means is you have a duty if you're given something precious to seal it in your heart, fix it there, develop the practice, and not let it deteriorate. So, if you go around collecting special instructions and then you just sort of say, "I just collected my new instruction; wow, I'm important," and then you never practice it, that's failing in your spiritual duty.

But if you say, "Wow, this is precious. I'm going to cultivate this. I'm going to work at it until I develop it." So, your duty is to integrate that as a realization of your mindstream. That's one part of "seal." Stamp it in your mindstream, give it the seal. The other meaning of seal is, seal your lips. In other words, you have a duty. You can talk about it, but you have a duty to talk about it in a way that doesn't cause the practices to lose their potency, or to degenerate. That's what sealing means.

So, if you talk about it only in conceptual ways because you really haven't practiced it, and you share it with people who are going to misunderstand it, and they do stupid practices based on how you shared it with them, then you failed in your spiritual duty. You have to talk about it in a way that conveys its preciousness and potency—not that you can't talk about it, but that's your duty. See the difference?

Student 3

Mm hmm.

Dan

So, for example, the most guarded of all the practices are the *tögal* practices, the Dzogchen bypassing practices that deal with all the visions. So, Lopon Tenzin Namdak once published a very precious root text on that practice called *Heart Drops of Dharmakāya*, for the West. It was the first time he ever offered something as secret as that. And he got sued. Because some Western idiot took the book, and there's a thing about sun gazing—you're not supposed to look at the sun; sun gazing doesn't mean you look at the sun. You sit at certain times of the day with the sun behind you, and you watch the surface of your eyeballs from the inside out, like movie screens. And you watch the dance of the visions on the surface, like watching a movie film. And the energy of the sun behind you will make all those visions dance, and they'll be easier to pick out once you know what to look for. You can do it without the sun gazing.

So, this idiot took the book and tried to practice on his own, and he stared at the sun like this [Dan looks up at the ceiling] and he fried his corneas and then sued Lopon Tenzin Namdak, which is a pretty Western thing to do, for damaging him. That's dumb practice.

So, your task in sealing it is not to talk about it with people who are going to do those dumb things. You see what I'm saying? So, if you think about what "*gya, gya, gya*" means in Western terms; if you're given a precious instruction, "Don't fuck it up." That's really what it means in Western terms. That's our closest way of understanding it. It's true. That's what he's trying to get at. So, you have a duty. That's why over time, we put things ... we've tried to word things carefully on the website.

But what I don't want is people taking the course, and then I get these emails from somebody I've never heard from before saying, "I heard that you become enlightened in your course." It's all conceptual rot. And somebody is obviously giving the wrong message about what they got out of the course. And it's harmful because what it does is it brings people who have essentially spiritual greed. That's not the kind of student [we want]. So, you have a duty, if you get something precious, to talk about it in a way that's going to send the right people to get those teachings who can use them to not do stupid practice.

Not everybody can do these practices. We like to make them available to everybody, and that's why, in Buddhism, they have this idea of different capacities. Menri and I, we have an ongoing debate about that. They teach at different levels of capacities saying you have to just not focus on getting people awakened. You have to focus on people who can't do that and teach at that level. And I say, that's the way you traditionally teach but, you know, if we take seriously the idea of buddha nature, then we have to single mindedly try and find a way of getting everybody there.

And his response was: "Good point," he says, "let me be alone with that one." But the idea is traditionally, you teach at a "level." I personally have the view that anyone can do it if you find the right instruction and we work hard to get them there. It's a more hopeful view of it, rather than limiting people about their capacity.

You don't want to have students who are just not going to get it. Some people, their original capacity, you can work with them, it just takes a lot of work to get them to the point that they can get something useful out of it. And that's when you can take them along stages in a kind of spectrum model like Ken Wilber does from basic student, then higher things, and they eventually can move into the higher things. So, a lot of people come here after therapy with him, but not spiritual practice at first.

In the Tibetan tradition, we say, if you're given the most precious teachings and they make sense to you in some way, it's because of previous lifetimes of practice; you have a karmic connection. We call you a *kalden*, a fortunate one. And a *kalden* means that you have previous karmic connection to this. So, when it's presented to you, it's not alien, it's something weirdly familiar about it, and you're curious about it, so you keep coming back for more.

So, many of you are *kaldens*. But some people, when they hear it, it just falls on deaf ears because they don't have that karmic connection. Not that they can't learn it. It'd just be layers over layers of clouds of mind you have to get through. That's Padmasambhava's "lion's roar" metaphor. It goes like this: "When the lioness roars in the forest, all the little lion cubs jump for joy at the thought of the lioness's milk. And all the rest of the animals run away in fear at the sound of the roar of the lioness. Tell me my friends, are you a lion cub or not?" Clear enough?

So, before we take a break, anything else about the neuroimaging stuff here? Did I snow you with this or are you following it?

Student 2

It's great.

Student 4

Dan, I actually had a question. It's about practice. So, when you were talking about compassion, and you were talking about the duty, one of the reasons that brought me into practice is that I work in mental health and I do some advocacy work, and I know that there's still a basis of a lot of emotional grab for me, like with people that hurt children and people that hurt animals, and it impacts my efficacy because there's so much emotional material around it. So, wanting to get to a place, not where I'm completely unaffected, but where I'm detached enough to be more effective. And so I'm wondering in terms of doing—the other thing that I've noticed is that often there's been a lot of moments of grab for me and one of your suggestions was to follow it. And I'm wondering if you had any more instructions on that.

Dan

Yeah. I'll try and give a brief answer here.

In my other hat as a clinician, I'm mostly a trauma and abuse expert. And I can clearly identify with what you're saying because having heard thousands of trauma stories, abuse stories, I went through a phase earlier in my career where I couldn't work with offenders. I couldn't work, particularly, with rapists. And I couldn't work with pedophiles, because I would just have way too much grab. It would evoke this rage and disgust.

And I used to run the Harvard Trauma Conference, which is a flagship conference where you invite the best trauma people and you share in a big conference of about a thousand people. I did that for about twenty years. And one time, when I was giving a conference, this woman therapist came up to me and said, "You're never really going to understand how to treat abuse survivors if you only treat abuse survivors. Until you actually engage in the treatment of offenders, you won't understand how their mind works, and therefore, you won't understand the impact of that behavior on your victims."

And I said, "You know, that's really a very well-intentioned comment; got me on that one." So, the next year, I invited in a woman and an author who has written the best things in that generation on treating offenders. And I invited her back twice to learn more. She would come in for the first time; she would teach by video tapes. The offenders would illustrate how and the strategies they used for victims, which was sort of funny because after watching the first day in total horror, these tapes, my counter transference was such that I went home and blew $5,000 on a security system for my house [Laughter] I had to use the next day because I was so terrified watching these tapes and how easy it is for them to get the victims. So, I was sort of amused by my own reactivity to that. But I started working with offenders and it changed how I worked with victims. I think I became more compassionate to both groups. But I had to look at the grab in myself.

I think I mentioned in one of these other classes when, years ago in the early '80s, when Erika Fromm and I wrote our textbook on hypnotherapy, there's a long case study in that book about a woman that she treated who was a victim of childhood sexual abuse who was successfully treated. That woman was somebody in the field. And what happened is that when she got better, she became an expert in treating sex offenders as a former victim. And she developed that larger metacognitive vision—wider vision of life—and a spiritual vision, when she got better. And she said, "Look, each one of these offenders affects so many lives. The most compassionate thing I could do was to learn to treat offenders because that's how you will curtail what they're doing."

It was an almost spiritual, larger vision of something, which I deeply respected. And I learned something from her: that we have to look at the larger picture here. And that means you don't have to condone their behavior. And I still get very disgusted with what offenders do. But that doesn't mean that I can't, at the same time of being disgusted, also try and practice compassion at their profound limitations.

Bob Thurman is sort of funny, and when he wrote his book on why the Dalai Lama is important politically, Debbie Solomon, who then was the *New York Times* book editor, interviewed him. She asked, "What do you do for compassion practice?" And he said, "I imagine myself as a mother and I have a young baby Dick Cheney suckling on my breast." [Laughter] That's the ultimate compassion practice, you see, right there! [More laughter]

Student 3

That seems really intense. I can't do that. [Laughter]

Dan

But sometimes I find that, you know, because we make people into … and we demonize them, but sometimes I find that I think if I want to feel compassion toward offenders, perpetrators, all I have to do is think about the last days as I had imagined in Sadam Hussein's life, who lived six months, basically, in a well in the ground. And the suffering of basically living in the same hole with no food, and shitting and pissing in the same hole, and not seeing sunlight, and coming out completely broken before they dragged him in the streets and basically tortured and killed him by a violent crowd.[6] That's not a good ending. And as hard as it is to muster up compassion, when I think of that vulnerability and pain, it's not hard to find something in my heart. I find that useful.

So, I suppose we'll all have to face that soon enough and we're beginning to do that as this trial starts, the Boston bomber. That's your test. Can you find compassion at all for somebody who is that violent? Affected so many lives and literally close to home? The man who runs this center, who teaches in the weeks that I'm not here, went to that marathon that day, with his kids standing there. And right next to him was one of the bombs that didn't go off. The sniffing dogs found it. It just so happened that the luck of the draw was that that one was one of the ones that failed to detonate, otherwise he wouldn't be here now and all of us would be affected by that. So, finding compassion for that is difficult, but not impossible.

Student 5

It seems to me that maybe nonduality is the biggest tool in that.

Dan

And common humanity and forgiveness practice.

---

6 Dan has here combined two stories, one is that of Saddam Hussein of Iraq who was found by American forces hiding in a hole and captured in December of 2003, tried and convicted of crimes against humanity, and executed by hanging in December of 2006; the other is that of Muammar Gaddafi of Libya who was found by the Misrata militia hiding wounded in a drainage pipe on October 20, 2011, where he was tortured and killed shortly thereafter.

March 11, 2015

Themes: Levels of Trust and Confidence; Virtue

Dan

Welcome everyone. You have a question?

Student 1

Well, I haven't been here lately, so this is a really big question. [Laughter] It's actually something I've been thinking about for a while now.

Dan

Uh oh.

Student 1

And it has something to do—it really encompasses a lot of things for me and perhaps for a lot of other people as well.

It has to do with, in life in general and in my practice and in the *sangha*, that over time so many things have changed and are changing constantly in my life and in the sangha. And, because we're not moving as frequently, what I've been thinking about, what I've been noticing in practice is that the trust is developing. So that I really have full trust in you, our teacher, and Rinpoche, in the *sangha*, in our practice, and that whatever presents itself is the right path. And, that things are happening for me—they're evolving in the way that seems natural. And so, I wonder if you would talk about the different levels of trust in the practice and in life in general, on the relative level and on the ultimate level.

Dan

Wow. What a super question. Well, there are three answers to that question. Each one has six parts, [Laughter] and each of those has four parts [Dan is here making humorous reference to the way that many Tibetan teachings are organized].

Students

[Inaudible comments and laughter]

Dan

Okay. Well, let's start out with the basics. There are positive states of mind, and those positive states of mind you might think of as potentiating factors—they potentiate spiritual growth. If you have them, then your practice tends to develop more rapidly and more thoroughly. And if you don't have them or have some missing, then the growth from the practice develops more slowly or may not develop. So, you can think of these positive ingredients of mind or the virtues of mind as necessary ingredients to support growth.

And there are many lists. There's the Seven Factors of Awakening in the older Theravādin literature: mindfulness, meta-cognitive awareness, lightheartedness, balance, sustainable energy, concentration, calmness, or non-reactivity or equanimity. And in the Mahāyāna Buddhism, there are the Six Perfections—generosity of spirit, considerateness, patience, enthusiastic perseverance, concentration, wisdom. And then there's a third list, which only has one ingredient on it, and that's trust, emphasized especially in Mahāyāna. And it's not an easy trait to translate.

Tibetans make a distinction between big trust and little trust. The Tibetan word is *dapa*, which is often translated as faith. But little faith is faith that requires an object, a buddha, a god, a teacher, a set of teachings. Big faith is a state of mind. It doesn't require an object. And there are two necessary components to it that I like to translate as trust, because faith implies an object, so trust is a better translation.

One of the components is an outlook component. When you have trust, you take the outlook that no matter what unfolds, it's good just the way it is. You don't have to do anything to it. Everything is perfect just the way it is. And the second component is what in Western terms we would call self-efficacy. Self-efficacy is your own belief that you have the capacity to do whatever is the thing that you're doing. Under self-efficacy there are two sub-components. One is metacognitive intelligence: that when you trust, you trust whatever meditation you are working on. Whatever the nature of the practice is, you trust that you have the innate metacognitive intelligence to figure it out. And the second component is resourcefulness, such that when you have trust, you trust not only your own native metacognitive intelligence, you trust your own inner resourcefulness, that you have the resources within you to implement whatever it is that you're doing in your practice.

Resourcefulness is important. In fact, a colleague and friend of mine, Adam Robinson, did a prospective study on what kids are successful at twenty, thirty, forty years later—looking for predictors of success in life. And the single best predictor of who was successful twenty, thirty, forty years later was resourcefulness, defined as a kid who can take whatever is at hand and use whatever he's got to resolve whatever the task at hand is.

So, when you have trust, you let everything unfold without having to do anything to it. You trust that it will unfold in just the way it needs to unfold. And that you, if you wait for that patiently, you will bring to that sufficient intelligence and your own inner resourcefulness so that whatever it takes, you'll figure it out. And it's said that trust is the cornerstone of all positive qualities of mind. Because if you have only that one ingredient, that's all that you need; because if you have trust at every level of the practice, you will figure it out. You don't need anything else.

The opposite of trust, on the cognitive level, is doubt. That's why we say that trust is the cornerstone of all growth in spiritual practice. And doubt is the main hindrance. "Am I doing it right? Is this what I'm supposed to be doing? Is that really what it means?" All that incessant doubt is a huge cloud that interferes. And on an emotional level, the opposite of trust is fear. So, when you can bring an attitude of trust with every step of this practice, and you go about this practice with no doubt, you practice fearlessly. That's when your meditation will gain. There's no place for fear of change. You have to confront yourself honestly and be open to the remarkable changes that this will produce in you. But some people are afraid of that, so they run away from it.

A wonderful passage I like from Padmasambhava is: "When the lioness roars in the jungle, all the lion cubs jump for joy at the thought of the lioness's milk. All the rest of the animals run away in terror. Tell me my friends, are you a lion cub or not?" Do you have the stamina, the openness, the courage, and the honestly to really take up the spiritual path? Because if you take it up, everything in your life will change. And as you look at everything in life, at the beginning, it's not very pleasant. Or as Chogyam Trungpa once said, "Self-knowledge is generally bad news." [Laughter] So, that's the cornerstone. All the good qualities of mind; it's all you need.

And it's not just applicable in spiritual practice. You can certainly see the importance of trust in the Olympics, in athletic performance. You all remember the gymnast Mary Lou Retton, where she had to get a perfect ten to get the gold medal. Nothing short of a perfect score would win her the medal. She went up there with an absolute confidence and an absolute trust and nailed it. Got a perfect ten. It's the same attitude. She absolutely knew what she was capable of doing and simply, without complication, did it. That's all it took.

So, this attitude of trust, it's a complex term. And it means something very specific. So, if you don't have that trust, then you have to cultivate it. You can do exemplar method. You can think of who the best exemplar of trust would be and imagine various scenarios where that person is manifesting that trust in a strong way, so you become familiar with the quality. We call that "becoming familiar with the quality through the eyes of the exemplar." Then you imagine the exemplar with you, and you change them into a bubble of light, and you put the bubble of light above your head, and then let it run down through your body into your heart. Then you imagine light rays bursting forth in all directions. And as the light continues to emanate, you imagine that quality developing in your heart and growing stronger and stronger until you develop that trust. If you do that as a regular visualization, you start to develop the view that you carry, that trust deep within your own heart, until there is nothing else other than that trust.

So, you have to cultivate. And there's a feedback loop with that. The more your practice is successful, the more it helps to contribute to refining and developing the trust. The more you bring the trust, the greater the likelihood that the practice is successful, and then that success fosters more trust. And that trust fosters more success, and it develops from there.

Strong practitioners have no doubt. They just listen to the instructions in an uncomplicated way and they just do it and they know they can do it. They don't have any doubt about it. I remember when I went to Burma in the 1970s; I was working on the *Visudhimagga*, the Path of Purification. And I only had a month. It was with a teacher who was eighty and I had a weird visa because Americans only had a week-long visa, but I had a special visa such that as long as I meditated, I could stay in the country. [Laughter] So, I had a weird visa, I had a teacher who was old, and every morning I heard the sound of the marching of the military troops, and I knew that this country was going to fold.

And I knew I would never ever have the chance to go back and do this again. So, I set the task of just doing it in a month. And it wasn't even hard to do, because I had no doubt. And in my exit interview with Mahāsī Sayādaw he said, "Look, right from the get go, there was no doubt that you were going to do this. You knew that right away and you just did it. And trust was the main factor for you and that's why it worked." And that was spot on. But that's not just meditation practice, that's anything that one would do in life.

Now, that's the first answer to your question. The second answer to your question is that if you follow the steps of this path, your concentration and emptiness practice, and you refine your emptiness to automatic emptiness, and you refine that to the natural state of the mind, as you know, and you set up your crossing over instructions in your view; and then, in holding that view, you then shift your basis of operation to awakening. However, that awakening may not be stable. If you get a taste of what Tashi Namgyal once called "little flames of awakening," however strong or however unstable that is—stable or unstable, or strong or weaker ones—if you get an authentic taste of awakening, then it changes everything, because you have found the path home. Just about anybody that we've ever had take these retreats who got a taste of awakening, almost everyone says, "This is very familiar to me. I've always known this." Because it's your true nature. Which will find the pathway home.

And of course, if you get even just the slightest flame of awakening, it changes everything. In some sense we say that's the end of the path because all that searching for what's missing, and all that longing, it settles all that. You've found the path in this lifetime, once you know that. But then we also say it's the beginning of the path. Because now you have to take that path of awakening and bring it to buddhahood.

But most people will tell you that having gotten an authentic taste of awakening, that something fundamentally changes about this trust thing. You know what I'm talking about. Because there's no doubt about what you're looking for anymore. It will move your heart when you open it up a little bit. And there's no doubt about it. So, you see, you know the path.

In the older literature, the Theravādin literature, that was called "distinguishing between path and not path." Once you know awakening, you know the true path, that everything other than awakening is not the true path. Or, in Mahāyāna terms, it's either *rigpa*, awakened awareness, or *marigpa*, failure to recognize awakened awareness. And in every moment of your life, you either recognize the awakening that's always here, or, in that moment you don't recognize it. Every moment. So, it's not a state where you say, "Yeah, I got that." You have to live it every moment and manifest it every moment. But even if it's not stable, which it usually isn't at the beginning because those nice clouds come back in and cloud over, most of us will get a taste of awakening and we lose it. Of course, you know that Dzogchen Ponlop once said, "Most people when they wake up, they put the snooze alarm on many times." You go back to sleep. But it's never the same again. Something has shifted. And the manifestation of that shift, amongst other things, in one way, is it brings trust to a whole new level. You know that it's there—or let me correct my language. You know that it's always right here. And even when it gets clouded over, you know that you can find your way back to it.

And if you keep opening up that awakening frequently, and for longer duration on and off the pillow, at some point it will seem perfectly ridiculous to you that you would ever lose it. And at some point, even in your worst moments of the day, when it's clouded over, that cloud is such a thin veil that all that's required is the intention to look at it with your metacognitive awareness. It's always right here again. It's as simple as that. All that requires is the intention to look and to remember, and you shift your basis back to awakening again—out of ordinary mind.

Now at some point, if you keep doing that, it will seem perfectly ridiculous that it could ever go away. And that's when you achieve what Tibetans call *dengwa*, which is often translated as confidence or assurance. You are assured that it's always right here, and it can't possibly be anything other than being right here. And it's always available even if it clouds over.

Now that's a whole other level of trust, to have *dengwa*, or assurance. Because when you develop that assurance, that it can't really get lost, ever, and all that's required is the intention to look with your metacognitive awareness and you're awake, then you pretty much have it most of the time, on and off the pillow. I mean you will still have moments where it will cloud over, but not much. You're done with that. You're confident about that now.

And that begins [the first of the] three maps—the beginning of the path to a taste of awakened awareness. The second is all the teachings that bring you from the unstable, little taste of awakening, to having it 24/7, on and off the pillow. And then, once you have that, the third map is how you take that continuous awakening and bring it to full buddhahood. So essentially, when you develop confidence, which is a kind of trust that comes directly from your experience, at that point, you see, that's a key that opens the door to the gateway of that third map that brings you to buddhahood.

Now, when you are working on that third map to buddhahood, almost everything unfolds automatically. And the next level of confidence is that you discover that not only does awakened awareness have liveliness—awakened awareness isn't a static, empty field—it's always expressing itself. All of this is lively awakened awareness, the whole show. It's all awareness, because awareness expresses itself to itself and knows itself through its own expressions. But at some point, you realize that awakened awareness has another property in addition to the liveliness. Especially when you get to that third map, it gets quite apparent that it has intelligence.

And that's when the whole path on that third map, almost everything, is automatic. And every moment you have an awakened mind, and whatever arises in the field of that awakened mind, we say, "The path shows itself to itself by itself." So, all you have to do is just not interfere with this automatic unfolding. And everything that you need to know on the way will show itself to itself by itself.

And I go back to the monastery to check in with His Holiness Menri Trizin, but I find that in the years I've worked with him now, I do that much less because the whole process is self-unfolding, self-manifesting, and self-correcting. It's almost completely automatic, and at best, as he can see into the nature of things, I show up at his room and he says, "Now do this." I never have to say anything about the state. Even if I didn't do that, it would self-correct anyway.

So, you see, that's another level of this trust. Now you're trusting not just in the unfolding of it, but there's an intelligent order to the unfolding of this. And when we get into the *tögal* visions where you see the different levels of visions, it's elegantly ordered. Everybody's mind has that orderliness to it. Everything shows itself to itself by itself in the same order. Because you're seeing the structure of reality.

So then, you see, the next level of trust is you see this whole bubble here that we take as the seemingly existing world, *jikting*, in Tibetan. We think this is all there is, but there's a certain point that you've got to open up all-at-once-ness; and there are multiple levels of reality here all simultaneously. And when you open up what's called all-at-once-ness and this limitlessness, the mind's awakened awareness saturates all those realms at once and they're all here all at once. So, your mind operates on many levels of reality simultaneously. Sometimes in Dzogchen that's called "cracking the eggshell" of this little seeming bubble of reality. The rainbow is the reality, all here at once.

Now, some of those realms are buddha realms and fields, where there are many teachers and buddhas and *bodhisattvas*, and some of the realms are *ḍākinī* fields where the laughing sisterhood of *ḍākinīs* offers teachings. And some of those realms are where previous teachers have manifested their complete sets of teachings. And you don't need to get the teaching anymore from an external teacher, because all of the wisdom that is built into the structure of reality is all there in that all-at-once-ness space. And you'll get complete downloads of teachings—whatever you need to complete the omniscience part of the mind.

None of that comes from "out there" of course—it's all a part of your own buddha nature. So, you've opened up that buddha nature. And then, there's certainly not any need to seek outside yourself for any further teachings. The whole path will show itself in its completeness, not just pieces here and there, in its completeness, always. So that's a whole other level of trust when you open up that all-at-once-ness. You trust that the omniscience of the buddha mind will come to you in its orderly, elegantly ordered unfolding. That's what is stunning.

So, those are the different levels of trust. See, there's a lot to your question; it's rather profound. Your questions help a lot. Good question.

But the starting point is trusting not in an external buddha figure or a teacher but trusting in your own innate intelligence and your own resourcefulness because they're part of your buddha nature.

Some of you know, but I'll tell it again for people who don't live here. A good example of resourcefulness was once when there was a concert at the Los Angeles Symphony; and I don't remember the piece of music, but they were going to play a long solo piece featuring Itzhak Pearlman. And they started the symphony, and they got off to the part that he was giving a solo, and he breaks a string right in the beginning of it. Now normally what they would do is pause the orchestra, the musician would walk off the stage, restring it, tune it, and then they would come back and pick up the symphony from there. But there was an awkward moment because, since he's disabled, everybody in the audience and orchestra could not believe he wasn't going to go off the stage. But he just didn't do that.

So, after a very awkward silence, he starts picking up and playing the piece of music minus the string. And he played it perfectly without the string which was nearly impossible to do. And the next day, a reporter from the Los Angeles Times asked, "How did you ever have the presence of mind to think of that?" And his response was very humble. "Sometimes an artist has to make do with what they've got." That's a clear example of resourcefulness—when you go about your practice and you understand that you have the added intelligence and resourcefulness to figure this out every stage of the way, and there is nothing that will get in the way.

But if you go about this practice and undermine your own intelligence and think, "Well, I have to get it from outside myself," or some source of teaching or teacher, and you start undermining your own intelligence and resourcefulness, and you don't get anywhere. All that looking outside prevents you from seeing that this is all built-in. It's part of the hardwiring. It's your buddha nature. The function of a teacher is to help you see that for yourself in yourself. Then, what else do you need?

When I was much younger, in my first group home with Geshe Wangyal, I lived with him over the summers for nine years while I was in school. He died when I was young, and of course at that age, I was not really able to appreciate what I had gotten. Over the years I sort of missed him, and when times in my life didn't go well, I wished I had a wise person like that again to go to. There's a famous scene in *Camelot* where the Round Table is sort of messed up. The vision didn't manifest itself, and Richard is sort of lost and goes to the forest to look for Merlin, and Merlin isn't in the forest anymore. And in these times in my life, Merlin wasn't in the forest anymore. And I longed for that. At some point along the way, I figured out what the message was. And that was not to long for that state of mind of the teacher, but to be that. Then there was no more problem. It's what you learn in guru yoga. The realized mind of the teacher and your mind meld in your heart and are inseparable. They're one and the same because they're not different.

Your awakened nature and the awakened nature of the teacher are one and the same. The only difference is that you can't see it. When you manifest it, you see it, and you manifest it and live it as conduct, there is no difference. And that is the best gift that you could give back to your teacher—to become it. Nothing less. And of course, that raises all the doubt, and you go right back to square one. First response is, "I can't do that." Why not? Where does that "I can't" come from? All that negative cultural stuff that we internalize. Just an empty idea.

So, think about times in your life when you really trusted yourself and you surprised yourself—in any endeavor. You went far beyond what your capacity was. It's not hard for most of you to think of examples of that. What if you did that all the time? As a continuous state of mind, imagine what your life would be like. Why can't you do it all the time? No reason other than your limiting ideas about yourself.

How we doing? Time for another question?

Student 2

Dan, we've talked about some of the virtues. There's a running distinction between the virtue of caring and the virtue of courage. Both of those require some wisdom to execute, but I guess I'm interested in whether there is a distinction, and second, how we cultivate that, because there are times when both are necessary.

Dan

Well, they can overlap, but when we think of the virtue of caring, we're already thinking of how it's part of the Peterson and Seligman list of the twenty-four major virtues, and caring is part of the virtue of humanity. It means putting aside your own self-interest for the welfare of others. You have a duty to put aside your own self-interest for the welfare of others. But in your field—the legal field—it would be called "fiduciary relationship." The senior party has a duty to put aside all of their own interest for the growth and development of the junior party. Parent-child relationships are fiduciary relationships. Doctor-patient relationships, teacher-student relationships, and minister-parishioner relationships are fiduciary relationships. And financial relationships. They're supposed to be fiduciary right? But my friend has been telling me, there's a whole serious debate about that now—most people on Wall Street don't think they have any fiduciary duties to their clients. Instead, they're just making money for themselves. Something went wrong here, but caring is about putting aside your own interests for the interest of the junior party.

In our culture, fiduciary relationships used to be strong foundations. But it has seriously deteriorated in every area. Welcome to *samsāra*. None of the people on Wall Street think twice about getting clients and sending all their money around, like stealing it or maybe using it to make money for themselves. All the priest abuse—there are obviously fiduciary relationships in the ministry and priesthood that have gone down the tubes as is the case for sexual misconduct in the health professions. We live in a culture of fiduciary violations rather than fiduciary relationships being upheld.

When is the last time you heard about fiduciary relationships being upheld? We don't even talk about it. So, we've failed miserably in the culture and ethics of care. I had the great fortune to benefit in this lifetime from having strong mentors who upheld the mentee relationships, fiduciary relationships where they were interested in my wellbeing. That's rare.

Caring versus, what was the other?

Student 2

Courage.

Dan

Courage. Well in the virtues and character strengths work of Peterson and Seligman, that's one of the other big virtues. But courage specifically is acting bravely in the face of fear. It doesn't necessarily just mean—certainly we see bravery in soldiers who put themselves at great risk to save other soldiers. We certainly see that amongst police officers and fire fighters and basically, citizens. And a good example of that kind of courage is looking at the film clips that are now being shown because of the trial of the marathon bomber.

What's for me the most heart-rending part of watching those films is to watch when the bombs go off that half the people run towards the source of danger and the other half the other way. There's your world right there. I'm more curious about the people who run towards the danger rather than away from it because they've got something special. They don't think about their own danger, they just do what's right. That's bravery in the face of great danger. And it certainly overlaps with caring because they were running towards the source of danger in order to care for others.

But courage and bravery extend to other areas, not just the threat of physical harm but the threat of reputation. I remember growing up in the '50s and '60s and being part of the whole Camelot myth of John Kennedy. When he came into office there was great hope for this country. And all that was shattered by his assassination. What was important, I think, about him—whatever we might think of Kennedy—one thing that always intrigued me is that before he became president, he wrote *Profiles in Courage*. So, he had given this a lot of thought. And there it was about people in politics who made decisions that were political suicide, but they were doing the right thing.

And they had the courage to stand up for what's right rather than what's going to get him re-elected. And he basically wrote that book as a series of case studies of people who had that kind of courage to do what was right in the face of their reputation and maybe even their job. It's rare. But nowadays we see that in terms of the abuse that most whistleblowers take. To be a whistleblower takes a certain courage to say what's wrong. And you find that in academic fields also, intellectual pursuits. Intellectual courage means you're willing to say what's truthful, not necessarily what's popular, what's going to get you a better reputation.

Many scientists won't do that. They only write about what's going to better their reputation rather than what's necessarily truthful. But in almost any profession, to have courage is the courage to live by what's true. For me, being a therapist, therapy is about saying what's true, sitting with that, and trying to find a way of presenting that in a way that the patient will understand it. But I can't do anything other than saying what's true. So, certainly they overlap, but bravery is specific to acting truthfully in the face of some feared consequences to whatever—physical integrity, reputation, whatever. And most people won't do that.

Student 2

I guess the follow-on is the cultivation of those characteristics. We talked about that a little bit but that's part of my question.

Dan

Then we get an East-West distinction because the modern work on virtues and character strengths is Chris Peterson and Marty Seligman's book *Character Strengths and Virtues* (for those of you who don't know that). Starting around 1990 and the 2000s was a kind of moving away from looking at negative states and behaviors of mind to a whole movement of research on positive psychology. And Peterson and Seligman got a grant from the Templeton Foundation to look at all the lists of virtues around the world in Buddhism, Hinduism, Confucianism, Judaism, Christianity, Aristotle, and Plato. They even looked at lists of virtues of Charlemagne, the Round Table, and the list of virtues in the Boy Scouts and Girl Scouts.

They looked at all lists of virtues. The task was to come up with a universal, cross-culturally valid set of virtues, and then give detailed descriptions of what each virtue was. The virtue was defined as a quality of mind that protects your growth of self and others, but never diminishes others, that contributed to the greater social good, and that was done for the sake of doing the virtue irrespective of outcome. Those are the basic definitions of the virtue. So then, they brought out this list of the twenty-four—there were six core virtues and four subtypes. So, you have twenty-four universally valued virtues.

And they wrote up a big thick manual of this that they call *Manual of the Sanities*. And it was supposed to be a positive counterpoint to the *DSM, [the Diagnostic and Statistical Manual of Mental Disorders]*; something positive that you do. But of course, with all of these things, if you take a narrow perspective of only this culture, it falls flat because the limitation of Peterson and Seligman's work was that they made the assumption testing it that the virtues are trait-like, like personality traits. So, the traits don't change very much. So, there's nothing in the *Manual of Sanities* that gives you a treatment manual for how you develop these virtues. They just assume you either got it or you don't; whereas if you look at all the writings in Buddhist *Abhidharma*, their version of psychology, and particularly in Tibetan Buddhism, then the whole idea is you use structured visualization to develop these virtues. And you cultivate them over and over again until you actually develop them into your strengths. So, you can develop and change them. In fact, in terms of spiritual practice, it's a necessity to develop these. So that's a huge difference because in the Buddhist tradition there is much more emphasis and, okay, let's take the ones you don't have and develop them.

Whereas in the West it's all about assessment—these are what you don't have, and that's as far as it goes. Like most Western medicine, we do great things on the diagnostic level, but then we don't tell people how to treat it. So what good is it to know what it is if you can't treat it? See, that's where I think we sell ourselves short here. You develop these things.

There's a story I often tell in my peak performance course. Some years ago, before free agency, the Patriots had [inaudible], name's Irving Prior. He was the number one draft pick in the nation, and he could run faster than anybody else. He was a wide receiver, and he played for the Patriots for around ten years, and he was very streaky. Sometimes he was great, most of the time he was mediocre, and sometimes he was just awful. He had a lot of off-year problems—he got arrested for illegal possession of guns three times, he had a domestic dispute with his wife the night before the Super Bowl when she stabbed him in the hands so he couldn't catch the ball—self-destructive.

So then free agency came along, and the Patriots dumped him. And he went to the Philadelphia Eagles, which in those days was not a very good team. He was then around thirty, and usually the body slows down, so he's not a very good wide receiver at that age, but for the next six years he was one of the top three wide receivers in the league even though he was ten years older than most of the other wide receivers. He was in the top three of about one hundred wide receivers. And rather than having off-field problems, he became a great community leader and devoted his life to working with violent street gangs in Philadelphia, working with the kids, directly teaching them nonviolent ways of conflict resolution. After he retired from football he went back to his Christian roots, became a minister, still does work with kids, and is committed to cleaning up violence. Complete turnaround.

What he did was that when he went to Philadelphia, he got hooked up to learn concentration meditation with the lama I used to teach with. And, of course, he didn't teach him just the Elephant Path concentration, he taught him all the visualizations about cultivating the virtues of mind. It fundamentally changed his character. That made all the difference in the world. He had the program of virtue training that the Tibetans used for spiritual growth, and you could see the results. Even after he went back to his Christian roots, he never lost the virtues in character training he was subjected to as part of his training.

And the reason why he became such a good wide receiver was that he was able to concentrate his mind so he's always just in the right place at the right time on the field. And the mental training gave him the edge over the decline of the mind and body even though he was ten years older than most wide receivers. So, this is an example of virtue training in the West using Eastern techniques. There isn't any reason why we can't do that with anybody. It's not enough to read the *Manual of the Sanities.* There's nothing in that book about how to develop these qualities. I disagree with Seligman and Peterson about that. If you can't train it, what good is it?

So that's another dimension that needs to be addressed. We all know about emotional intelligence and social intelligence (Danny Goleman's work), and Bob Engler has put together, based on that, spiritual intelligence. So, when you do practice, you should do it intelligently. The opposite of spiritual intelligence is fundamentally a kind of *nyamtak*, unquestioning acceptance without looking into the nature of things at all.

One of my colleagues put together a definition of fundamentalism: "low on the fun, high on the mental." Every religion has its form of fundamentalism. It's spiritual practice "blind" and it's "dumb trust." And it's destructive—destructive to the individual because basically it erodes any kind of sense of self and judgment, and it's destructive of the various social groups and can destroy entire cultures in the name of fundamentalism. And we have our own versions of dumb trust besides fundamentalism in terms of spiritual teaching. So blind trust is when you uncritically accept anything the teacher says—you do the strangest thing because you think he's a "guru." It's the disease of idealization in this culture. People have done the most bizarre things in the name of spirituality.

My first Root Lama, Geshe Wangyal was Mongolian—he wasn't Tibetan—he was a Mongolian horse trader, and he was very shrewd. He said, "Finding teacher is like buying horse. You don't just buy a horse; you check out the hoofs, you check out the teeth, you have to check out what you're buying." You don't just accept. So, you have to have some critical judgment about what you're getting, otherwise you're just blindly accepting some things that are obviously off, and we just dismiss that notion. So, when you dismiss the stuff that seems off and you go along with it, it leads to enormous destructiveness in terms of sexual misconduct and misuse of power, the accumulation of wealth and self-importance, all in the name of spirituality. What's wrong with that picture?

Think about it in terms of metacognitive awareness. When you practice concentration, it's not enough to just focus on the object. You have to constantly use your intelligence to look at the quality of that meditation. A Sufi tale says, "A log sits very quietly on the woodpile for years, but logs don't realize God.

So don't sit like a log, sit intelligently." We're always looking into the nature of it to bring out the best quality, and self-correcting how we go about our meditation practice.

Now, in neuroimaging terms, concentration is activation of the anterior cingulate cortex. You have to adequately focus on one thing and tune everything else out. But the metacognitive awareness center in the brain is the right dorsolateral prefrontal cortex. That's where we can see into the nature of something and evaluate the quality of it, not by thinking but by seeing clearly and truthfully what it is. When they did a study comparing the difference between advanced and beginning concentrators, both activated the anterior cingulate cortex, but only the advanced meditators activated the right dorsolateral prefrontal cortex. What made them better meditators was that they're constantly looking into the quality of it, trying to better it; they were self-correcting their mistakes. In fact, that's the difference between hypnosis and concentration—both are heightened states of awareness that activate the anterior cingulate cortex, but in concentration, you're constantly putting metacognitive awareness online and refining it, sharpening it; whereas in hypnosis you take the right dorsolateral prefrontal cortex offline, so you're uncritically accepting every suggestion the [hypnotist] gives you, even though you are in a heightened state of concentration. That's the difference.

Practice smart. That's spiritual intelligence. That's another way of saying "spiritual." So, trust isn't "blind" trust, it's really trusting in your own intelligence to see things the way they are. Don't misunderstand trust with the kind of blind belief in somebody by way of uncritical acceptance. It's almost the exact opposite of that. Otherwise, we make lots of messes.

Think of the excesses we've got in this culture—like Rajneesh. He's got a funny name, and he comes from India. That makes him a guru? He basically ran a bookshop, never meditated a day in his life. He's got a funny name, and he stops talking. He gets thousands of followers. He even tried to take over a town so he could run the town with [an election]. And when he thought he didn't have enough votes, he brings all of these great busloads of homeless people because they could vote there, but after they vote, they still didn't get the election. And he basically dumps them on the street. Now this place is a homeless culture. How compassionate is that? When it's not so clear he's going to win the election, he basically put salmonella in the water supply so people couldn't vote. How many thousands of people follow this guy? But then they caught him in twenty-seven million dollars of tax evasion. And then he reinvents himself in India and does the same thing again.

Who is at fault here? All the people who follow him as much as he is. They have jointly participated in it because they suspended basic, honest judgment of the situation. And that's dumb practice.

Smart students test their teachers as much as the teachers test them. So, you better watch out for the disease of idealism in this country. Just because people come over and have a funny name and are from another culture, we think they are gurus immediately. Most of the stuff, two thirds of it, is outright crap in the name of spirituality. It's embarrassing the way we behave in spiritual traditions. So, don't suspend your critical judgment. Metacognitive honesty is a necessary ingredient on this path—it keeps it honest. If you give it up, then essentially, your religious practice is basically a cult. That's true in any culture, not just here.

May 27, 2015

Themes: Working with Physical and Emotional Pain; Rainbow Body

Dan

Hi everybody. You have a question?

Student 1

I have one question. There's several parts.

Dan

Okay.

Student 1

The difference between the physical pain and emotional pain, and sometimes one is more, sometimes one is less and how … Is it the same for all the people or different? Which one is worse or how does it work in general?

Dan

Oh, that's a good question.

Student 1

And the other thing is as you mentioned about the death. When someone who is very close to us is leaving us, it's a very painful experience. Practicing emptiness is very good meditation and it helps a lot, and you realize that you're letting your grab—and it's your desire and it's your grab basically.

Dan

Yeah, there's a body here somewhere. [Dan smiles]

Student 1

But it still bothers you. On a different side, the pain is still there. And on the top of that, I noticed that many times with other people and when it came to me, there's always guilt. It's like it's always there. It doesn't matter if we've done something wrong or not, we always think about that. Maybe something else should be done more or better or different, and it's always there. We can tell our self that everything has to be in peace, and it's not up to us when people come and when people go, but it's still there. And on another side, we live in a big society and it's multicultural, and many traditions and people have different beliefs. And sometimes, unintentionally, we can hurt people and it's not like we want it, but it just happened that way. I should probably stop now.

Dan

Well, there are two big issues, separate issues, somewhat … physical versus emotional pain. Let's answer that in Western terms because I'm not sure that they're that different. Some of the earliest and best work on pain in the 1970s and—most of the 1970s—was done by Jack Hilgard at Stanford. He said that pain had two components to it. There is a sensory component, the pure sensation of pain, and there was an emotional component, a cognitive-affective component to the pain. So, there's the pure sensation and then there's the cognitive-emotional reaction to that sensation. And he thought that those were concomitant or co-arising features of any physical pain experience.

It turns out that if you look at modern neuroimaging studies where we can take live action shots of the neurocircuitry in the brain, if we induce pain from what's called "cold pressor pain," like taking your hand and circulating it in freezing ice water and asking for a report on a one to ten scale of the amount of pain; most people go "one, two, three, six, eight, ten," and after a minute, they take it out. You can induce pain that way. You can take a metal rod and heat it up to the point that it gets uncomfortably painful. However, you can take a tourniquet and produce ischemic pain. Those are the usual laboratory ways of inducing short-term intense pain that doesn't damage people, and it allows you to study pain in a laboratory. But now, we have—while people have laboratory induced pain like that—we've looked very carefully at the neurocircuitry of that.

And physical pain is a little different from other sense systems because with the other … There are five sense systems, right? The other four sense systems have end organs. Eyes for sight, ears for sound, tongue for taste, nose for smell. But what about touch? Where's the end organ for touch? The problem is that the way that "haptic" system or touch system works is that it reads completely phenomenologically distinct sensations. Cold, heat, immediate pain, secondary pain.

Immediate pain is your banging a nail into the hammer, and you hit your thumb. Your "aaah!" That's immediate pain. And then it goes away after about a minute, and then about three or four minutes later, you get this throbbing pain which is a secondary pain. So, cold, heat, pressure, movement. First order of pain, second order pain. So, how does the body-mind experience that many different varieties of sensation when there are no end organs or nerve endings for either one of those things?

The way it does it with what's called "gate control," not in the central … not in the brain but at the dorsal root of the spinal cord there's a little software package. And depending on whether the input is ascending or descending, intermittent or steady, how intense it is—there's a whole series of criteria at very high speeds in terms of milliseconds—it sorts those sensations into cold, heat, pressure, pain, movement. Then it sends the signal already classified up to the brain.

And in the brain, when it comes up is a pain signal, two different neurocircuits get activated. One is the primary and secondary cortices, sensory motor cortices. That's pure sensation. It's a sensation of pain, but at the same time, the limbic system lights up and certain parts of the prefrontal cortex. The limbic system is the emotions of the brain. The parts of the prefrontal system is how we think about that pain. So, you see it's a kind of neurobiological corroboration for what Jack Hilgard said a long time ago. There's the pure sensation and then there's the cognitive emotional reaction to that sensation.

He called the pure sensation the "sensory component" to pain, and the cognitive-emotional part the "suffering component" to pain. In other words, the signal is just the signal. It could be more or less intense but is not necessarily painful. What makes it painful is the interpretation of that signal. And that's partly individual differences. There are personality differences in how we interpret those sensations and how we tolerate them. There are cultural differences in terms of what we consider pain, and there are contextual differences.

If you're having a bad time in your life and you're depressed, for example, and you experience physical pain, it's probably going to be more intense than otherwise would be the case. But, if you're an athlete playing a game and you get hurt, you might put aside the pain.

Since we live part-time here and part-time in San Francisco, I've been watching the Golden State basketball game which I had to miss tonight to come here. [Laughter.] See, if I made the decision about which of those two things I'd do for the sake of all sentient beings, it probably should be the basketball game. Anyway, I'm here. [One of their star players, Klay Thompson] had this horrendous injury. It looked like a concussion. It's one of the worst falls I've ever seen the other night. It was horrendous to watch. And he came back and played. For him, he didn't experience any pain in that context, and we see that in a lot of athletes.

So, how much we experience pain is somewhat contextual. If you hurt yourself, if you have broken a leg or something like that, and you're chasing your kids around the house, you don't feel that pain when you're chasing the kids around the house because you can't. So, there's a strong contextual component to pain and all of that is about how the mind interprets the pain. And there are two separate systems in the brain that light up: the sensory motor system, pure sensation, and the cognitive-affective circuits, the suffering component to the pain. Do you follow me?

Now, in Buddhism, it's not very different. In Buddhism, there are the same five main sense systems: sight, smell, etcetera, but they add a sixth. They call it the mind consciousness. And the mind consciousness, the *yishe* in Tibetan, is what appraises and assigns meaning to sense experience. So, if I look at this [Dan holds up a large bowl] with my eye consciousness, this is color and form. But if I look at integrating the eye consciousness with the mind consciousness, this is now a bowl. You see the difference? The mind consciousness assigns meaning to this as a bowl. And then in what's called "the eight consciousness" model in Buddhism, the seventh is sense of self, or what's called the "afflictive consciousness" because that gets into reactivity and emotions. And the eighth is the memory system. So, that would be a bowl that has certain personal meanings. If I had my meditation bowl that I use for my retreats, it's one that I bought in a father and son trip to Japan with my oldest son. We bought it in Kyoto and it has personal meaning to the self. So, now it's color and form; it's now a bowl that's meaningful to me and it has memories associated with it. All eight consciousnesses are involved. Follow me?

So, in that sense, the idea that the mind interprets pure sense experience and overlays onto that a whole conceptual and emotional story is not that different from … between Buddhism and Western psychology, except that the Buddhists make it more explicit to the areas of the brain to do that kind of thing. And their model is actually closer to modern neuroimaging than the Western model is.

But, if you think about what I'm saying, what that suggests is that since all physical pain has a very strong overlay of a cognitive-emotional reaction to it, and what causes the suffering is mostly the cognitive emotional reaction to it, not the purest sensation, then you see the distinction that you're making between physical pain and emotional pain isn't that clear because physical pain has a strong emotional component to it, the same way that emotional pain does. So, maybe they're not so different after all at least in terms of how we know how the mind works. They're not different.

Now, how do you work with that pain? In Western terms, one of the studies that Jack Hilgard pioneered was hypnosis. I can have a person put their hand in circulating ice water and every ten seconds they give me a number about the degree of pain from one to ten and they go, "1, 3, 5," and after a minute most people pull their hand out because they can't stand it. Now, what Jack Hilgard found is he said … After demonstrating that, he said … he hypnotized them and told them that they wouldn't feel the pain. They might still feel some sensation, but it wouldn't be painful. So, what does that hypnotic suggestion targeting?

It's targeting the cognitive-affective part of the pain. Cognitive-emotional part, right? Then people who are reasonably or highly hypnotizable would put a certain hand in the circulating ice water and then go, "1, 3, 5, 2, 1, 0, 0, 0." Then after five minutes, they still have their hand in it and they're not feeling any pain. That's been done a number of times. We replicated that study some years ago. It's impressive.

But, if you look at that study with hypnosis—in looking at it nowadays, forty years later, with all what we know about brain neurocircuitry—that when the hypnotized person is not hypnotized … and they're in a waking state, and they put their hand in, they activate the primary and secondary sensory motor cortices, and they also activate the limbic system, the emotional part of it. And after they get a hypnotic suggestion and they put their hand in the circulating ice water, neither of the primary and secondary sensory motor cortices get activated. Nor the cognitive-affective limbic system. In other words, they've shut down all the neurocircuitry, and what gets activated is the ACC, the anterior cingulate cortex, which is how we pay attention to things. It's the same area of the brain that is activated in concentration meditation.

So, what are they doing when we give them a hypnotic suggestion that they might feel something but not pain? They activate that area of the brain, not consciously, that has to do with attention control, and they divert their attention away from it in such a way that they stop processing it with higher cognitive areas, higher brain areas, but it never reaches up to the sensory motor piece. It never reaches the limbic system. They shut it off at that gate [in the spinal cord] simply by diverting their attention to it.

I worked with hypnosis for many years and that was something that I was once quite interested in. So, one time I had oral surgery, and I wanted to try this out. So, I convinced the surgeon that I would hypnotize myself rather than have an anesthesia. And he took out four impacted wisdom teeth. It was a six-hour operation, and I went through the whole thing by hypnotizing myself. And I lasted about four hours into the post-op and then it was [hurting?] a little bit, and after ten hours I was tired, so I took one Percocet. That's all I took.

I needed to show myself that I could actually have this mind-body effect with hypnosis, and I didn't feel anything. In fact, the surgeon gave me a running commentary on everything he was doing and I found it terribly interesting. I simply focused on what he was doing. I didn't feel the pain.

Now, many years ago, when we were doing research on the early generation of mindfulness people at Barre,[7] we repeated the cold pressor experiment, the laboratory experiment, with people who were skilled in mindfulness. So, I

7 Insight Meditation Society in Barre, MA.

brought my little cold pressor tank up to IMS in Barre. And we had the people who went on three-month retreat. We tested them the first day, and then we tested on the day they came out. What we found was after three months of sixteen hours a day of mindfulness training, they would put their hand in the ice water, and they would feel a sensation. And it would vary in intensity. And at no point did they feel pain. It was just pure sensation. Now if we would look at that study again today, which other people have done, in terms of what we know about neurocircuitry, we'd found out the following: the ACC, the anterior cingulate cortex gets activated, and the primary and secondary sensory motor cortices get activated, but not the limbic system.

So, mindfulness is actually affecting the pain completely differently from hypnosis. In hypnosis, you basically stop any higher processing, both emotional processing and sensory processing, but with mindfulness you're simply more aware of the sensation, but you shut down the emotional processing.

In other words, in Jack Hilgard's original terminology we would say, you still have the sensory component, sometimes even stronger, but you don't have the suffering component. You follow me? It works totally differently. And that's why somebody like Milarepa can say if you work with pain with emptiness practice and you push it to its limit, pain is like bliss. It's not negative anymore. It's just strong sensation. It's terribly interesting. And it has no positive or negative association to it. It just is what it is and it's just wonderful to watch all this stuff happening. It's just not pain anymore.

So, if you add to this equation not simply trying to block it out with hypnosis and not simply become aware of it, which is the second method of mindfulness, but to practice emptiness which is a third method, emptiness does something rather different to it because then it's no longer a neutral experience, it's a positive experience. It's like bliss. And you get to the pure essence, what we call "the pure energy of manifestation" of pain.

All these practices, mind-body practices—hypnosis, mindfulness meditation, emptiness meditation—all affect the experience of physical pain, but the end result is quite different. And I'm not sure all of them are equally useful. For example, years ago, Bill Morgan, a psychologist at the University of Wisconsin who was into sports psychology, studied marathon runners and the strategies there, because if you run for twenty-six miles, you get a lot of bodily pain. And what he found is that inexperienced marathon runners used largely dissociative strategies. They would find some way of distracting themselves or taking their mind out of the discomfort. And he found there was a significant correlation, positive correlation between using dissociation strategies for pain and being injury prone. In contrast to that, the top marathon runners didn't use disassociation strategies but the opposite—they used awareness strategies. Rather than trying to put their mind on something else and blocking out the pain—because if you do that in the short run, you may be able to run longer, but you're not getting the feedback from your body, so that you're much more prone to injure yourself.

But the best athletes figured out along the way that what they really needed to do was put their awareness fully on it, like a mindfulness strategy. By doing that, they had continuous feedback, and the body sort of took care of itself and regulated itself, so they're far less prone to risk. I think that's a pretty good model for what unfortunately never translated down to professional sports because we have many talented athletes who are constantly getting injured. Probably what's missing for them is the mindfulness of the body. And the people who are the iron men of sports like Cal Ripken who played for so many years in Baltimore without ever getting injured. He played more games without injury for any other player in history. Probably it's because they're present to their bodies and they get that constant feedback, and they don't get injured that way.

Now, I'm suggesting that … what I'm just saying for physical pain is also a metaphor for working with emotional pain. It's no different. They're different strategies and they don't always end you in the same place. So, if you want a short fix, blocking out the pain through some dissociation strategy or hypnosis is probably the easiest thing to do; that's why it's used a lot, for example, as an accompaniment to surgeries or to childbirth. But, in the long run if you're depending on your body for your profession, as an athlete is, probably the worst thing you want to do is use dissociation strategies; and mindfulness, being aware of your body, gives you constant feedback of what it's doing so you're less likely to get injured. Then that's a better strategy.

I think the superior strategy of all three of those would be emptiness practice because it's mindfulness plus something else. Because then it's not just an idle sensation. It's something deeply positive. And there's no need to avoid anything. So, it does a much more thorough job than the mindfulness does. So, that's what I would say to first of your questions. Give me the second one again to refresh my memory.

Oh, yeah. The loss. Again, I don't know what to say about that from a Buddhist perspective. Again, the answer would be that you practice emptiness around grief. But we have, in Western psychology, very good protocols for working with grief, and they work. The very first work on grief in the West was good old Sigmund Freud, and he talked about the difference between melancholia and grief, mourning. He's noticed that the symptoms were the same but one was acute and one was chronic. And what he noted correctly was that when people have chronic melancholia, or what we now call "complicated bereavement" versus "simple bereavement," the reason why it goes on, and on, and on is it's usually because there was some conflict. Either conflict about the way the person died, unfinished business around that, and or conflict about the nature of the relationship. There's unfinished emotional business there. In short term work, if you set the context for people to do that unfinished emotional business, then you can clean that up.

I remember once reading an article that came out in the hypnosis literature in the late '80s in Australia where they took sixty-three cases of complicated bereavement and all of them were resolved between one and three sessions. That raised my eyebrows. But as is often the case in the literature, they didn't exactly give the wording of what they did in any detail. So, we took the protocol and revised it. And I was surprised that it worked. I don't think I've ever seen anybody for more than two or three sessions.

And we've used it for hundreds and hundreds of people in bereavement. So, I think there's a simple way of working with that clinically, and I don't agree that it lasts forever. It lasts as long as you don't set up the context to work on it. When you process the relationship in a way that comes to an endpoint, then the grief symptoms go away. It's that simple. But you have to set the context for that to happen. Maybe we'll do that as a visualization because everybody probably in the group has some grief thing that they could deal with, and so we'll do it as a visualization. That's part of the conflict issue. That's exactly what I'm saying. So, we'll get to that.

Yeah?

Student 2

If pain is a mere sensation arising in *rigpa* … you kind of pointed out pain is also a feedback system. It's giving us, at times, really useful information and if it's just bliss, we might be ignoring an important symptom that might require medical intervention. And I've actually thought about that, like, "Am I ignoring something just because there's no emotional reactivity and as I get older is that something that has the potential to have a medical consequence?"

Dan

It's a nonissue. The issue here is doubt and fear interfering. Here's why: If you look at the history of development of the biofeedback field in 1970s and '80s, you can give people feedback about their moment-by-moment fluctuations in brainwaves, heart rate, heart coherence, smooth muscle tissue response from the gut, whatever electrodermal response. We know that smooth muscle tissue in the body learns. And if you do something like heart rate bio feedback or EEG brainwave biofeedback or heart rate or heart coherence feedback, or striated muscle feedback, we know that those systems learn. Some tissue is smarter than others. Striated muscle tissue is quite smart because it's more under voluntary control. Mostly in five or six sessions you can teach different muscle response. Smooth muscle tissue that makes up the vascular system is slower. It takes about twenty weeks to stabilize learning in that, but it learns. And if you do something like vasomotor biofeedback for headaches or for blood pressure, people learn it. You get your classic third/third split. A third of the people don't ever get an effect and the other two-thirds do.

And one of those thirds, if you ask them what they did, they can articulate clear strategies. "When I was getting the feedback, this is how I went about changing the machine," which is basically changing your muscle response. Then the other group, the other third has no idea what they did. They can't articulate their strategy, and it works just as well for them. And the third group who fails has no awareness of what's happened. Since that's a robust finding across many, many studies, what does it tell us? That the effect isn't so much the feedback because there are a number of studies that were done with so-called false feedback.

If you give people false feedback, it still works. Is that a placebo effect? Well, sort of yes and sort of no. What it really suggests is the key is awareness. Those two thirds of people who used the metaphor of the biofeedback machinery to put their awareness on the bodily processes, the awareness regulates the bodily processes. It knows how to do that. It has its own intelligence. The whole thing is a trick to get people to be aware of their bodily processes in an ongoing way, and the body takes care of itself.

And the people who fail can never put their awareness on processes. You see what I'm saying? So, what does it suggest here? It suggests that the issue isn't bliss. The issue is the quality of your awareness of the body processes. And all of those body processes arise out of that awareness and regulate themselves. That's the key to the mechanism both in Western and Buddhist terms. The whole thing gets you to look at the awareness and if you do that, you can trust it's going to take care of itself. Just don't get in the way with an overlay of conceptual doubt and fear.

It's quite profound. Now, there are different levels of awareness, as you know, and each one of those awarenesses has a completely different effect on bodily systems. So, it's a question of how far you want to go with that. That's pretty interesting. There's a whole path there. I don't know if we want to open that one up tonight.

Do you want me to go more on that one?

Student 2

Sure. It's kind of mystical what you're saying. You're saying that depending on the level of awareness, if there's a sensation, awareness is present, then the body will basically heal itself.

Dan

If you bring your awareness to the body and you continuously do that like in Burmese mindfulness practice, you bring a kind of presence to the body. What happens is you develop first nonjudgmentalness and nonreactivity. Pure mindfulness, right? And if you do that consistently as a strong practice then, essentially, you're getting pure sensation without all that judgment. You're getting what we called before the pure sensory part of it, not the cognitive-affective overlay. Okay? That would be the first level.

The second is if you combine that with emptiness of self-practice then there wouldn't be all that self-reactivity to the sensation. That would be a superior practice. Now, what if you let all that sensation arise within an ocean-like, changeless, boundless awareness, and along the path of what we call "spacious freedom." You can do that just as I'm talking. Then whatever arises at what used to be pain, it has no grab to it whatsoever.

Now, what if you had awakened awareness? The body that arises isn't solid anymore. The body is just within that vast domain of ocean-like, changeless, boundless awakened awareness—the body just hangs within that vast domain of space. It has no substance to it. It still appears—we say "like an empty glass bottle filled with light"—as clear light body practice. There's no reactivity there.

What you're experiencing mostly is an energy body with no substantiality left to it. That's a strong practice.

That's why I can still, at my age, do this stuff with advanced arthritis, because if I lived an ordinary mind then maybe it wouldn't be comfortable enough to sit. But if I'm in clear light body then it's not painful anymore. It's just the energy is more dense than it was before. So, it's better to hang out in clear light body. Otherwise, the suffering would be too difficult. Now, you can continue to do that, and you can transform that body into complete light. But, it's the last thing to go.

In the tradition there are three versions of that. The first version of that came up right after the teachings of Shakyamuni Buddha after he got enlightened under the bodhi tree, and for the first two hundred years after that, mostly, what the tradition was concerned with was preserving what he was saying. And many people use those teachings to not just get awakened but to enlighten, to become buddhas. There are a lot of buddhas walking around.

Then they had a whole debate for about three hundred years about how you could mark the authenticity of realization. What were the markers to tell you that this was a valid buddha, as opposed to somebody just thought they were Buddha or said they were? And one of those debates had to do with how many multiple levels of reality you open up simultaneously. You open up one hundred thousand or five million. It was a serious debate in terms of degrees of all-at-once-ness.

The other debate was more interesting. It had to do with what you find in the *Lalitavistara Sutra*. And it was the characteristics of the thirty-two major and eighty minor marks of a buddha. An enlightened buddha has thirty-two major marks, and the reason why they call it major marks is because they're physical characteristics. If you're a buddha, you have long ear lobes, you have a big tongue, you have a soft step. What were they really talking about? For years I thought this stuff was so weird. And what they were talking about is a kind of, you know, like Woody Allen's movie, *Zelig*. They were serious about this. There's a certain level of enlightenment, not just awakening, where you actually refine the enlightenment so much that it changes the physical structure of the body. So, if you talk the speech of the body, you have a bigger tongue of the *dharma*. If you listen to the teachings, you had bigger ears.

They were serious about this. The physical structure of the body actually changed as the outcome. Now not all Buddhists can do that. So, it was considered that the degree of your enlightenment was measured in part by how much or what degree you changed the physical structure of the body. That was the first model.

The second model that came up in Dzogchen in Tibet was the *zakme* model. *Zakme* means no outflows. And I learned that one when I was translating the Akhrid system with Asonam. And *zakme* usually means no karmic outflows—you've gone beyond the point that you're making any new karmic impressions that would ripen and influence your experience over time. And that's how I translated it. He said, "No, you translated it wrong." This was a section of our text that we translated that was towards the end of the text. And it was about buddhas. So, I said, "What does it mean?" He says, and he got a little nervous because he didn't know how to describe it because he was a monk. What he really meant—he says, "Buddhas don't go to the bathroom."

Zakme meant no outflows. Buddhas don't have snot. They don't piss. They don't poop, but they can intentionally make tears out of compassion for other beings. That's an intentional *zak*. But what they're talking about is that there's a certain level of realization, if the body so much transforms into light that it's not really solid anymore, so the usual physical operations of the body don't exist. That's the same level of practice where you can do *chudlen*, which are the secret practice to extract what's called *dungpa*, the elemental energy directly from *dharmakāya*, awakened *dharmakāya* space, and fill your body with that so you don't need to eat food. You just take another … You use the universe as your energy source rather than eating. All the cave yogis did that so they could go for years in retreat without having any food.

There was a guy, and they proved he didn't eat—and there's no sleight of hand—that he didn't eat or drink anything for an entire month. And they did a daily CT scan on his gut. Then they had a physicist come in and he said, "Well, we don't live on food, we live on energy"; and these people have obviously learned how to extract energy in different ways from the universe bypassing the gut, which is essentially when I got the secret *chudlen* text and they had me translate it—that's exactly what it says. We know something about this works now.

But, the last model, which was the refinement of this model, is really the rainbow body model that a great master can transform himself into rainbow light so that when he dies, at the point of physical death if he goes into retreat, usually after two or three-days—sometimes a great master can do it almost immediately—the body disappears and pops into rainbow light and disappears in space. And the only thing that's left are the hair or the nails. In Dzogchen, that's considered the ultimate test of awakening, if you have rainbow body. And if you can produce rainbow body at the point of dying, then that shows that your realization was to the ultimate, to the far end of this path, which means that you basically transformed the body right down to rainbow light.

Some great masters can transform their bodies into rainbow light before they die. The guy who showed me the pointing out teachings did that. After he showed me all the teachings, he popped into rainbow light and then popped back into his body. That got my attention. He died three weeks later. So, he was clearly working on a rainbow body practice.

Shardza Tashi Gyaltsen—the person I'm doing all the translation of all these texts from—he was a documented partial rainbow body when he died in 1936. The trouble is, a student screwed it up. He was doing rainbow body practice, and he went into his cave and told him not to disturb him. And then the students doubted it, so they opened up the cave in three days to see if he did it because they were impatient. And he had shrunk his body down to this size [Dan gestures with his hands, one above the other by about fourteen inches], but it hadn't completely dissolved and disappeared yet because they opened it too early.

But he wrote a rainbow body text which I have on my list to translate. So, at some point I'll be able to tell you more about how this works, but I haven't done this thing, obviously. But one of the students, before he did it, died, and he gave the instructions to the student. And the student got full rainbow body. So, we know it can be done and these were two cases that were fairly well documented that are somewhat modern.[8]

When we went and visited Lubrak to Yungdrun Gyaltsen's meditation hermitage, the one who gave us the secret cave yoga instructions for extracting energy out of the universe, that … there's a lineage of people … there's a cave in his hermitage where people go to achieve rainbow body, and they teach it there. So, they still do this stuff. That's the ultimate of this. You got to change your body into light. And it's not really restricted to this tradition. I mean, all you have to do is look at a picture of the Virgin Mary and you can see a halo. Right? Other traditions understand that ultimately the body is light if you work on these practices.

---

8 Although Shardza lived well into the twentieth century, he lived within what was still a pre-modern Tibetan culture.

In a very different tradition, there's not much left of it, but this was well developed in the Daoist tradition. There's a front channel and a back channel. You spin that cycle with your awareness and then there are six other inner channels, and you spin them all at once. It's called "spinning the smaller and spinning the larger heavenly cycle." And you open up that system and it regulates all the energy systems in the body. But they were using it for what they call "immortality."

Now, there's a secret channel system in the Daoist system that's not taught [inaudible]. It's called the Shen channel system. If you do the regular channel system, then it regulates health and you live very long, but if you do the secret channel system, you transform your body into light, and the body disappears, and your consciousness becomes a star. In the Daoist system, stars are living forms of consciousness and they can come and take a form anytime. Now, that's dangerously close to what some contemporary physicists say now. The universe is conscious and alive. So, it's interesting that if you transform yourself in that system, which is a completely different discovery, you become light. Only the light is stored in star forms.

June 4, 2015

Themes: The Natural State; Crossing Over; Recognize the Shift; Emptiness-liveliness

Dan

Hi everybody. You have a question?

Student 1

I don't know if you're able to do this, but I'm going to ask it anyway. Could you describe … maybe it's two questions. Is there a consistent experience in doing sky gazing in terms of the contents of what would be … what would appear? And, if it is consistent, can you describe it in as much detail or what the "subjective" experience would be in a sky gazing experience?

[Silence…] It's about practice.

Dan

First of all, you don't need it; it's a prop. The question you're raising is how you set up a view that helps establish the direct realization of an awakened mind. The prerequisite is you have to have the mind in its natural state. And there are at least five conditions of the natural state of the mind. First, you have to have done the foundation of concentration and the foundation and special insight practice, emptiness practice, to the point that you have the skill of automatic emptiness—everything arises immediately and as soon as something comes up—at the head, not after it's elaborated, it immediately arises, it automatically expresses itself as empty every moment by moment by moment. That's the first precondition.

Second then, there's no duality between what arises and the knowing of what arises. So, secondly it has to be a nondual state. If there's any duality, it doesn't work.

Thirdly, you have to refine that natural state so there isn't a shred of doing anything. And that's a little bit more complicated because oftentimes in Dzogchen you'll hear, "settle the mind" or "relax the mind," which all implies a kind of strategy of doing something. That's why automatic emptiness is so important because if you genuinely have automatic emptiness, as soon as something arises, the moment that it arises it's automatically empty.

So, if you notice any tendency to make anything happen, that's empty upon arising. If you notice any tendency to stop anything from happening because you think something else should be happening instead, that tendency is automatically empty. If you notice any tendency to focus the mind at any point, that's automatically empty upon arising. If you engage in any strategy, any doing, that's empty upon arising. You see, automatic emptiness because becomes a kind of clearing agent for all instances of doing. And when all instances of doing are immediately made calm, then that is what Gampopa calls "making the mind simple." Simplicity.

[Fourthly] now, the other thing is that one of the things that clouds over the mind is all the incessant conceptual thought … dualistic conceptual thought. So, if you have strong automatic emptiness, at the very moment that any conceptual thought arises, at that instance it's expressed as empty, and it becomes calm. That's why it all settles out of the mind. As soon as any conceptualization about state or outcome comes up, it's immediately expressed as empty. In that sense, automatic emptiness is a clearing agent for all conceptual thought. And that's what Gampopa calls "freshness." As all conceptuality settles out of the mind, Tilopa says, "The mind remains like a crystal-clear pool of water when all of the mud settles."

[Finally,] something about the nature of the field of awareness that remains becomes obvious, obviously lucid. So, the lucidity of that field of awareness is more distinct than it was before because you strip the outer layer of conceptualization from the mind.

So, those are the five conditions of the natural state: automatic emptiness, simplicity, freshness, and what ensues from freshness, lucidity, and not a shred of duality.

You can't do sky gazing unless you have the natural state. Otherwise, it's just an artificial technique. It just won't work. If you try and conceptualize and do methods without having that natural state, then it becomes conceptual, and it actually hardens the mind and precludes awakening and makes it harder to actually have the experience of awakening, which is why this stuff is kept secret. It's to protect you from fucking it up. To use it right, it works, but if you just try and screw around with it and don't have the right requisite state, it doesn't work. So that's why you have to begin with the natural state. That's your foundational state.

The whole idea is, as you know, awakened awareness is always right here. It's part of your buddha nature. Everybody has it. So, we're all awake all the time, but it gets clouded over by layers and layers of stuff in the mind that gets too solid and substantial. So, when we say "emptiness is the vehicle," emptiness is the view that makes everything less substantial, as being without inherent nature, without independent self-existence. And therefore, the seemingly solid structures of the mind, seen as empty, don't go away, you just see beyond them into the deeper nature of awakened awareness.

So, when there are no clouds left … emptiness is like cloud clearing. When there are no clouds or few clouds left, then awakened awareness can shine forth in its true radiance, which it's always doing. But here's the issue; the last cloud is your information processing system. Every part of your information processing is just … the way it acts from slowest to fastest operations, in that instant, partializes, and if you're operating out of partial mode, you can't directly experience the unbounded wholeness, the vast ocean of awakened awareness-love that's always right here. You can't operate on partial mode and grasp wholeness. That's the essential key point.

Any conceptual thought delineates. If it's this, it's not that. So, any moment of conceptual thought clouds over awakening. You can't conceptualize awakening. Any time that you direct your attention or do anything, that instance of doing something or directing the mind in any way clouds over the unbounded wholeness because directed attention partializes. And the fastest operation of your information processing system is to particularize, *yilajepa*. It's the tendency of the mind towards something.

The way to understand that is … in Western psychology we start perception, we stimulate perception, we see something, we react to it. We apprehend it, we praise it, and we react to it. But Buddhist psychology starts pre-stimulus. It starts with the tendency of the mind to go towards something, the outcome of which is stimulus perception. Whatever you want to call that thing. I call it "particularizing." The mind tends in a particular direction and the outcome is to pick out something in particular that it perceives. In Western terms, it's like an action potential.

That high-speed operation—if you want to see how that works, take a panoramic view of everything in the room right now. Take in everything all at once and nothing in particular. And hold every moment that same view of all-at-once-ness. And you can't do it because as soon as you try and hold the all-at-once-ness, you watch the mind doing this. [Dan holds up his hand and moves it from one position to another.] And you can actually see particularizing happening at high speeds. So, you're not going to get rid of that, it's the basis of your information processing system, but as you know, emptiness practice isn't about getting rid of, it's seeing beyond. If you take a certain view, you can see beyond that. The way you see beyond that is to look at all … by taking the view of the unbounded wholeness that is this vast ocean of awareness. You orient your view towards the ocean of unbounded wholeness of awareness. And that's the little trick.

If you do that, what happens? If you do that, you start to see all that activity is none other than just part of the wholeness. It doesn't obscure it anymore. You see beyond it. So, when you hear a crossing-over instruction like "do not particularize," it doesn't mean you're going to stop the particularizing. You're going to hold a certain view that allows you to see beyond the looking glass. And what happens is you shift your … you have a huge shift in your basis of operation—out of localizing individual consciousness and your information processing system and, whoops, you're operating out of being the wholeness. You can sense that shift. We call that "the shift to non-localizability."

So, if you use what are called "crossing over instructions," you set up a view of the infinite vast expanse—the unbounded wholeness is the view, and then you orient the awareness towards the unbounded wholeness and you hold it. If you try and do that without having the requisite foundational state of the natural state of the mind, you will just conceptualize, harden the mind, and you may never awaken because you get it wrong. That's why you have to do this in the right way at the right time with the right guidance. But if you have that requisite natural state, and you set up your crossing-over view, it will work. In Mahāmudrā we call those "non-meditation instructions." And in Dzogchen we call it *trekchö*, "thoroughly cutting through the ordinary mind" instructions.

And there are many versions of how to do the same thing. We try and give different students different methods, so hopefully one of them will work for them, and you know. That's where ... so that's the preface. That's where ... in Dzogchen, methods like sky gazing comes in. It both helps and it doesn't help. It's a prop—you don't need it. If you have the natural state and you set up your view ... what we call the Lion's Gaze ... if you don't know Lion's Gaze, it means that if you throw a stick, the doggy chases after the stick, if you throw a stick to a dog. If you throw a stick to the lion, the lion doesn't chase after the stick, the lion looks to where the source of the stick came from and chases after the source. So, if you orient awareness back to the totality of awareness, and that's your view, that's what you're looking at every moment by moment-by-moment undistractedly, then you have "the gaze of the lion"—you're looking to the source for everything it expresses from. So, if you set up your view of Lion's Gaze, that's the essential ingredient.

Another; in Mahāmudrā, they say, "like a child viewing a temple." Unlike the adult, when the child goes in the temple with all the colors and all the statues and the books and the candles and all that stuff, the child goes, "Ahh," and takes in everything all at once, and nothing in particular. All of these metaphors are designed to get you out of partializing mode to seeing the unbounded wholeness as direct seeing, and not conceptually. Sky gazing is like one of those metaphors; it's like the child viewing the temple.

The view that you hold won't work if it's partialized, if it's narrow. It has to be the totality of awareness. Huge. It has to be vast. So, think about what happens if you were to ... I remember, some of you were not with us, but when we went to Rahob's place, Rahob Monastery, with Rinpoche—or if you haven't been there, then the other way of thinking about that is thinking about climbing a mountain. Most of you have walked up a mountain of some sort. And when you get to the top of the mountain and you look out into the space, what is it like? What's your experience at that point? It's vast. Right? It pulls for that vastness. So, if you look into the surrounding sky, it helps; it assists you into holding that wide view of the unbounded wholeness just by virtue of the sky being very spacious, especially from a mountaintop. That's what I mean by it being a prop. But you're not looking at the sky; you're looking at awareness-space.

So, if you want to do sky gazing, first of all, you have to set your foundation in the natural state. Second of all, there can't be a shred of out-there-ness. So, you're not looking at the sky out there, which is another way of saying you have to establish a strong foundation of nonduality. And thirdly, you have to do mixing. The sky gazing instructions originate, so far as we can tell, from Sri Singha, a Chinese master who was Padmasambhava's teacher. You mix your awareness into the sky, into the surrounding space, and you mix the surrounding space into your awareness. So, you want a field of awareness, empty awareness-space, and there's no duality in it. When you do sky gazing, you take this vast ... your mind naturally gets pulled to this vastness.

You can set up the view yourself, but if you're lazy, it's better to look out there into the atmosphere because it will ... that spaciousness on top of a mountain will pull for that large view if you are not smart enough to set it up right. Without it, that's when you use a prop. So, it pulls for that; it makes it easier for you to understand that part of it. That's the positive side of sky gazing.

The downside of that is the tendency, like the metaphor of the child in the temple, to recreate duality like you're looking out there. And you're looking into the space and not seeing it as a nondual field. So, you have to correct that. So, the metaphor, the prop, both helps and doesn't help. If you tend to not have duality and you tend to take a more narrow view and not a view of the unbounded wholeness ... and sky gazing is a good technique for that kind of mistake. But if you tend to have duality and wholeness is easy, then sky gazing wouldn't be the best match for you. Work on the issue of duality separate from that, but not looking out and seeing it out there—you see what I'm saying?

So, if you set up that view on top of a mountain, then ... and hold that unbounded wholeness, the mind naturally gets pulled to being elevated. So, you don't get dull; so it keeps awareness nice and bright, and lucid. It tends to pull for this vast expanse as your view. So, it's just easier to hold the view for some people by using sky gazing. However, there are specific instructions about what to not do when sky gazing.

For example, the trouble with sky gazing is that there are very few times that there are ideal conditions to really use it. If, for example, the sky has a lot of clouds in it, you're going to start particularizing the clouds. So, you have to find a sky that has a cloudless sky—it's not often the case. So, how often in the year do you actually have days you can use it? You see, that's a problem, because if you just try and use it, it's going to screw it up because you're going to go with the clouds and other things in the air. And there has to be certain conditions of light. You certainly can't do sky gazing at night because if you look at the stars, you're going to particularize the lights and keep looking at all the stars. And you don't want to do it in a strong sun because you'll fry your eyeballs.

That actually happened with some stupid kid when Lopon Tenzin Namdak published *Heart Drops of Dharmakāya*, which is a very precious root text by Shardza Tashi Gyaltsen Rinpoche about … it's a primer, it's a very condensed primer on the *tögal*, the bypassing visions. And there's a section, a very small section on sun gazing. And some kid read the book and just thought what he should do is look straight in the sun in midday, fried his eyeballs and went blind, and then sued Tenzin Namdak for giving him a bad practice. But no one ever represented it, the teacher never represented himself that you should go out and try to do this on your own. It's like being stupid and reckless. Anyhow.

Student 1

Just for the sake of the conversation. Imagine a cloudless sky at the beach.

Dan

Alright, so imagine a cloudless sky. It doesn't have to be at the beach, it can be anywhere.

Student 1

It was the beach. [Group laughter]

Dan

You're asking this because you were trying this on your own?

Student 1

Let me be really clear. I wasn't trying anything, so that's why I'm asking about the content, because I wasn't trying anything.

Dan

You're not a bad doggy. [Laughter]

Student 2

It was on the Cape when it happened. [Laughter]

Dan

Your eyes just happened to be pulled to this view spontaneously and naturally, without self. [Dan laughs]

If you have the right external conditions, then your mind is naturally pulled to this, the unbounded wholeness, and if you can be mindful to have no duality in that and you've established the natural state, you hold that view uninterruptedly. But here's the issue: whether you're doing sky gazing, or whether you're doing the more traditional setting up of Lion's Gaze in any environment, it's not about the environment, it's about setting up your view. Then … the important part is not just setting up the view. There's one other thing that has to happen. You have to recognize the shift in your basis to awakened awareness. You have to know that at some point you've shifted so you're not operating out of the narrow localization of individual consciousness, but that you're operating out of being that unbounded wholeness.

So, what does that mean? What it really means is that you have to put your metacognitive intelligence online. So, it has to be a moment of direct … metacognitive awareness is not thinking—it's directly seeing the way things are in your mind. So, there has to be a moment of recognizing the shift in your basis of operation.

And we say, "There are two pathways to recognition." First is the pathway of non-localization. Which means that at some point, if you just hold the view, you don't do anything else. Bill doesn't awaken, as you know. You can't think your way into it. If you hold the view uninterruptedly and set up awareness so it's oriented towards the totality of awareness and unbounded wholeness every moment by moment by moment by moment, what happens is because of the intention of your own buddha nature to show itself to itself, then that awareness will keep opening itself to itself … keep opening itself to itself, awakening itself to itself. Just don't get in the way.

But at some point, there will be a moment of metacognitive recognition of a shift in your basis. One pathway is non-localization. At some point you'll notice a shift in your basis of operation so you're no longer operating out of the constraints of your individual consciousness but operating out of being the unbounded wholeness—the place there is no place, has no location, no reference points.

And the second pathway is the pathway of lucidity. There are certain descriptors of awakening that you can actually look into this field of empty awareness space and see the awareness as distinctly different from ordinary awareness. And the descriptors are things like: awakened awareness compared to ordinary awareness has *dongpa*, brightness. It has *gnar*, intensity. It has *hrige*, awakeness. It has *danpa*, sacredness. It has *bole*, softness.

Now, if you make any one of those qualities into a thing you're particularizing, it screws it up. But if you use them as guidelines … them as guidelines but not as things, they guide metacognitive recognition that there's something distinct about awakened awareness as compared to ordinary daily awareness.

Either way, whether it be the pathway of localization or the pathway of lucidity, you have to notice the shift in your basis. So, you're operating out of that lucid, awake feeling of ocean-like awakened awareness-love and not operating out of these little narrow confines of the individual consciousness. Using the ocean metaphor, you're operating out of being the ocean and your individual consciousness is like a bubble in that ocean, but you're looking at it from a perspective of the ocean, not from inside the bubble.

That's the big difference. When you shift your basis of operation, that's not where your … *chulyu* means basis of operation—where you're coming from. You're not coming from operating out of the information processing system and seeing localization anymore. You've shifted out of that to being the unbounded wholeness. Simple as that. That's the whole point. If you have that experience of awakening, you have the confluence of all the teachings. They all come down to that same experience. You have to refine it and develop it.

So, you can … in my experience with students, some students screw up the view because they can't get out of duality. It's more the exception that they screw up the view because they can't hold it as vast and unbounded. In that sense, sky gazing isn't the best match because most people don't do that thing. They can get the vastness enough. If that were the case, then a teacher would assign that person sky gazing.

But in my experience, holding nonduality is more difficult for students. So, that's why I don't make a big deal about the sky gazing. It's not what we see as the main issue. The main thing that we see … and that's where I listen for it because if people describe their experience, how do we know its authentic? And it's not so easy, because it's easy to conceptualize about it, as you know. But if your experience is accompanied by spontaneous compassion or gratitude or devotion, you're probably on the right track.

But, conversely what I listen for as a teacher—and I try and tell the other teachers to listen for—is that when somebody describes what they think—I mean that literally—is awakening, it's not because they're conceptualizing it. What you listen for … what I listen for is whether the description is strongly particularizing. If they're describing it as something particular, as a thing that's particular, then they're not in awakening. They can't be. They might think they are, but it can't be awakening. It's not that hard to tell, more often than not; it's sometimes difficult, when somebody's still operating out of particularizing mode. At least that's what I've learned that helps as a guideline to how we can evaluate the authenticity of a realization.

But we're still … I'm still a work in progress to trying to figure it out. I'm glad the last couple years I've been friends with Hogan and Chozen Bays from the Zen Center in Portland. I think, as you know, they come to a lot of our courses. But what I like about what I've learned from Hogan and Chozen Bays and the Zen center out of Portland, Oregon—as you know, they come to a lot of our courses—but what I like about what I learned from Hogan and Chozen in the Zen tradition, it's sort of this … they're sort of minimalistic in instructions and step-by-step stuff; we do a better job of that. One of our students said this approach is like GPS for the mind. It is GPS for the mind. That's a good way of describing it.

But what I think they do better than we do … we do better with the map, but I think what the Zen tradition does better with is they have a much longer tradition of trying to authenticate descriptions of realization. They're very good at that. In fact, they take that quite seriously. So, I've learned a lot from Hogan and Jan about how they go about that. I think we just take people's word and what they say more at face value and sometimes it creates false beliefs of people thinking they're awakened and they're not. And even if you are, of course, you lose it.

I'm working on a very precious text at the moment, which I like a lot. And it talks about if you have a taste of awakening, [there's] thirty-five different ways you could screw it up. [Laughter] And go off track. So, it's really detailed about … and we see every one of these. I was saying "yes" every time I was translating. We've seen every one of these in our students. So, it's the … at some point, I'll just go dedicate teaching to that particular part of the text, but I'm still learning it. It's okay with your question?

Student 1

Yeah, I could elaborate, but I don't want to take time. I'll let someone else have …

Dan

Finish it up.

Student 1

No, but … does anyone else have anything?

Dan

What do you have? There's more to this; go ahead and say it.

Student 1

Well. Partly the reason I asked the question … I framed it the way I did, is because I'm hesitant to talk about my experience obviously. But I guess maybe the question is, I don't think I understood. I was ignorant about really what sky gazing was because I never tried it.

Dan

You can talk about your experience. You know I like busting your frame. [Laughter]

Student 1

I'm not trying to be busted. [Laughter] Save that for another conversation, too. So, maybe the question's about automatic *thigles*. And really what … because I definitely had … what we describe as a visual phenomenon experience just looking at this cloudless sky, without trying to do anything. And I've always sort of questioned what exactly a *thigle* is, and am I having an experience of *thigles*? But this is very … it's something I …

Dan

It's a good question. I'm glad you asked it.

Student 2

I've had it before …

Dan

No, no, this is important.

Student 2

There was something about, like something about metacognitive awareness that said, "Is that … ?" … because again, it wasn't, like, stunning, it wasn't awe inspiring.

Dan

Okay, let me … let me answer this question, because what you're saying is quite important. I'm glad you raised it.

If you keep setting up the view, say, Lion's Gaze or something comparable for you, the task to keep setting it up is so that becomes a learned pathway, so you can shift your basis of operation to awakening more quickly, more frequently, and for longer duration. Ultimately, through this path of learning, doing it many times and setting up the view, with just the intention to set the view you shift your basis to awakening; that's all it takes. Okay? That's important.

Now, every time you set up the view and you shift your basis to being the unbounded wholeness, what you're shifting to is what we call the ground aspect of awakening. All right? But if you keep doing that many times, it sort of gets redundant after a while. You're trying to … If your basis of operation is awakening most of the time, why would you keep doing that? Because you're already there. Or here. [Laughter]

So, that being the case, we say that what naturally happens is there's shift from the ground aspect of awakening to what we call "the appearance aspect of awakening." Then you have to tweak your view. The view is no longer Lion's Gaze. The view then becomes what we call "liveliness." Because awakened awareness isn't just a static empty field. It's alive! It's always expressing itself.

Everything that appears, everything that arises is none other than the liveliness of expressed awakened awareness. The whole show is lively awakened awareness. Every thought is lively awakened awareness. Every emotion is lively awakened awareness; it might even seem more lively. Every sight, every sound, every smell, every taste, every body sensation. The whole show inside and outside is lively awakened awareness.

So, you'll naturally turn from opening up the ground aspect of awareness, which is space-like, the unbounded wholeness, to the appearance aspect, so you start to see everything as lively awakened awareness, uninterruptedly. A continuous uninterrupted flow of lively awakened awareness in all times and all situations. Okay?

So, now, if you keep doing that, at some point we change our language a bit. Because it's so alive and nothing sticks, and nothing is substantial, everything is lively awakened awareness, has a kind of radiant hue to it—or a sacred hue to it—and nothing is substantial. So, more and more, if you hold the view of liveliness, the seemingly solid world turns to light and energy. That's when we change our language. We stop talking about awakened awareness as liveliness, and we start talking about it in terms of what's called "primordial wisdom energy." Because the deeper realization is all of this is generated by primordial wisdom energy. Primordial wisdom has an energy of manifestation—*yeshe*.

And even awakened awareness is an expression of primordial wisdom energy. At that point, we start saying that what you're seeing is primordial wisdom energy and how it expresses itself, how it operates. And another way is we say, "You're seeing the seat of *bodhicitta*." You're seeing the intention of the mind to awaken itself by showing itself to itself for the sake of its own realizations. You're seeing the intention of an awakened mind to reveal the whole show, the whole magical display for the sake of training compassion. So, what you're seeing is the intention of bodhicitta. And the energy of manifestation of that every moment-by-moment, and at lightning speed, instantly every moment.

Now, what you're describing here is that transition. Okay? And it's the transition from the world seeming solid and out there, to the world being all energy. And it's not … I wouldn't word it so much in terms of *thigles*, although that is certainly accurate. It's better to take the view that you're seeing liveliness. The energy of liveliness. Or you're seeing the activity … the expression of primordial wisdom energy.

Now, and more and more as you refine your practice, that's what's going to happen and is happening, which is what you really described. But here's the rub. When you start to see all that, you have to be careful not to go back to particularizing mode. Because as soon as you do, you're right back in ordinary mind again. And you might not last in ordinary mind. You can set up the view and shift your basis to awakening. And as soon as you start looking at this energy and *thigles*, you're seeing particular things and you're partializing and you're back in ordinary mind again.

So, what has to happen is you have to use traditional emptiness practice to make sure that you're not seeing any of that as a thing. And then you have to look into that as liveliness expressing awakened awareness, or as primordial wisdom. What's going to keep you on track … and this gets into a whole other discussion then, but it's worth going over here. What's going to keep you on track is the tension of what, in the tradition, is called self-emptiness and other-emptiness. So, let's review that.

There's a huge debate within Tibetan Buddhism about two schools of thought, self-emptiness and other-emptiness. And as a dry academic debate, it's boring. And what people have lost is they've lost the liveliness, the heart of that debate. Because both views are necessary as part of a necessary tension in your ongoing practice. The self-emptiness position is that all phenomena, all relative phenomena, are empty. That's called the self-emptiness position. You see that in the Prāsaṅgika Madhyamikas. And you see that particularly represented in Tibetan Buddhism, rather than Indian Mahāyāna Buddhism; you see it represented in the Dalai Lama's Gelugpa tradition—Tsongkapa.

So, everything is empty. Nothing is substantial and independently existing. And you apply your sword of emptiness everywhere. Even awareness is empty. Prāsaṅgikas criticize the Mind Only school because you can reify the mind as not empty. You can reify awareness as not empty. You can reify emptiness. So, you have to practice emptiness of emptiness. You level everything as empty. Any tendency to reify, of course, means you're under-applying emptiness. The Dalai Lama says one of the big errors ... and what all these schools of thought are really discussing is that there's some area of your experience that you under-applied emptiness to. You made it into a substantial thing. So, you have to constantly look at ... that tendency to make it into a substantial thing, because we have a habit to do that kind of thing. It's how the ordinary mind works.

Now, the other-emptiness position is equally important. And what it means ... the term other-emptiness means that all relative phenomena are empty, like the self-emptiness position. All phenomena are empty of other relative phenomena, but they're not empty in the sense that ultimate reality is not empty. It's only empty in terms of other relative phenomena, but not empty in terms of ultimate reality. Ultimate reality is not empty. What does it mean?

It means if you use emptiness everywhere, there are certain aspects of ultimate reality that keep shining forth and you can't get rid of them. If you clean up the clouds, there's a certain intensity, a certain brightness, a certain awakeness to awakened awareness that's not going to go away, it's going to get stronger. If you practice liveliness, there's a certain energetic aspect of primordial wisdom that's not going to go away, it's just going to be more energetic—it's going to be intense all the time.

So, you see, the other-emptiness position was first put forth by a lama called Dolpopa in a text called *Mountain Doctrine*. And, unfortunately, when he put it out there, the view was a little extreme. It had a lot of good stuff in it. And there was a lama at the time who hated it. He trashed it. He was really competitive and aggressive. But we know that Dolpopa, even though he was the one who coined the term other-emptiness, lived at the same time as the third great Karmapa, Rangjung Dorje. And on at least two or three occasions, they met and discussed their views.

So, even though Rangjung Dorje never mentions the term other-emptiness, he wrote a whole text on the view that's representative of the Kagyu, Mahāmudrā tradition. It's clearly an other-emptiness text. Or, if you take the component of our elephant path, Asanga, it's other-emptiness even though he never used the term. So ... it's also the major position within Dzogchen. In other schools of thought, other-emptiness, even if you call it that or not, is a very important position. It means that the more you negate things as empty, the more that certain aspects of ultimate reality shine forth and it becomes something that goes dangerously beyond the tradition of the extremes.

And the two main extremes are nihilism and eternalism. Because basically the position is that ultimate reality is permanent. You lock into it. By doing emptiness and getting to these practices, you lock into the stream of ultimate reality, which is called "the three kayas" or "three enlightened bodies of ultimate reality." You're not going to make that one go away, you're just going to get stronger and stronger the more you apply emptiness.

So, this broke down into a debate, a competitive debate between different schools. And it got nasty. And part of the reason why I have to say that is, historically, the first Tibetan Buddhism—modern Tibetan Buddhism—that came to the West was really in the '60s and '70s. And the first doctoral dissertation on emptiness was Jeffrey Hopkins' *Meditations on Emptiness*, which represents Tsongkapa's position. And Tsongkapa's position is extreme. And he's not fair to his sources. He'll say, "Some people think this," and then he'll shoot them down. But they didn't really say what he said they said. He's not fair to his sources that way.

But that was the first view, so the self-emptiness position is all we knew in the West. Now Jeffrey has corrected for that. He's written three textbooks on other-emptiness. In fact, he translated Dolpopa's massive text on *Mountain Doctrine* because he wanted to give a more fair representation of this to the West. And now we know that the reason why Tsongkapa was so intense in going after the other emptiness position was that the lama who originally went after Dolpopa was Tsongkapa's main teacher. So, they have axes to grind, we get into things that sound much like Western academic debates, and all that infighting that goes on about different theories.

And, of course, in doing that, we lose the heart of this. Because I see it as a necessary tension. In other words, if you start going off and looking for lucidity properties, you start looking to see if you can recognize awakening by looking at awakeness, and looking at brightness, and looking at softness, and looking at sacredness; as soon as you make them into a thing, you're off track. Then you have to go back to the self-emptiness position and see all those qualities as empty, because you're particularly back into particularizing mode, and they're not empty anymore. You're reifying. You follow me?

Student 1

Mm hmm.

Dan

And then, on the other hand, if you just do emptiness everywhere and everything is empty, you've failed to look for the obvious of ultimate reality that's staring you right in the face all the time. So, you can go too far with emptiness, and it starts to shade off into nihilism. So, you need the other-emptiness position to know what positive qualities to look for and try to bring forth with your metacognitive awareness. And for the rest of your lifetime, you're going to ride that tension. Sometimes you're going to have to be reminded to do more emptiness practice: self-emptiness position and correct for that tendency to reify. And then sometimes you're going to go too far with that, it's going to shade off into nihilism, and you'll have to start looking for the positive qualities as guidelines to open up awakening again. And you've always got to ride that tension. Don't believe for one instant that it ever goes away. Because the tendency for duality, the tendency to particularize, are a part of ordinary information processing, are deeply ingrained, and they're going to come back.

That's why all the Dzogchen bypassing practices are usually kept as a guarded secret. Why? Because as soon as you start seeing that fantastic display–"ahhh!"—you create duality. And as soon as you look at anything, you're like, "Oh, well that's a *thigle*! Look I got a *thigle* there. I found a *thigle*." [Laughter] As soon as you do that, you're back in particularizing mode again, and you're back in ordinary mind. So you see, the paradox here is the more fantastic the display gets, the more it all turns to light. And at some point, it gets to what we call "blazing splendor"—ah, it's wondrous. And the tendency to see that as a show "out there" and to greet [it], to particularize that show, is so strong that you keep screwing it up.

And that gets into another prop. Okay? The other prop is dark retreat. If you're doing the four levels of the bypassing visions, if you listen to what the yogis say about that, if you do *dharmadhātu* exhaustion and everything that arises in the vast expanse of universal ground, every moment, if you do that 24/7, and whatever comes up is left completely alone, you don't engage, because engaging [is] causing karmic impressions to form. If you set up that view absolutely correctly and it becomes automatic, you have what I call "automatic *dharmakāya* release." Everything arises by itself and is immediately released and liberated by itself. Every moment. Nothing sticks, "like writing on water." Or "like snowflakes melting in an ocean."

If you do that all the time, and if you practice, not as a strategy, but as part of the view—leave-it-alone-ness, with no mental engagement—you've got to get that one just right. If you do that all the time, because you're not forming any new karmic impressions for the first time, it forces the mind to dip into the storehouse consciousness and automatically release the previous storehouse of karmic impressions at a rapidly accelerated rate. You do that for say, on the average, six years, you'll clean out the storehouse bin. That's why we call it *dharmadhātu* exhaustion. There's no negative states left and you only have positive states because the negative states obscure the positive states, the pure states. At some point, when that balance relatively shifts, all eighty positive qualities of the mind flourish.

No negative states and the flourishing of all positive qualities of the mind—that's what the word "Buddhahood" means. In Sanskrit, *buddha* means realized one. But when the Tibetans translated it, they didn't translate it that way. The Tibetan term for buddha is *sangyé*. It's a compound term. *Sangwa* means completely purified; *gyewa* means flourishing. So, the word for buddhahood in the Tibetan language literally means the one who has established the eradication ... the purification of all negative states so there's none left—*dharmadhātu* exhaustion—and cause, therefore, the flourishing of all positive states. So, buddhahood literally means, in Tibetan language, it means purified and flourishing mind. Okay.

Now, here's the issue. What the yogis will tell you is if you've done your practice of *dharmadhātu* exhaustion, at some point the relative balance shifts so you're staying in pure states of mind most of the time. There are not a lot of negative states left at a certain point, because they don't come up so much. The tendency does ... it doesn't stick very much, even in daily experiences that are stressful; it doesn't stick.

So, if you have that, then when you try and do your *tögal* visions and bypassing visions, they naturally arise because they're obvious, because they become obvious when there are no clouds. When the *dharmadhātu* exhaustion is such that you've eradicated the negative states, you just see them as naturally self-occurring. It's part of the natural intelligence of the mind showing itself to itself. If you want to cut corner—and it's really cheating—then you can do props again like dark retreat. You can either force the vision before you have *dharmadhātu* exhaustion. Because if you put yourself in a sensory deprivation environment like that, and you keep doing that for forty-nine days, and at some point if you get the visions generated, you get the point in complete darkness and you're seeing everything, it's just like now.

And you can see it's not generated from out there because there's no "out there." So, it helps you to do that, but it's sort of like cheating because you're trying to force the issue with strategies, and that's going to come back to bite you. Because if you do it with the natural flow of this—this is where the GPS map comes in again—if you do it in the right sequence, at some point, you don't need all those props, because it's obvious to see. But the reason why the *tögal* visions are kept mostly guarded is because there's a very strong tendency—because the display is so fantastic, as soon as you go, "Aahh," you're back to out-there-ness, you're back to particularizing.

Student 2

Is it correct though, at that point you see the particularizing as the same thing?

Dan

If you hold the view uninterruptedly and correctly then, if you can see that instance of particularizing as the liveliness of awakened awareness, then of course you're seeing beyond it, so it doesn't stick. And even though the tendency arises, you're right back on track again. Self-correcting. And you need it to be automatically self-correcting. Follow me?

Then you get the visions right because there's a strong tendency to particularize and you attest to that. I've been there and done this. I know, I make mistakes. Menri is great with me. When I was first working on the *tögal* visions, it all started to open up. Much like you, I was like, "This is really exciting." So, I went to see Menri, and I said, "The visions are opening up." He said, "Ahh, you get one vision, you get another vision, no big deal."

Student 1

I want to be clear, it's like a … not like you, I wasn't excited about it. I actually was questioning whether or not this wasn't some sort of just …

Dan

But there's a reaction in the mind.

Student 1

It wasn't while it was happening. It was just an observation. It was really afterwards that I thought, "Oh, is that just some sort of optic nerve thing?"

Dan

There's no "afterwards." You're going to keep doing this every moment.

Student 1

Well, I understand, but while I was sitting on the beach and this appearance occurred, or without trying, no doing. I could certainly see … I knew it wasn't out there. I could even describe it as, like, a visual hallucination if I wanted to approach it from that perspective. But it was really the question … you said this to me last week, "Is it doubt?" I mean, am I doubting? I mean, something happened. But should I take it as …

Dan

It happened because the mind has the natural intelligence to recognize its own display and leave it at that and not think about it.

Student 1

But that's what I was asking you about, the content of it.

Dan

The content doesn't matter. It changes every moment. There's no content; it's all a continuous flow of liveliness. In that sense it all has sameness. Don't particularize the content. Don't differentiate the content. It's just all liveliness, a continuous uninterrupted flow of lively awakened awareness in all kinds of situations. Or, as you know in Lion's Gaze, the other way of saying the same thing is, "it's all in the ups and downs of *dharmakāya*." Or another way of saying the same thing you've heard in one of Milarepa's songs, "It's all pure like river flow." Like that. Then, it's just liveliness, so no big deal. There's no attachment to particularizing any aspect of that. And it's really important that you set the foundation of this now, because the display is going to get brighter. It's going to be more splendid. It's quite a show. Because once you get up with the *tögal* visions, it's like one huge acid trip that never stops.

June 10, 2015

Themes: Conduct 24/7; Karmic Memory; Flourishing; Cracking the Eggshell

Dan

Welcome everyone. You have a question?

Student 1

I've been watching the way conduct arises, and what I've been noticing is that there's no thought, there's no doing. And it always arises in conjunction with compassion. And they seem inseparable. So, I wondered if you would comment about that.

Dan

Wow. Another question with depth. So, the general issue is *choepa*, conduct, and how conduct appears—that is, how we behave. And conduct means a couple of things. It means how we act or comport ourselves with respect to our own practice. More specifically, it is what are you actually doing to improve your practice with your conduct.

For example, I've just been translating the great Bon master Shardza Tashi Gyaltsen Rinpoche's material, and he has a trilogy of texts on conduct. The first is how advanced practitioners act during the daytime in terms of how to increase the depth of their meditation experiences and realizations. How you use the stuff that comes up like thought, like emotions, like external perception, and use that as a vehicle to deepen your realizations. The gist of that is you see it all as the liveliness of awakened awareness. So, the view is liveliness.

And the second of the volumes is on conduct at night. How you conduct yourself during deep sleep and dreaming, so that the task is essentially to train awakened awareness so that you are awake while you're deeply asleep, and that you have awakened awareness when you're dreaming. I mean, we have a literature on lucid dreaming in the West. People are aware of the fact that they're sleeping and in a dream while the dream is going on. But the difference is that's just ordinary awareness. In this practice it's awakened awareness during the dream, which is different.

So, the task is to extend your practice so that you are awake 24/7, throughout all the variations of your diurnal rhythms. You practice during the day. You practice during sleep, deep sleep. You train yourself to keep awakened awareness and bring it into deep sleep. And then train yourself to keep awakened awareness and bring it into when you're dreaming.

And the third of that trilogy has to do with conduct with respect to the dying process. That is, how you use everything you've developed in your life and in your meditation practice as preparations through time. But the true test is how you put it into practice in your dying process so you don't get caught up in all of the intense states of body and mind, so that you forget that you had a practice and that that practice is something that is the true test of your practice—this is how you face dying. So, there's a detailed manual on how you do that.

Now, all that would be conduct with respect to one's practice, and the task is to develop that practice and move it along. There are some more details, both in Dzogchen Great Completion practice and in Chagchen—Mahāmudrā, or Great Seal practice—there is a literature on what's called *thun* practice. *Thun* means session-based practice. And it means something very specific. It means that you organize your practice around certain times of the day and evening, not simply around diurnal rhythms, but the fact that the entire experience of your mind and body changes in interaction with the environment.

So, in each time of the day you do a different practice; so, you enhance and develop your meditation experiences and your realizations. So, for example, at night when you're dreaming, the previous store house of karmic impressions gets activated. And as karmic traces ripen, they manifest as spontaneously emergent states of mind, which we call dreams. So the content of dreams is essentially the ripening of the karmic impressions, certain karmic impressions of the store house. Why some as opposed to others? That's very much like what Freud, in his first work on dreams in the West, called "day residues."

Certain experiences in the day trigger certain karmic memory traces. And those get activated and ripen, and that's the content of the dream. But if the first thing you do when you wake up in the morning is *dharmadhātu* exhaustion, a practice where you take a certain view that everything that comes up is left completely in its own way with no mental engagement, then all the karmic impressions as they arise disappear immediately, leaving no trace. So, you clear it out for the day.

Now that does two things. If you were to leave all those ripening karmic impressions alone, it creates a certain heaviness of mind. You know, when you wake up in the morning and you've had a bad dream, there's a certain heaviness that goes through a lot of the day. Well, if you did that kind of *dharmadhātu* exhaustion practice, and you do it every morning first thing when you wake up, and as the last thing you do … the last cycle of sleep is a dream cycle, then all of those ripening karmic impressions, you clear them up—it takes about twenty minutes—so they have no influence on your day. It's clean, what we call stainless mind, *drime*. That matters.

Now, then the next part of the day is the morning, not dawn, but early morning to mid-morning. There the sun is not very hot, but it's arising and it's bright. So that would be a time to use the energy of the sun. So, if you were doing *tögal* visions, bypassing visions, all that energy would dance before your eyes by doing a practice like sun gazing. You don't look into the sun; you have the sun behind you. So that's a good time of the day to actually train working with how to deepen your realization into the nature of all appearances as being insubstantial and like light.

Then, in the late morning, when the sun's hot, to midday, and midday to early afternoon, you don't want to practice outside. Then it's a good time to go inside and to do something like central channel practice in a cool, darker place—get the fire going there. Then, in the mid-afternoon to late afternoon, you do another round of sun gazing, best time for that. Then you train up the *tögal* visions. Then in the early evening, as you watch everything get to dusk, you watch everything shade, that's a pretty good time to look into the nature of external appearances, because they appear less substantial when they're fading. And you're deep in your realization of empty: insubstantiality and impermanence.

Then, when you get to the late evening you might want to do another practice of *dharmadhātu* exhaustion to clear all the karmic impressions that set forth that day and clear it out so you're not forming any new karmic impressions; that will enhance your progress of *dharmadhātu* exhaustion. And then, deep at night like at midnight and thereafter, if you're still practicing, that's the best time for generation stage practices, tantric practices, visualization of the deities of the mandala to keep out negative influences, or protection practices.

So, you see, for advanced practitioners, your whole day is organized around which practices are more likely to be enhanced at certain times of the day. And most advanced practitioners who do this full time do that kind of thing. And all of what I talked about so far is really conduct to enhance your practice, to develop it. The Tibetan word for it is *chungwa*, which means to protect. Sometimes it's translated as nurture. You've got to take care of your practice; you've got to nurture it; it's precious.

So, then we get to the larger issue about how you behave in the world towards other people: conduct with respect to others. And how you act depends on the level of your practice. The general principle here is, in terms of action towards others, as in the Mahāyāna tradition, you serve the benefit of other people. You don't do your practice just for selfish gain. It's about serving other people. But how you do that depends pretty much on your level of practice.

If you are practicing at anything less than Dzogchen practice or Mahāmudrā practice, if you practice with the common vehicle of Mahāyāna or Theravādin practice, then in Theravādin practice, the foundation that's the oldest practice is really *donpa*, restraint, in Tibetan. There are certain behaviors you don't engage in because they cause too much destruction to your own spiritual practice and to those around you. So *donpa*, restraint, means "just don't go there." So, the Seven Restraints are: you don't kill, you don't steal, you don't commit sexual misconduct (although a lot of gurus seem to forget that), you don't lie, you don't engage in abusive speech, you don't engage in divisive speech—the kind of speech that causes divisions in others or causes their practices to deteriorate—and you don't engage in meaningless speech, idle chatter and gossip. And I think it's interesting that of the Seven Restraints, four of them are about speech, because we don't mind our mouths enough and it causes harm. And out of those, I think it was Tsongkhapa who said the worst of those is divisive speech. If you talk to other spiritual practitioners in a way that makes them have doubt about what they're doing, or causes the practice to deteriorate, then you're doing something really harmful. Leave the practitioners alone or help them. But don't directly actively interfere with a practice in a negative way by what you say.

And that's something that needs to be said particularly in the West, because we have lots of teachers in lots of centers. And of course, what happens as soon as you institutionalize this stuff—because you have to support your center or support your own teaching, and it becomes a livelihood—then people compete or try and get students for their center. And then it goes down the tubes. You can't institutionalize the *dharma*. It is not for sale.

I think I told you my first Buddhist teacher was a woman, Terry Davis, who was the main student of Carolyn Rhys Davids of the Pāli Text Society from the late 1880s. And they first translated all the texts in Pāli of the Buddha and brought them to the West for the first time. Terry Senior came to the US, and in the mid-1930s, she was offered an endowed chair at Yale in Buddhist studies. Now, women didn't get professorships in those days, certainly not endowed chairs. But even more irregular was the fact that she declined it because she said that Buddhism can only be lived, you can't teach it in the classroom setting. That's walking the talk.

So, we have to be careful of that because the West is very competitive, and then it becomes a profession. Then it creates difficulty. That's why I like being a nomad and wandering where our students ask us to go. This isn't my center here. I just pay rent. There's no center. We're not going to institutionalize this.

So, in the first layer of Buddhism there was this notion of restraint; you just don't do certain things. But that was more like in the realm of social mores. But how you act and not act is still very much based on self. And the idea was that if you acted positively, you accumulate positive karmic memory traces; those are called "merit."

And the accumulation of positive karmic memory traces eventually ripens so your mind is just lighter and easier, and that makes it more easy to engage in meditation practice without major interferences by all your "stuff." That's why people did it. In Mahāyāna, there was greater emphasis on developing the aspiration to serve the benefit of other beings, not just your own spiritual gains, and focusing on emptiness of self. So, that's the difference.

Let's take something like compassionate action: if you have the idea in your mind that you should act compassionately towards other people, you're acting out of self. There's still conception and that is limited. Because if you're acting out of self that means you have preferences, likes and dislikes. And it's more narrow in terms of your scope. But if you practice emptiness of self, and you have what's called ultimate as opposed to relative compassion, then that state of mind that you're operating out of doesn't include self. It's just a pure way of being, arising out of ocean-like, changeless, boundless awareness—or even better, awakened awareness.

We say the difference between relative compassion and ultimate compassion is that if you're practicing ultimate compassion, it is like being the sun. The sun has inexhaustible energy. The self gets compassion fatigue, gets burned out if it gives too much or reacts to all the suffering. If you're acting out of that ultimate compassion of the great expanse of the universal ground of being, it doesn't get burned out. And like the sun, it has inexhaustible energy. Also like the sun, it's impartial. The sun has many, many rays. It doesn't decide who to shine on, [like] it shines on these people and not these people. It shines everywhere equally. So, ultimate compassion is a better state of mind to practice on. But still it's cast within ordinary consciousness and still accumulates merit, only more merit.

But then, there's a point at which you have awakened awareness. What that means is that always right here, like the sun that always shines, is an infinite ocean of awakened awareness-love which is your true nature; it's part of your buddha nature. It's always here. We don't see it because of all the heavy clouds of the mind, the heaviness of thought, the heaviness of self, the heaviness of the construction of time, the heaviness of perception. And all those serve like dense clouds. When the clouds clear you know the sun's always been shining; it never stops shining. Through emptiness practice where you see the insubstantiality of all of your constructions of mind and clear them enough to see beyond them—not to get rid of them, to see beyond them—you see that the radiant nature of an awakened mind, the brilliant lucidity of awakened awareness, and its infinite, unbounded wholeness; the expression of awakened awareness-love is always right here.

Now if you stabilize that, so that's where you're operating out of, operating out of being the ocean rather than something in the ocean; if your basis of operation is shifted to awakened awareness in a stable way, you have to develop that. So, it's not just like "a little flame" as Tashi Namgyal says. You have to develop it so you have it at all times, in all situations—a continuous flow of awakened awareness and its liveliness all the time. Now if you do that, there's no duality and you start to see, as you stabilize awakening, that all of what's out there is part of the same field of that big mind—awakened mind. So that starts to give you a different experience of what seems to be individual consciousnesses of all of you in the room here, because you're not out there anymore.

We all participate in that same field of the unbounded wholeness of awakeness, awakened awareness-love. And once you have the direct experience of that, one of the things you see is that everything and everyone is interconnected, and you'll directly understand what Tibetans call *wang*. The word literally means influence. Everything you think and do affects everybody else—what the physicist David Bohm, who was a student of Krishnamurti, once called the "implicate order." Everything implicates everything else. Every thought you have, every behavior you engage in, affects the entire field around you. You're not separate.

Now if you really understand that directly, that'll change your ethics because you can't live in a vacuum anymore. But it's not an idea; it's a direct experience of that interconnectedness. And if you move beyond all conceptualization so you just see it, then you begin to start to notice people in a different way. You start to see what they need, and where their vulnerabilities are, and what they most need. Because it doesn't come from thought; it doesn't come from self. It comes from the field of big mind.

Now still, that seeing is clouded by all of the accumulated negative karmic traces in your mind. But let's say you get as far in your practice as to practice *dharmadhātu* exhaustion. So, what does that mean? It means that every moment when something arises in our mind and we first perceive it, it's like what in Western psychology we will call stimulus perception. As soon as you recognize something and make contact with it at very high speeds in our information processing system, we act on it. We have to engage it. We have to decide whether to process it further or not. It's not an intellectual decision. It's very high speed.

We either have to engage it enough to process it further—and that's called "accepting" or "taking it up"—or we have to engage it enough to say, "That's the end of processing; we're going to dump it in the bin." Whether we accept it or reject it, those two things are two sides of the same coin. They're ways of engaging, at very high speeds, something to make a decision to process it further or not. And if I engage it, then I start to form a memory trace to it. So, in Dzogchen particularly, we have *langdor*: "do not accept, do not reject." What they're talking about is that as soon as you accept it or reject it, either way, you're engaging it enough to form a karmic memory trace.

But if you have pretty much continuous awakening all the time—or not all the time, but most of the time—and you have *dengwa*, confidence, that you'd never lose this awakening, after a while this stuff, the usual habits of mind, will cause it to cloud over. But you start to see that that clouding over is a thin veil, and all it takes is the intention to look. And you're back in operating out of an awakened mind again. So, it can never really go away if you have that confidence that everything is just the manifestation of the liveliness of awakening, at all times, in all situations. Then, on top of your view of liveliness, the view in your meditation practice becomes "let it all arise." Take the view of this vast expanse of space—it's like the groundless that everything arises in—and let it arise, and leave it completely alone. You take the view of leave-it-aloneness. But it's not a strategy because strategy is about doing. It's just a natural outcome of that level of realization that everything arises in its own place and immediately disappears because you're not engaging it. You broke the link to engagement.

And what that does is, if you do that practice 24/7—and the practice doesn't involve doing it [but rather] taking a certain view because as we say in Dzogchen, "The view is the meditation, the view is the meditation." It's the perspective you take. You've got to get the view right. If you take that view all the time and you're not forming any new karmic impressions again, well, you might get a little, but generally you don't, right? You know what I'm talking about. Then it forces the mind to dip into *kunzhi namshe*, the store house consciousness, and cause the rapidly accelerated release of the entire bin of karmic memory traces that would otherwise ripen—karmic memory traces from this lifetime and from all your previous imprint of lifetimes.

And if you do that practice of leave-it-aloneness, 24/7, everything arises and immediately disappears leaving no trace. We say it's like writing on water—it disappears right away—or snowflakes melting in a vast ocean; as soon as they land in the ocean, they disappear. So nothing sticks anymore; you just watch everything leave no trace. No reactivity to anything, nothing sticks anymore. And if you do that all the time, [after] on the average of six years. there are no negative sates of mind left. And over time you tip the balance, the ratio of impure states that spontaneously arise in your mind to pure states.

And it gets cleaner and cleaner in there. The subjective experience of this field of boundless, lucid, awakened awareness will start to feel squeaky clean. The Tibetan word is *drime*, which is often translated as stainless mind. What does that sound like? What does that mean? It's clean! That's what it means. You can feel it. It's clean. And there are no negative traces left.

Now, I remember years ago when Jack Engler and I gave Rorschach ink blot tests to people at various stages in the practice. The great masters that we gave Rorschach ink blots to, they didn't do something ordinary. Because they were completely absent of any negative states, consistent with this idea of *dharmadhātu* exhaustion. And what was remarkable was there was no aggression or any aggression-related emotional states. They cleaned it out. So technically, in Buddhism, that means "*dharmadhātu* exhaustion," which means you exhaust the storehouse, *dharmadhātu*, [which] is storehouse mind; you exhaust the storehouse of all stored karmic memory traces from your entire continuum of existence over lifetimes.

Now, those impure or negative states mask the positive states, which are part of your buddha nature. So, as you slowly, over that span of six years—or you can do it more quickly, you can do it in two years if you do certain energy meditation practices—but whatever, when you do it, however long it takes, over that time you shift to more pure states. They're not masked anymore. And there's a flourishing of all those positive states and no negative states left. It was first recorded in the *Lalitavistara Sūtra*, and those are called the eighty minor marks of a buddha. There are eighty positive states of a buddha mind. And they flourish! You get them all. But they're not something that just develops. You just see that they were there all along. Like trust, like beauty, like concern, etcetera, etcetera. They're all part of your nature. There's nothing missing.

So, at that point, you can see beyond the negative states to the deeper, positive core of your nature. It flourishes. And you find that in the Tibetan word for a buddha, [different from the] Sanskrit. Buddhism developed in Sanskrit and Pāli, where the word for buddha was *bud-dha*, from the root *budh*, which means realized one. So, in Sanskrit, the name for a buddha is a realized one. But when those practices got transferred north to Tibet, the Tibetans were very careful to accurately translate from the Sanskrit. But they made a couple of exceptions that are sort of notable. They didn't translate buddha as realized one. The word for buddha is *sangye*, it's a compound term. *Sangwa* means completely purified, and *gyewa* means flourishing. So, the name for a buddha is someone who's mastered their meditation practice sufficiently so that there are no negative states. They've purified all negative states. And positively, they've now caused the flourishing of all eighty positive states of a buddha mind. That's sangye. Now, if you've gone beyond simply being awake and gone beyond being awake most of the time to be far along the path of *dharmadhātu* exhaustion, when you see beyond the clouding and the delusion that comes from all your negative states of mind, there's almost nothing left of that.

Then, in that field of big mind that we all share, where does conduct come from? It doesn't arise at that point from self, doesn't come from [you,] "Leslie." It doesn't arise at that point from an idea, because you're not operating out of conceptual mind. The awake mind is stripped of all concepts. It's direct knowing awareness, *sherig*, knowing awareness. There are no thoughts involved in any of that. Your conduct isn't an idea then. Your conduct isn't clouded by ideas; it's not clouded by thought, and it's no longer clouded by impure states of mind in the self. And since now you are a part of that field of big, awakened mind, then your conduct towards others arises spontaneously from the vast expense of awakened *dharmakāya* space. It's spontaneous conduct. You don't think about it; you just have it. And it arises as the best fit to the situation at hand. That's real conduct.

So now we say that conduct is spontaneously emergent, *lundrub*, spontaneously present. So, there's not a plan of action here. Your conduct is whatever is the best fit for the situation at the moment; with your own continuum and who you are as the best match to the need of that given individual or group of individuals at that time. That's more profound, because it is like the rays of the sun.

Now, nevertheless, there is a something beyond that. At that level of conduct, you, as Leslie, as reflected in that larger awakened mind, are acting spontaneously as the best fit for the situation of whoever you're with. You know what I'm talking about. You do that with your clients. It doesn't come from Leslie. And it's likely that you're going to see about what a given individual needs. But there are still boundaries here because you still have the tendency, by virtue of the habits of the ordinary mind, to segment that unbounded wholeness that has edges and space. So, there's one more level of practice beyond that.

You see this bubble here; we take this bubble to be all of our reality. We include in this bubble not just this room, but Newton and the earth and whatever we imagine beyond the earth and the cosmos, but it's still one bubble. And it's got boundaries to it, however small or large it is. And at some point, you start to see beyond the bubble, and you open up the experience of what's called "all-at-once-ness." You see, if you remove the subtlest edges of boundaries of this bubble through emptiness practice, through what's called the practice of "opening into the space"; if you do that practice, which is very specific, then what happens in Dzogchen is called you "cracking the eggshell." This bubble, this seemingly existing world that you're living in is like an eggshell, and we're chickens trying to get out of it. And once you crack the eggshell, you open up the direct experience of all-at-once-ness—that all realms and times are here simultaneously. And each realm, and all the beings in it, and the knowledge in it, are all available at once. And that's a huge shift, huge. You get little glimpses of that; then eventually you open it up more stably, like anything else we've talked about—just like opening up awakening.

If you open up that level of mind, then it's not just the conduct towards beings in this realm of reality. Now you have truly big mind. Now the conduct opens up simultaneously to thousands and thousands of realities, simultaneously. And the conduct is completely spontaneous, to benefit all beings. Then you're truly like the sun with infinite rays.

Now you're manifesting one of the five wisdom energies that is called discriminating wisdom energy. Every intention you have towards any being on any plane of reality is like a ray of light. But you have infinite rays of light across many planes of reality simultaneously. A buddha mind shines like that all the time, like the sun. Buddhas don't just help people in this plane of reality. There are other planes of reality they're acting simultaneously in. That's huge.

Now the conduct is completely spontaneous, and it's unceasing. And every action illustrates what in Tibet is called *gonpa*—sometimes translated as the intention of a buddha. The intention of a buddha is for all beings in all places of reality to simultaneously manifest whatever it takes for the benefit of their own realization and for the benefit of helping in compassion. That's big compassion. Now when you get into that range, there's no self, there's no thought. You're protecting all beings in all planes of reality simultaneously. You work uninterruptedly to keep this whole thing going here before we destroy it. Then you've achieved the status of a protector, a protector of all species.

So, the fruition of that is buddhahood. It's profound. But the reason why your question is so important is, as you know, it's very hard to judge realization based on verbal report because realizations can come out of conceptualization. Realizations can come out of [a] need to reinforce or call attention to the self. Those aren't realizations. But all the time we get students who want to be awakened. And they talk about fantastic meditation experiences that are really wonderful. And not any of them could talk about it in a way that's awakened because they're particularizing. They're making their experiences into things.

Those kinds of reports generally force [us] to mistrust; they're not genuine. So, any time you're hearing a student talk about what they think about awakening, when it comes to particularizing in any way, it's not awakening, whatever they'd like to think. But, on the other hand, if they're not particularizing as they describe it, and it's accompanied by compassion, spontaneous compassion, or gratitude or devotion or love, then they're probably more on the right track. But as Rinpoche says, as many of you know, the way you test realization is when you find yourself in the most difficult of life circumstances.

If your realization was largely conceptual, it will fall apart. If it was genuine, it's likely to deepen in the most difficult of life circumstances. Great yogis intentionally put themselves in the most difficult life circumstances as a way of enhancing their realization. That's called the Samādhi of the Heroes, or Heroic Samādhi—*jangpa chongchu papo tenzin*—the *samādhi* of the hero, the heroic *samādhi*; *Śūraṅgama Samādhi* in Sanskrit. And hero practice means once you have pretty stable awakening, you intentionally put yourself in the worst of life circumstances as a way of deepening your practice, as a way of benefiting others the most.

You see, in the transfer of all these teachings to the West, you all have a great opportunity. This is the best *samsāra*. And if you want to test the reality of your realizations, put yourself in the thick of all this crap. And develop the practice there. That will test you. Because if you can't do it there, then it's just conceptual. It's important. So, difficult life circumstances, it's a good test of hero practice. You know my clinical work is largely, and has been for the last forty years or more, in the abuse field. And I do a lot of work in the courts. That's how I test it. And I keep my realizations during vigorous cross examination with asshole lawyers. And if I can't, then I've done nothing. I'm not helping anybody. I'm not helping my clients. Because they're mostly—in my expert witnessing, they're mostly victim identifying. Today the Pope came out and said he's been fighting child abuse. A bit slow on the uptake, I think.

Student 2

It's also a five-year timeline to get the committee going.

Dan

Yeah, right. It's all for show. So, that's part of hero practice, to live in the real world and the worst of it. And it's very well suited for the West because we have a lot of crap. It's not an accident these teachings are coming here at this time because we need them.

Now real hero practice, if you want to put yourself not only in difficult life circumstances to deepen your practice, the most difficult of life circumstances is your own dying. That'll test your practice.

I have some students who studied with a Western teacher who really had what seemed to be quite strong realizations. He taught a lot of good things over the years. And what they told me is that when he was dying, he lost everything and turned on them in a mean way and really damaged them. If you can't sustain it during the dying process, then it doesn't really have a reality to it, however good he might have done before that point. He caused a lot of damage.

My first Root Lama, Geshe Wangyal—the great gift was he let us be with him when he was dying of advanced liver cancer at eighty-seven. And he gave us a running commentary, as much as he could, through the whole dying process until he couldn't talk anymore. His last teaching was to show us how to die. Amazing. Didn't flinch. He was more concerned that we learn something in what he was going through. That's a big test.

But, the ultimate test of conduct, or the ultimate test of realization rather, is how you live your life. Great beings leave a wake of positive influence behind them. They don't make an issue of it; it's just how they live. They don't have flaws. Many of you have seen *Digital Dharma*, the documentary on Gene Smith's life. He was a great being. He was also a good friend. He died in 2010. When the Chinese took over Tibet in 1959, they had their version of *Kristallnacht*. They spent, for one week all over Tibet, twenty-four hours day and night burning all the sacred texts and destroyed about one hundred thousand volumes of a literature that was collected over three thousand to seven thousand years.

We can think of Isis destroying great treasures. It's not the first time in history this has been done. This was a scriptural tradition, and it was entirely destroyed. And one man, a Westerner, took it upon himself to reconstruct that library. In his lifetime he reconstructed about eighty thousand of the hundred thousand volumes of Tibetan literature. Since they don't have a country anymore, he digitized the whole thing. You can get the entire tradition now on a stick or a hard drive. Even in Tibet where it's hard to get around from place to place, you have to walk over big mountains, and it's slow. Even the Tibetans, for all of their years of practice, never had more … only ever had a small number of texts to practice from. Now any Tibetan or Westerner can have the whole thing.

When I went into TBRC, the foundation that Gene formed at Harvard, they said, "Bring me a 500gig hard drive and we'll give you the entire thing." And that's never been available to anyone before. It's amazing. One person left that behind. No one even knows who he is, except the Tibetans. If you asked Gene about his practice, he was a serious Dzogchen practitioner. He studied for twelve years and lived with Dudjom Rinpoche, the great Nyingma Dzogchen master. He never talked about his practice, ever, because he had no spiritual pride. He just kept it to himself. You want to know about Gene's practice, look how he lived his life.

He left a legacy behind of an entire spiritual tradition that will last now across lifetimes, and that was nearly almost completely destroyed in a single lifetime. That's positive influence. William James in his great book, *The Varieties of Religious Experience*, over a hundred years ago was asked, "How do you tell the authenticity of mystical experience?" And his response was, "By their fruits ye shall know them." The only true test of realization is how you live your life.

So, if you're operating out of awakened *dharmakāya* space—and more and more as you are noticing that the conduct isn't coming from Leslie, the conduct isn't coming from thought, it just is—then you're well along the path. And you're getting little glimpses of all-at-once-ness, but that's not stable yet. But at some point, that will be stable, and when you "crack the eggshell," that will stun you. Totally stunning. Then your conduct will shift to a whole other level. There isn't so much beyond that. Why isn't that opening up? That will only work with *dharmadhātu* exhaustion; and you're not far enough along with it yet. Clear enough? You know exactly what I'm saying.

Good question, important question, it's all about conduct.

July 8, 2015

Themes: Beliefs in the Background, Negative or Positive

Dan

Welcome everyone. You have a question?

Student 1

I left Christianity at about eighteen because the story that Christ was doing something for us that we couldn't do ourselves didn't make sense to me, and I couldn't find much method. That's when I went to Zen. And usually, seeing the people that I've known who are Christian, often I'm seeing them trying to apply the principles of living well but very stuck on their beliefs.

So, two weeks ago, my cousin's wife died very suddenly. She had just passed a fourth-year post-breast cancer checkup, and a week later, she became very, very fatigued. That weekend she was diagnosed with an aggressive leukemia, and she died that Monday night. My cousin who—which is what's prompting all of this—was just as steady as anyone I've seen with an advanced Buddhist practice. He and his wife, who had been very active in their Methodist church—he is a lay minister there; and as I talked to him through the process and then at the funeral, he was just deeply at peace.

He explained it in a way very different than I might. He explained it in terms of, "My wife's now with Christ and he can love her better than I can." But his heart was completely open through the whole thing and through the ceremony, and the only tears were tears of just gratitude that he'd had twenty-three years with her. He was just kind of unshakeable, and yet I know that it's important to him that he defines it according to those particular beliefs.

It seemed to me that he just lived with them with enough sincerity that his consciousness was transformed in the way that we're trying to. So, I'm wondering if you can comment on that.

Dan

Well, that's a good question. There are two issues here. The first issue has to do with beliefs as a system of knowledge acquisition, and there are two parts to that. First, as cognitive psychotherapists would tell us in the West, experience shapes beliefs. Unlike negative self-talk, which is a sort of a moment-by-moment negative evaluation of our state, beliefs develop very slowly over time. And the funny thing about limiting beliefs, or even positive beliefs, is that we acquire them slowly, and once we acquire them, they're remarkably stable. But they operate in the background of awareness, and they have influence, whether they be positive or negative. Once beliefs develop, they're relatively impervious to change. So, if you have a limiting belief and it's stable, and you encounter some new experience that runs contrary to that belief, the natural human tendency is to throw out the new experience and fail to assimilate it and keep the belief intact.

So, in that sense, we don't learn from new experiences. That's what Albert Ellis, Western psychologist, tried to write about when he said there's an inherent and irrational component to those beliefs. Because we stop learning. We live in a world where we keep the beliefs intact irrespective of the nature of the experiences. A lot of our limiting beliefs are shaped by early experiences, and they have an emotional component to them. That's why we don't call them beliefs, we call them schemas. So, from that perspective, you see, beliefs develop slowly, and they have limits to them. But they have a profound influence.

I like to think about limiting beliefs as kind of minimized windows in your computer. If you have background programs running but they're minimized, you don't know that they're running, and the only way that you know that they're running is when you make some command that's incompatible with that background program and then your computer crashes. So, you don't really know what your limiting beliefs are until something exposes that, and then there's a certain immediate dysfunction to your experience and it's hard to account for.

If you want to get an appreciation for how limiting beliefs operate, you can look at how limiting beliefs are interchanged in couples, because each spouse has certain ideas in their mind about how their partner is supposed to behave, but they're never explicit. They're always in the background of your awareness. But you know when you've not operated out of that belief (that your partner wants you to operate out of), when you do something that's contrary to that belief, because you get an immediate reaction, right?

Student 2

I guess. [Laughter]

Dan

Everybody knows what I'm talking about. That's when you expose these limiting beliefs. And it's like each partner would have to read the mind of the other to know what these are because by definition, they operate in the background of awareness. But they have profound influence. They have influence over our sense of self and what we think is possible. They have influence over what we think is and is not possible in relationships, and how the world of unfolding experience happens, and what we think is and isn't possible. Core beliefs are beliefs about self-world and the world of others. Now, all of those beliefs develop slowly over time. They don't change much. You can change them, but it's not so easy. That's the perspective that beliefs are conditioned by experience. But it goes the other way around too.

The experiences can also change our beliefs. So, if we have new experiences, then that can lead to fundamental belief changes. That's essentially what a lot of motivational speaking is about. If you take the Tony Robbinses of the world, every one of his books is an infinite variation on the same theme: to introduce new experiences you wouldn't think of because that changes the underlying limiting beliefs. So, you begin to think anything is possible and you can accomplish anything. It's the heart of all this motivational speaking stuff. It makes a lot of money, and it's based on the other, the flip side of this equation, that new experiences can fundamentally change beliefs.

Now, how do beliefs function? In the negative sense, they limit our experience. We narrow the confines of what we think is possible for self. We have limiting ideas of what we think we're going to get out of relationships, and we select relationships to get exactly those limitations rather than what we really want. We limit how we see what's possible to get out of life, so we don't even try going beyond that. That's the negative side of beliefs. The positive side of beliefs is that beliefs serve as central organizing principles, and that people need stable internal beliefs.

The more stable the beliefs, the better the mental health. In the '60s there was a classic book by Jerry Frank called *Persuasion and Healing*, and what he was looking at was that it doesn't make any difference whether it's placebo effect, a quack, a shaman, a psychotherapist, or a doctor, all treatments have about the same effectiveness, irrespective of the truth value of the treatment itself. They all work pretty much the same. So, what he was looking at is that what really is working, what's really healing, is that whatever the system is, however legitimate or crazy it may be, if you give people a clear explanation, if they're sick physically or mentally, they need a clear explanatory model. If you clearly say, "This is what's wrong with you," even if it's total fiction, they tend to get better, because beliefs have an organizing effect. There's a central organizing principle to explain all these weird things so they're not sick anymore. Hence the title *Persuasion and Healing*. Persuading people that there's a certain view that they can take that organizes and explains all these symptoms is healing.

Also, in the '60s there was a way in which people looked at how cultural belief systems actually operated in the service of mental health and physical health. People who have a clear explanatory model do much better. If you want a clear example of that, let's talk about religious beliefs. How many people have had mental health breakdowns, how many people have had serious depression, psychotic episodes, or serious addictions, and then they found God and they're better?

There's something about adopting a consistent belief system, however crazy it may be. It has a central organizing principle. It explains things in such a way that they're not sick anymore. I remember when I was working at Cambridge Hospital, and I was on call for the psych emergency room. Our catchment area was Harvard Square, so we saw all the weird people from all over the East Coast. It was a good place to work if you want to learn about mental health. And I remember one Latino man coming in, in his early twenties, and he had all of the early signs of psychosis.

This guy was going to be crazy out of his mind three days later. But he didn't want to stay in the hospital, so he left. And then I saw him a week later on the street and I was talking with him. He wasn't psychotic anymore. After he left the emergency room the next day, a Jehovah's Witness knocked on his door, and he adopted the system totally. And as rigid as the system is, for a mind that's coming apart and getting disorganized, the rigidity of the system actually worked to organize his mind. It worked better than neuroleptics. You see what I'm saying?

Cultural belief systems organize mental health. As some people say … like the psychoanalytically bent sociologist Phillip Lief once said, if your cultural systems organize health and mental health, how many potentially aggressive and violent men are out there that we don't see in the clinic for violence? Because what they do is they spend all day behind the controls of a bulldozer. And that organizes all that aggression. Makes it actually constructive. I remember seeing a guy who was quite psychotic, and his Rorschach … it was extremely violent. And he was passionate about becoming a cop, and he was pre-psychotic.

I thought he was going to be the most dangerous cop in the world. But he was hell bent on going to the police academy. And so, there was an ethical dilemma for me. How do I get him to not do that because this is going to be a big-time mess? Because he's going to kill somebody and justify it. So, I went to my supervisor at the time who was a mad genius, and he said, "Here's what you're going to do. You're going to give him the Strong-Campbell test, which is going to tell him what jobs are the best suited for him. And you're going to tell him based on the findings, which we already know what that's going to be. You're going to tell him that what he really needs to do is not be a cop. He needs to be a paramedic. Because now rather than blowing people apart, which is where all his fantasies go, he's going to pick up all these people on the streets that are blown apart, and he's going to learn how to put them back together again, and in the course of, that he's going to put together his own mind."

So, I mimicked what my supervisor told me to do, and said, "This is what the tests show," and he became a paramedic, and he became a rather damn good one. And he never went psychotic and he was never violent. Because now we have a cultural belief system, an organized set of activities that organize the mind. So, you see, from that perspective, beliefs are useful and they provide meaning. They provide action plans, so we organize our behavior toward meaningful ends and goals.

What Philip Lief said is that the cultural systems largely work to organize health and mental health for most individuals. The people we see in the clinic are the ones it doesn't work for, and that's a rather small minority. I remember once, with this same supervisor who liked to think about cultural systems, seeing a woman who was very bright; she went to college, had a degree in anthropology and then started teaching. And she was also a talented pianist. Quite good. Then she got married and left all that stuff and raised three kids, but she never developed a sense of self. She had a subtle, what we call, "false self-organization." And when the third kid left home, in that empty nest she had a massive psychotic depression and made a very serious suicide attempt. Now I could have sat down with her and tried to treat her depression, but I had this supervisor who thought about cultural systems. And he said, "Look, she never really organized a sense of herself, but what's the best self-organization she ever had? It was when she was independent in college doing really well, and when she was playing the piano and she had a lot of accolades for that. And, where she organized most of herself around was being a mom, so, you've got to reinstate that."

So, here's what his instructions were. "Go out and find a college where she can volunteer and be a dorm mother." We don't have those anymore, but in those days, we did, "and let her have a bunch of kids to take care of. But those kids will come and go every year so she's going to learn to let the kids go and have new ones come in, unlike her own kids. And put a piano in that dorm, and let her discover her music again and she'll start developing a sense of self." And that's exactly what we did. We organized a cultural system around her. And we didn't see her back in the hospital. Understand what I'm saying?

That's how cultural systems and belief systems work. They organize health and mental health. Now, that goes directly to the example that you gave about how in the process of somebody getting a serious illness and dying, belief systems, in the best sense, provide meaning and have an organizing effect. It guides grief in the right direction, and that's useful. I would say in this country, about a third of professional athletes in professional sports are seriously Christian, many of them fundamentalist in their base. And that organizes them so they can play better.

So, that's the positive side of beliefs. Not all beliefs are created equal. Robert Emmons, in his work *The Psychology of Ultimate Concerns*, says that people who have a larger overarching belief structure about what provides the ultimate meaning in life—spiritual, humanitarian, civil, philosophical, whatever your central purpose is—people who have a well-articulated sense of purpose have greater psychological wellbeing, they have greater physical health, and less internal noise in the system, less internal contradictions about different goals. They're happier.

When I do my performance excellence course for judges, one of the exercises I always do with them is trying to articulate the larger vision of their work, which for them is usually humanitarian, around justice and things of civil responsibility and justice. And when they can articulate that and hold that in the backdrop of their awareness, they're more resilient, they're happier on the bench, and they can take all the crap and not get swayed by all the stress that they deal with. And that always works for them. So, the more you can articulate that larger vision in life, the better.

Now that leads into the second part, and that is that right now, we're framing knowledge in terms of belief structures as if that were all that we have as knowledge, but it's not. If you think about here, the West again, most of our theories of intelligence, modern theories of intelligence, go back to Piaget—sensory motor, preoperational, concrete operational, and formal operational thinking. And in formal operational thinking, in about adolescence, you discover all the infinitude of possibilities, as the existentialists say.

You start seeing larger relationships and interconnections. But a number of people since Piaget said, "Look, adult mature cognitive development doesn't stop with adolescence." That's ridiculous. So, there's an articulation of stages beyond that as what are called postformal stages of cognitive operations. Some of that stuff is pretty complex. The best research on that is by Suzanne Crook-Greuter, and she tries to articulate some of the higher systems. Or Ken Wilber's work. But he takes all the higher stages and smushes them all together as integral without unpacking them.

But the basic idea here is that the more cognitive development matures, what you're opening up is wider and wider perspectives. So, the first postformal stage of intelligence is you see beyond the information given. You look deeper within the system. You see things that are not obvious. The next stage, second postformal operation, you go to a larger system, and you appreciate the entirety of the system at once, not just the operations within it, but the whole system itself. In your meditation practice, the first, going beyond the information given, would be special insight practice and emptiness practice. The next level beyond that is when you see that there's a larger whole beyond all of those interrelationships, and that would be Ocean and Waves practice—developing ocean-like, changeless, boundless awareness, beyond the convention of time, and seeing everything arise within that ocean of changeless, boundless awareness from the perspective of that changeless boundless awareness. You see the difference here?

So, every one of these shifts is like a larger perspective of cognitive development. Yeah, but now you're looking at the larger picture. You're looking at the pieces from the larger picture. The next step beyond that is where you see that the whole perspective and all that's within that, that it's varied and pluralistic, that all of it is the same structure, nondual. So, the next step would be nondual perception.

And when you open up nondual perception, you open up another funny thing—and this goes beyond a lot of the Western stuff—because that's the stage where you transcend representational thinking. And now your knowledge acquisition is pure awareness. It doesn't come from your secondary cortices. It's not about thought and representation. It's true, direct awareness. So, anything from nondual awareness up is direct access. Now you've gone beyond all beliefs.

It is not an accident [that] the last practice in Mahāmudrā that you do at that level of practice is sealing the underlying beliefs. You look at all the stories you made, all the limiting assumptions as empty ideas, until there's nothing left. The underlying beliefs, the whole house of cards collapses. Now you're operating out of a pure, immediate awareness every moment. That's a big shift, nondual awareness. But you're still operating within a system, and what you realize from a cognitive perspective is it's not all relativism. That's an immature view, from a higher level of cognitive development. There is a "whole" behind all those relative things, and you begin to get a sense of that with nondual perception when you begin to get a direct sense of that with awareness, not thinking about it because you can't think your way through that.

But now if you set up your crossing over instructions, like say, Lion's Gaze, and you open up a direct perception of awakened awareness, now that's a huge shift. You're operating out of being that unbounded wholeness. You shift from any kind of partial view to wholeness. In Western cognitive terms, what we would say is that you're not looking at the interrelationships between systems, you're operating out of a larger field that includes all those systems, you're operating out of being that field. So, that larger perception of the field supersedes all systems, which is why awakening is such a big shift.

Now, if you refine that awakening so you have it all the time, eventually you see that this little bubble of reality is just one little bubble. If you do certain meditations that open this up, you have all realms and times all at once. There are no boundaries between past, present, and future. No boundaries between different realms of reality. Everything is here all at once. That's a major shift. Now you're operating on thousands of realities simultaneously—all distinct and all seen from this larger field—or all-at-once-ness. All direct, now, no conceptualization. Then, the next shift is you lock into the structure of the being—enlightened buddha bodies. You are the whole show. Every individual mind is the whole show. But you're still in the physical body. And ultimately, you can transform that into light, like in rainbow body practice.

There are seven levels of development, each including larger and larger perspectives on the field that Ken Wilber talks about in terms of integrative levels. Each one of those you can open up with a meditation practice. But when you get to nonduality or beyond, none of the direct immediate access to awareness has anything to do with representations or beliefs. Now as Westerners, we like to get over-identified with thought, so we don't even think that exists. Even in Cook-Greuter's research, she'll say that when you get to that level of, say, what we're calling nonduality, maybe only 3 percent of the population can manifest that.

Well, that's not surprising in the West because we don't have the tools to teach how to do that. But we do in Tibetan Buddhism, and it's explicitly laid out, every one of these steps. As Westerners, we have to be open to the fact that there are levels of awareness that transcend all conceptual thought, and that's a better way of accessing things and being in the world. More importantly, these larger perspectives that have to do with, say, awakened awareness, have far more important implications for mental health than the organization that ever comes from any particular belief in any kind of religion. And in most religions, including Christianity, you move beyond beliefs, but that's something that's not really explicit in Christianity.

See, in Tibetan Buddhism we have a lineage tradition. These things are passed on for thousands of years from heart to heart in the same way because they work. But Christianity isn't a lineage tradition. There was a great tradition of the Desert Fathers in Syria and Egypt, starting at about the year 100 AD, peaking in about 250 AD. About 150 years. But there are several problems with the Desert Father tradition. One was that the yogis in the Christian Desert Fathers tradition rarely wrote anything down, and what we do have that survives are notes taken by students. Some writings of Evagrius [Ponticus], Macarius, or the Egyptians, some of the better yogis, were written as a series of scratch notes by students. That's all we've got left. Whereas in lineage traditions in the East, you get people talking about this stuff, writing texts, writing commentaries on the texts, and passing down a great literature. So, a hundred thousand volumes in Tibet on states of mind. That's remarkably different from the scratch notes of the Christian Desert Father yogis.

The second problem was that the live tradition of meditation practice of the Desert Fathers turned out to be a terrible threat to the church that was developing. There was a time at around between 200 and 250 AD where lots of people were running off from the cities like Alexandria to study with the Desert Fathers, and the church was terribly threatened. So, they commissioned a great scholar of the day whose name was Lucius Palladias to go out and live with the Desert Fathers for two years for the sole purpose of discrediting them. He lived with them, and he came back, and he wrote this book which is like the *Autobiography of a Yogi.*[9] It's all a miraculous description of super normal abilities that he observed: Desert Fathers flying through the air, living for months without eating any food, raising people from the dead; it's like a travelogue of super normal abilities. The church was terribly embarrassed because he didn't discredit these teachings—he gave them a strong billing. So, they didn't publish his work, they suppressed it.

Palladias, I later found out, was enamored by these teachings. And unlike what most scholars say, the Silk Road was much more advanced earlier than we thought. So, he actually hitched a camel ride on the Silk Road, and went to India to a place close to what's now Rishikesh, and wrote a second book of observing the same kind of miraculous things by the Indian yogis in India. And he spent the rest of his life studying this stuff.

Having failed in the mission, the church then had to seek much further to find a second great, respected scholar, and his name is Johannes Cassianus (John Cassian). He lived with the Desert Fathers for two years for the sole purpose of discrediting them. But he didn't. He wrote two works. The first one was much more threatening than Palladias' work. It's called *The Institutes.* So, the church for many hundreds of years suppressed it. Because what he was saying is that, look, if you look at the first generation of Christian yogis with St. Anthony and all the people around St. Anthony—if you did these practices, you became Jesus.

---

9 Classic volume by Swami Yogananda.

Now that's not terribly different from Buddhism where everybody has Jesus nature, like buddha nature. Anybody who does these practices becomes that. Now the church was terribly threatened by that theology, so they got him to change it. And what he changed it to was, well, you don't really become Jesus, you really become an art changer like Gabriel or Rafael. But that's not what he meant. And later it got watered down such that the only thing that happens is you get a glimpse of the Godhead, but it stays out there. Not much changes at all. So, they kept watering it down. But why? Because they were terribly threatened that a live tradition of practice would threaten the development of the church and what the church eventually became. Because look what it became, particularly the Roman Church. It became the seat of power and wealth. And as sick as that is today, with all of its depravity, it's a bankrupt tradition. And all we have to look at is their attitude towards abuse. It's a bankrupt tradition.

If you look really carefully, and you read the newspapers in Italy, you can see how much money the church has laundered in the last years. Fifteen years ago, the prime minister and all of the cabinet members of Italy, with mafia people, were siphoning off a quarter of the gross national product to private bank accounts in Switzerland and then a judge blew the whistle. A lot of people got killed. But they investigated and that was the first time that Swiss banks opened up the bank accounts; and [they found that] all the money was laundered by the Catholic Church at the Vatican.

So that's what it became. And I'm not saying it's any different [in Buddhism]. There was just as much struggle with fat lamas who were interested in power and money and accumulating fame for themselves in Tibet, as you have with priests and bishops in the Catholic Church. It's no different. Then we lose the heart of it. East or West. But as a live tradition, it moves beyond belief systems. You have to practice this stuff. You've got to see how it works in your own experience, and none of that has to do with beliefs anymore. If you want mature spiritual practice, it's always beyond belief structures in any religion.

The more rigid beliefs then may be an organizing principle, but at some point, it comes back to bite you because they're rigid. As one of my friends says, "A good definition of fundamentalism is low on the fun and high on the mental." And fundamentalism, in any religion, is destroying this planet. But fresh experience is never conceptual. You have to look into your own mind and see.

See, where the church went wrong is St. Augustine was a great yogi, but his mother, Monica, had ambitions for him to be the most powerful bishop. And she pressured him, badgered him to drop all of his meditation practice, and he did. And then he was rigid against any of that. And at that point, mysticism got cut away from the Roman Church. It survived in the Eastern Church. But since then, you only get pockets of it. Like the Spanish mystics, like John of the Cross and Teresa of Avila, or the German mystics Suso and Tauler. But you never get a lineage tradition because it was just an aberration at certain times in history, which is why many people look to the East because the traditions are much more evolved.

This practice doesn't have anything to do with beliefs. You've got to look into your own mind. See for yourself. And the sooner you get out of conceptualization, the better—you can't think your way into awakening. And you have to move beyond all thought. Otherwise, awakening won't happen. That's why the crossing over instructions are often kept secret. Because if you spill them out there too much and people try and think their way through it, they actually harden the mind and it's harder to awaken. The heart of this practice is always the direct experience of awakening. We say, "It's the confluence of all the teachings."

So, you see, we can talk about levels of knowledge at the lower to mid-levels of knowledge, healthy belief systems have an organizing effect on the mind, but eventually they're limited; at the higher levels of knowledge, all higher levels of knowledge are not based on knowing some conceptual thought or beliefs—they're always direct awareness and refining that.

So, that's what I would say to your question. Good question. There's a lot to it. Anything else? We have time for a brief question.

Student 3

How about when you feel resistance to something? What's the best way to deal with that?

Dan

You've got to say more. What does that mean?

Student 3

Even if it's something that you enjoy doing, but you put up blocks for some reason, is it—should you just make it emptiness?

Dan

I remember years ago when I was trying to write my doctoral dissertation, I had so many pencils I could sharpen. They would distract me from sitting down and writing. [Laughter] Like that.

Student 3

That's what I mean.

Dan

Yeah. Well, first you have to decide whether the task at hand is worth doing. You have to know what your motivation is for doing it. If it's important and you're resistant to what's good, either for yourself or for others, really the best practice is impermanence. I find these days I get far more done than I could, say, ten years ago, simply by virtue of being older. Life is not infinite anymore.

Realistically, I've got limited time left, and so the things that are important to do, I don't sit down and futz about it anymore. There's nothing like that perspective. Always, always keep death in the background of your awareness and it will keep what you do fresh and honest. That's the most strong practice I think.

I remember growing up in the '60s and '70s and reading the Castaneda books. We all did that, right? And him saying, "Let death have a seat on your shoulder at all times. Then you'll act authentically in the world because there's no time to waste."[10]

I remember I was supposed to be in Nepal, but we had to postpone the trip because of obvious reasons, like the earthquake. So, there was a forty-second-year reunion for the freshman class where I went. Forty-two years—that's a long time. We even went back to our old dorm rooms. They looked little. And I thought, my god, those forty-two years just went by like that …

[Impermanent,] like Geshe Wangyal. He came over to the US before Tibet was taken over, which is sort of interesting. He lived in the Delaware Water Gap

---

10 This is most likely from Castaneda's first book, *The Teachings of Don Juan: A Yaqui Way of Knowledge* in 1968 as a work of anthropology, though it is now widely considered a work of fiction.

in a beautiful area, and probably had about a dozen students over the thirty years he was here. And the thing I found most refreshing about living with him in summers between college and graduate school over a nine-year span was, this is a guy who never played the guru game. Actually, no one had heard of him. But look at his students: Jeffrey Hopkins, who probably was the most influential scholar in modern Tibetan Buddhism in the West. He was working with University of Virginia's doctoral program that he set up. Bob Thurman, myself, all of us have had a lot of influence, and he never played the guru game.

In fact, he gave one public talk, and why he gave that talk, I don't know. But it was interesting. I think it was something like 1975, which is sort of early in this whole thing, and there was the first international yoga conference. That was before yoga was popular, and it was like a sideshow. There were about three or four hundred different people doing different kinds of yoga and meditations and all this kind of stuff, and they all had their little workshops. It was like a huge smorgasbord of spiritual practice. And he actually accepted the invitation. Which amazed me.

When he got up to talk, he walked up on the stage, he was an old man, and he said, "I'm not going to talk to you about meditation. There are lots of people who show you all sorts of meditation practices and yoga practices. That's not my purpose here." He says, "All I'm asking you is that when you sit down to meditate, take a moment and examine your motivation. Why are you doing it? And make sure you have a clear answer to that. That's all I have to say." And he walked off the stage.

The brevity made the point. Why do we engage in anything in life? What's your motivation? If it's to develop your spiritual practice, if it's to improve yourself, if it's to help all beings, then you're probably on the right track. And if you can establish that motivation, then you're going to get it done. You're not going to futz around and be resistant to it. But when your practice or whatever you're doing in life loses that motivation, that's when you start resisting. Because it doesn't come from the heart anymore. You've lost your way with it. So go back to your motivation. It doesn't take long to fix that one. Understood?

But, it's often the case that when you look at motivation and try and clarify it, the immediate reaction to that is the bump across your limiting beliefs. And we're right back to where we started. So, if you start in Buddhist practice, you set up your posture and the first thing you do is you set your motivation with *bodhicitta*. Okay? You make a promise to yourself that the purpose for doing this is for the experience of awakening.

Why do we start with that? Because if you start the meditation every time by setting the intention towards awakening—that's literally what *bodhicitta* means. *Citta* means intention, *bodhi* means awakening or realization. You start the practice by setting the intention. If you do that, it serves like a central organizing principle, so as you go through the rest of the twenty minutes or a half an hour, whatever you do, always in the background of your awareness, you're doing this because it leads to awakening. You can be a little more careful with your practice.

And secondly, you're doing it because this realization may serve the benefit of others. You tend to work a little harder if you're doing it for others. You've heard me say that before. I think the thing I've learned most about being a parent was there's something remarkably self-transcending about it. If your kid's sick and they wake you up for the tenth time at night, the first impulse is, "Oh God, not again." You want to roll over and go back to sleep. But you never allow it. No matter what it takes, you get up and you attend to your kid.

So, when you practice with *bodhicitta* and you practice for the benefit of all beings, it's like being a parent for all beings. No matter what it takes, no matter how hard it is, you get out of yourself and you just do it. So, start with setting the motivation. Now the first thing you do when you set the motivation is … you're going to bump across whatever limiting beliefs are there. So, as Westerners it's, "Well, awakening, oh, I can't do that." Or, "I don't deserve it" is one of the common things, or "I can't do that." The Tibetans have their version of limiting beliefs. "It takes lifetimes, so don't even bother to practice this lifetime. It's okay to be lazy because, of course, it takes so many lifetimes."

Ultimate reality isn't defined by ideas. All those are ideas. They're useless. So set aside the limiting ideas as empty constructions of mind. Burn with your practice. Then you get somewhere. But then you have to change that intention depending on your level of practice. If you can stabilize awakening, or you have a taste of awakening, you don't set the intention towards awakening, you set the intention to have awakening all the time. And worse, if you have awakening all the time, then you have to set the awakening towards being a buddha. That's going to raise your limiting beliefs! "I can't be a buddha." Why not? This is the time that all the teachings are coming to the West. We need buddhas.

I can't retire until there are seeds planted in the mindstreams for twenty-five buddhas in the West. That's my duty. So, help me out here. That's all we need. You understand what I'm saying? They're just ideas. They're useless. With the right teachings and the clarity of how you approach them, anything is possible.

It's all about motivation. If you're resistant, go back and look at your motivation. Examine it honestly.

July 22, 2015

Themes: Karma Theory; Intention Matters; Compassion & Conduct

Dan

Welcome everyone. You have a question?

Student 1

I have a question about karma. It's been coming up in my daily meditation, like a dilemma around the idea that we're not supposed to think about killing anything or detesting anything, and yet it's summer, and I do not want …

Dan

Those flies. [Gentle laughter]

Student 1

Oh, mosquitoes. And I have a termite service that takes care of my house for the mice that are prevented from coming in, and there's a little poison in the corners here and there. So, I don't know how to make that work with the idea that I should be one with even those mosquitoes and mice.

Dan

[Smiling] I'm not the right person to ask. [Laughter] When Asonam was staying with me for a month, he wanted to have local food, so I gave him lobster, and I'm still getting busted about it. But actually, it's a good question.

First of all, let's talk about what karma is in general and then we'll get to the specifics of this.

Some days my reflux is bad, my voice goes out, and I can't talk so ... Today was one of those days, so that's why I do this. [Dan drinks something and points to some foods in front of him.]

Karma means that anything that comes into your field of experience, at the moment that you engage it, you form a karmic memory trace called *bagchag* in Tibetan, or *samskara* in Sanskrit. And what causes you to form that impression is mental engagement. In Dzogchen you'll hear a phrase, *langdor*, or *langdor mēpa*. And *langwa* means to move toward something in order to process it further. It's often translated as accepting it but doesn't quite capture what it means. It means that every moment, things come in rapidly in our field of experience, and the moment that you engage it, you fix it in the memory trace. Or the opposite is *dolwa*, which is often translated as rejection, which means you engage it to stop processing it. Either you engage it to process it further or you engage it to say, "No, done with that one."

Both of those are two types of mental engagement. The alternate possibility is it just passes through and you leave it alone, do nothing to it. At which point it immediately decays. In that sense karma theory in Dzogchen isn't terribly different from Western psychology.

After the 1960s and '70s, which were the beginnings of the days of information processing theory in Western psychology, a popular way of studying information processing was with a machine called a tachistoscope or T-scope. And it's an electronic board with a stationary viewing hood, and it flashes events in terms of thousandths of a second. And you can study the speed of the mind with a T-scope.

One of the things that was discovered with a T-scope was what was called iconic memory. If I flash an event, it decays in about one hundred milliseconds, tenth of a second. Then it's gone, unless I engage it. And if I engage it—it's not like a leaky sieve—if I engage it at all, it doesn't run through, it gets transferred to short term memory. Then if I attend to it—which is a much slower process, a much more deliberate process—if I attend to it, then I transfer it to long term memory. So we go from immediate iconic memory, to short term memory, to long term memory. So, it's not so different from karma theory, you see. What it means is that everything runs through the mind, and nothing will stick unless I engage it. And even if I engage it, it will stick a little bit longer, but it won't last unless I really deliberately attend to it. That's why if you're in school and you're trying to memorize things for an exam, the best way of memorizing things so they stick in long term memory is rehearsal: you keep going over and over it. Then it lasts in long term memory; it has greater memory strength.

So, in Dzogchen, it's like an iconic memory theory. What it means is that every single moment you engage something, you make another memory trace. That means [that since] we engage things a lot, we get thousands and hundreds of thousands of memory traces developing in the storehouse mind, in the course of a lifetime. And in Tibetan theory, we store those memory traces from all of our lifetimes, not just this life. Then you have what's called ordinary storehouse consciousness. The matrix of the mind is *kunzhi*, universal ground, the groundless ground, the structure of being. *Kunzhi* is like a vast expanse of empty awareness space; it has no content. As an overlay on that, we fill that storehouse, that groundless ground. It's like a depository for millions and millions of memory traces. Now, awakened groundless ground becomes ordinary storehouse consciousness because it has content—all of the memory traces from every previous action of the mind. That's a lot of actions of the mind.

And if you engage actions with greater behavior—like if I don't just think of something but actually play it out—the more I play it out in behavior, the more I rehearse it in mind, and the more I rehearse it in behavior or do it many times, it has greater strength. So not all karmic impressions are created equal. Some have greater strength than others, okay? We call it *chuk*, the force of the karmic trace, or memory trace. Now, karmic impressions get activated and they ripen, *minwa*—to ripen, in Tibetan. And what gets ripened from the millions of memory traces has a lot to do with things that you encounter during the day.

Certain things become reminders, and then certain karmic impressions ripen more than others. It seems somewhat random, but it's not. It's similar to the idea of a day-residue in dreaming in Western psychoanalysis. And once karmic impressions ripen, they manifest as spontaneous states of mind. So, the reason why most ordinary people ask about the spontaneous emerging states of mind where they say, "Oh where does all this junk come from?" It comes from the ripening of karmic impressions. And the reason why it's skewed towards the negative is that mostly what we engage and involve ourselves in are negative states and behaviors rather than positive states and behaviors and virtuous states and behaviors. So, for most people in the ordinary mind, the relative ratio of pure to impure states is skewed in the direction of spontaneously emerging negative states.

That's why when we talk about spiritual practice, there's a whole world of preliminary practices which are designed to "build the vessel," which is another way of saying you have to shift the balance to more positive states emerging spontaneously than negative states. Otherwise, you play out on the pillow all the crap that you play out in your everyday life, which is why you don't usually start with concentration or meditation practice, you start with preliminary practices to shift that balance.

Karmic impressions that ripen that have the greatest strength manifest first as spontaneous states of mind. Then they manifest as behaviors. But usually there's an influence on behavior indirectly, and ultimately as direct behaviors. And if karmic impressions have great strength, they actually ripen in the form of the events that occur in your life. So, the fact that we're all here together is good fortune. It's the ripening of certain karmic tendencies from your previous life that allows you to hear these teachings.

You are then what's called the *kalden*, one of fortunate karmic connection. But it doesn't come from nowhere. It's all based on previous engagements. So, that's the theory of how karmic impressions develop and why our mind, over the accumulation of lifetimes, becomes filled with junk. It's a big depository.

Now there are several implications of karma theory for spiritual practice. One is that all mental engagement forms karmic impressions. Two, karmic impressions at some point or another ripen, they get activated and they ripen. Three, as they ripen, they proliferate in their effects. And their effects are not immediately one to one. They come up in various ways. So, it's not so easy to trace the cause-and-effect trajectory of ripening karmic impressions. Four, if you engage in actions that have greater karmic memory trace strength, the ripening has greater force. And fifth, if you don't engage in the action, you don't get the karmic effect. That includes mental actions as well as physical actions, and something as subtle as engagement.

So that has implications for practice. First, what the recommendation is, is to avoid negative behaviors that have the greatest negative karmic strength. In traditional Buddhism, those are called The Seven Restraints, *donpa*. You just don't go there. No killing, no stealing, no sexual misconduct, no lying, no divisive speech, no abusive speech, no meaningless speech or idle speech or gossip.

Those are the big seven. I find it interesting that when they developed this list two thousand years ago, they struggled with the same thing that we struggle with; in other words, in four of the seven restraints, the predominant category is speech, because that's the hardest one for people to control.

Now, what your example was about is the first of those, no killing, because killing has great karmic strength. But remember, it's not just physical acts; it's also the intention. That's also a kind of engagement.

So, when I'm sitting out on my porch and watching the sun go down over the water in Gloucester in green fly season, and the little monsters are going to create welts that are going to last for weeks, my first impulse is to really swat that green fly—swat the shit out of it. But, you know, that impulse has, pretty much, strong karmic strength anyway. So, whether I do it or not is less the issue because the fact that my intention is to do it, I've already created the karmic thing. So, don't beat yourself up over it.

Also, intention matters, not just actions, including the intention to do better. So as a regular practice you don't go out and try and kill things. But relatively speaking, some types of killing are more harmful than others. And in certain situations, killing is compassionate. Like there was a time in the old Tibet when Tibetan Buddhism had just flourished for about two hundred years and then one of the successor kings decided to kill all the practitioners and kill all the teachers to get rid of it.

And then after wiping out about 80 percent of what was left of the practices in old Tibet, one of the surviving monks killed the king out of compassion, to stop the reign of terror. He took on that karmic debt. It's still a karmic debt, but the intention matters. Intention matters.

You do the best you can with these things. As it's said, all of the smallest creatures, right down to the smallest insects, all have awakened awareness. But only humans have the metacognitive capacity to recognize awakened nature. That's why human birth is so precious, because it's the only brain, the only mind that can recognize true nature. That's why you want to get a human birth, so you'll have the chance to recognize that and develop it. Insects can't do that. But, if you've come up with your mind, with the impulse, it's there anyway. So, it's best to work on looking at the impulse as empty.

If you have a strong urge, if you bring it into your awareness, that has some positive karmic effects. See, not all karmic impressions are negative. Every time you practice, you form positive karmic impressions. That's what's called *gendor*, virtue practice. The art of this is that through ordinary practices, you develop an accumulation of positive states of mind, which is the ripening of all the positive spiritual practices that you've done. That's called the accumulation of merit. You see the ripening of positive states based on doing spiritual practices as opposed to something neutral or something negative, and in the mind, the balance shifts towards more pure states, so it's easier to practice. That's why you do it. But ultimately, the best practice (it's quite an advanced practice) is to do *rangnang rangdröl*, which I like to translate as: "arising in and by itself, left in its own way, so that it becomes immediately liberated by itself."

So, you view everything arising from groundless ground, the matrix of being, like a vast expanse of space. As soon as something arises, you don't engage it. You don't accept it; you don't reject it; you just let it pass through because there's no self that's doing anything to this. Just watch the show without a watcher. And if it's left completely alone … leaving it alone isn't a strategy, because if you try and leave it alone, you're engaging in a strategy, which is a kind of mental engagement, and that's not really understanding the practice.

At a certain point, the practice of leave-it-alone-ness becomes part of the view. The view is the meditation, so it's not a strategy anymore. It's just how you see it. And if you mature your practice to that view, everything that arises is left completely alone every moment without engaging anything. And then as soon as it arises, it immediately liberates itself. We say *rangdröl*, liberating in and by itself, immediately.

So every moment, nothing sticks. So, the metaphors that are used are like writing on water, or like snowflakes falling in a great ocean, this vast space-like awareness. Everything just arises and falls like snowflakes in an ocean all the time. And then you do that practice all the time, 24/7. That particular practice, if you understand it—of course, there's a lot of preparatory work to be able to do that, but if you get it completely right and you do it 24/7, you have now opened up the gateway to this third map to buddhahood. And it's the key practice. And you initiate a process that's called *dharmadhātu* exhaustion.

In other words, if you are not engaging anything every moment, by moment, by moment, by moment, you, for the first time in your life or maybe lifetimes, are not making any new karmic impressions. So, what it does is it forces the mind to start automatically releasing all the karmic impressions that would normally ripen from the storehouse at a rapidly accelerated rate. And you just watch the whole show without a watcher, without doing anything.

And if you do that 24/7, on average for about six years, you've exhausted the bin of all the karmic memory traces that potentially ripen across lifetimes.

The storehouse is emptied out. That's why it's called *dharmadhātu* exhaustion, because there's an endpoint. It's finished. And since those negative states mask the positive qualities of mind, the *yonten*, at the point that the balance, the ratio shifts much more to pure rather than impure states, all those positive states flourish. And there's eighty positive states of a buddha mind.

The word buddha means "the realized one" in Sanskrit. But when those practices came to Tibet, that's not how they translated "*budh*." The Tibetan translation is *sangyé*. It's a compound term: *sangwa* and *gyewa*. *Sangwa* means purify; *gyewa* means flourishing. If you do *dharmadhātu* exhaustion as your practice, at some point you purify all negative states so there's actually none left. And then there's a flourishing of all eighty positive states. That's what your mind becomes; there's no negative states anymore.

So, that's technically what it means to be beyond karma. It doesn't mean that, "Well, now I can do anything I want." It means that you have exhausted the influence of what would heretofore be previously ripening karmic impressions; it just doesn't happen anymore. There's no more influence of that. But you're not beyond karma, you're beyond forming new karmic impressions and beyond the influence of ripening or potentially ripening previous karmic impressions.

But here's the catch—because that's your level of realization, all conduct arises spontaneously from universal ground as the exact fit for the situation at hand. So, conduct is not something that you do or a strategy that you engage in. It's spontaneous, and it comes out of the realization, so all conduct is for the benefit of others, naturally speaking, and it's all compassionate. So, the realization leads to conduct. So, it's not like you say, "Well, I'm beyond karma. I can do whatever the hell I want."

What's built into the structure of the universe is [that] the action is always for the benefit of others, it's always helpful. It can't be anything other than that if the realization is genuine. You can't act like an asshole at a certain point of your realization even though you might still want to. [Dan laughs] Although some people do a good job with that still. You know what I'm saying. You can't.

We have a fun thing with that … sometimes in the mixing practices that we do in one of the courses where you're operating out of awakened awareness, and we have you engage in trash talk or negative speech about someone; and you really can't do it in quite the same way, because it doesn't work in that state, that awakened state. And it becomes hilarious.

So, it's a good question. And there's several levels to your question depending on the level of practice. If you are doing sutra-based practice, at that level of mind, lesser capacity practice, sutra-based practice, then you try and restrain from at least negative behaviors that have strong negative weight, karmic weight. So, you don't kill, you don't lie, you don't commit sexual misconduct, you don't trash others, you don't be abusive with your speech. And that includes idle gossip, useless talk. And the worst of that list from a practice perspective is divisive speech, where you talk in ways that plant doubt in other practitioners' minds about their practice or about other practitioners or about their teachings or teachers. No place for that kind of crap. Tsongkhapa says that the blackest deed is to intentionally talk in ways that interfere with other people's practice. So that's a restraint. And it's really something rather simple. You just don't go there because it's disruptive to the harmony of your inner life.

And if you go there, it's disruptive. If you swat a mosquito, you're probably not going to go to the Avici hells in the next lifetime. But if you sit there—"Oh my God, what have I just done?" It's disruptive. I'm trying to say something here that's important. It's about intention. If you do something and it bothers you, that has a partially corrective effect on the otherwise ripening of that karmic action. If you do it being somewhat oblivious, and you bring it into your awareness, that has a positive muting effect or buffering effect. So, it's not like one to one. There are all sorts of—in Western language, we call them mediating variables—that mute karmic ripening.

There's a funny story—you guys know this from Gloucester—but there were two Tibetan lamas who saved up a lot of money and what they did is they went around Gloucester and they bought every live lobster. And they went out to the harbor, and they had about 600 live lobsters to let live, and it's all in the National news, and of course all the lobster fishermen would wade out there, wait for them to release the lobsters, and by the next day almost every lobster released had been caught again. So, they interviewed the lamas about that, and they said, "Well, our intention was to give the lobsters a chance; we did what we could. If the lobsters are stupid enough to get caught again, we don't have any problem with that." [Dan laughs]

Student 2

There's a different version of the story and truly … What some Buddhists did was to get a whole bunch of lobsters—like a lot; dozens and dozens, not six hundred—and released them with the rubber bands on their claws. Stupid compassion.

Student 3

Yeah, that's idiot compassion.

Student 2

Yeah.

Dan

It's New Bedford, what do you think? [Laughter] It's the water supply. It's all those PCBs that we grew up drinking. [Dan laughs] Look, my *Sandlot*[11] baseball field was a PCB[12] dock. I didn't know that. I'm still alive.

What? You have another question? Sure. Go ahead.

Student 1

I'd like you to comment on how compassion seems to arise from groundless ground, yet at the same time is present already. And how in relative life we experience compassion, and, at some point, it is the view without focusing it on "I" as the view.

Dan

Another simple question. Wow! Well, thank you for the sutra!

Well, in Dzogchen we say that ultimate reality as symbolized by the primordial Buddha Kuntuzangpo (which literally in Tibetan means "everything good") has *gongpa*. It's difficult to translate. I like to translate *gongpa* as intention. But the trouble with that is the intention of a buddha mind is not the same as an intention of your mind or my mind. And in a dialogue—a respectful

---

11 A 1993 baseball movie, *The Sandlot*.

12 PCBs are a family of highly carcinogenic and long-living compounds made by Monsanto that were used widely in various industrial and consumer products until they were banned in 1976.

dialogue I had with Jean Luc Achard, who's a good translator of Bon material, his view was that we shouldn't translate it as "intention," we should translate it as "contemplation" because realized buddhas are in round the clock, 24/7 contemplation about the nature of sentient beings. So, they're always doing it

So, I don't know how you want to translate it, but basically … the simple way of explaining it is that in the Dzogchen view of the mind, intention is built into the structure of ultimate reality. And ultimate reality has the intention of showing itself to itself on the one hand for the sake of its own realization, and two, on the other hand, for the sake of compassion training. So, this whole thing—the way it appears here is like a giant video game. And the whole video game is set up for it to realize itself to itself. And if you come at that from the wisdom side of the equation, every instant of the mind is another invitation to you to see it just the way it really is, as opposed to the way you're likely to see it, which is deluded. But if you get it right, then game over. And every intention in this massive sea of what seems to be suffering to us, is an intention to show you this way (even though it's deluded). It looks like this for the sake of training your own compassion, so you'll be a softer being.

That's how the video game is set up. So, in Mahāmudrā, that's where the word comes from; it means great gesture or great intention. Every moment is a gesture to you, an invitation to see it just the way it is. Every moment is a gesture to you, to train your compassion. So, there are no mosquitoes, there are no lobsters; that's all an illusion that's set up for you to say, "Wait a minute, what am I doing here?" But ultimately to say, "This is what the nature of reality is." There is no suffering. It only appears that way because we don't see it right. But there are millions of beings there who don't see it that way. If you see it that way, that's where your compassion comes in. It's that pain of the depth of your realization. The longing and the wish that everyone else will come to this realization, that's the basis of compassion, until every being is emptied out from *samsāra* into awakened *dharmakāya* space.

You can't be satisfied until every being is that way. So, this is a massive relocation project, to relocate all beings into awakened *dharmakāya* space. And you are the engineer of that relocation project, each of you are. The structure of ultimate reality is intention—the intention to show itself to itself for the basis of its own realization, for the basis of its own development of compassion. That's why wisdom and compassion are two sides of the same coin. But it's the nature of reality. It's not a large conceptual structure here.

Think of Western psychology. I remember in college having a wonderful professor in history of religions who walked us through Martin Heidegger's *Being in Time*. It's a fantastically difficult book. And his conclusion is absolutely remarkable, because at the conclusion of this massive intellectual project is the structure of being—in German, it's *fürsorglich*, caring. Care is built into the structure, the impulse of being, every moment! What a remarkable piece of work.

But look at his life. As an academic he was a strong supporter of the Nazi party. It shows you [that] you can't do this intellectually. As brilliant as the work was, based on conceptuality, and he came to a conclusion similar to what we were talking about with intention; he couldn't live it with conduct, just the opposite of that. So, there is a fundamental disconnect between the conceptual thought, which isn't a bad structure, and his actual behavior. That kind of disconnect is not possible for spiritual practice, because at some point in Western psychology—and Western philosophy *does not* realize this—at some point you transcend all conceptual knowing. There is direct-awareness knowing that transcends representational thinking.

We're not good at that in the West. Even the people who talk about postformal, mature types of cognitive development in adults have a hard time moving anything beyond representational thinking. But you go beyond it. No place for it. And that's why our conceptual structures in the West, as well-intended as they are, never translate into conduct. And it's certainly the case that we have a disconnect from conduct in the West. That's the missing piece here, because conduct can only come spontaneously from direct-awakened awareness and primordial wisdom energy, the energy of primordial wisdom. Then, conduct is self-regulatory. The spiritual practice takes care of itself; it has its own intelligence. You can't screw it up at a certain point, because you don't get in the way of it. It has its own intelligence of unfolding.

And the more you manifest that realization as awakened awareness, the more it begins to shape your conduct. It's not conduct that comes from self; it's not conduct that comes from ideas about how you're supposed to be; it's not represented, *migmay*. It just is, as an expression of the intention of the structure of ultimate reality. That's different. So, it's this stupid Western stereotype that practitioners, yogis, get crazy because they get beyond any responsible conduct. It doesn't happen like that. Those are nuts. Your conduct comes *more* in line with the structure of ultimate reality, not an aberration from that, the further you have realizations. And it's not something that you strategize or do or develop, it just unfolds that way because the path has its own intelligence.

That's why conduct is always the ultimate measure of this realization; can't be anything other than that at that level of practice. But that's pretty advanced practice. You can get a taste of awakening and it's not necessarily stable. Then you have to develop that awakening so you have it all the time. Then you have to do *dharmadhātu* exhaustion so you change the structure of the content of your mind, so it's pure states rather than impure states. Then you have to open all-at-once-ness, so your mind opens at all levels at once. At that point, conduct is spontaneously arising from awakened *dharmakāya* space as the best fit on multiple levels of reality at once, but only at that point.

And at that point conduct is not represented; there's no action plan here, only at that point, which means that you can have legitimate realizations prior to that, and not have those realizations matched by conduct. We've all seen many examples of that with spiritual teachers. We don't question the reality of their realizations, but the conduct is abominable because they haven't gotten there, to that level. Had they gotten to that level, then that kind of conduct, sexual misconduct, accumulation of power and wealth at the expense of others, it just can't possibly happen. Not possible.

But those people [who have matured to that level] in a society where, essentially, morality has seriously degenerated at this time of the Kali Yuga really badly, those people are such rare beings they stand out right away. Ordinary people can see that because there are so few moral exemplars in this time, in this plane of reality, at this time of the Kali Yuga, it stands out immediately. No delusion about that. You can see it. That's a good thing, because we're all built with the nature of awareness to see that and recognize it for what it is, just like you're all built with the capacity to recognize awakened nature.

Is there more to your question? Let's go over it again.

Student 1

No. I don't think there is more to it, I think what I want to comment on, though, is I feel like it's maybe crystal clear in the sense that one becomes aligned with one's own true nature and the nature of reality.

Dan

More and more aligned with that.

Student 1

So, I appreciate your saying that.

Dan

And the nature of that ultimate reality is basically transmitted through lineage. So, another way of saying what you're saying is you get more and more aligned with lineage. That commands respect. And you can see the difference right away with that. There's lots of Western self-important dharma teachers out there, but they're not aligned with lineage. That's the difference.

My task in part is to show you that lineage, which is foreign to our culture, can be conveyed in a legitimate way and understood by Westerners. Some of you understand what I'm saying. It's important. But you can't mess with that. And the power of that is unsurpassable. And it's only that that's going to bring the quickness and depth of these realizations that we're talking about.

You can't engage in misconduct and represent a lineage. You can't, if you truly represent that. It's not possible, because you're never apart from that, so how could there possibly be such aberration? Not possible. And when you see it in others it breaks your heart. You know what I'm talking about. We see it all around us all the time. But you won't ever be apart from that kind of compassion. Realization is not exempt from pain. You just don't experience it as that kind of pain, as ordinary pain. It's not exempt from pain. It's built into seeing the true extent of ignorance. But it's not overwhelming. It just is.

Yes?

Student 4

What advice do you have for those of us who are unrealized beings, about conduct and intention? Because if it arises from realization, that's helpful, but in the meantime, what do we do?

Dan

Well for you, based on that comment, my advice to you would be to look at the limiting belief there as just a story. It's a story. And as long as you keep operating out of that story, it's going to limit your practice. Practice is boundless. It has no limits unless you impose conceptual structures, which are always limited. To say, "My practice is necessarily limited this way," as soon as you've done that, you've boxed yourself in. How can you possibly go beyond that box if you're living in that box? But, if you see the box as just an empty structure of mind, then you're back to boundlessness, limitlessness, or as the Sufi poet [Rumi] said, "It's not hard to find the door when there are no walls."

So, what we do in our conceptual mind is we keep creating boxes. There are lots of boxes. You can't stop making boxes because that's what the ordinary mind does. But if you see them as all empty boxes, the house of cards collapses, and then there are no walls. So, the smart practice is to look at stories you're generating for yourself as limiting beliefs. They're just ideas. Ideas don't define ultimate reality.

August 26, 2015

Themes: Prayer East and West; Gift Waves of Influence

Dan

Welcome everyone.

I found out more about the mind reading thing that His Holiness Menri Trizin does and apparently, there's a text on how to do this. It's called *The Sadhana of the Baby Tigress*. And apparently, Menri at one point was trying to teach it to people and he stopped teaching it because he said, "Look," he said, "most people's minds are much worse than you think, and you just don't want to know." So, apparently the only two people on the planet who know this text anymore is he and Lopön Tenzin Namdak because they stopped teaching it.

I don't know, I have to talk with him about it. But I don't want it to die out. It's important. It's a really important thing. So, we'll see.

Yes?

Student 1

This is something I've been thinking about.

Dan

I always brace myself when she says that.

Student 1

I come from a tradition of prayer in the religious tradition that I was in previously, and so I've been thinking a lot about this; and Rahob Rinpoche talks about that there is not a God out there, but several years ago when my grand-nephew was born and ended up in the hospital with pneumonia, I was concerned, and I shared that concern with him and he said a prayer, whatever that means. And more recently, I feel as though when I do guru yoga that it's sort of in the form of an invitation; and also in some of my past religious experience, I've heard people talk about how it's like their prayer is an integral part of their lives.

So, what I was wondering about is what would you say is the relationship with prayer and our meditation practice?

Dan

Well, you've got two questions here. The more limited question is the function of prayer. Good question. And the more backdrop question is who is that directed to? And is there a fundamental difference between Buddhism and, say, Christianity around the concept of gods, deities, and a God. And I'm not so sure. I think we oversimplify these questions. I'm not so sure that the answer that Rinpoche gave you covers the whole thing, because it's in a specific context.

So, let's take the larger question first and then we'll take the more limited question about prayer, because in Buddhism, it's not the case that there aren't deities. In fact, deities or non-ordinary beings—let's say it that way: non-ordinary beings play a huge role in Buddhism, in Tibetan Buddhism, at least. You have the deities of the *mandala*. There are many types of peaceful deities. There are many types of what are called wrathful deities, or what I like, Bob Thurman's definition for *trola*, which is terrific deities. They're terrific. So, you've got classifications of peaceful and terrific deities.

Then you get non-ordinary beings who have certain *yonten*, certain positive qualities that are the qualities that you need to develop in your mindstream to strengthen your practice. And those are matched to you. So, if you have four or five positive qualities that you're weak in, the lama will give you a *yidam* [deity] who has those four or five qualities strong, and you practice with that *yidam* on a regular basis to develop those qualities within yourself.

Then there are the *ḍākinīs*. Most of the teachings are conveyed to humans from *ḍākinīs*. They're *ger kandroma*. *Ger* is a funny word. It means wild but it also means laughter. So, we talk about the *ḍākinīs* as the wild laughing sisterhood. And in Tibetan, *kandroma* means the female wisdom energy forms who dance through the portals of wisdom space to convey teachings to humans. And they can either temporarily take a human form, like a shape shifter, or they can convey teachings through what's called the warm breath of the *ḍākinīs*. They whisper in your ear.

So that's why in Milarepa you see him like this [Dan tilts his head slightly and holds his hand to his ear]. That's the ear whispering *mudrā*, because he's taking in the complete teaching, downloaded from a *ḍākinī's* warm breath. You know, in the Level 1 course when we do the crossing over instructions from Tilopa, the Gangama, teachings at the Ganges, those teachings were ear whispered and downloaded to Tilopa from a *ḍākinī*.

So, we can't say that Buddhism lacks its non-ordinary beings and deities. There's a huge population in the assembly of beings that are not of this plane of reality. So, there are lots of deities of the *mandala*, so to speak. But, where Buddhism is at is that these are all constructions of mind—that the mind constructs physical reality that we take to be out there as real, and that the mind constructs deities in non-ordinary planes of reality in the same way it constructs physical realities. Ultimately, they're all constructions. So, from a Buddhist perspective, they're all empty. But on a relative level of reality, the deities exist in the same way that seeming external reality exists. And that's what justifies prayer. Okay?

As to the ultimate question, "Is there a God?" Buddhism comes in a little bit more humble than Christianity in that sense. Because what it says is you can't know the answer to that question with the apparatus that you have. Because the mind, by nature, represents; any answer to the question, does a God exist, is a representation. So, the only thing you're knowing is your own representations. Beyond that, you can't know. It's through the conceptual mind. And in that sense, they look at God representations in Christianity or Judaism as simply that: representations, constructions, empty of essence. And they don't prove that that means that a God exists. They just prove that we can represent. And amongst everything else we represent, we represent a God in the same way we represent the external world. We make it real. We reify it. But ultimately, can you know that through constructions? No. So, they don't go there because they don't think that's useful, because conceptual knowledge is too limited.

On the other hand, let's suppose you get a taste of awakened awareness. Always right here is an infinitely vast ocean of awakened awareness-love. You are never apart from that. But most of us don't recognize that because we have layers and layers of constructions of mind that, like dense clouds, cloud over us so we don't see it. Much like when we say, "The sun just came out." After the rain clouds clear, you can see the sun. Well, it's not true that the sun just came out. The sun was always shining. You just didn't see it because of the rain clouds. And like that, the radiant nature of an awakened mind, the brilliant lucidity of an awakened mind, and that knowing awareness [that] is always right here, like the sun that radiantly shines all the time. But from your perspective of ordinary mind, with the layers and layers of clouds, you can't experience that. So, we don't know that the sun is there when we're looking through the clouds and not seeing beyond them.

On the other hand, let's suppose you directly recognize that awakened nature, and more important that recognizing it, it becomes your basis of operation. So, you step out of the limits of your individual consciousness and its seeming localization in time and space, and you become that infinitely boundless ocean of awakened awareness-love. So that's where you're coming from. And that is a place that has no location, no reference points. So, you're being the unbounded wholeness and there's no location in that. And let's suppose you refine that awakened awareness so it's not just a state that you have temporarily, but you have it all of the time. And let's suppose you refine that to enlightened buddha bodies. You lock into the structure of ultimate reality itself and you become that structure and manifest that structure of ultimate reality.

Now, if you lock into the buddha bodies, all at once there's this infinitely vast, empty knowing-awareness space that pervades everything. It's the groundless ground of your being. And out of that is this lively energy of an awakened mind that's there as the potential of everything, and out of that are all forms of all realms in time that you hold in your mind all at once, not just this little bubble. What if you crack the eggshell of this bubble? Once you crack the eggshell, you open up what we call limitlessness. And all realms and times are here all at once—thousands and thousands of realities simultaneously. And the enlightened mind holds the scope of all that at once, and it's the structure of your being. Breathtaking. Truly awesome.

And what you realize when you lock into enlightened buddha bodies is that every moment of the activity of that liveliness of an awakened mind has the intention of benefiting other beings. We say that ultimate reality has *gompa*, it has intention. There's a wisdom side to that intention and there's a compassion side. So, every moment of an enlightened buddha mind on many levels of reality simultaneously operates within what we call *trinlé*, enlightened activity, acting inexhaustibly to serve the benefit of other beings. And every moment that that mind unfolds, it unfolds in a certain way as an invitation, as an opportunity for you to see it just the way it is, and for all beings to see it just the way it is.

Enlightened mind has the intention of showing itself to itself for the sake of its own realization. [You as an ordinary, named individual] don't get awakened. You just have to set up the right conditions or the right *dawa*, or the right view. And awakening shows itself to itself. The path has its own intelligence. The further you get, the more you appreciate that and at some point, the whole path in all of its wisdom shows itself to itself by itself. Just watch the show without a watcher.

Now, when you get in to something like that and you see that the intention of every moment is for the structure of being to reveal itself to itself for the sake of its own realizations; and every moment is a test of your compassion and to strengthen and deepen your kindness and compassion towards other beings inexhaustibly—at that level of realization, how different is that from a Western notion, from a Judeo-Christian notion, of a God? I'm not so sure those distinctions are so clear cut anymore, you see. Is it the same? Not exactly. Is it different? Not exactly. But the difference is that you cannot realize that with a conceptual mind, with a mind that represents.

See, part of the problem here is it's really an epistemological problem, theories of knowledge. And in Buddhism, the great logicians, like Dignaga and Chandrakirti and others, laid a very careful infrastructure to say that there are two ways of knowing. There's conceptual knowing and there's knowing that comes from direct awareness. We have a very strong bias in the West toward conceptual knowing. We think that's the only kind of knowing there is. And the fact that you could operate out of pure awareness, cleaned up of conceptual mind, is something very foreign to Westerners. But almost all the advanced realizations in Tibetan Buddhism don't come from the conceptual knowing, they come from direct awareness knowing.

That's metacognitive. Metacognition means stepping back and seeing and evaluating the nature of your own state. Not with thought. Through direct seeing. If you're training concentration meditation, you have to keep directing your mind back to the concentration object and tune out all distractions. In terms of the neuroimaging of concentration, you're activating the anterior cingulate cortex; it's the concentration center of the brain. But advanced concentrators do something else. They're constantly evaluating the quality of the meditation. They can see very quickly when they go off track and steer it back to the concentration object. And that monitoring of what they're doing is with the right dorsolateral prefrontal cortex, the metacognitive center of the brain. And the difference between beginning and advanced concentrators is that they activate the metacognitive center of the brain.

Everybody's awakened, but most people can't recognize their awakened nature. At the moment that you recognize that infinite vast expanse for what it is, that recognition is metacognitive. We say that all animals, even the smallest of insects, have awakened awareness. But only humans have the capacity to recognize it. The difference is that humans have metacognitive capacity. But thinking is the secondary association cortices. Metacognition has nothing to do with thinking, and if you think of the neurocircuitry of it, even in Western terms.

So, when you evaluate the quality of your own state of mind, to keep your meditation on track, it's going to be more advanced, quicker when you use that metacognition to recognize your true nature. Through directly seeing it for what it is, you're using your metacognition. When you lock in to the structure of enlightened buddha bodies, lock in to the structure of reality, and recognize that it's always right here, you're using your metacognition to do that.

But you see, where we get in trouble with this in Western psychology is we don't believe that there's any kind of knowing other than conceptual. And the idea that we could have levels of mature, adult cognitive development that are completely nonrepresentative and go beyond all thought, and even the more radical idea that those might be better ways of existing in the world than operating out of thought mode, that's foreign to us as Westerners. We are so over identified with thought that we think that thought is all there is. We mix up thought and awareness, as if they're one and the same thing. If you take a high-speed electronic board like a tachistoscope and flash events in thousandths of a second [equal to a millisecond] to subjects, you can show that most thinking occurs at around 500 to 3000 milliseconds, and, in similar luminance conditions, directing your attention to something takes about 200 milliseconds.

Awareness is [or seems to operate] at the speed of light. It takes no time. You can't measure it. The fastest the machine will measure is ten milliseconds. So, the intention of awareness is much higher speed than directed attention. Much higher speed than thought. But in our ordinary, everyday experience we smush those three things together as if they're one and the same. We think that paying attention and thinking are the same thing. We don't even see that awareness is different from both of those things.

That's where concentration comes in. Because if you constantly bring your mind back to one object over and over again, the side effect of that is that all that thought elaboration activity winds down and eventually stops. So, at some point in your direct experience, it will dawn on you that there's a way of knowing that has nothing to do with thought activity. You've separated out pure awareness as a mode of knowing from conceptual knowing. We use a good Tibetan metaphor here: separating out the yak curds of thought from the pure milk of the yak. The pure awareness milk of the yak. Because usually the curds and the milk are all mixed up together as one thing and you've got to separate them out.

I remember when we went to Tibet with Rinpoche and stayed with his family, we'd see that a woman would get up and milk the yaks every morning at about five in the morning; and then her husband had this machine and he would churn the yak milk and churn it over and over and over again; and finally you see all the curds separating out from the pure milk. And the young boy who was with us and I would have our yak hot chocolate. [Dan chuckles] Yak milk hot chocolate.

So, you have to learn to see in your direct experience that awareness has nothing to do with conceptual thought. And learn to operate out of awareness. And then you see that awareness has *gongpa*, it has intention. You can direct awareness with lightning speed towards anything. And whatever it goes to it goes just to that, for as long as you intend to put it on that, with *Ma Gag Pa*, no interference. Like a ray of light touching upon something with lightning speed and great precision. It's much better to operate out of awareness than to operate out of conceptual thought.

But then you'll learn that awareness has other properties. Not only does it have the capacity to know—we call that *sherig* [sounds like "shay-rig"], knowing awareness—but it has the capacity of intelligence. So, the further along the path, the more you refine that awareness, the path starts to show itself to itself by itself. Even when you do crossing-over instruction so you use all that careful activity of the ordinary mind to set up the right view in just the right way so you can shift your basis to awakened awareness.

Well, that's a lot of work. But after you keep opening up that pathway and every time you shift your basis of operation to awakened awareness, out of ordinary mind, and into awakened mind over and over again, then after a while, the only ordinary cognitive activity that's required is a subtle kind of cognitive activity to maintain the undistracted view of Lion's Gaze.

But then after a while, maintaining awakening becomes completely automatic. We say that *rigpa*, awakened awareness, takes over its own operations in order to maintain itself to itself. Then, you see, that's when you start appreciating this intelligence. Because then at that point, the path shows itself to itself by itself. Just watch the show without a watcher. And all of that is built into the structure of being and it's called *gongpa*, intention.

So, if the larger universe that we, our minds, share or participate in, has this intelligence to show itself to itself, and its impulse every moment is to act inexhaustibly for the benefit of others, maybe these distinctions, East and West, are not so different, are they? Somewhat different. Somewhat not different. Hmm? Does that mean that there's a God in Buddhism? Absolutely not, in the ultimate sense. But in answering the ultimate question—East and West—is there an intelligence built into this universe that you directly lock in to? Is the intention of that intelligence one of love? I think the answer's pretty much the same. So, these distinctions, they become unfortunate divisions. They're useless. Whether the distinctions are East and West, or within Buddhism itself.

I'm thinking that studying with His Holiness Menri Trizin, the lineage holder for all of the Bon teachings, has sensitized me to the oppression of the Bon over the years. These people have been the most oppressed and they've given us everything.[13] That's usually the way it is, isn't it? You know, the Bon are from a large, massive kingdom of Zhang Zhung, which in the old days included western Tibet, all of Afghanistan, all of Pakistan, Tajikistan, the eastern two thirds of Iran—that was all one kingdom. That's where all the original Dzogchen teachings came from, the Bon Dzogchen teachings.

There was a small kingdom separated from that—a very small area that was Tibet—a separate kingdom. Trisong Detsen, the thirty-eighth Tibetan king, decided to make a great empire, and he realized that he couldn't make that great empire and realize his ambitions when the Zhang Zhung empire was so much larger. So, he did two things. One is he invited Indian Mahāyāna Buddhists to come, and that's when Śāntarakṣita and Padmasambhava came, as competition with the Bon. And two, is he spent a lot of money hiring one of the young

13 By "everything," Dan is here referring to the most precious and formerly secret teachings of the Bon Tradition.

wives of the Zhang Zhung king to poison him so he could take over this large empire without having to go to war. The reasons that Mahāyāna Buddhism ended up in Tibet were largely political and rather crass because they had to do with ambition to develop an empire.

Trisong Detsen understood that you control people through religion. So, if you brought in Indian Mahāyāna Buddhism as a way of taking over the Zhang Zhung empire, that meant pushing out all the Bon practitioners that were the indigenous people. And there's this great speech, where Padmasambhava debated the Bon teacher who happened to be his twin brother. We won't go into the fight or the family dynamics here. But it was decided ahead of time—it was a stacked deck—that the Bon teacher had to lose. And it's one of those great speeches in history that's like the Martin Luther King "I Have a Dream" speech. Because after losing, all the Bon either had to convert to Indian Mahāyāna Buddhism or they got kicked out. Many of them left. So, this great tradition got dismantled based on political ambitions. And in that speech, he says, "What are we doing here? It's the same state. And if you are making any distinctions at all or divisions here, then you do not understand this state," but those words went unheard.

Even the notion in Buddhism of the two truths, relative and ultimate reality, you move beyond that, too. You move beyond all distinctions to what's called the *nyachik*, the one great sphere of ultimate reality that transcends ultimate and relative reality wherein all realms and times exist simultaneously, and all beings within that realm are interconnected by loving filaments of *bodhicitta*. We are all one large, interconnected organism. That's the nature of this love. There are no separations here, only the separations that come through conceptual distinctions.

And something similar was put forth in some of the Christian mystics, particularly like Meister Eckhart, who said there is the God that we represent and then beyond all representations and distinctions is what he called the Godhead, which has no characteristics; it cannot be represented, but it is the structure of ultimate reality. It's not so different.

So, that's the larger question. So, the smaller question is then, what about prayer? And in Buddhism, the question about prayer is around the Tibetan word *wang* [pronounced "wong"], which has often been translated as empowerment, which is a terrible translation. But the word *wang* in Buddhism literally means influence. And another term that's important is what's called *chingilap*.

A *lapa* is a wave, and *chingwa* means giving. So *chingilap* literally means waves of giving, or sometimes we call it gift waves. And what does it mean?

In relative reality, where this seems to be real—and also in the relative reality where deities seem to be real and non-ordinary beings seem to be real—if you call forth non-ordinary beings, they are compelled to come to your call. They're curious. So, if you call forth Padmasambhava, who we have over here [pointing to a *thanka*], he will appear in non-ordinary space. He wants to know why you call him. If you chant or sing, they like the melody. So, they tend to come more curiously if you sing a pleasant song as a prayer. And they want to know why you're calling them forth. And then what this is all about is what's called gift waves of influence. If you call a non-ordinary being forth and you put the intention into making a request—the Tibetan word is *solwadeb*, which literally means throwing out a request, you're putting it out there—so if you put out a request, that intention, that *gongpa*, of your own mindstream, necessarily requires a response from this non-ordinary being.

And here's what they can do. They can do three things. Number one, they can directly intervene in your unfolding mindstream and clear away *dripa*, obscurations. Number two, they can activate the *yongtan*, the positive qualities in your mindstream like patience, non-reactivity, light-heartedness, concentration, strength, trust, and all these things that potentiate your practice. And number three, they can implant the *dawa*, the right view. If you set up that view correctly, it will open up the mind to the direct experience of awakened awareness, or the view that will help you to see the liveliness of awakened awareness in everything—all sights, all sounds, all thoughts, all emotions. Or the view that will help you to rapidly release all karmic ripening impressions to what we call the path of *dharmadhātu* exhaustion, so you exhaust the storehouse of all the negative states so there's no negative states left. Each of those levels of practice and levels of realization require a very precise view. The view is the meditation, and the meditation is the view.

So, you see, when you call forth non-ordinary beings, what you're doing is you're requesting that they plant the seed of that right view in your mindstream so that it blossoms, and then you can directly have the realizations. But you can't just throw out the request. If you throw out the request, non-ordinary beings, in the request of your prayers, they have to respond. Okay? But [how] they respond is by giving you that influence. But it doesn't last unless you match it with your own practice.

So, if you go and get an empowerment, which is really gift waves of influence, as it's sometimes called, a Tibetan teacher comes and there's all this ritual, and you get this empowerment. It's like a window of opportunity. So, you get all this stuff and you say, "I just got this empowerment," and you don't even practice because you collected that empowerment [thinking that's enough]. Well, then next week the influence of that is completely gone. It's sort of like a matching grant. You have to match it with your own effort. You have to match the lama's influence with your own effort; and if you don't, you lose it. And it's worthless. So, however many empowerments you collected in your lifetime is junk if you don't practice it right away.

Now, I suppose when you think about it—and I'm not trying to be reductionistic because I also appreciate the differences here—there is some interface between *chingilap*, gift waves of influence in Buddhism, and the concept of grace in Christianity. Because you're allowing a higher power to directly influence your experience in each case. And you're receptive to that. So, in that sense, there's an affinity here. They're not exactly the same. And I think the difference is around this matching grant idea. Because, I mean, there are different definitions by theologians about grace in Christianity but, generally speaking, when we think of grace in Christianity, we think you don't have to do anything. It's a pretty good deal. You can be completely passive and get grace. And you're not required to do anything on your own. That's where Buddhism is very different because you've got to put in your work. If you don't put in the meditation work, that gift wave of influence is useless.

Now I think that's a very important distinction. And a rather good one. And I think that's missing in Christianity. Because what I see a lot of in Christianity is people say, "Okay, I've been forgiven. I'm saved." And you don't have to do squat. That's not good enough in my opinion. And so, it's a way for people that develop a conception that they're really doing okay to justify a lot of bad conduct, and then they can get saved. And they don't have to do anything different. That's one huge difference.

And the other difference is a self-other distinction. In Buddhism you have to put the work in and do that transformation yourself in reaction to getting the gift waves of influence. But in Christianity, it's always that you're getting the grace from something out there. So, who's causing the transformation is that mechanism out there, whether it be Jesus or whatever.

But you see, that's subtly undermining of you. Because if you're always getting it from out there, where does your own responsibility come in? Because

Christianity has gone rounds and rounds and rounds with that, how good will fits in. But in Buddhism that's required. You don't get it for free. You've got to do the work. And ultimately, that's empowering because it's not disempowering, because you're not assigning it over to some power, like, "I don't even have to worry about it because Jesus is gonna save me." We've rationalized lots of really bad behavior with that one throughout history.

But in this way, in Buddhism, the issue of conduct is central. In fact, conduct is the authenticity of realization. The greater your realization, the more it manifests as good conduct. East and West, William James understood that over a hundred years ago in his great classic, *The Varieties of Religious Experience*, when they said, "How you judge the authenticity of a mystical experience?" He said, "By their fruits ye shall know them." Genuine spirituality, people with genuine spiritual experiences leave a wake of positive experience around them. That's how you tell.

East to West, there's no difference. So, there's lots of false prophets, East and West. If a high lama comes to the West and he has great teachings and we all go "gaga," and he has fifty counts of misconduct, sexual misconduct, against him, and a collection of Ferraris and Lamborghinis, I'm not convinced by his conduct. Any way you cut it, it's crap. There's no place for this. East or West. There's no place for the distinctions and the differences if you have realization. None of us are different. All of us are interconnected. We're loving filaments of *bodhicitta* in one great ultimate sphere of reality that we all participate in. If you understand that, there can't possibly be any distinctions. Ever.

But it all comes down to where you're looking from. We're back to basis of operation. Are you looking from ordinary conceptual mind? Is that where you're operating out of? Are you operating out of ordinary time and space? Are you operating out of self or personal identity? Are you operating out of none of those, an ocean-like changeless boundless awareness? Are you operating out of nondual awareness? Are you operating out of unbounded wholeness of awakened awareness-love? Are you operating out of a mind of *dharmadhātu* exhaustion where there are no negative states left and only positive states? Are you operating out of a level where you've opened all-at-once-ness, and your mind operates out of thousands of planes of reality at the same time? Are you operating out of an enlightened mind, across all those planes and with inexhaustible compassion towards all beings? It all comes down to where you're operating out of. And each one of those levels of mind is always right here and rather simply accessible with the right key to open it up. You see, at some point it gets rather simple.

So, prayer is the intention of the mind towards either non-ordinary beings to receive gift waves of influence, or prayer can be directed towards people or beings and sentient beings in relative or *samsāric* existence, with the intention of having them have a better state. We can pray for others.

There's two types of prayer. And the common factor in both of those types of prayer in Buddhism is *gongpa*, intention. So, when you pray, you may be praying for a better state for others, physically or emotionally, or a better lifetime. When you pray, you can pray to receive the gift waves of influence. But always when you pray, in both those instances, your prayer represents the intention of ultimate reality. You are manifesting that intention whether you realize it or not in that impulse of prayer. So, you see, prayer is a good thing.

When we went to Tibet the second time, Michelle interviewed the kids to find out how they learned to concentrate, and then she did the same thing in Nepal. And what we discovered is that in both situations in Nepal and Tibet, the kids learn to pay attention by memorizing longer and longer prayers. They learn every day to do slightly longer and longer prayers. So, it's a device that has secular benefits because they learn by every day doing longer and longer prayers; they learn to exercise and develop what we would call in the West working memory. Working memory is like RAM in your computers. It's like how much memory space you've got online to do a task at hand. And they, by learning these prayers over and over again, develop good working memory capacity. And ultimately, when they get very good with this, some of the older kids, at around [age] nine or ten, go and do standard concentration training in certain settings in certain monasteries.

So, paying attention is built into the structure of the culture in their educational system, unlike here where kids don't learn to pay attention for anything anymore. We don't teach them in the school system, and they certainly don't learn at home. Paying attention means watching videos.

In that culture, the prayers are important. The kids learn them. Not only because they have secular benefit like paying attention, but also because they have spiritual benefit. They are learning to train the intention to be compassionate towards others' needs and to pray for others. So, they develop compassion training. They learn to manifest that ultimate reality and the impulse to do that prayer at a very early age.

In Nepal where we're working, none of the kids in the school system learn their own language any more. They all learn Nepalese and English. So, in this generation, all of the teachings will die out in Nepal. The last of the Tibetan transmissions will die out in this generation because the kids can't do their own prayers and speak their own languages. That's why we're sponsoring all these kids to go to school and learn their own Tibetan language and their own prayers and history again. So, this is a good question. Really good question.

September 9, 2015

Themes: Self-emptiness and Other-emptiness; Levels of Mind

Dan

Welcome everyone. You have a question?

Student 1

Dan, I'm really seeing in my practice that there's an auditory experience that … "silence," there is no such thing, and I'm not sure what to make of that. There's an underlying sound that is always there.

Dan

So, the question is what? What is that sound?

Student 1

Should I attend to it? I don't know if it's something that's distracting me or if it's something worth letting be as part of my felt sense of the body, if you will.

Dan

So, you hear a specific sound like a car, a bell.

Student 1

I hear those also, yes, but…

Dan

Those are episodes of sound, right? For a short period of time, you hear a car horn, you hear a bell, and then there's a beginning, there's a continuity or staying of the sound. And at some point, there's an endpoint of the sound. Most sounds are discreet episodes like that—you perceive them as if they're occurring out there in the external world. But if you listen really carefully, you can hear something other than those discreet sounds. You can hear the sound behind the sound.

Student 1

That's what it feels like. It's a constant background.

Dan

And it's constantly on.

Student 1

Yeah.

Dan

Technically, what you're listening to there is the sound of liveliness. Awareness is lively. It's always creating itself to itself. You're hearing the sound of liveliness expressing itself. You're hearing awareness. And it's constantly lively. It's a continuous flow of liveliness.

Student 1

There's beginning to be, also, a physical sensation that's a similar thing. I wouldn't even know how to describe it, but there's a sensation …

Dan

Try.

Student 1

Okay. Especially in paying attention to the felt sense of the body, there's a sensation of—like the sound is a wave. It's a vibration. There's a physical vibration in my body that is similar; it's a background. I mean, they're a sensation like—okay, there's an itch or my eye blinks or whatever, but this is a background to that. It's always on.

Dan

It's always on.

Student 1

And I'm hearing it and feeling it now when I'm … like even now.

Dan

It always changes. It always changes.

Student 1

Okay.

Dan

If you want to amplify the perception of the sound of liveliness, then take your thumbs and put them in your ears. It's pretty lively. It never stops. Now, if you continue to do that—let's say, for example, you plugged up your ears for a day or two and you did nothing but listen to that sound, there's a whole world in there. And there's not a discreet or a series of sound, it's a continuous flow of liveliness. If you push that to its limit, it's what we call ultimate sound. It's the sound of lively awakened awareness expressing itself to itself. It doesn't stop.

You tend to become more aware of that undercurrent, if you will, when you take an inward orientation and stop seeing sounds as out there or stop seeing sounds as specific events that are interpretable, things like a bell. You're really hearing the sound of awareness expressing itself to itself and knowing itself through its own expressions. It's lively. It's very lively.

Student 1

Do each of us have a different harmonic like that?

Dan

You mean, does that sound have a unique signature?

Student 1

To you or you or you, yeah.

Dan

It might. I don't know that. Not in the yogi literature, but I don't see a reason why that couldn't be the case. It's just not how they emphasize it. But there's Western material on that. Did you ever see the film *As It Is in Heaven*? It's one of my favorites. It's a story of a boy who grows up in a small town in Sweden and he's very different because he can hear the music of the spheres. But he is so different that he gets bullied mercilessly and beat up a lot in the small town, where there's lots of abuse and alcoholism.

And he's raised by a single mother who watches him get too bullied too many times, so she takes him away from this small town and they go to the city and he becomes one of the greatest composers and orchestra conductors in the world at a young age. And having become world famous as a composer and conductor, he has this substantial heart attack at the age of thirty. He's so weakened that he's not going to live that long. So, having given up the fast-paced lifestyle, he's a little lost.

So, for some inexplicable reason, he makes it back to his place where he grew up, where he was bullied. Nobody knows him anymore. And he takes a job teaching the choir at the local church. But when he gets to know all the people, all of whom are vulnerable in some way or another, and he knows them, he composes these songs for each of them that fit their harmonic. That's how he loves them. And each of these people blossoms.

Student 1

That's a great story.

Dan

It's a wonderful story.

Student 1

Tell me the title again.

Dan

As It Is in Heaven. It's a good *dharma* movie.

In other traditions like the Hindu [and Sikh], they'll talk about the sound behind sound or the sound of silence.[14] But, in Dzogchen it's very specific. You're listening to the sound of awakened awareness as liveliness. Everything is lively awakened awareness expressing itself to itself and knowing itself through its expressions. It's all one big, magical show, but there's a sound, a vibratory quality to that, but it's not specific sounds. It's the sound of everything coming into creation every moment. That's incessant and wondrous. So, when you stop looking at specific sounds, this undercurrent of what is [is] more obvious to you. Okay? Maybe we'll do some exercises with that.

Yes?

---

14 See "esoteric meaning of *shabd* (Sanskrit)" in Wikipedia (under *shabda*), it is "the sound current vibrating in all creation."

Student 2

I'm reading a commentary by, I think, it's Thinley Norbhu Rinpoche. He died a couple of years ago. He's a Nynigma master, on the Seven-Line Prayer. And in the first part of it, he sort of debates away a number of other views that aren't Dzogchen. And I got to one that I had a real question about because he's talking in general about those that err either on the side of nihilism or eternalism. And he's talking about one that refers to—I believe he called it the *purusha*, referring to the sense of being that moves through the lifetimes. It sounds similar to what you've talked about, but he's describing that as a non-Dzogchen point of view that it's erring towards eternalism.

Dan

Correct.

Student 2

So, I wonder if you'd comment about that.

Dan

Well, it depends on what view you want to take. I understand what you're saying. What you're saying is that in Samkhya Yoga, which is the philosophical underpinnings of the great tradition of *The Yoga Sutras of Patañjali*, there is the matter of the world and the stuff of the mind which is *prakriti*. It's the observable elements of the mind and the particles of the world. That's the stuff of life. That's *prakriti*. Then there's the kind of Self, with a capital S, which is like mind, and that's called *purusha*, often translated as self.

So, we have this mind and matter thing. When you refine your meditation practice in yoga, you refine it down to the finest elements of the mind, the *prakriti*. Then, you go beyond that. You can see beyond the most refined particles of the mind and the universe to *purusha*. And that is eternally existing. So, Samkhya Yoga is an eternalist position. There's something that's eternal.

In Buddhism, with Mahāyāna Buddhism particularly, you get a notion of what's called the doctrine of two truths. There's the world as we perceive it, which is relative reality, and it looks this way because we all share a similar perceptual apparatus and a similar brain. But then there's ultimate truth which is that everything is just a construction. What we're really seeing is our own constructions of mind. You can't see anything beyond that. You see things because the mind represents through visual perception. You hear things because the mind represents sound. You're seeing, hearing, tasting, smelling and sensing your own representations.

So, from an ultimate perspective, although they exist because there are certain causes and conditions and interactions that cause the world to appear this way, ultimately, they're just all representations. They're all empty constructions. That's the view that you get in Mahāyāna Buddhism. And your Dzogchen practitioner is refuting the fact that there's not the extreme of nihilism, which means that nothing exists. But that defies our senses. Relatively speaking, things exist. We all see the room here, and we all seem to exist together in this room. The nihilistic position goes too far, as if this isn't what we can perceive, but of course, we perceive it in relative reality.

But it also refutes the position of eternalism, that there's some independently existing stuff that's out there apart from how we perceive it. We perceive it because we create it with our representational capacity. So, ultimately, it doesn't exist. Now, that's where the *purusha* model is different because what they say is there is some permanent structure of reality called purusha that you can realize when you refine away all the finest particles of the stuff of the universe in mind, the *purusha*, and then it's obvious.

However, one could make the argument that even within the Essence traditions of Buddhism, you'll find a similar position. That's the "other-emptiness" position. Self-emptiness means that all phenomena are empty of themselves. This isn't the bowl, it's just the representation in my mind and I construct it and give it a label and called it a bowl. This [Dan strikes a metal bowl with a stick] isn't a specific sound of a bowl, it's a construction in my mind, and I represent it as a specific sound, and I assign meaning to it as a gong from a bowl.

So, the nature of the mind is to construct. And when you say something is empty, you're seeing it as not a sound that's independently existing out there, but relatively speaking it exists because my mind constructs sound representations. So, I'm hearing my own sound representations. I'm seeing my own visual representations. I'm perceiving my own thought representations, my own emotional representations. I'm operating out of my own self-representation. It's all representations. So, to say something is empty means it's just a representation. There's no big self out there. There's no "out-there-ness." Out-there-ness is a representation. Seeing things as empty means they lose their solidness. They lose their independent existence.

Then, Dölpopa came along and the third Karmapa, Rangjung Dorje. And Dölpopa took a different position. What he took was the position that's known as the "other-emptiness" tradition. What he said is that all relative phenomena are empty of themselves. That means they're just constructions, and they're empty of other relative phenomena (that's where the term "other-emptiness" comes from), but they're not empty of relative reality.

What he means by that is if you negate things as just constructions, and you keep doing that and you take it as far as you can go, there are some things that don't go away. They shine forth more and more clearly. If you negate thought as just an empty construction every minute, and emotion is empty construction every moment, there's something about the field of awareness that shines forth. If you negate time as a construction, you negate your information processing system as a construction, then you negate everything as just constructions.

What's left is more interesting because awakened awareness will shine forth, and it has certain properties. It's much brighter than ordinary awareness. Awakened awareness has a certain intensity of manifestation compared to ordinary awareness. It has *hrige* (sounds like "hree-gay"), it has awakeness; it has *danpa*, it has a sacred hue to it; it has *bole*, it has a softness to it. And the paradox here is the more that you negate these things as just constructions and labels, the more they shine forth. So, what emerged in the other-emptiness tradition is this view that the structure of ultimate reality is permanent. And the more you negate things as empty, the paradox of that is the more that shines forth in its true nature. You can't negate it. Emptiness is only relative to relative phenomena.

The Essence traditions like the *tantras*, Mahāmudrā, and Dzogchen are essentially other-emptiness traditions. The third Karmapa never uses the term, but all the Mahāmudrā practices are based on the other-emptiness position. It's clear that Dölpopa and the third Karmapa, Rangjung Dorje, met on at least two or three occasions in their life and they talked about this together.

The tradition that's vehemently opposed to other-emptiness is the Gelugpa—which is the Dalai Lama's school—and the originator of the Gelugpa, who was Tsongkapa. And that goes back to personal issues, to where when Dolpopa was developing his *Mountain Doctrine* and the writings on other-emptiness, the guy who hated it and trashed him the most turned out to be Tsongkapa's teacher. So, Tsongkapa trashed this position rather badly. And, of course, since Tsongkapa's teachings were the first teachings in Tibetan Buddhism to come to the West, no one knew about this other-emptiness thing until Jeffrey Hopkins, who originally translated the self-emptiness position for his doctoral dissertation—which is basically Tsongkapa's position—later in his career, decided that it might be fair to give the other side a debate, so he translated a lot of the other-emptiness stuff.

Now, where this is relevant is not as an academic debate—it's a tension in practice. Every time you make something into a thing, it clouds over awakened nature. If you start looking for brightness and make it into a property of light rather than the alertness and the brightness of knowing and being awake, as soon as you look for it as a thing, you've reified it. Therefore, you need the self-emptiness position in terms of seeing it as just a construction of mind because that's what it's become. And you keep doing that. But you can go so far with negating everything and seeing everything as a construction that you forget to look at what's here. It's what's left.

With all emptiness practice, what we call the affirming negation, you negate A in order to affirm B. And what you're affirming is always and necessarily about the nature of awakened awareness. Each time you clear up some seemingly solid structure of the mind, what becomes much more clear is what shines forth, cleaned up of that structure. So, if you clean up the convention of time and see it as just a construction, so things don't come and go, you end up with this changeless, boundless ocean of awareness, because you see through that construction of time and you see beyond it.

And if you clean up all the operations of your information processing system that always partialize, you see beyond that to the unbounded wholeness, this limitless ocean of awakened awareness-love that's always right here. It's like if you clear away the clouds, you find out that the sun has always been shining. And the brightness of that becomes apparent just like seeing the sun after the clouds clear. The brightness, the awakeness, the intensity, the sacredness of awakened awareness, is like seeing the sun that's always shining after you clear away the clouds. But that doesn't ever go away.

So, when you get into the other-emptiness position, you see, it's not so different from the *prakriti-purusha* position, is it? Even though the Buddhist would like to say that they're in this middle path thing, I wouldn't call it a strong eternalist position. But in practice, what it means is, at some point, if you really carry this down, you get a taste of awakening. Awakening is always right here. You're never apart from that. So, since it can't come and go and it always shines forth whether you see it or not, it's like locking into something that's on a different level than the ordinary distractions of our mind.

If you carry the refinement of that, and you're listening to the sound of awakening creating itself and seeing all the patterns as lively awakening, it's all a lively flow. You're seeing that awakened awareness is, from the mind perspective, an infinite vast ocean of awakened awareness-love. It's the knowing aspect, brilliantly knowing everything just the way it is. But from the event [perspective] side of the equation, it's liveliness. Awakened awareness is always creating itself to itself and expressing itself to its own creations and knowing itself through its own creations. That expressive aspect of this field of awakened awareness is what we call *tsal* [sounds like "sell"], liveliness. It's always here.

You can hear it, which is what we were talking about earlier. You can taste it. You can see it, but you're not seeing patterns. You're seeing the field of lively awareness. All these patterns are lively awareness. It's all the dance of lively energy. You can reduce the whole world to that, and you live in a world of light, light rays and ultimate sound, which is the sound of liveliness. Nothing solid, and it's all a big magical display at that point.

If you refine that liveliness so you have it all the time and then go one big step further to buddhahood and lock into enlightened buddha bodies, when you're locking into the structure of being, that is permanent, and you will never be apart from that. And when you know that, in terms of enlightened bodies, it never goes away and it's like locking into the structure of being. Is that a strong eternalist position? No. But, is it permanent and always here? Absolutely.

You see, yes, some Dzogchen people like to debate in the classical sense, but that's at a lower level of mind. In the *tögal* system of bypassing, if you master all five levels of what we call the visions, the last is called *thigle chenpo* or *nyakchik* in Tibetan. It's the one great sphere of ultimate reality. And within that, there are infinite worlds and infinite beings, and you are the entirety of that. And all those beings across all realms and times are all intimately connected with loving filaments of energy, *bodhicitta* energy.

That entire show is manifested as your enlightened mind. That transcends this notion of both relative and ultimate truth—it's all one big bubble, but the mind encompasses that big bubble. You are, at that point, the entirety of that show. The only expression of that realization is *trinlé*, enlightened activity. The intention is to bring everybody within that interconnected reality because they're all intimately connected within this field of awakened mind; the intention is to bring everybody along, to guide them to the same realization.

So, you see, from that point of view, I'm not so sure it's so different. But, so it doesn't deteriorate into some academic debate, I like to see this tension between self- and other-emptiness as a necessary tension. If you're negating everything, even emptiness is empty. Awareness is empty. Then, there's a tendency to shade off [into nihilism] and to fail to affirm that when you negate, you're clearing away the clouds so that you can see the sun. If you negate too much, you have to take the other-emptiness position and see the qualities of awakened awareness as they shine forth as always right here. You don't want to negate so much that you lose the lucidity of this, or the awakeness of this, the sacredness of this. Then you've gone too far.

On the other hand, if you start looking for those qualities as things, they cloud over the mind. As soon as you look for awakeness as a quality and reify it, as soon as you look for a brightness as a quality and reify it, making it the light that you're looking for out there, then you have to go back to the self-emptiness position and see that that's just an empty construction you put up.

So, you'll go back and forth in that necessary tension—sometimes negating too much, you want to go to the other-emptiness side of it and look for what needs to be affirmed in terms of these properties of awakeness. And then when you start making those into things, you have to go back to the self-emptiness position and say, "Hey, wait a minute. These are constructions. I'm starting to reify these again." Like that. Then, you're always riding that edge. If you do that, how can you possibly go off track? Not possible.

Student 2

Thank you.

Dan

So, you see, it's necessary. I understand that he was giving you a traditional Dzogchen debate point of view, but at a certain point of realization, it supersedes that debate. It's not relevant to fully awakened or enlightened mind. It's a lower-level position. All positions are relative to the level of mind. The realizations and the thoughts that you have are relative to that level of mind, that level of realization.

Student 3

So, how much lightness do I want to keep in my perception?

Dan

There are different levels of awareness.

Student 3

Oh, okay.

Dan

So that your perception of what awareness is … is relative to the level of mind that you're in. So, what are the different levels of mind, okay?

The first is the coarse level of mind. That's the world of ordinary content. You have specific thoughts. You have specific emotions. You have specific sights. You have specific sounds. All those are representations or constructions. Right? If you were to deeply concentrate, the tendency to elaborate and construct all that stuff winds down. And at some point, you leave the mind in an unelaborated state.

All those constructions are built up of very quick bursts of energy and movement called mind moments. If you were deeply concentrated, you'd be operating at what we call the subtle level of mind—one hundred thousand blips of energy and light in the blink of an eyelash. And you stabilize it, the subtle level of mind.

If you do emptiness of time and move beyond the convention of ordinary time and space, then you're operating at what's called a very subtle or extraordinary level of mind—Ocean and Waves meditation. You are operating out of a boundless, changeless ocean of awareness, and whatever comes up within that massive, spacious field, it comes up without any grab whatsoever like an ocean looking at its own waves. That's a big shift. Most of Mahāyāna practice and Essence practices are done out of that level of awareness. It's called the very subtle or the extraordinary level. But you're still operating within the constraints of individual consciousness which you seem to localize, and within the constraints of your information processing system.

If you shift your basis to awakening, that's the next level. Awakened awareness isn't limited or localized. At some point, you'll notice the shift in your basis of operation so you're no longer operating within the seeming constraints of individual consciousness and your information processing system but operating out of being the unbounded wholeness—a place that is no place, has no location, and no reference points. There's your awakening.

If you stabilize that awakening, and then you can hold the view that always right here is this vast expanse of groundless ground of being and everything that arises is none other than the liveliness of awakening expressing itself. And if you hold what we call the inseparable pair of liveliness and groundless ground and the expanse, then everything that arises within that expanse arises in and by itself and you don't engage it. It just goes its own way. There's no self to engage it anymore.

And because you're not engaging anything that comes up, you're not making any new karmic memory traces, so everything immediately comes up and dissipates, immediately comes up and disappears. We call that arising in and by itself, liberated by itself, *rangnang rangdröl*. If you have that, and then that process, and you've set it up right and it's automatic, you start a process called *dharmadhātu* exhaustion; because if you hold that view all the time and practice 24/7, you're no longer forming new karmic memory traces so it forces the mind to dip into the storehouse of all previous karmic memory traces and release them at a rapidly accelerated rate. And if you do that 24/7 for on the average of six years, you'll clean out the storehouse.

Dharmadhātu exhaustion means that there's no negative states left. And because those negative states masked the positive states, you get a flourishing of all the eighty positive states of a buddha-mind, *sangye*—purification of all negative states, flourishing of all positive states—the Tibetan word for a buddha.

Now, once you do that—the stainless or what we call the clean mind—the mind's cleaned out; then the next task is you need to look at how we construct seeming boundaries on the nature of reality. If you look out here to this out-there-ness, it looks to us as if there's a bubble out here and we're in that bubble. And whatever the boundaries of that bubble are, that's our *jikting*, that's our seemingly existing world.

But, if you start looking at that with a certain view and a certain practice, because the view is the meditation, what begins to happen is you begin to move beyond the boundaries. Wherever you have boundaries, you move right through them. It's like basic space. And wherever you see these edges of boundaries, you keep moving through that. It's basic space. If you keep doing that, it busts the bubble. In Dzogchen, that's called cracking the eggshell.

So now, there are thousands and thousands of worlds here simultaneously, all at once. And you open up the next level of mind which is "all-at-once-ness" or simultaneous mind. Now, the mind operates on thousands of levels of reality simultaneously. That's a big shift. And when you keep pushing the envelope with that, until there are absolutely no edges and boundaries, the end point of that is limitlessness. As you open up limitlessness, then, at some point, you'll see that the structure of being is right here; and you lock into that and you're locked in to what we call the enlightened buddha bodies. Then, game over. Enlightened buddha bodies the last level of mind.

So, you can move up these levels of awareness like shifting gears in a car, just shifting your gear ratio. But the key is you have to recognize what level you're operating out of. You need your metacognitive awareness to tell, "Oh, yeah. This is a different level of awareness than I was at previously." You have to recognize it. It's not enough to just sort of say, "Well, this is all awareness," because that's not going to get you anywhere.

At each level of awareness, you have to see beyond certain seemingly solid structures, the clouds of the mind, until you can see beyond it to another level of awareness, until you take the journey through all levels of awareness. That's the hyperspace journey to buddhahood. Then, game over. There's an endpoint.

So where do we spend most of our time? Coarse level of mind. We think that's all there is. It's a problem. Each level of practice, you could say, opens up another one of those levels of awareness, and each one is more profound. That's, as you know, not all of those levels, but at least the ones up to awakening are summarized in the Heart Sutra. That's why the little mantra for the Heart Sutra is so popular because it defines the path.

Gate gate pāragate pārasamgate bodhi svāhā

Gate gate pāragate pārasamgate bodhi svāhā

Gate gate pāragate pārasamgate bodhi svāhā

"Gone, gone, gone way beyond, gone way, way beyond, ooooh, what a realization." That's what it means.

First, the mind gets clouded over by thought. We think that thought and awareness are the same things. We mix them up. So, you have to use your concentration to calm thought, to separate out pure awareness from thought, so you'll learn to operate out of awareness rather than operate out of thought. That's the first gate. Awareness gone beyond thought.

But then, we're still operating out of personal identity, so I still operate out of Dan. Then with emptiness-of-self meditation, I go beyond Dan, and I learn to operate out of pure awareness, freed up of Dan. Awareness itself gone beyond personal identity. That's the second gate.

Then, I have to come to see that this idea that things come and go in conventional time is its own empty construction. And if I see beyond the convention of time, I open up a changeless aspect of this field of awareness. And since time and space are related, not only is it changeless, it's boundless. So, now I'm operating out of changeless, boundless ocean-like awareness. That's a big change. Then, everything is contained within that ocean. [That's *pāragate*.]

But I still localize it. I still think I'm operating out of my information processing system. But with the instructions to cross over to awakening, I shift out of that to being the unbounded wholeness of awakened awareness-love. It's always right here. That's awakened awareness—gone way, way beyond the constraints of your individual consciousness. And since that's a much bigger shift [*pārasamgate*], *bodhi svāhā*. Oooh, what a realization.

Now, if we kept going with that, then having operated out of the unbounded wholeness of awakened awareness, I'd have to see to that I'm still … that unbounded wholeness is actually bounded—it's a bubble. When I bust that bubble open, there's billions of bubbles right here, and I'm operating out of simultaneous realms all the time. And then, if I push that to its limitlessness, then it opens up so you lock into the structure of being and open up the enlightened buddha body.

That's the path. Each level of practice shifts you to a different level of awareness until you reach the end point. Simple. It's not even hard to do. But it never occurs to you to do it. And then, most of us have limiting beliefs that say, "Not me, I can't do that."

Why not?

Is it any different from a buddha mind? Buddha did it. In fact, there are many buddhas. After Shakyamuni, there were hundreds and hundreds of buddhas and *bodhisattvas* who followed the same practices. It wasn't just one buddha. And there are many buddhas before Shakyamuni because we all have buddha nature. So, it basically means it's built-in, anybody can do it. But it has to occur to you, and you have to try it. Then, you have to get the right instructions that show you how to do it.

December 2, 2015

Themes: A Violent World; Going Beyond Fear; Common Humanity Practice

[Dan is speaking here in the context of a terrorist attack that took place earlier in the day in San Bernadino, California where fourteen people were killed.]

Dan

From a meditation perspective, human life is precious, and all life is precious. But in Dzogchen, as we say, all creatures, even down to the smallest insects, have awakened nature, but only human beings have the metacognitive capacity to recognize it. So, from a Buddhist perspective, the reason why human rebirth is so important is because you have a shot at using your metacognitive capacity, which other beings don't have, and that in this life you could use it to recognize awakening and develop your mind fully to enlightened buddhahood. So, to snuff out the preciousness of human life is the worst thing you can do. You take away not only life, you take away an opportunity to evolve that life into something that matters for the sake of all beings. So, you never know, when people get killed, what the potentials of those people are that were killed.

I'll tell you a brief story that's from a different tradition. One my favorite books, it's not very well-known; it's called *Interlinear to Cabeza De Vaca*. It's a Spanish book, very obscure, and it's a true story. It's a letter, and it was written by a Spanish conquistador, a great explorer at the height of the Spanish Empire when they were exploring the new world. And he's a nobleman, so he takes all of his money and his self-importance and outfits his ship—three ships actually—and they come to the new world based on a rumor that there's a city inland that's made of pure gold called Tenochtitlan, and they're filled with this vision of greed about discovering a city of pure gold and bringing it back to the king and queen and getting great honor as a nobleman.

And they sailed to the New World, or a place off of Southern Florida. They don't know where they are. And then as they go inland, to basically what we know as the Everglades; it's not exactly what they expect, and some of them get picked off by the elements, some of them get picked off by the gators and the snakes, some of them get picked off by disease, some of them get picked off by the Indian arrows. And it was only at the end of a year, there's about two dozen left. They make it out of the Everglade swamps and back to the ships, and a lot of them get excited and they launch one of the ships, but the ship's been sitting there for a year, and it rotted, so it immediately sank, and most of the people died. And then there's about maybe three or four left of what were three full ships.

And then they see the Indians on the sands looking at them curiously, and the Indians start crying, and they are amazed that these poor creatures could find pity for them, these noblemen and their plight. And the Indians take them in even though it's a harsh winter and everybody starves. And it's somewhere in the process, the Indians come to them and tell them that they have to heal their sick; and they don't know what to do, so they make the sign of the cross and they dig down deep in themselves and they discover, when they get stripped of their identity, they get stripped of their nobility and their self-importance and all their ideas about themselves. They get back to the basic, raw nature—that they actually have healing ability—and they go from village to village healing Indians, and they become great healers. Until one day, a band of new Spanish conquistadors picks them up as Indian slaves. But they were curious about how these Indian slaves who dressed like Indians and looked like Indians speak fluent Spanish.

So, the book was written as a letter to the king and queen about their episodes and what they learned about how self-importance wasn't terribly important. And when they stripped themselves of all the self-importance, what they found is an innate natural tendency to heal others.

And there's a famous line about when they're standing there and one of the ships that the first very eager conquistadors were going to launch is rotten, so it sinks and they all go to their death. And the line is, "Who knows who was lost on each one of these ships? Another Cervantes, another Magellan, another King

Ferdinand?" etcetera. So, when you snuff out life, it's like that. Who knows who was lost in San Bernardino today and what their life would've become if it wasn't snuffed out. But whatever might have evolved was cut short. There's no place for that. There's no place for that in humanity, in any sense of the word. It just can't happen.

Human beings are the only species that have metacognitive capacity to recognize awakened nature, and they're the only species that can kill based on an idea, a thought. We're strange creatures. People can think themselves into a state where they kill and think that that's all okay. It's never okay. But who's at fault? Is it some deranged individual? Or maybe a group of them? Is it the culture that supports it? Is it all the profiting from guns that make them so readily available that we won't stop it even though we know it's wrong, because too many people make too much money from it? What if we took away all the arms trafficking around the world? What do you think would happen to the culture of violence if we took all the money out of it? But we won't do that because there's way too much money involved in it, including for many American businesspeople. Nuts.

What is the justification for ... Yes, I know that in America we like to have the right to bear arms. I don't have any trouble with that. But what's the justification for the right to bear an assault weapon, or hand grenades? Why are they readily available to anyone? Because we make money from it and because there are powerful lobbying interests? That's not good enough. It's just not good enough.

It's difficult, because we have a more and more violent world. And I think what's difficult for people to wrap their mind around is intentional mass violence, where one or several individuals will go on a rampage, whether they're just deranged or whether they have deranged beliefs. It doesn't make any difference, does it?

What is the motivation here? To inflict terror and fear through massive violence. What's the motivation for that? It's interesting. What do people really think they're accomplishing by inflicting terror on lots of innocent people? Do they really think it's going to improve their condition in life? It's nuts, anyway you look at it. But human beings are the only creatures that can actually, based on concepts, kill others and kill themselves.

So, I don't know what else to tell you. From the Buddhist perspective, there's no place for it. But we have, deep in our hearts, to find some compassion for how people can go so deranged and so off-track that that's what they become.

But I think you have to balance that with finding compassion for the victims and the victims' families. Otherwise, we lose sight of something terribly important: the suffering that people go through, which is immense.

So, we'll all hear on the news about what the profile of the perpetrators are in the next couple of days, and they'll all get a certain self-importance about that, and we'll hear almost nothing about the victims and the victims' families and the impact on these lives. So, there's something wrong with the way we cover this in the news, and that's why it keeps happening, because you can get more self-importance by being a killer than you can by being a victim. It's difficult.

But there's something to be learned from it. I've worked in the trauma field now for over forty years, and there isn't any godawful story about what people do to each other that I haven't heard. And I think if you hear that many awful stories, the best that it does is that it helps you to evolve to a higher level of moral development, which is on pretty much a low point in this culture. If you hear so many stories, you sort of get it right about how people are and are not to be treated, and there are certain things that are just not compromisable.

That's one of the reasons why I spent so many of my professional years treating victims, because after a while, when they work through all the pain of their own victimization, they evolve to a higher level of moral development, because they know how people are and are not to be treated. They paid for that with the pains of their own victimization, and they turn out to be the moral spokespeople for this culture. It's important. It's just uncompromising after a while, and they have important things to say about how people are to be or not to be treated.

If you look at moral spokespeople for our culture, people come to mind like Nelson Mandela and his own prison time, the years of incarceration; Dan Ellsberg who released the Pentagon Papers. Every one of them has their own trauma story and they worked it out to change history. So, from that perspective, we have a lot to learn from victims. If they work it out, they have a lot to say about the moral compass of our culture—or lack thereof—that merits being listened to.

As you know, as a trauma expert, I've spent lots of time in the courts. I've done seventy priest abuse cases against the Church. They have a bounty of unlimited funds to discredit me. I take that as a compliment. But what sort of organization systematically continues to try and cover up everything and take no responsibility? Whatever the Church once was, it has no spirituality left in it. The coverups have been massive, and if you look in the last two years and you read carefully about all the money laundering that the Vatican has been caught doing in terms of millions and millions of dollars, then the idea that they have spirituality left is a travesty. It's a front for an organization that became very powerful and very concerned with maintaining their power and their considerable money. And if there are a few good people left in the organization, they're greatly eclipsed by the status quo.

For me, that's evil. Because the worst evil is the evil disguised as spirituality. There's no place for it, so I'm compelled to fight back, whatever the odds may be. And after doing that for over thirty years, I'm still standing, so that's good. But the stories aren't ... they're not pretty. I'll spare you the stories.

So, I think what I've learned personally from the so many trauma stories over the years is a certain fierceness of being protective. It's just uncompromising. So, that's a good thing, I think. But I don't know that that's going to change. You're evolving a culture of power and violence, and I see those things as interrelated. Right now, 1.5 percent of the population on this planet owns 95 percent of the wealth. That's all happened in the last twenty years, so now we have a world oligarchy, so what we have is extremes now with no middle path anymore. There's no middle class.

We have people who own way too much, and more and more people who own nothing; and the powerless think that violence is a way of getting their recognition and influence. So, the remarkably skewed distribution of the wealth has to be factored into this whole thing about the culture of violence and mass violence at the moment. When people are disempowered in one way or the other, what do they do? They engage in addictions, they engage in violence. That's what the world's becoming.

So, some people would say that the problem here is a social structure that allows for this. We're all victims, but not just of the violence. There are different kinds of violence, including economic violence. Someone once put it to me, they said, "Look. What do you pay in the US for taxes?" And I said, "Well, I have a small business. I pay 48 percent. Now, if I add the sales taxes, that's probably about 55, 60 percent," which is what most Europeans pay, but they get social medicine, and they get their colleges paid for their kids. We don't get any of that here.

So, why should I pay 48 percent and work my butt off for most of my life, and pay all the sales tax in addition to that, and Apple Computer, Microsoft, Google, and Facebook pay no taxes in this country and most other countries? Apple didn't pay any taxes for about twenty years in this country. And all you have to do is take the money that Apple could've paid in twenty years—I did the math one time. Google, Facebook, Apple, and Microsoft—four companies; there's your entire national debt right there in back taxes. It's a farce. We sold this country. And people don't even realize it. We sold it. It was once a precious democracy.

And, as a parent, I'm concerned about the fact that we have nothing to pass on to our kids and to our kids' kids. Most of them won't be able to buy houses anymore. They won't be able to afford to have their kids go to college. What does it cost to send your kid to a private school here now? Thirty, thirty-five, forty thousand dollars? Okay, so that's three or four hundred thousand dollars, and every one of those private institutions are collecting that and they're double dipping because they're getting all that research money, too. And what they're doing is socking it all away in endowments and investing the money. It's a double dip any way you count it. And that's all okay? At some point, you have to say, truthfully, this is just wrong.

So, these are all symptoms of a larger problem with the social structure, as I see it. And we're just pissing away what used to be a very precious country. So, as I see it, it's a much bigger issue. It's not good enough anymore to just sit back and let it happen.

So, that's why, in these traditions, it's not about sitting on the pillow. The mark of any realization is conduct. What you do with your life matters. And either you take from others selfishly or you leave behind a wake of positive influence. You have a choice about that. So, how you act towards others matters.

So, I've learned in this process, it's sort of interesting, that moral degeneration is so strong in this culture. If you try and lead a good life, it doesn't take much to be an exemplar. I'm not a very good exemplar, but relative to what we have as a standard here, [Dan chuckles] I suppose it stands out in some sense, and that has, I've learned a curious thing about that, it has influence. If you try and mean what you say and live life accordingly, that's so rarely done, that people listen more, so the teachings matter a little bit more preciously to people.

I think what those of you who know me well, probably more in this role, but certainly in the court arena, you know I can't be bought. I never take on a case unless it's got merits. It's never about the money, and I'm fierce about it. And I found out that that scares people, because you can't be bought. And it scares people in a good way, because it invites them to be honest, and either they'll rise to that occasion or they'll show their worst colors, and then we'll see how that goes, but it has an effect.

So, each of you is responsible for your own conduct. And in the face of mass violence, try and be compassionate, the best you can. One of our students was part of our first response team here for the Boston Marathon bombing; and you can see people's conduct immediately on the film. Half the people, when the bombing took place, ran the other way, and half the people ran towards the bombs. That pretty much defines people's character, doesn't it, in situations like that?

So, enough said. I don't know enough about this situation yet, but unfortunately, we have too many of them. And with a wife who was a hostage thirty years ago, every time a shooting happens again, we have to relive it, because in those days nobody dealt with it.

Questions?

Student 1

From the same question of these things that are happening in the world, I have been thinking myself about the nature of fear, and the responsibility I have to make sure I do not sort of succumb to it.

Dan

Good question. Yeah.

Student 1

So, I'm not sure what to make of that because I haven't come to any conclusions, but …

Dan

No, I think you're on the right track, that the whole M.O. behind terrorism is inflicting fear so people are afraid to live normal lives. I just was teaching in Israel for the last couple of weeks, so it's interesting, because terrorism happens all the time there. However, unless you're living in the West Bank, you don't see it most of the time. We see it more on the news here than you would see in Tel Aviv or most places in Jerusalem or outside. But the new strategy is to use a knife and just to go up to people randomly who are waiting at bus stops or places and just stab them, and the whole strategy is to inflict fear on a population.

But the Israelis have lived with this for a long time, so what they've managed to do, most of them, is say, "Yeah. Terror things happen, violence happens each week, but you don't stop living. Life goes on. And hopefully the odds don't catch up with you." We have a tradition in Israel that every time we finish the Level 1 course, then all the people go back to Tel Aviv and we go dancing all night and it's very spirited. It's the only place that we do that. And it says something about the culture.

Now, I suppose they could bomb the dancing club, but no one is going to stop to think about that. You have to live life fully in the face of the fear. And that's the lesson, because if everybody embraced life fully, then terrorism doesn't work, does it? So, your question, it's the heart of the matter. Look into the nature of that fear until it's empty, and embrace life fully in the midst of that.

I remember when I first worked for the International War Crimes Tribunal, it was a little weird because it was during the Yugoslavian War, and our first case was against the head of the Croatian SS. He was not a nice man, a sadistic machine. And they wanted to stop the tribunal because the war was still going on, so they thought they could intimidate the tribunal. So, I would fly over to Schiphol,[15] and the plane would land and the UN Security Forces would escort me off the plane after not sleeping all night because I would get in at 6:00 a.m., and every day I got off the plane—I had to commute back and forth[16]—I had a different car with a different route and a different bomb watcher. You have to testify while you're simultaneously translating into seven languages, and you testify in a plexiglass bomb-proof bubble; and if I went to the bathroom to piss, then they would watch over me with Uzis. And every note, every piece of scrap paper was shredded and burned. Nothing went out of the tribunal.

But it was a constant environment of fear of getting bombed, which was constantly on my mind, having young kids at home, but I didn't let it stop me. And I think the intensity of that fear became a remarkable point of single-minded, determined concentration. So, it was probably my best testimony

---

15 The main international airport of the Netherlands.

16 The court is located in The Hague, thirty minutes South by car from Schiphol airport.

ever. But it involved working with that intense terror that any moment I could get blown up. And the outcome is we set a standard for what would constitute reliable memory of severe victims of atrocity. It's been the standard for seventeen years. We have a 93 percent conviction rate. It's been appealed five times, always unsuccessfully. So, that fear, put in proper perspective, was a useful thing. It became a fierce determination that nothing could stop me from helping these victims, and nothing did.

Student 1

It's that fear seems to be the block to an awareness of our own, of my own divinity, and that's why I have to keep remembering it.

Dan

Yeah. The problem with fear is that we inhibit ourselves, in all sorts of ways, rather than mastering the fear, and being more single-minded and determined about what's right. That's your responsibility, that's everybody's responsibility. You have to work with that fear, and embrace life fully in the face of it, and embrace everyone else and help everyone else along, fully in the face of it.

Like the film of the Marathon Bombing. There's two types of people: those that are caught up in self and they're selfish and they run away in fear, and the other people don't think anything about the fear; they run towards it because the only thing they can think about is how to help. It's a diagnostic test right there for who the genuine spiritual people are and who's not.

Student 2

Back to conduct.

Dan

Back to conduct.

Student 3

Dan, I've heard you once say that fear isn't one of the three or five poisons. Can you talk maybe a little bit about that?

Dan

Yeah. It's not. It's on the list of fifty-one mental factors as one of the negative ones, but it's not one of the big five. So, I don't know how to explain that. The big five poisons: desire, hatred, ignorance or non-awareness, jealousy, pride. Fear's not on the list of the big five, but it's certainly, there's an expanded list of negative factors and it's on that, but it's not seen the same way.

Student 3

There isn't a kind of symmetry between desire and hatred, like attraction-aversion, or …

Dan

Yeah, but fear's not part of that; it's separate.

Student 4

Dan, one thing that I … something in me tends to find troubling is, in times like this, we have a tendency to divide, have a duality of people; like there are good people and there are evil people, and I'm wondering …

Dan

I wouldn't say good people and evil people. I think there are good people and there are people who are really ignorant—they've lost their nature, they've lost touch with their nature. I see it in terms of ignorance.

Student 4

Okay. So, the question has to do with are there—I guess, what do you think would be the best practice to bring into that as far as when we view people as evil rather than ignorant or different in some other way?

Dan

It's difficult. You have to practice forgiveness. And forgiveness doesn't mean you condone their behavior. There are several—there are a number of steps in the forgiveness process. There's a lot of research in positive psychology on forgiveness and what works. And forgiveness occurs when there's been some sort of significant moral transgression, when you've been transgressed against. So, first you have to review the actions, the transgression. You have to look into the nature of what was done to you that was so bad, that seems so bad.

Then you have to process the feelings about it. Because what we know with people who are traumatized or victimized, they distance themselves from the feelings and they disrupt the processing of it, so it goes on, and sometimes for months or years because they never really process the feelings. Then you have to process the underlying feelings, the ones that you really never get to, or in whatever the conflicts are.

And then, if you go that far and process all that stuff, then something begins to shift. Then you contextualize it. You get them to take a perspective and look at the larger issues here. And once they've processed the feelings in an effective way, then they can step back and look at the larger picture and they might start to see why that person might have acted that way. And they come up with some way of contextualizing it, put it in a larger context of what that person was dealing with and what might then have made them act so badly. That doesn't mean you condone the action, but you can at least understand it at that point.

Then, if you can take a wider, even spiritual perspective, you can see our underlying common humanity. And at that point, things will start to shift. The common humanity is that even with our worst enemies, we all want the same things out of life. We all want to be healthy, live a full life. We all want to be happy. We want our family to be healthy and happy. We all want to be prosperous. Even mass murderers and terrorists want that for themselves and for their people. They don't want anything different from what we want. We fundamentally disagree with how they go about it, but it's not different. So, you have to look at the underlying common humanity.

And then, if you can take an even wider perspective, you might see some spiritual merit in the act of forgiveness itself. I think it was a case where there was a kid who got murdered, and the parents came to the courtroom and pleaded for mercy for the shooter. Earlier this year it happened. It was very moving to watch that.

Student 5

Was it Charleston, South Carolina?

Dan

Yeah, the Charleston massacre. It was very moving to watch that, because they were operating out of a larger spiritual perspective that hatred was consuming. And if hatred becomes the response to losing your child, then essentially, you're consumed. Then the terrorist wins. And that was a remarkable larger perspective to be able to take, to take that point of view when you just lost your kid. Most people can't do that. I was really moved by it. And it was genuine.

So, no matter how bad the atrocities are, we're still left with having to work through our own fear, our own hatred, in response to those atrocities. Or, as was once said, "The only real enemies are those within our own hearts." So, all of this becomes an invitation for you to work with your own fear, your own hatred, and move beyond it to a more compassionate response precisely because it's that difficult. It's difficult.

I remember working on a priest abuse case. It goes back to the '50s. And the priest abused a boy four times, and the last time, he was in the boy's bedroom in his home, and the father walked in, and the priest was anally raping the boy. The father caught the priest in the act. And the father being in the military immediately got his guns and was going to blow the head off the priest, but the neighbors called the police, and they got there quickly and prevented another act of violence. And the priest went to trial, and he was convicted. This was in the '50s before we knew a lot about abuse. And then in the sentencing hearings several months later, the bishop came on behalf of the priest and pleaded with the judge to have mercy because this was a one-time offense, saying it would never happen again and that he was truly remorseful, and since it had never happened before, he should be compassionate. So, the judge, in the '50s, let him off.

Now, we tracked that priest over thirty years, in four states, and there were at least one hundred victims that we identified. God knows how many more there were. But the real problem here is that what we later found out was there was another victim that had come to the attention of the bishop four years earlier by the same priest, and when he went to the sentencing hearing, he actually knew that there were other victims, and he intentionally perjured himself and lied to the judge. So, who's the perpetrator here? Is the perpetrator the sexual offender, basically, a pedophile? Is the perpetrator the bishop who intentionally lied to cover up for him? Or is it the larger Catholic Church?

What happened in that case is that we now have a smoking gun. We finally catch the bishop in a coverup. So, they bought their way out of the case for seven million dollars in exchange for a gag law by the victim. He couldn't talk about it. They bought their way out of the coverup. And right after that, in that state, they claimed bankruptcy so they couldn't get any more claims against them. There's our Catholic Church. So, who's the perpetrator here? It's the whole culture of it. I can tell you many stories like this, but that was a particularly pernicious one because we actually got them with a smoking gun, finally. Yeah?

Student 6

I'm thinking of your comment about the folks at the Marathon and how some ran toward the blast and some ran against the blast, away from the blast, and the comment that that speaks to the character of those individuals, and I feel like I want to put a shout-out for trauma survivors whose nervous systems have a reaction that isn't in line necessarily with their character. When their frontal cortex goes offline, for example, and sympathetic nervous system takes over and there's a fight-or-flight response, and trauma is so pervasive. We have amazing experts in this room who have worked tirelessly …

Dan

You know as well as I do that most of the people who were running away weren't running away because they were trauma victims. That's the problem.

Student 6

But I think that … I don't think it's so black and white. I don't think you do either, which is, like you said, living with somebody who survived a hostage experience; whenever there's a shooting, it's relived, and I think there are so many layers of complexity to all of this.

Dan

I think that's true, but I think that ultimately—where Buddhism comes in—is that you're responsible for your behavior. Either you work with your conduct and try and change it, improve it, or you don't. And if there are states of mind that make you limited in your behavior, then you work with those states.

Student 6

So, along those lines, if there were a buddha who was a psychotherapist who wanted to really do everything that they could do to help in this world at this time, what would their job, his or her job, look like?

Dan

Well, it's a rather exhaustive job description, isn't it? [Laughter]

That's why Buddhism's coming to the West, because Buddhists have to be psychotherapists in the West. I remember when we went the first time with Rinpoche to his monastery in Eastern Tibet; he got up to his throne as the emanation of Padmasambhava and did a traditional Seven-Line Prayer. But the second time we went with him, which was to consecrate the philosophy school that we helped build, he didn't do that. He got up there and he talked about why he stays in the West.

And what he said was the West has a great tradition of studying the mind with psychotherapy, and that his experience was that Westerners, in the best sense, are motivated deeply to look into the nature of the mind. And that's why the teachings were coming here now, because that's a good motivation. Whereas a lot in the East, these traditions have deteriorated into sort of rote prayers and monastic rituals and people aren't looking into the mind anymore. So, it's a cushy, monastic lifestyle. He was wasn't subtle about it.

So, you know, psychotherapy is our preliminary practice. Right? And it's a good match for this culture. But in terms of these traditions coming to the West, it means that we have to use them in a way that works in the West. But I think we each learn. The West learns from Buddhism and Buddhism learns from the West, but certainly Buddhism doesn't deal with emotional issues very well or psychotherapy issues very well. There's no tradition in Buddhism to deal with trauma.

But I think that what we need to learn from Buddhism is that this notion of karma is that we are responsible for our actions, and some ways of acting in the world are better than others. Most people don't think about their actions or the consequences of their actions. We live in a selfish, self-involved culture where we do whatever we want for ourselves. That doesn't work. And most people who are selfish aren't very happy being that way. There's lots of research that shows that people who are more civic-minded and involved in community projects and the social good actually are happier people. Like His Holiness the Dalai Lama says, "When I'm acting compassionately, personally, for me, I'm happier."

So, there's a lesson here to be learned. We have to evolve better behavior, and we have to evolve better behavior in the face of all these reminders. Otherwise, what's the alternative? We become more inhibited and more fearful? Put our heads in the sand and do nothing? That's what we've become and we're wasting what was a precious democracy here. It was Thomas Jefferson who said, "To maintain democracy requires an enlightened culture." Maybe he meant that more literally than we thought. Maybe that's what these teachings are about.

Because it does require a certain participation to make this work, and we've seen that with one failure after another, painfully, in the last two or three years with most of the Middle Eastern countries, who are clueless about how to get a democracy to work. But it's not for us to be judges of that, because we're not doing a very good job of it anymore either. We sold this country to corporations.

December 23, 2015

Themes: Heart-mind; *Dharmadhātu* Exhaustion; Visions; Non-meditation

Dan

Welcome everyone. You have a question?

Student 1

So, this is what I've been wondering about, that as one gets farther along the path, there seems to be a sense of freedom from conceptualization, and what it verges on, is a sense of purity, as in the purity of awareness and a sense of pure knowing. And so, I'd like you to comment on that, if you will.

Dan

[Dan laughs] In twenty-five words or less? Well, okay. That's a good question. Another good question.

Okay. In Buddhism, the Buddhist logicians like Chandrakirti and Dignaga, spent a lot of time in Buddhist logic, laying the foundation or infrastructure for the fact that there are two completely different ways of knowing things. There's conceptual knowing, which is what we favor in everyday life, certainly in the West. And then there's knowing through direct awareness, and that's completely non-conceptual. It transcends conceptuality. And it's not a way of knowing that we easily acknowledge in the West.

If we think about higher stages of adult mature cognitive development, we can talk about non-representational knowing, but it's not something that's very elaborated in the West, whereas it's very elaborated in Buddhism. When you know through direct awareness, you don't go from thought. It's different. Another way of conceptualizing the same thing isn't with Buddhist logic, but with Dzogchen, the Great Completion *tögal* practices, or bypassing practices. And if you open up the Heart Lamp,[17] if you focus on the space in the center of the physical heart region, and you do that in the right way, it will open up a vast field of brilliant awake awareness—lucid, bright knowing awareness. And that is located or abides in the center of the physical heart. And if you're operating out of that direct knowing awareness that's in the heart region, it bypasses the brain and thinking. It's a completely different way of knowing.

So, if you think [Dan raises his hands, palms together, and holds them differently according to the three locations he mentions, descending from head, to throat, to the heart] body, speech, mind ... look where the mind is. Heart-mind. And heart-mind knowing is a different way of knowing of things other than conceptual knowing. It doesn't use the secondary association cortices, the brain.

Now, Western psychophysiology doesn't preclude the idea that we can know through the heart. In fact, one of the best measures of moment-by-moment information processing is heart rate. Because when we take information from the world, heart rate decelerates. And when we process that information, or we act on it, the heart rate accelerates. So, you can actually detect the moment-by-moment changes, and taking it in and responding by the variability in the heart rate.

So, the whole heart and circulatory system is a way of knowing the world and processing it. But we don't go any further than that as part of basic information processing, whereas Buddhism is much more elaborated. You're looking with awareness, not with thought.

See, in the ordinary mind we confuse three things. There's conceptualization. There's direct attention. And there's the intention of awareness. And in

---

17 *The Six Lamps* is one of the main Bon bypassing Great Completion practice manuals from the Oral Transmission lineage.

our ordinary experience, we confound those things. We think they're one and the same. So, we think that the only way of knowledge is thought, because we mix them all up.

If you use a high-speed electronic board, a tachistoscope [with which] you flash events, you can calculate the speed of recognition. Thought is rather slow; it's about a half a second or from five hundred milliseconds to about three thousand milliseconds. Directed attention takes about 250 milliseconds. It's about twice the speed. Attention is about twice the speed of thought. Awareness has lightning speed. It's the quickest machine we have. Awareness has intention and directionality, so if you're operating out of the intention of awareness, it's much, much quicker.

If you want a practical example of that, and that's sometimes talked about, take a major league baseball player. A fast ball comes out at the plate at ninety miles an hour. That's four hundred milliseconds to a decent player. If you're standing up there on the plate and you're thinking about the location of the ball, you can't hit it, because the fastest thought is five hundred milliseconds. It's too slow. But if you train yourself to operate out of attention, it's about a little bit ... almost four and a half, twice the speed of the ball. So, you should be able to attend. But when batters get into the slumps, it's when they're thinking too much. They can't see the ball. But if you really wanted to hit it, you train yourself to operate out of pure awareness, with lightning speed—then, it's much quicker.

Tony Gwynn, who hit the second-highest batter average ever in baseball—for over three years, he did that—he would have tennis balls lobbed in and out at fifty miles an hour. No bat speed could match that. But he wasn't about to hit it, he was just standing at the plate and locating, with pure awareness, the location of the ball. And after several hundred balls like that, he would have the pitching machine throw him regular hard balls, fast balls, ninety miles an hour. And with operating out of pure awareness, not with thought, not out of attention, but pure awareness at lightning speed, those balls were slow. So, he could hit one or the other out. And based on training himself to do that, which he figured out on his own, he hit for the second-highest career batting average ever. He did what the yogis do. They train themselves to operate out of intention of awareness rather than on attention of thought. So, all higher modes of knowing were based on direct awareness, where you see things as they are.

Now, as you know—and that's the other part of your question—in Buddhism there are three paths. There's the set of instructions that takes you from the beginning of the practice up to a taste of awakening. But it's not stable. There are the practices that stabilize that awakening so you have them all the time. It's a whole other set of teachings. And then once you have continuous, uninterrupted awakening pretty much all the time, then there's a third map that takes you from continuous awakening up to enlightenment, full buddhahood. And that path is sort of interesting. That's what you're talking about. Because all knowing is direct awareness knowing, and what you're really talking about is how the mind gets more … it returns to its original purity as part of that third path.

There are two main processes on that third path. The first is what happens to impure mental states like emotions and thought. And the second is what happens to perception, starting with emotional states and thought. If you have directly perceived the *kunzhi*, the universal ground of being, like a vast, infinite expanse of empty knowing awareness space—the ground aspect of awakening—and if you can then watch everything arise within that, as the lively expressiveness of awakened awareness expressing itself to itself—and knowing itself through its own expression—if you set up what we call the inseparable pair of the expanse of ground and the liveliness of what arises within that ground, then you hold both of those views simultaneously. Then, other than holding that view uninterruptedly, you do nothing. So, whatever arises, you don't engage. You don't move towards it to process it further. You don't move away from it to stop processing it. It's left to go completely in its own way, without any mental engagement. So first you have to set up the view; then you have to hold that view without any mental engagement, every moment.

Now, mental engagement is what causes us to form karmic memory traces. So, if you're at that level of practice, and you hold that view correctly, you're not forming any new karmic memory traces. So, what it does is it forces the mind to release the entire storehouse of karmic memory traces at a rapidly accelerated rate. You just watch everything go through. We call that *rangnang rangdröl*: arising in and by itself, left completely in its own way without any mental engagement, immediately liberating by itself, leaving no trace, like writing on water, or like snowflakes falling in a great ocean. It immediately disappears. So, nothing sticks.

If you set up that view of *rangnang rangdröl*, self-arising/self-liberating for short, and it becomes automatic, and you do that all the time, on and off the pillow, then you initiate a process called *dharmadhātu* exhaustion. You initiate the rapid accelerated release of the entire storehouse of karmic impressions over lifetimes. And there's an endpoint. At some point, the entire storehouse exhausts itself. Over time, what does that look like? *Drime*, in Tibetan, often translated as stainless. I like to translate it as clean. The field of awareness gets squeaky clean, because there are no negative states left.

And if you finish that process, the outcome, if you do it all the time, it takes about six years. You can accelerate the rate of that if you do some of the central channel practices. But if you do that all the time, there's an endpoint. And there are no negative states left. And since those negative states mask or obscure positive states, all of the positive states are here all at once.

In fact, that description of *dharmadhātu* exhaustion is what the Tibetans ... how they translated the word buddha. In Sanskrit *budh* means realized one. So, a buddha is somebody who has a realized mind. But that's not how the Tibetans translated it. They translate it with a compound term, *sangyé*. *Sangwa* means completely purified. *Gyewa*, means flourishing. So, if you hold the view correctly, the view is the meditation. If you hold the view of *rangnang rangdröl* correctly, the outcome of that process is that at some point, there's complete purification and eradication of all negative states. And there's a complete flourishing of all the eighty positive states of a buddha mind that finishes the causes of *dharmadhātu* exhaustion. There are no negative emotions left in the field of experience. No negative thoughts, no negative memories. There's an endpoint—the fundamental transformation of the mind.

Years ago, we gave a workshop, and we had lots of people at various stages of the path. The masters who had achieved *dharmadhātu* exhaustion, they didn't do anything on the Rorschach that we'd ever seen before. They were completely absent of any negative states, any conflict. I've never seen anything like it before. *Dharmadhātu* exhaustion.

Now, with respect to perception, what happens to ordinary perception? There's another part of this third map—how perception returns to its own original purity, just like thought and emotion return to their original purity. And that pathway of the transformation of perception is most articulated in a version of a Dzogchen practice. In Dzogchen, Great Completion practice, there are two sets of practices. There's *trekchö*, thoroughly cutting through the ordinary mind to awakened mind, and the other is called *tögal*, or bypassing practices.

And the *tögal* practices use the energy currents in the heart as the foundation for the practice. So, if you were focusing on the Heart Lamp against the backdrop of a universal ground, and you continue to focus on the Heart

Lamp, at some point, by holding pinpointed focus on the center of that space, what would happen is the field of awakened awareness would get brighter and brighter and brighter—they say like the first dawning of the morning sun. And if you continue to hold that view, not only does it get quieter, it also starts to have an energy that sort of flares up.

And then over time, that energy starts to course; it sort of revs up. And it starts to define some pathway. And it will shape its own pathway. You don't have to visualize the pathway at this point. It will shape its own pathway—from the center of the heart, it will flow back, up what we call the *kaṭi* tube channel. It will automatically turn up and go up the other part of the central channel. And just above the Adam's apple, at the back of the neck, it will split into two side channels. It will come up the back of the side of the neck, over to the top, and loop down into the eyes.

And if you keep opening up that channel, it will be suffused with a constant, infinite supply of energy, awakened awareness energy. And then the eyeballs are like fluid sockets. They're like crystal balls. And if you then set up all three or four Lamps simultaneously against the backdrop of the infinite expanse of empty awareness space, you visualize, pinpoint your focus on the Heart Lamp and wait for that energy to surge and course through the central channel—the *kaṭi* tube channel as we call it—up to the eyes. And you do all the Lamps simultaneously; and there's a continuous resurgence of that energy; and it will start to shape and pattern itself. If you look at that point, out from that vast expanse, if you look up to the border of the eyes, it's like looking at … the inner part of the eyeball has a surface, a little like looking at a movie screen. And you watch the visions dance. And the first level of visions is what's called the increasing of or proliferating of visions.

So first, what you're going to get it is like little energy drops, *thigles*. And it looks like boiling water. It goes very quickly. You can see all the little drops and bubbles. And they scatter and they move all over the place. And they dance and they have a lot of energy. And then you get bursts of filaments, threads, and spheres that look like cells under the microscope. And sometimes you get bursts of color—sometimes muted colors, sometimes very bright. It's not likely that you get all of the colors. Usually, the colors that emerge and which don't emerge have to do with the imbalance of elements in your body. But over time, as you watch the visions dance at the surface of the fluid eye Lamps, then they get more prolific, the colors tend to get more bright, but you tend to get a larger range of colors. You tend to see more spheres and filaments rather than just dancing energy. And it starts to slow down a bit.

And then, in the second level of visions, if you look into those little [visions], taking the energy drops, you'll start to see that they suggest shapes and patterns. Triangles, squares, circles, partial bodies which look like buddha bodies. Then you get lots of emerging shapes that are much more specific patterns and shapes. And what you're seeing is that awakened awareness not only is lively, it has its own organizing capacity. You're watching it shape perceptual forms before your eyes.

The third level of visions is much more dramatic. You get it all; you open up all the buddha fields. You get complete celestial realms with buddhas that are directly lucid, all the beings of the mandala. All the realms and times, you hear all at once. And at that point, you open up all-at-once-ness. Everything opens up—many levels of reality simultaneously. It's like looking in a kaleidoscope, where you can see many different angles with the same thing. It's all complete realities.

Then, in the fourth level of visions, they actually wind down and come to an end. We say the visions reach full measure. And they finish, just like the process of *dharmadhātu* exhaustion for emotions and thought, the visual perception reaches its endpoint. The visions burn out when they come to an end. There're no more visions. And then, that's the fourth level. The visions reaching full measure—*sepa*, in Tibetan.

And then the fifth level, the last level, is called *tartuk*, the visions reaching an end. And what's left is this one humongous, huge sphere of ultimate reality. And all realms and times are contained within it. And all beings across all those realms are all interconnected by loving threads of *bodhicitta*, of filaments of love. And the entire sphere of ultimate reality, everything and everyone is interconnected. Sometimes it's called Indra's net.

And it transcends the notion of ultimate and relative reality of the two truths. It's one integrated sphere at that point, with all realms and times being integrated within that. At that point, your mind has vast scope. And then *nyakchik*, or the integrated sphere of ultimate reality, or *thigle chenpo*, as we call it, is one of the perspectives on unified light. There's an endpoint. Thoughts and emotions exhaust themselves; ordinary perception exhausts itself. You become a buddha.

And all the activity of the mind is no longer something that's observed. All the activity of the mind is directed towards all beings who haven't realized that.

So, then you spontaneously manifest *trinlé*, enlightened activity inexhaustibly towards all beings.

So, if you have a taste of awakened awareness, then you see that it's not just a static space. It's light, and it's always expressing itself to itself for the sake of its own realization. But then, with the opening up of the visions, you come to see that awakened awareness has its own organizing capacity, organizing entire worlds.

And then you discover, somewhere along that path of *dharmadhātu* exhaustion, which is what you're talking about, when the visions which are happening to you, somewhere you figure out that not only does the path have liveliness and organizing capacity, it has its own intelligence. It has its own *gompa*, its own intention. And the whole show shows itself to itself, for itself, for the sake of its own realization. At this point, there's nothing to do. Just don't make the visions "out there"; make sure there's not a shred of duality. The process will happen automatically. And the next stop is buddhahood. Game over.

So, you're sort of now sensing that that has its own intelligence. And it's not an easy concept … because, we say, you've stripped the mind of its outer layer of conceptualization. You've torn down the net of self, so the mind isn't localized, packaged within the self where you deal with individual consciousness. It is that unbounded wholeness. And everything is contained within that lofty scope.

It's quite profound. You can see for yourself. And when you get a glimpse of the *nyakchik*, the ultimate sphere of the way things are, it commands awe and respect. If you get a glimpse of that, nothing will ever be the same. But you've got to stabilize it. But there's nothing you have to do other than just get out of the way and watch it happen. So that way, when you get a taste of that, we call that basis. We get caught up in it. It keeps showing itself to itself, and gets caught up in the path. And at some point, even that comes to an end. And you have fruition. There's nothing beyond that.

So, you see, it's already happened. Please don't get in the way. It's simple. Everything happens to itself by itself. You don't have a shred of duality; there's no reasons out there; they're all nondual. Everything is self-generating, self-grounding. If you remember only that and you stay on the path, it's that simple.

But the visions get rather wondrous, so the tendency is to see them "out there," and what you do is you screw it up. And everybody does it, which is why there's so much emphasis on seeing it as self-arising. Then don't screw it up. See what happens. You already know where it's taking you.

There isn't much to say beyond that. It's so awesome. It commands enough respect, so there's not much to say about it beyond that. It's happening. You don't turn it back.

Good. If Buddhism is going to come to the West, we need buddhas. Take it seriously. That's where the path leads you to. And at this point, there isn't a shred of it that's conceptual. Not a shred of it. All direct perception, direct awareness. And you can see that the mode of knowing is much more lucid, because you see things just the way they are. It's not clouded by conceptualization at all. It couldn't possibly be at this point.

Now, it doesn't mean that thought goes away. It means that thought transforms itself back into its original purity. If you operate out of the lightning speed of the intention of awareness for long enough, and not out of thought, a funny thing happens. Thought transforms itself back into its original purity, and then it's not different from the intention of awareness, because in fact, thought and the intention of awareness have certain common features. Both have directionality. We can think along certain lines. We can intend with lightning speed a certain direction. In that way, thought and awareness are not that different.

So, what's the main difference between thought and awareness? Speed. Thought is much slower. But, when thought is transformed back into its original purity, thought becomes the lightning speed of intention, awareness. It's one of the five wisdoms. We call it, *sozha tokpa yeshe*, discriminating wisdom energy. And what thought has that perception doesn't have is directionality. And that's useful, because if you transform thought back to its original purity, it has lightning speed and it has directionality, and it has another property that thought doesn't have—*Ma Gag Pa*. It's unobstructed. The lightning speed of intentionality does something that thought can't do. Nothing interferes with it. So, if you intend to put your awareness on something, with that lightning speed it goes only to that, and just to that; nothing gets in the way of it. Whereas, thought, you can branch off to another thought, and you can sort of veer off and go in different directions with that. And you can lose the thread. You never do that with awareness. Whatever it goes to, you just go with that.

So you see, thought, when you transform it back to its original purity, is actually helpful because it becomes one of the five wisdoms, discriminating wisdom. That's how Buddhists know how to help people. Because they use the discrimination of the lightning speed of directionality and the intention of awareness to see what's in the mindstream of that person, to know how to best help them according to their capacity.

That's how buddhas can read minds. All you have to do is put the intention to look at the entire array of what's in that person's mind and that displays itself. Not that you want to see it. [Laughter] It's certainly not going to help them. So, it's useful.

Menri said that he tried to teach the mind. There's a text on it and a whole set of teachings on it. Some of the monks, they gave up, because they were horrified by what was in people's minds. [Laughter] It had such a reactivity to it that he just felt that he couldn't handle it, so he stopped teaching it. So now there's only two people on the planet who knows these teachings, which is unfortunate, because it will die out. But that's how buddhas work. You have to know how to read people's minds, to see what they need.

So, if a thought is useful, you don't get rid of it. You transform it back to its original purity, discriminating wisdom. Very discriminating. We say thought is like rays of light. It goes right to the source. Nothing gets in the way of it. And there's infinite rays of light for different beings. It's like your mind is like the sun, with infinite rays of light, inexhaustibly shining, to discriminate what people need and to respond accordingly.

Now, the whole process, when you're looking at the transformation of perception through *dharmadhātu* exhaustion, or you're looking at the transformation of the visions of the five levels of visions, the whole thing is based on *rangnang rangdröl.* Set up a view of the infinite vast expanse and simultaneous to that, the view that whatever arises and has the liveliness of awakened awareness, hold the view as an inseparable pair, and let everything arise without engagement in every moment. Let it go its own way.

So that's the path, you see. That view is the path—the whole map through buddhahood. So, it's rather simple, you see. If you know that practice strongly, then never waiver from it. You've already caused the sprouting of the seeds of buddhahood. And the rest of it just flows.

So, it's not a hard practice. Once you get it going, it goes by itself. Just hold the view and let it finish. You don't know when that is. And when that occurs, I'll know when it is.

Good. The question reflects your practice and has a lot of depth. It's right to the heart of the matter. What's the mode of knowing that's going to bring you to buddhahood?

Good question.

Anybody else? Yes?

Student 2

With regard to this, what I've been thinking about recently is the idea that I can include everything. That is, all … the practice of not having the dualistic point of view, that all that's included is feeling like home now. But I then question, what do I do with—like you said, if you could read minds in the way that you wouldn't want to know what's going on in somebody else's head, what do you do with the preferences and the tastes? It's easy when it comes to …

Dan

They all drop away.

Student 2

Okay.

Dan

Okay. If you can set up emptiness of time, and then do Ocean and Waves, where everything arises like waves, viewed from the vantage point of ocean-like, changeless, timeless awareness, and you look with the speed, the lightning speed of awareness, so you can catch everything as it forms, and you can see it. And if you bring that practice up to automatic emptiness, so that everything that arises is the natural expression of emptiness-liveliness as soon as it arises, then you go … in Mahāmudrā, you go to what we call—when you don't have to do anything anymore, because all doing is immediately expressed as empty and all conceptualization is immediately expressed as empty, automatically, you enter what we call the natural state.

And where it becomes completely what we call automatic emptiness at every moment, that non-doing and that automaticity is the gateway, it's the key that opens the gateway to what we call the great meditation of non-meditation. You don't have to do anything anymore. It goes by itself. *Gompa*, meditation of non-meditation.

Now, when you have non-meditation, everything that gets expressed is empty. Everything has the same taste, emptiness liveliness. So, there's no preferences anymore. If you want the neurobiology of that—in concentration meditation, when you focus on one thing and tune everything else out, you activate the ACC, the anterior cingulate cortex. That's the piece that's activated in concentration meditation. The ACC is what's underactive in children and adults with ADHD. Concentration activates the ACC. We hypnotize somebody, you activate the ACC. When an athlete goes into the flow state or peak performance mode, it spontaneously activates the ACC. The ACC is associated with a heightened concentration of one thing and tuning out everything else.

Mindfulness meditation—that is, Burmese mindfulness—deactivates the PCC, the posterior cingulate cortex. And the PCC is how we categorize experience, like when we label a scenario where "this" is a fantasy, and "this" is actual perception. We like "this," or not, as good or bad. All categorizing, perception categorizing of experience, is done by the PCC.

So, when people do Burmese mindfulness and they try and open up a field of the nonreactive awareness, they basically partially deactivate the PCC, when in Tibetan meditation, if you do pure non-meditation meditation, the PCC deactivation is much more robust, much stronger. You're really shutting it down. And there you're doing a practice where there's actually no preferences. There's no good. There's no bad. Anything beyond that point, like what we talked about earlier, there's just no—you don't make those distinctions: good, bad. You shut down that whole system. There's no good. There's no bad. There's no neutral. There's no discriminations of like or dislike, of pleasant or unpleasant. Every moment has the same taste. It's all into this liveliness. And you move beyond all preferences.

And so, for the rest of the path, those preferences are irrelevant. We don't really mind those anymore. And with *rangnang rangdröl*, if you set up that view correctly at that point in your practice, you move beyond the formation of any new karmic impressions, and ultimately, as you're going along the path of *dharmadhātu* exhaustion, you move beyond any influence by former karmic impressions. You're beyond karmic impressions. You're free.

Student 2

So, preference is just more karmic impression?

Dan

Yes, you're engaging.

Student 2

Engaging.

Dan

You're engaging, either positively or negatively; it's still engagement.

Student 2

Because I'm thinking how it's easy for me to think, "Oh, red, blue, green. I love them all." But when it comes to personalities, I like some. I don't like others. And I have conflict with that.

Dan

Yeah, that's true. But you can go beyond that too.

Student 2

Ah, okay.

Dan

I once asked my first Root Lama, just before he died. I said, "Look, you've practiced all of your life. What was the hardest practice?" And he said, "Treating everybody the same."

Student 2

Ah, good, yeah. Okay.

Dan

And social psychologists tell me we make impressions of people, like or dislike or neutral, within three seconds of interacting with them. Basically, we make the impressions based on no interaction. And they don't change that much after that. So, it's discouraging.

Student 2

Yeah.

Dan

And it's all in our head. You know, all constructions. They have nothing to do with people. You have to move beyond that, otherwise you can't open up yourself to being sensitive to or helping anybody.

Student 2

Yeah, okay.

Dan

So, we don't really help people. We help people so it can make us feel good. That's the difference between relative and ultimate compassion. Ultimate compassion is impartial. We say it's like the rays of the sun. The sun doesn't decide who it shines on. It shines on everybody. If the sun said, "Well, I want to shine on these people today," we'll be like, "Oy." You've got to be like the sun, with inexhaustible, impartial light rays in the direction of all beings.

January 6, 2016

Themes: Metacognition Is How You See Your Basis of Operation

Dan

Welcome everyone. You have a question?

Student 1

I've been thinking about the idea that we are, in our meditation, peeling back the layers of karmic traces.

Dan

Okay.

Student 1

And wondering how I'm to know the difference between that and thoughts that are coming up. Is there an identifying way for me to say, you know, "be quiet" or "not be quiet" and let them happen?

Dan

Well, that's an interesting question.

Student 1

Well, there was a second part of that, too. After the last time I saw you, I went home and thought about this whole notion of ... I asked about preferences and tastes and that it would be something that would disappear all the time.

Dan

You went home and thought about it. That's always dangerous. [Dan chuckles]

Student 1

I know, maybe I shouldn't ask the second part. [Laughter]

Dan

No, go for it.

Student 1

It's part and parcel of the same thoughts, you know. I don't quite understand the way to be nondualistic. And if there's something I can do in my practice to promote that more or just meditate and play it out.

Dan

Okay, so, the heart essence of your question is about metacognition. And metacognition means the capacity to step back and to correctly be aware of, in, or monitor your state of mind and to know what that is. Now, metacognition in the West has a checkered history here. The introduction of metacognition as a concept in the history of ideas in the West began in 1979 with a psychologist at Stanford whose name was John Flavell, and he was probably most famous for his translation and interpretation of the Swiss child psychologist Jean Piaget's work. Then, later in his career, he got interested in metacognition, which he defined as thinking about thinking. And now we know that that's wrong. You're not thinking about thinking, you're aware of your thinking or you're aware of any other state of mind.

You see, what we presume in the West is that the dominant model for knowing is thought, conceptual knowing. Whereas in Buddhism, the Buddhist logicians like Dignaga, Chandrakirti, and others set a strong infrastructure to understand that there are two modes of knowing. There's knowing conceptually and there's knowing from direct awareness, which is nonconceptual, it's nonrepresentational. And we don't acknowledge direct awareness knowing, or metacognitive knowing as something that exists in the West. If we step back and look at our state of mind, it means that we're thinking about our state of mind. Well, that's way too slow.

In terms of these two ways of doing metacognition—thinking about thinking, or direct awareness of and monitoring an evaluation of your state—the neurobiological evidence strongly favors the Buddhist position because the metacognitive center is the right dorsolateral prefrontal cortex, and that's activated in meditation. So, if you're doing good old concentration meditation and you're constantly, with effort, bringing the mind back to the concentration object, like the rising and falling of the breath as compared to chasing after thought or sense experience that's distracting, what allows you to see when you get distracted is metacognitive awareness. What allows you to know when the meditation is off, and you need to self-correct it because you've gotten into some bad habit is metacognitive awareness. What allows you to know when the meditation is set up right so you can know what those conditions are so you can set it up right the next time—and keep setting it up right—is metacognitive awareness.

Now, if you look at the neuroimaging of standard concentration meditation when people actively or effortfully focus on one thing and tune everything else out, they activate the ACC, the anterior cingulate cortex, part of the prefrontal system. Then in one study that was done out of Richard Davidson's lab, what distinguished between beginning and advanced concentrators (and that has nothing to do with time of meditating, but rather it has to do with level of skill; some people can be advanced concentrators after a month and some people can be beginning meditators after ten years), what distinguished the two groups based on skill was not only the activation of the ACC but the activation of the right dorsolateral prefrontal cortex.

Smart meditators are always looking into the nature of the quality of their concentration and making corrections. Or as you pretty much said before, the old Sufi saying is, "A log sits on a wood pile very quietly for years, but logs never realize God, so don't sit like a log, sit intelligently." The best meditators, when they're concentrating, are always evaluating the quality of the meditation. Not with thought in terms of metaphors of neurocircuitry. The right dorsolateral prefrontal cortex is part of the executive control system and has to do with awareness. It has nothing to do with the secondary cortices that have to do with thinking.

So essentially, this idea that metacognition is thinking about thinking from a neurocircuitry point of view, is wrong. The right dorsolateral prefrontal cortex is direct, immediate knowing of your state—just seeing into it and knowing it. The Tibetan equivalent for that is called *shé zhīn*, which the Dalai Lama now translates as metacognitive awareness. It's one of the necessary ingredients for awakening. But the use of metacognition is something that's necessary in every stage of the path. You can't just sit and practice. You always have to look into the nature of the quality of your practice and keep improving it.

So, when you're concentrating, what does that mean? It means two things. First, recognizing more and more quickly when you get distracted; thought is too slow to recognize that, but awareness isn't, because awareness works with the speed of light, metacognitive awareness. And secondly, being able to evaluate when you're off so you can self-correct; and through doing that, you will constantly improve your concentration.

But when you get to the special insight series of meditations, most of those practices are about different levels of awareness. And what's required there is the same metacognitive recognition of which level of awareness you're operating out of. Okay?

So, there's two technical terms there. One of those technical terms is *chu yul*. It's hard to translate. I like to translate it as "basis of operation." Where are you operating out of? Where are you coming from? What's your operating system at this given point in time? In our everyday life, what's our basis of operation? A lot of the day, it's operating out of thought mode rather than awareness mode. A lot of the day, it's operating out of self. Sometimes it's operating out of emotions. But what you learn through emptiness practice is to shift your locus, to shift your basis of operation. So, you're operating out of some level of awareness. But the key, metacognitively, is to know with immediate perception what level of awareness you're operating out of. And that's the key to understanding your question.

Because you see, as Rechung, the main student of Milarepa once said, there are different levels of awareness. Okay? So, what are the different levels of awareness? *Rigpa*—there's awareness that's separated out from thought. In our ordinary experience we mix up thought, directed attention, and awareness as if they were all the same thing. But when you calm thought, awareness is still there. And if you concentrate enough and you calm thought enough, you realize that awareness has intention and directionality, except it has much quicker speed than thought does. So, through calming thought through concentration, you'll learn to operate out of pure awareness and its intention with lightning speed, *rigpa*. But, even if you separate out awareness from thought and make awareness your basis of operation, different from operating out of thought mode, the likelihood is you're still contaminating that with sense of self.

So, I'm not sure at that point whether I'm operating out of awareness or if I'm operating out of Dan. But if I do emptiness of self correctly as a meditation, I learn to shift my basis of operation. Then I'm operating out of a level of awareness that's cleaned up not only of thought but cleaned up of the sense of self or personal identity. So, we have linguistically marked that as *rang rigpa*—awareness itself gone beyond personal identity. But, you see, I have to be able to have some metacognitive awareness to recognize whether I'm operating out of thought mode, self-mode, pure awareness mode beyond thought, or pure awareness mode beyond thought and self. You see? And that's all about metacognition.

And still, if I'm operating out of a level of awareness that's beyond self, and it does the meditation now rather than Dan, it probably does a better job than Dan does. Still, that level of awareness is mixed up with the convention of time. So, if I practice emptiness of time and I shift my basis of operation, then I'm operating out of a level of awareness that's actually timeless and changeless. And because time and space are related, I'm operating out of a level of awareness that's not only changeless and timeless, but it's absolutely huge and vast. So, we call that ocean-like, changeless, timeless awareness. But I have to recognize that awareness as my basis of operation. So, if I do emptiness of time correctly, I shift out of time mode and I shift into operating out of a timeless, spaceless mode—ocean-like, changeless, boundless awareness.

Nevertheless, if I practice Ocean and Waves, the standard Milarepa meditation, while I'm practicing Ocean and Waves, I'm holding as my vantage point, or view, that ocean-like changeless, boundless awareness. That's where I'm coming from. And within that field of ocean-like, changeless, boundless awareness, I let everything arise—thought, emotions, sights, sounds, etc. And whatever arises, arises within that vast spaciousness with no grab. That's spacious freedom. That's the beginning of what we call the path of spacious freedom.

But the problem with that is as things arise there's some residual tendency to still see it as "out there." So, the next step to develop is that all of the view, the feel of all the surrounding empty space, all of the objects in that space, and the knowing of those objects is one single, unified, nondual field. So, beyond ocean-like, changeless, boundless awareness, I have to recognize nondual awareness. It's a different level of awareness.

Still, that nondual awareness is packaged in individual consciousness. I seem to localize it somewhere. And if I take the crossing over instructions for awakening, I shift out of any localization to a place that is no place and has no reference points. And when I recognize that shift to becoming the unbounded wholeness of that ocean-like, infinite expanse of awakened awareness-love, I've shifted to another level, to awakened awareness. But I have to metacognitively be aware of that shift. It's not enough to just set up the view. You have to recognize the shift in your basis.

Then, if I have awakening and I'm operating out of that unbounded wholeness of awakened awareness-love, and I stabilize that so I have it all of the time, within that vast expanse, then whatever arises, arises as the liveliness of that awakened awareness itself. It's all awareness. And I set up the view of what we call the inseparable pair, the universal base, or groundless ground, the vast expanse and the liveliness of whatever arises within that. It's all the same nondual field. And if I let everything arise and let everything go its own way without reacting to it or engaging it at all, then I set up another view, which is called self-arising, self-liberating. Everything arises in and by itself, left completely in its own way without any mental engagement, [and] immediately liberates itself, leaving no trace.

If I set up that view correctly, and I do that all the time, then that's the view that allows me to no longer form any new karmic impressions, because it's the mental engagement of whatever comes up that forms new karmic memory traces. So, if I set up the view just right so I'm not forming any new karmic memory traces, then it initiates the mind to release all the previous karmic memory traces from lifetimes at a rapidly accelerating rate. We call that process *dharmadhātu* exhaustion.

Now, you have to look for the signs that you're doing it correctly. First, everything disappears immediately, nothing sticks. We call that leaving no trace, or like raindrops falling in a great ocean and melting into the ocean. The next sign is it becomes completely automatic, it just goes by itself. And the next sign is what's called stainlessness or clean mind. All of the karmic impressions release themselves so that the ratio of impure to pure states shifts. The balance shifts to purer states.

Nevertheless, although those things happen, I still have to be metacognitively aware and recognize those shifts as happening. I have to be able to recognize the signs. So, you see, for every one of these shifts in awareness, it requires a kind of metacognitive recognition of knowing precisely what that shift is. You can't just be oblivious to it. It's not enough to produce the states; you have to know with metacognitive awareness what those states are when you have them at that moment. Not with thinking, but with pure capacity to be aware and recognize them for what they are.

In Dzogchen, there's a whole set of teachings called differentiation practice. And what it means is you learn to sharpen or discriminate your metacognitive awareness to know what level of awareness you're operating out of.

So, as you see, that's what's behind your question. It's metacognitive awareness of your level of awareness. How do I know when it's nondual? Well, you see it; or you learn to see it. How do I know when I'm doing *dharmadhātu* exhaustion? Because you see it. How do I know if I'm getting it right? Because there are these three signs you can look for that you can see.

As you know, we talk about best capacity, middling and lesser capacity students. And what differentiates capacity is, in part, metacognition. The best capacity students have metacognition, so they can recognize and see clearly what's going on here. If you don't have it, you can learn to sharpen and develop that metacognitive capacity.

A simple way we teach students to do that in everyday life is go around your daily life and ask yourself the question, "What's my basis of operation right now?" Ask that many times during the day and see it for yourself. In one of the advanced courses, when we're trying to teach people to stabilize awakening, one of the assignments we give, which is a lot of fun, is we take everybody's cellphone, and we put it in a hat. And they grab a random cell phone of somebody else in the course. And that's their *rigpa* buddy. [They record their number for future texts or calls.] That's their awakened awareness buddy. And what we ask the person to do for the next six months is to randomly text their buddy in different times of the day and say, "What's your basis of operation right now?" It really helps because you start training your metacognition; you start thinking like that, and training your metacognitive awareness to look.

There's a funny sideline to that when we were teaching that instruction in the course that Rinpoche and I did in Switzerland on Lake Lucerne. And one of the students put a little note in Rinpoche's shoe: "What's your basis of operation right now?" [Laughter] So when he put on his shoe he had to read it. But he got the point of what we were trying to do.

So, if you understand the essential point I'm making, then progress along the path is necessarily about metacognition and sharpening your metacognition, whether it be about concentration or about insight practice—knowing—to be able to discriminate what's your basis of operation and what level of awareness you're operating on at any given time.

I'll give you an example of that. I had a student who was very motivated, and he had a taste of awakening at a lot of the courses, and I followed him over time. And about a year later I talked with him, and he said, "I've been trying to take it off the pillow when I think I've been awake all the time." And I said, "Well, how do you know whether you're operating out of awakened awareness or nondual awareness or Ocean and Waves awareness?" And he said, "What's the difference?" And I said, "Ocean-like, changeless, boundless awareness is changeless and boundless, but it's still cast within duality, and it's still cast within the localization of seeming localization of individual consciousness. Nondual awareness is changeless, boundless, and nondual but still cast within localization of individual consciousness. Awakened awareness is changeless, boundless, nondual, and nonlocalized, and brilliantly lucid. So, using those criteria, what do you think?"

And he was quite honest. He said, "I've mostly been in Ocean and Waves and sometimes in nonduality and probably never in awakened awareness." And I said, "Well, how do you know that?" He said, "Because based on your description, what I've learned is I'm using the wrong criteria. I've been using boundless as just the criteria." And boundlessness is not a criterion for awakened awareness. That's a common mistake. Nor is nonduality, and that's important because there's a lot of people out there teaching nondual practices in Dzogchen now. I've even looked at their websites rather carefully, and they give the false impression that nonduality is awakening. It's not. It's a precursor. But it's not the same because you're using the wrong criteria again. Nonduality is still localized, and you're still operating out of your information processing system. It can't be awakening.

So, it's important to sharpen your metacognitive awareness, and not as a "need to know," but [that] you need to know. Know the difference here. You still have to do it correctly. Because I think if you read between the lines, sharpening metacognitive awareness is what differentiates the best capacity students and the ones who advance the quickest on the path. That's well established in the neuroimaging studies on concentration, and it has nothing to do with length of time. The best concentrators use not just training concentration, but they're sharpening metacognitive awareness to know when they're concentrating well and how to self-correct, and to know when they go off and not get lost in it.

The best people doing emptiness practice know what level of awareness they're operating on, and they can tell immediately through metacognitive awareness, not thinking, what their basis of operation is, and they've sharpened that. But you've got to use the correct criteria. It's all about metacognitive awareness. "A log sits on a woodpile for years very still but never realizes God, so don't sit like a log, sit intelligently." Metacognition makes all the difference. That's really the question.

Student 1

Yeah.

Dan

Do you understand what I'm saying?

Student 1

I do. It's a confrontation. It's like, okay, so just sit down, concentrate, and keep …

Dan

Not just concentrate. Concentrate and monitor the quality of your concentration, not by thinking about it or doubting it, but by seeing into it with clear awareness, metacognitive awareness.

Student 1

Right. It almost feels like "get back to basics."

Dan

Okay.

Student 1

Yeah. Okay.

Dan

Also, as a Western psychologist who has spent ten years doing outcome studies on meditators, what we saw particularly when we were studying mindfulness practitioners in the '70s and '80s is that people in the mindfulness tradition weren't advancing very much. And what was happening instead is that they were creating lots of bad habits and getting stuck on the same-old, same-old, and never changing it because there was nothing either in the teachings or in the tradition or how they're being taught that would allow them to develop metacognition. So, they didn't advance. And they would make lots of subtle and not so subtle mistakes and get stuck there for years, sometimes decades.

I mean, examples of that would be partial staying, where you're dividing your attention between the object and the background noise, the distraction. And they were doing that for years and thinking they were deeply concentrated because technically, they were following the cycles of the breath. But only twenty percent of the mind was on the breath, and the other 80 percent was still on the background noise. That's not very good concentration.

But then we point it out to them, and they say, "Oh, I never thought of that before." Then they would move beyond it. But unless you have the criteria of what to look for, how are you going to train your metacognition? That's where good teaching comes in, teaching that will explain to you that this is what you look for, and these are the pitfalls you look for, and how do you know? But people who keep making the same-old, same-old mistake over and over again, many people who sit for years and years and never reflect on the quality of their practice, they just uncritically accept it because that's what they were being taught. It might not even be good practice.

So, you have to match the practice with some intelligence about what you're doing. You don't leave your intelligence outside the door. If you do, you are very vulnerable to creating bad habits and getting into those bad habits in a way that you never get beyond them, whether it be concentration or insight practice, either way.

Yes, you had a new question. Didn't you have your hand up?

Student 3

I did. This whole discussion has raised another question for me, but I'll go back to the original question.

Dan

Either way.

Student 3

My question is, going through the stages and recognizing where you are in terms of your awareness and having that interrupted by things that you have very deep attachment for, particularly relationships and what …

Dan

Relationships are the path. [Laughter]

Student 3

Okay.

Dan

The teachings coming to the West means we do them in the context, in the midst of all of *samsāra*, which for Westerners means a lot of that's about relationships. If you can't do it in relationships, what good is your practice?

Student 3

But relationships I find particularly loaded in terms of … [Laughter]

Dan

They are loaded. Look at popular music. They're all about attachment and relationships, every song. It's dominant in our culture.

At the turn of the last century and the late 1800s, there was a popular movement (which didn't last very long—maybe about twenty years), called introspectionist psychology. And the reason why that failed with great proponents like William James and others was the problem of the stimulus error. When they did something like testing or measuring pain threshold, or visual recognition threshold, they came up with the problem of the stimulus error.

When a person gives you a verbal report of a recognition threshold for pain or for sight or whatever else, how do you know that that's an accurate report of the actual threshold, or if it's a report about their idea about the threshold? And the way that the human mind maybe works is to overlay perception with cognition. So, it's so intertwined that you can't separate it out, so you can't get through perception; you get ideas about perception. And because that bogged down the field of introspectionism, it died out rather quickly after exciting beginnings for about twenty years.

Now that was around the turn of the century. And in that zeitgeist, that's when Sigmund Freud was doing his first discoveries of psychoanalysis. And he came up with a weird term called "object representations" as a description of people. That's a somewhat weird term to describe people if you think about it. You are an object representation?

But why was he doing that? Because he was writing in the zeitgeist of the failure of the stimulus error, and what he realized was that people perception was not different from pain perception or visual perception. Essentially, when we look at people we don't see people, we see our ideas of people, and the ideas are so intertwined with the perception of people that we mostly see our own ideas.

So, to make that distinction very clear to people, he called that object representations. We're not seeing the person; we have an object in our mind about the person or an idea in our mind about the person, and that's what we're really seeing; we're seeing our own ideas about that person. And that was so compelling to him when he started doing analysis and he saw how those ideas got projected in therapy, he called that transference. And then most of the relationships were distortions. So then maybe about 5 percent of what we know about people is accurate, and the other 95 percent is our own constructions and our own distortions. You better keep that 5 percent accurate because it's not very much! [Laughter]

And social psychologists since, with a very different approach to the matter, came up with a similar answer; that if we look at things like human like and dislike, we make those decisions usually within about three seconds of meeting someone. And we rarely change them after that, and it has absolutely nothing to do with knowing the person or the interaction even. It's all in whatever immediate impressions get activated in our mind. It might have nothing to do with the situation or the person.

So, we live in the world of our own representations. We don't see what's there. It's hard for us in the West to get back to pure perception. All visual perception is like that. That's what Jean Paul Sartre, the philosopher, was writing in his novel, *Nausea*. And what he was trying to say is that we don't ever see things; we see our own representations of things. So, the proponent in the novel, Roquentin, at one point looks at a tree, and what we normally see, if I say, "Look at a tree," is the idea of a tree in your mind. But Roquentin looks at the tree and he actually sees the raw perceptual data absent of the idea. And he was so unused to looking like that that it stunned him so much, he got sick. Because so much of our visual perception, and our sensory perception, and our perception of people, is our own ideas about it. And we don't get back to see things just the way they are.

And that belies an underlying bias in the West that the only mode of knowing is conceptual. Meditation doesn't take that view. The real mode of knowing is direct awareness, or metacognitive awareness. But you have to train that over and against your biases, otherwise you're always seeing them as your own projections. You have to move beyond seeing your own projections. That's especially true around people, because the projections have more of an emotional overlay to them.

The Tibetan point of view would be that all visual perception, all sensory perception, all perception of people, people perception, is all deluded; it's all distorted by all the stories and constructions and projections—especially so with people, because you have all the five poisons. And we get a strong emotional overlay to those constructions. All the more necessary that we sort out perceptions of people and see them the way they really are, apart from all our projections and what gets activated, and all the karmic memory traces that get activated. That's how we interact with people in a way that has nothing to do with them.

So, you see, in terms of the *dharma* coming to the West, this is the cutting edge of practicing. To live in the midst of *samsāra* and in *samsāric* relationships and to work it all out, and to see it the way it is. I don't think it's any accident why the teachings are coming to the West. This is what will change the Buddhist teachings. In coming to the West, it will become relationally based teachings.

If you practice the *dharma* around relationships, then you have to look at your own constructions metacognitively. You have to look at all of the strong emotions that come up, metacognitively, see them all as empty constructions of mind, and move beyond them. Then, you have an opportunity to really see the person for who they are—direct awareness of who they are, rather than through all the projections and stories and all that kind of stuff. That becomes the basis of compassion. You can genuinely be open to and kind to someone for who they are because you work out all of that stuff.

Student 3

I think I'll go back to my cave. [Laughter]

Dan

This is not a time for caves. You know, my first Root Lama, I really respected him. He came over here in the mid-1950s, before Tibet was taken over. The first students with him, people like Jeffrey Hopkins and Bob Thurman, were monks. They didn't last long. Bob Thurman was a monk for about two years. His main teacher was Ling Rinpoche, the Dalai Lama's senior tutor. And he had to come back to the States to do something and Ling said to him, "You won't make it back to the States before you break your vows."

Bob thought that was stupid, and didn't take it seriously. He had a flight back, and had about a four hour stopover in, I think, London. There he met his wife-to-be in the airport. It was the end of his monk-ness. And they've been together ever since. And Ling saw that ahead of time.

My first Root Lama, Geshe Wangyal, used to say, everybody who lived with him in his retreat house was involved in terribly messy and complicated relationships. And he used to say, "This is the West. It's not a time for monks anymore." And even though he was a monk, I really appreciated what he did, because he actually had a girlfriend. He was in his eighties, and she was in her late seventies. She would come out for the weekends, and they would hang out together and probably had an intimate relationship together for about ten years. If you asked him about that, he'd say "Well, how can I teach in the West when I don't know about this relational stuff?"

And rather than committing sexual misconduct on all of his students, he did something which was honorable, which I've always respected as a model. He got somebody his age who wasn't a student and had a regular intimate relationship with her so that he could learn why this was so important to Westerners. He wanted to know, as a former monk. That was a great teaching.

He was sincerely interested in what all this relational stuff was that we all get so caught up in in the West—we all get caught up in it—and when I was with him in my twenties, I was really caught up, as was everybody else was at that age. This is the stuff you work with. It's the hardest stuff to work with. There's a level of practice called *bapo ting ngé dzin*, heroic *samādhi*. And heroic *samādhi* means a level of practice where you can intentionally put yourself in the most difficult of all circumstances.

The three advanced *samādhis* are King of Samādhi: pinpointed focus against the vast expanse. That's the first. The second is automatic mastery—every moment, whatever you put your mind on, it does just that, and only that. And the third one, the most advanced of all, is a heroic *samādhi*. Can you intentionally put yourself in the most difficult of life circumstances as a way of deepening your practice? So for the West, that would mean putting yourself in relationships, [laughter] and especially family relationships. Now we're past the holidays, we need to overcome the holidays. [Laughter] There's your practice. I figure if I can get to the point of my practice that I don't have a lot of grab around my kids, as a parent, then I'm probably getting somewhere. But I'm not there. [Dan chuckles]

So, you see, it's a very good question you asked. But that's the vehicle of your practice, because relationships give us the best opportunity to look at all the constructions and how the mind constructs and projects, and has strong attachments and strong emotions. It's the best source of it. *Dharma* coming to the West means relational-based stuff. Our great traditions of growth and psychotherapy are always relationally based. The best cutting edge of teachings is to do it in the context of relationships.

In a different tradition, when mindfulness was just beginning to get popular in this country in the 1970s, Jon Kabat-Zinn wrote his first book on mindfulness. He took the title of his book from a line from *Zorba the Greek*. He called it *Full Catastrophe Living* because Zorba, at one point in the film, talks about how his passion in life was to evolve himself completely steeped in the "full catastrophe" of everyday life. That's Western *dharma*. And Zorba the Greek is our western lama.

It's a good question.

January 20, 2016

Themes: Enlightened Mind Is an Invitation; Inexhaustible *Bodhicitta*; Set the Intention

Dan

Welcome everyone. You have a question?

Student 1

I'd like to say that this is something that I've been thinking about, but it's more something that I've been noticing. And it has to do with noticing how liveliness is suffused with compassion. And so, it seems as though *bodhicitta* is expressing itself through liveliness.

Dan

It's not really a question. It's a statement of reality. It's a good observation. So, in Dzogchen or Great Completion practice, the primordial buddha state is epitomized by Kuntuzangpo, or Samantabhadra in Sanskrit. And *Kuntuzangpo* means everything good. *Kun* means everything, *zangwa* means good. So, it's the expression of ultimate reality. And the primordial Buddha Kuntuzangpo has a property of mind called *gongpa*, and it's difficult to translate. The closest translation in English is "intention," but it would have to be continuous, uninterrupted, eternal intention—it never stops.

And the intention of the enlightened mind of primordial Buddha Kuntuzangpo is to express reality for the sake of wisdom and compassion. So, every moment of the expression of an awakened mind, a fully awakened mind, is a gesture. It's an invitation. And since Kuntuzangpo has a mind that operates by encompassing and saturating all levels of being, all realms and all times, then that intention, from our perspective, appears in the form of the way we see this world—how it appears to our mindstream. And to every being it appears a certain way as a gesture, as an invitation.

So, the world looks this way to you as an opportunity, as an invitation, as a gesture to see it right. And it will patiently and inexhaustibly keep presenting itself basically to itself over and over again, until you get it. That's why in Mahāmudrā … the word *Mahāmudrā* means great gesture or great invitation, because every moment is another gesture, another invitation to you to see it correctly, and through that to evolve your own mind. That's the wisdom side of the equation. And every moment the seemingly ordinary world of *samsāric* existence appears the way it does is an opportunity to develop in your depths your own compassionate mind.

If there were no suffering beings, there would be no compassion development. So, from an ultimate perspective—there are no suffering beings, from Kuntuzangpo's perspective. But from our perspective, caught up in *samsāric* existence, it appears like there is an entire array of enormous suffering. And that's an opportunity to train your own compassion. And when you develop your wisdom and compassion to its ultimate condition, your mind and the fully enlightened mind of Kuntuzangpo are inseparable. They're one and the same. At that point, there's no suffering, there's no delusion, and you have the full enlightenment of Kuntuzangpo's mind as the same. So, with respect to cyclic existence at that point, game over. Finished with that. But insofar as we're still caught up in the web of cyclic existence, the world will still appear the way it does, and every moment is another opportunity to use. Hmm? That's from the side of awakened Kuntuzangpo space.

Now, for those who are unfamiliar with the terminology here, *bodhicitta*: *bodhi* means realization, and *citta* can mean mind, but it's the honorific for mind, so it means it's close to intention again. So, when you practice *bodhicitta* at the very beginning of your meditation practice before you sit, we can call that relative *bodhicitta*. You're practicing from the perspective of an ordinary mind that's caught up in *samsāric* existence. But the first thing that you do is you set the intention. You set the intention towards awakening.

Now, that has several effects. The first thing that happens is if you set the intention for your practice towards awakening, there's going to be a reaction against that. You're going to bump across all those limiting beliefs: that awakening isn't something that you can get; the Western belief is that you don't have the capacity, or you don't deserve it; the Tibetan limiting belief is that it takes lifetimes, so don't bother to do anything in this lifetime. All of those are just ideas, and ideas don't define ultimate reality. They're just interferences. So, the first thing you do when you practice is you set aside those limiting beliefs and set the intention, because it's like if you were trying to shoot an arrow at a target; if you want the arrow to hit the target, you have to aim the arrow at the target. So, if you want your meditation to go in a positive direction towards awakening, and ultimately towards full buddhahood and enlightenment, you've got to start by aiming your practice and setting the intention.

So, if you start your meditation practice with that intention, it serves like a kind of central organizing principle in the backdrop of your awareness. So, you make every moment of your meditation count a little bit more carefully, because any one of those moments could be a moment of awakening to your true nature because awakening isn't measured in the convention of time. So, you practice a little bit more carefully, and you take yourself more seriously, that the practice matters. It's not good enough to just sit. If it's aimless sitting, what is the goal? Do you think the goal is to be quiet? To reduce thinking? That's just a very mundane goal that's never going to get you out of cyclic existence. So, now you can be a little bit quieter and more still within the realms of cyclic existence. So what?

So, you have to start with, "Why am I doing this?" And set it right. Most people today never think about that, because in the Western culture, meditation has become an end in itself. It's our way of relaxing. We never think about the goal of what these practices were designed to do, so we've lost the heart of it.

I remember my first Root Lama, Geshe Wangyal. He was very unusual, and I lived with him nine years in summers while I was in college and graduate school. And what I liked about him is he rarely played the guru game. He lived his life; he very rarely gave public talks or public teachings. He had a small group of students, and that changed everything. And I remember once, he actually accepted an invitation to a talk. It was somehow in the mid 1970s, I think it was. I think it was in Chicago, if I remember. And it was the first international conference on yoga and meditation, way back when, in 1975. And there must have been about 4,000 or 5,000 people who attended this thing, and it was like one sideshow after another of different meditation demonstrations and yoga demonstrations and all sorts of weird yogis. And he came to it and accepted an invitation to talk.

And his talk was unforgettable because he got up on the stage and he said, "I'm not going to give a talk about meditation. Most of you came here to learn how to meditate and there are many people who will show you how to meditate. But what's more important than just meditating is: when you start to meditate, the first thought that comes through your mind is, 'Why am I doing this?' Make sure you know how to answer that question right. Think about your motivation, and if you're doing it for the sake of your own realization, and better, if you're doing that for the sake of how it will help others; that's a good way to start your meditation. It's the most important point."

That was the end of the talk, and he walked off stage. And because it was so brief, it was unforgettable. And with all the yogis and the self-importance of the yogis, what struck me is the simplicity and utter truth of his message. And he didn't care what people thought about him. But he said what needed to be said, because nobody at this conference was talking about the end point: awakening the mind and developing that awakening to enlightenment. So, he had foreseen what would be very much the heart of how we go about that in this culture, aimlessly. It made the point. At least, it did to me.

The second part of that is, when you set the intention towards *bodhicitta*, and the intention towards awakening, you're practicing and doing this not just for your own realization. In the Mahayāna vehicle, you open up simultaneous mind, where everyone and everything is interconnected. If everyone and everything is interconnected, then that changes the way you treat people, because you can't live in a vacuum anymore and it's not "your" practice. You're doing it for the sake of how it helps others, and ultimately, if you evolve your own mind, that has influence, because in the field of big mind, awakened mind, we are all interconnected and everything that we think, feel, and do affects everyone around us in the field.

It's not like if you awaken then everybody on the planet wakes up along with you, but it is like the strength of your realization is planting a seed in every mindstream. It will ripen eventually into the eradication of all negative states and the flourishing of all positive states. Everyone's practice affects everyone else.

So, from that perspective, you never practice in isolation. And it's never about personal gain, but how it contributes to the greater good—that aspect of *bodhicitta* as you've heard me say before is like being a good parent. The one thing about being a parent is that it's self-transcending. If your kid's sick, and you're dog tired, and your kid cries out for you at night, you don't sit there and think, "Well, I don't really feel like getting up." Whatever it takes, however many times you've been woken up, you just do it. There's no other life experience that's quite that self-transcending. It gets you out of yourself. And that's useful because if you take that wider perspective, when the meditation practice is hard, you don't sit there and say, "Well I don't feel like doing it." No matter what it takes, you put a little bit more care into it. Because always in the backdrop of your awareness is that you're doing it to evolve your own practice for the sake of how that contributes to the greater good.

What if you cultivated that view that everything that you're about is designed to contribute to the greater good? What if everybody started doing that? Then we would transform selfishness because, you see, without *bodhicitta*, the opposite of *bodhicitta* is selfishness—more and more accumulation of wealth and power, material goods, for one's own sake. Look where that's going. 1.5 percent of people on this planet in the last twenty years now own 95 percent of the wealth. Most of us sense that there's something fundamentally wrong here. That's not going to go in a good direction.

Do you think those people are happy with all they've accumulated? It leads to nothing good—just more greed, more accumulation of power and money, more selfishness. The Dalai Lama was once interviewed in a series of interviews by a psychiatrist, Harry Cutler, about compassion, and he said, "Personally, when I practice compassion, it makes me feel better about myself. It makes me happy." And there's some research to suggest, there's a lot of research now on compassion, that people who practice compassion are happier. So, it has a nice side effect

One of my favorite novels—and I would recommend it to you if you've never read it—is *City of Joy* by La Pierre, or the movie that was Patrick Swayze's first movie and made him famous. The book's better than the movie. It's about a young pediatric surgeon who is very idealistic and very perfectionistic, and he watches one too many kids die on the operating table. And he gets so angry and disillusioned that he just gives up the practice of surgery, and he's completely lost. And what do you do if you're lost in life? You go to India. [Laughter] So he finds his way to Calcutta. And the first thing that happens is he gets mugged, worked over really badly; so now he has no money and no medical care. And he gets treated in a free clinic with lots of poor people around him.

And as he's recovering, he gets caught up in the lives of the extremely hard-working, decent people who carried people by foot all day in a rickshaw, and most of what they earn gets taken by the people who own the rickshaws, and they get just a very small amount of what they make during the day for their family. And they're decent, hardworking people, and eventually they protest and strike against the slumlords who own all the rickshaws. And he gets more and more caught up in their world, and eventually, with a great deal of anger and resistance, he starts volunteering in the medical clinic. They have no supplies, and it's impossibly difficult. And you can see his transformation. He's happy. He finds meaning in life just by selflessly serving people. It's a good story.

So, relative *bodhicitta* is the practice of compassion in everyday life. But it's based on the ideas of still having an ordinary sense of self and what we think is helpful to others. There's nothing wrong with that. It's just limited, because if you operate out of self when you're compassionate, even if you are primarily aiming it towards helping others, then it's partial. It's not impartial. And if you do too much, you end up with compassion fatigue.

Now if you evolve the mind, and practice in a way that there's no self, no substantial self, and you move beyond the sense of self, you open up the very subtle level of mind, an ocean-like, changeless, boundless awareness where everything and everyone is interconnected. And then you open up awakened awareness, so you're operating out of an awakened mind. You're not operating out of self. We call that 'you shift your basis of operation.'

Your basis of operation is like where you're coming from, where you locate your knowing. Oftentimes we locate our knowing in thought—we're "lost in thought," and that's our basis of operation. We locate our knowing in the sense of self, in my case Dan-ness.

But as you know, if you do these practices, you shift your basis out of thought. You shift your basis out of self, and even though they're still there, that's not where you're operating out of. You shift your basis out of the convention of ordinary time. You shift your basis out of your seeming localization in individual consciousness and the operations of your information processing system, so that the basis becomes what is always right here: an infinitely vast ocean of awakened awareness-love.

Now if that's where you're operating out of, then it's like being the sun. The sun doesn't decide who to shine on. It shines on everyone equally and impartially. The sun has inexhaustible energy. So, if your *bodhicitta* is what we call ultimate *bodhicitta*, and is derived from an awakened mind, or even a fully enlightened mind, then it's never partial, it's always impartial and it's inexhaustible. It's the way of being every moment. It's not a thing that you visualize and imagine yourself helping suffering beings. It's the spontaneously present expression of ultimate reality every moment. And that translates into conduct. The spontaneous conduct that arises is called *trinlé*, enlightened activity of an enlightened being—always acting towards helping others and guiding them, subduing their out of control mindstreams, calming and "taming" them.

Enlightened beings have four ways of helping other beings. In their peaceful aspect, they do it by calming the mindstreams of all thought and all emotions; they calm everything. In their peaceful aspect, they activate and help the flourishing of all positive qualities in all sentient beings. They bring out all the positive qualities like trust, and patience, and lightheartedness. That's the peaceful side of enlightened beings. That's how they act.

The wrathful side of enlightened beings, or what I like to refer to as the *troa*—I like the way Bob Thurman translates it. He likes to translate wrathful as "terrific." These are terrific beings. Terrifying, but they're terrific. It's a better translation of *troa* than wrathful. It's much more positive. And they guide beings by influencing the mindstreams, directly intervening and influencing, clearing away obscurations in the mindstreams of millions of beings. And lastly, by what are called the *dokpo*, intense means. They're the ones that give you the no bullshit instructions that will just awaken your mindstream, the pith instructions. So, this is a codification of how enlightened beings act to guide all those beings that are caught up in cyclic existence along the path. That's ultimate *bodhicitta*.

Now what you're describing is if you develop your own mind, and if you stabilize awakening; if you set up your view so that you can shift your basis out of ordinary mind and your localization of individual consciousness into being the unbounded wholeness of this always-right-here field of awakened awareness-love; if you can set up your view so you open directly to that, and recognize that, like recognizing the sun when there's no clouds, then you have to stabilize that. It's not good enough to have a taste of awakening because the habits of the ordinary mind will come back, and you'll cloud it over again.

I like the phrase from Dzogchen Ponlop who says, "Most people who wake up put the snooze alarm on many times." But if you keep setting up the view, you'll open up awakening more frequently and for longer duration, and eventually you'll have it all the time. And somewhere in that process, the mind shifts away from the ground aspect of awakening, which is this infinitely vast field of empty awareness space, *dharmakāya* space. And then what naturally occurs if you've opened up awakening and it's stably where you're operating out of, or where you're coming from, being the unbounded wholeness rather than being a little drop within it; if that's your stable basis—where you're operating out of—then after a while, the mind naturally turns to how things arise within that vast expanse of empty awakened awareness space. We call that the shift from the ground aspect of awakening to the appearance aspect of awakening.

Then what you come to see is that everything that appears is lively awakened awareness expressing itself. Awakened awareness isn't just an empty field of knowing space. It has liveliness. It's dynamic. It's always expressing itself. So, all thoughts are lively awakened awareness. All emotions are lively awakened awareness. All sights are lively awakened awareness. All sounds are lively awakened awareness. All smells, all tastes, the body, all body sensations. It's a whole magical display as a continuous flow of lively awakened awareness expressing itself to itself, and knowing itself through its own expressions. That's pretty lively. So, after a while, the view isn't the Lion's Gaze that opens up awakening, the view becomes a continuous, uninterrupted flow of the liveliness of awakened awareness, its appearance aspect.

Then when you can do that as a practice, then you do both at once. You take what we call the inseparable pair of the vast expanse, that empty awareness awakened space and the liveliness of whatever arises within it. You do both at once. From that perspective, when you stabilize that view of the inseparable pair, whatever arises, you don't do anything to. There's no self that gets in the way of it. And there is absolutely no reactivity to anything. If you just let it spontaneously go by itself, then everything that arises immediately arises, you don't engage it, and it immediately disappears. You just watch the show without a watcher.

The key there is not to do anything. You leave everything alone but leave-it-alone-ness isn't the thing that you do. It's not a strategy. It's part of the view. And if you set it up right, you're not forming any new karmic impressions, and what happens is all the previous storehouse of millions of karmic impressions will start releasing themselves at a rapidly accelerated rate until there's nothing left—the path of *dharmadhātu* exhaustion. And the end point of that is *sangyé*, the Tibetan word for buddha, the eradication of all negative states so there's none left. And because those negative states obscure the positive states, what flourishes are all of the positive states of mind. There are eighty positive states in a buddha mind. Now you're getting close to being like Kuntuzangpo's mind because you have all those positive qualities, what we call a *yonten*.

Now, as the mind spontaneously and automatically releases everything, somewhere along the line, with your metacognitive intelligence, it dawns on you that you're now caught up in the path that will automatically and naturally take you all the way to buddhahood. And that every moment of this path has its own intelligence of expression. So, it's not like you're sort of doing a meditation thing here, like your twenty minutes of meditation every morning. It doesn't ever stop. And every moment is another gesture. Every moment is the presentation of things just the way they are. In the path, every moment becomes another moment of realization of the true nature of the way things are.

In academic Buddhism, we have these terribly convoluted terms like "suchness," but if you think about where that originally comes from, it was a yogi term. At that level of practice when everything unfolds, every moment, expressing itself in its true nature—and it's wondrously stunning—what else can you say other than "such as it is"? It's not hard to understand what the term really meant, but it got sort of abstract there. This wasn't what it was about. "Such as it is"—what else do you say? And every moment is the expression of *bodhicitta*. The path is now showing itself to itself by itself for the sake of its own realization, and all of that will soften you and open your heart.

Now, ultimate *bodhicitta* is gone beyond being in a state that you realize when you step out of ordinary mind into awakened mind that you have some of the time but not most of the time. Now you understand that ultimate bodhicitta is a way of being in every moment, and you're inseparable from that and are never apart from that because that is who your real nature is. Now you are much more close to approximating the state of mind of Kuntuzangpo, you see, because your mind every moment then becomes the expression of ultimate reality. You just have to open up the one little cloud left: all-at-once-ness.

We think that this little world here is a little bubble that we exist in, that it is like an eggshell. In Dzogchen, you have to crack the eggshell like you're the chicken inside. Then there are millions of worlds here all simultaneously, millions of worlds. And you open all that up, the whole show, and the mind operates on all those levels simultaneously with enlightened activity towards all beings. Every moment in that vast array, every moment is a gesture of compassion until all beings are emptied from the six realms of cyclic existence and repopulated into awakened *dharmakāya* space.

Now, you see, ultimate *bodhicitta* isn't a state. It's the structure of ultimate reality. And it's become your way of being. So, we have relative *bodhicitta*, which comes from self. We have ultimate *bodhicitta* that's a state that's associated with unstable awakening. And we have the living embodiment of ultimate *bodhicitta* every moment as a way of being where your mind and the mind of Kuntuzangpo are now inseparable.

So, imagine all that starts with the simple setting of your intention at the beginning of your practice. These little things turn out to be so important. Hmm? Don't practice aimlessly. You have to aim [Dan raises his arms as if holding a bow and arrow] at the target. And you have to keep that focus at every moment of your sitting practice, and ultimately every moment of your life. Practice isn't sitting on the pillow. Practice is what you do with your mind every moment, in every one of those gestures to you, how you come to see it. How you come to see it.

We translate that term into English from Tibetan as "insight"—insight into the mind, but that's not what the term means. The term that we translate as insight in Tibetan is *lhagthong*. *Tongwa* means to see. *Lhag* means beyond. Every moment is an opportunity for you to see beyond all the seeming solid structures of the mind into its deeper nature, into the awakeness of this mind that's always right here. Like the sun that never stops shining. But you have to see through the clouds to know it's shining. But, if the sun is clouded over by clouds, you're never going to see the sun unless you look for it.

So, we're back to setting your aim. Where you look, the intention you set towards looking, matters. Don't practice if you're not going to see that it takes you somewhere important. And that's not just relaxing and sitting quietly. You can relax and sit quietly in front of a TV set, but that's not going to get you to develop the mind.

Now you can—if you want to see the real liveliness of this, there's a little aid that you can use; we say the central channel from the heart up is "the seat of *bodhicitta*." So, when you have the vast expanse, put the intention of pinpointed focus on this upper central channel, the *kati* tube channel, like King of Samadhi practice—pinpointed focus against the backdrop of the vast expanse. And watch the activity of the liveliness at that location. Do the Heart Lamp first. But then let it open up into that space in the upper central channel. And, in your own experience, see why it's called "the seat of *bodhicitta*." The depth of compassion that you'll come to realize by holding the mind that way will literally melt your heart. See for yourself. You can do that practice. Then we'll talk about it, if you have anything to say.

Good question, as usual. But at some point, if you keep going, we'll have to switch roles here. I'm going to have to start asking you the questions and you're going to have to give the answers. [Dan chuckles] Yes, it's like that.

Anything else?

Student 2

Thank you. So, to start with, a comment. I've been reading a book on cosmology by a particle physicist which describes, among other things, the patterning of matter and energy in the first few seconds after the Big Bang. And there's a graphic in there that has these clumps of matter that look for all the world like Indra's Net. And so, I'm very moved by the cognitive contemplation of this other language that describes the origins of patterning in the universe. It's really stunning. And the question I think is—it feels to me, in a kind of knowing way, that this is real, and it's the same kind of underlying patterning in the universe that one perceives directly in the practice of meditation. My concern is that maybe I'm getting caught up in phenomena, which I think I seem to do …

Dan

Oh, no, not at all, not at all.

Student 2

I shouldn't worry about that?

Dan

No.

Student 2

Okay.

Dan

It's a good question. In the tantras, you often hear *chinang sangwa*. *Chiwa* means from the perspective of the outside. *Nangwa gonay* means from the perspective of the inside. And *sangwa gonay* means from the perspective of the secret [purified] view—outer, inner, and secret. So, if you were to explore external reality and break it down, you can see that it's not really substantial. The whole thing is like a mirage. It visibly exists but it's not solid, it doesn't independently exist. And if you push that external perspective to its limit, like the particle physicists do, you're going to get an external view of Indra's Net.

Now if you are a yogi, and you open up, say, *The Six Lamps*, you open up the ground of being, the infinitely vast expanse of empty awakened awareness space. Then you open up the Heart Lamp so lucid awakeness of an awakened mind dawns like the first morning sun, and it gets brighter and brighter and more lucid. Then you open up the *kati* tube channel. You watch all that awakened bright lucidity become more and more alive. It flares up. It starts coursing in the center of your heart, and it starts defining a pathway; it flows back into the upper central channel and flows up and eventually it connects with the Eye Lamps.

Then you do all the Lamps at once, as you know, simultaneously, against the backdrop of the vast expanse, pinpointed focus on the heart where awakened awareness gets brighter and brighter and flares up and courses, and the channels define their own pathway themselves, by themselves—you don't have to visualize the channels; there's no visualization here. And then you do it all simultaneously, and all that energy from the real aliveness of an awakened mind fuels the Heart Lamp, it fuels the Eye Lamps.

Then you go through the five stages of visions. Everything dances; then you get patterns; then you get entire buddha worlds; then the visions sort of come to an end point—we call that "the full measure" of the visions. And then what's left is *nyakchick*, Indra's Net. It is one vast sphere of ultimate reality, the great sphere, the great *thigle* where all realms and times are contained within that. And all beings are interconnected by loving filaments of *bodhicitta*. That's as far as you can take it. Its one ultimate reality and its vast scope is one living organism, one living universe. And you are that scope at that point. And you've arrived at that from the internal perspective. It's no different than the external perspective.

Or if you just start with the inseparable pair of universal ground, groundless ground, and liveliness, you follow the path of *dharmadhātu* exhaustion, which is much quicker to get there, and you will arrive at the same end point, on the secret path in Dzogchen. And no matter which way you do it—*chi*, the external perspective, *nangdu*, the internal perspective, or *sangwa*, the secret perspective—are [simply] three different ways of looking at the same ultimate universe that you are. So, where's the contradiction here?

You understand it now. The light went on there. Clear enough. There's no place for doubt. Doubt is just another reminder to you, it's just another gesture to you to see it just the way it is. It gives you an opportunity to sharpen your realizations. That's right. So, take doubt as path. Doubt is your friend. Use your friend.

February 3, 2016

Themes: Don't Jump Ahead; Using the Gaze; Positive Qualities

Dan

Welcome everyone. You have a question?

Student 1

I have a somewhat strange question. Of course, I did the one week retreat a few weeks ago and have maintained, mostly daily, sometimes getting to forty-five minutes or an hour, and still doing the *kundalini* stuff. Things have gotten really bright, to the extent that …

Dan

What are you doing in your practice, your daily practice? Let's go through the steps.

Student 1

Twenty-five minutes by myself, I think getting to the Lion's view and a little beyond that; and King of Samādhi and then Tilopa after that. Doing that mostly consistently, if not rotating the Tilopa with a cherishing or compassion meditation. Just found that things are very pixilated, colored pixels. Occasionally, when I close my eyes and when I'm meditating, a I see little focal point of blue light, which is very strange to me and frankly, a little distracting. Just curious what that might be, or if that's just something good to ignore.

Dan

Well, I would caution you on jumping ahead. In your daily practice, a good practice would be to set up your premeditation routine, which includes setting up your posture, setting the motivation; the intention towards awakening and serving the benefit of all beings, *bodhicitta*; calling forth your retinue of masters; making the request for the gift waves of influence; taking a positive quality and cultivating it through the exemplar method; then doing a brief version of emptiness of self (so you go into the concentration meditation not with you doing it as your personal identity, but awareness doing the meditation). Then do your three- and seven-point concentrations. At the end of that, do one of the versions of emptiness of time, so you can shift through the very subtle level of mind and Ocean and Waves, and look more quickly so that you can seal and bring your practice to automatic emptiness.

Then we have to refine the automatic emptiness to the natural state. Don't jump into the view if you do not have strong automatic emptiness in the natural state; and if you try and use the Lion's Gaze, you're going to conceptualize about it, and however legitimate your awakening may or may not be, over time it will deteriorate in conceptualizing about awakening. It hardens the mind and it makes it harder. You have to get rid of that striving towards getting the goal, because it's getting in the way.

The reason why it's getting in the way is because what's happening is your view is deteriorating, however clear it might have been in the course, because it's becoming partialized. What that means is you're describing phenomena from a perspective of duality: there's blue lights, there's various kinds of brightness. What you're doing is that … awakened awareness is now clouded over by luminosity, and you're describing experiences and things rather than awakened awareness. See the difference?

Student 1

Yeah, that's helpful. Thank you.

Dan

What we ask people to do in daily practices, as I said in the course, is to do your pre-meditation routine, do your concentration, because it stabilizes the view. Do Ocean and Waves at least. If your practice is strong and you can go beyond that to automatic emptiness, that's fine. If you can go beyond that and refine that to the natural state, that's even better. But don't use the Lion's Gaze or crossing over views in any way until you can very easily set up the natural state so quickly that just by the intention of looking, you can shift to the natural state. When you have that pliancy of mind, then as part of the teaching relationship, we'll give you the crossing over instructions and how to use them. But if you do it on your own, it's coming out of self and striving and it's going to deteriorate.

The self can't awaken—*can't.* But if the self arises as immediately empty so you see beyond that, if all moments of particularizing arise and you see beyond them, and you don't get caught up in any of that stuff, then it stays fresh. Now, you've not completely lost it, because the more you stabilize awakening, the more it gets accompanied by special states. You get luminosity, and you get bliss, and you get deep stillness, and you get all three at once, which is quite spectacular. But as soon as you see them from a dualistic perspective, you've lost it and they're just states. The languaging you're using says—how you describe it, it's about stuff that you're seeing out there. It's based in duality. You see what's happening? It's deteriorating.

Student 1

Yeah.

Dan

Go back, set the foundation, don't jump ahead, and see all the striving as immediately empty upon arising. Automatic emptiness is a clearing agent. Any instances of doing anything, as soon as they arise, they're expressed as empty upon arising. Any conceptualization, as soon as it expresses itself, is empty upon arising. If you have that automatic emptiness strongly, then no doing, no conceptualization can possibly get in the way. And there's no duality. If you maintain that throughout and set your view up, as we say, on top of that, then the view can't go astray. But if you set it up based on a memory that you had a compelling shift to awakening, or what Tashi Namgyal calls "little flames of awakening," they're not stable, however compelling that experience is, and as soon as it becomes cast in an idea or memory, you get further and further away from it. You see the difference?

Student 1

Yeah, that's very helpful.

Dan

We call that "the flaw of representing in memory." You have a very compelling experience, not just about awakening. It could be a deep *samādhi*. Then the next time, rather than setting up the conditions for that to happen again, what you do instead is you try and remember your way back into it. That doesn't work very well, because you get further and further away from it and you go off track. This summer, Asonam and I translated the main, very large commentary to the foundational practices, the main practices in the Akhrid system, the pointing out instructions for awakening and for cultivating awakening so you have it automatically all the time. One of the things that Shardza Tashi Gyaltsen Rinpoche does with that, which I found very valuable, is once you get a taste of awakening, which is not usually very stable, he lists forty-five ways that you can lose it and go off track.

When we did the Akhrid course, we went through all of those. We asked the students to do their own checklist of which of these applied, because it's common. You're not doing anything different from what most people do with this. So, as soon as there's a striving to push ahead, you're missing the mark.

It's not hard to fix. Understand what I'm saying?

Student 1

I'll probably do a little more Ocean and Waves to get that natural state of mind.

Dan

Just the foundation is Ocean and Waves. On top of that, increase the quickness of the speed of your realization so it becomes automatic emptiness, and then refine it. The natural state is automatically empty—not a shred of duality, simple—which means that all doing is empty upon arising. It's fresh, which means all conceptualization is empty upon arising, and the consequence of that is the field of awareness as inherently, obviously, or transparently lucid because there's no layer of conceptualization to cloud it over. Those are the five conditions of the natural state. The reason why it's important is that if you set up that natural state as your foundation, then the view works, because no conceptualization can get in the way. No trying to look at something in a certain perspective or to fix your mind on anything that can get in the way. There is no reference point. There is nothing to look at. All striving is immediately empty upon arising.

You're using Tilopa. Remember what Tilopa says: "When you don't try and see it, you will see everything there is to see." If you try and see it, that screws it up. It's not a thing that we grasp at. It's always right here. You're raising a very important question for all practitioners. That's why it's important to be followed, because no matter what you realize, there's a strong tendency to go off track with it. Some people just don't get it in the first place. Other people get it, and they go off track. They get lost. They deviate from the path. There are a number of corrections for that. The best one is … for those at best capacity … the best correction is sharpening your own metacognitive intelligence. [That way] you can actually see when you're off track. You can use the same criteria that I'm using. Language matters. It reifies.

If you describe a realization from a partialized point of view, it's not realization. If you're describing a duality, it's not realization. It's not a hard criterion to follow. All I do is listen to how you describe it. You can do the same thing. When you see it, in terms of whether it has duality, whether it's partialized, or whether it's the unbounded wholeness, that discrimination you can make yourself. If you can't make it yourself—or better—until you sharpen that ability; then that's why the relationship with the teacher matters, because then if you go over it, and you're thinking that you're getting the realization but it's exactly that, thinking, then we'll send you back to the drawing board to work on it. In this relational style of teaching, of pointing out, we'll explain to you why it isn't that, and go back and have you work on it. If we're in the Zen tradition, we'd hit you over the head with a shoe or something like that. [Laughter]

Student 1

Thank you very much.

Dan

Understand. Now the other way of doing it is what's called *kyongwa* or protecting or cultivating practice. At the end of your meditation, you don't come completely out of it. You ease up enough to allow your discursive ordinary mind to come back, and then you reflect on what your actual experience is. In a traditional *kyongwa* practice, you compare your experience to the descriptions in the authoritative texts. But since we're not reading the texts, then the next best option is that you compare your experience to what your teachers pointed out to you. There's lots of experiences—you can go all over the map. But there's a particular way we're trying to take you along here, because it leads somewhere important.

It's sort of like you have a TripTik [AAA travel planner] and you're trying to go to a certain vacation spot, and you keep stopping on the way because there are all sorts of interesting things along the way, so you never make it to the vacation spot. We're trying to get you to say, "Remember, this is where you're going; only have the experiences pertaining to staying on that road. Don't keep veering off and making detours somewhere else." There's lots of detours. But they're not what we're looking for.

But you see, I'm not worried about it. Yes, you're jumping ahead. You're not patient. That comes with age. As soon as I tell you that, you have almost immediate recognition of the problem, and you have a sincere motivation to go back and fix it. Where's the problem here? You're going to do it. I don't have any doubt about that, and neither do you. You'll fix it, and then you won't do it in quite the same way.

Even at this age, I'm not any different. I remember when I was working on the bypassing, the *tögal* visions, and it takes a while to get it just right to get it started. All the visions started unfolding and I got really excited, and I went to see His Holiness and said, "Oh, the visions are starting, the visions are started." And he goes, "Ah, they're just visions. You get one vision and you get another vision. They're just visions. No big deal." And it suddenly deflated my balloon, and I sort of dragged my tail out of his room, and I got the point. If you're reacting to it, you're off track.

Then, it was pretty clear. I didn't stray off track after that, because I understood. And that generally happens when you open up some new shift in your mind because your metacognitive intelligence tells you the magnitude of the shift. You know it's important, so you get excited about it. And of course, it's really hard to set that strong foundation in nonreactivity or equanimity of mind. And as soon as we react to it, we're back in duality. And you'll fall out of the view at that point.

A lot of people, particularly in the West, when they get a taste of awakening, the first response when it starts opening up and it's so huge: they get terrified and they shut it down. [Dan chuckles] That's why we say compassion is the gateway, because if you have a strong foundation in compassion, when it starts to open up, you get excited about it and you embrace it for the sake of all beings, and the implication of the strength of that realization, and what it will do in terms of the influence it will have.

So, you come at it with a whole different attitude and there isn't any fear anymore. So, that kind of reactivity, when you shift, is not uncommon at all. If you lock into the structure of reality of the enlightened buddha bodies, that's the magnitude of that shift; it is just awesome, and even there, the tendency to react to it is even greater. So, it's always the same lessons, and you learn them over and over again.

I appreciate your honesty, and your reaction shows a certain sincerity to get it right, so, what more could I ask for?

Student 2

Two questions. One is about … I'm kind of more heady and I'm looking to be more embodied and more compassionate, and on Saturday I heard a talk about meditating from the heart, so I was wondering if you could expound on that, and the other question is just simply that the luminosity is causing my eyes and contacts to dry out fast. And …

Dan

They will.

Student 2

Is there any trick around that or …

Dan

No. First, if you are strongly heady, then *tsalung* practice on a daily basis would help with that.

Student 2

What is that?

Dan

The energy practices.

Student 2

Like the five-channel ones?

Dan

The five main branch channels are pretty safe to do.

Student 2

Yeah.

Dan

So, if you look at Tenzin Wangyal's book *Awakening the Sacred Body*, there's a CD in there that tells you how to do them. You would've done them before in class. I'm sure you've been exposed to them. What it does is two things. If you do them when we do them in class, it sort of slows it down, so you don't get the full impact. You have to slow it down to explain it. But if you do the *tsalung* practices quickly—there are five of them—and if you do all five of them say, three, or even better five, sets each without interruption, and go one to the next to the next, it burns up a lot of that conceptualization. And then the consequence of that is the field of awareness will get very lucid and alert and bright. So, that's the quick way of calming a too active thought mind. And then if you do that as a preparation, you can do the whole thing in ten minutes. And if you go right into your meditation from there, you'll have calmed all that thought mind.

Student 2

So, I do less concentration? I would need less concentration?

Dan

No, just add it on as a preliminary.

Student 2

Okay.

Dan

And doing it that way, that's the best way of handling it; it sort of strips the mind of its conceptual layer. The other practice, if you have too much thought, is to do emptiness of thought.

Student 2

I do that, actually. That's part of my practice.

Dan

So, then you don't get caught up in thought so much.

Student 2

What was that book again, the ...

Dan

Awakening the Sacred Body, by Tenzin Wangyal. It's very well-written. See, there are central channel practices that would use the central channel and the two branch channels. But those are risky, because if you don't do them with a teacher, then you can really screw yourself up badly. But then there's the five main branch channels. There's an upwardly moving channel, there's a life force channel connected with the heart. There's a fire channel connected with the navel. There's an all-pervasive channel connected with the skin, and there's a downwardly moving channel [connected to the lower body functions].

And all of those five channels are connected to the juncture of the central channel, but indirectly. So, if you regulate the energy by doing these movement meditations while you're sitting, it redirects the energy flow of the winds into the central channel in a way that's completely safe, the way that the inner fire practice isn't. So, it's pretty safe to do, and you can do it on your own, and it's a good practice to sort of get out of thought mode, because you're really completely into your body and the body's energy system burns up thought. Then when you practice, there's just less background noise; all that activity and junk is not there to work with, so it gets quieter, so it's just easier to do the concentration, it's easier to recognize the field of awareness.

Student 2

Would it be possible to do that one tonight?

Dan

Sure.

Student 1

It's just that I've only done it once, that one time, one month ago.

Dan

Don't try and be too exacting with them. When Gretchen and I learned them, we learned from three different lamas, and they're all slightly different from the others, so there's no exact way to do them. The intention is what matters.

Student 2

Okay.

Dan

So, that's what I would suggest.

Student 2

Anything else for the eyes or is that just something you learned?

Dan

Yeah, the eyes … the eyes tend to dry out if you have eyes open; so, the best way of handling that is very pragmatic. Intentionally blink every now and then. It washes the eyes. If they really dry out, then use the eye drops, but just don't get distracted so you're always sitting there every moment in the background of your awareness, dividing your attention between the concentration object and the worry about your eyes. The best thing to do is from time to time, disengage from the meditation object, blink, wash the eyes, use drops, and come back to it.

Student 2

Okay, that's what I've been doing.

Dan

In very advanced practices, when you're doing the bypassing or tögal visions, one of the risks if you do the levels of visions all the time—where it's like this fantastic display—is the eyes heat up too much. I suppose in Western terms, we would call it inflammation. But they described it in terms of the concentration of the winds in "the fluid Eye Lamps," and it's like the eyes are on fire. And if your eyes start burning up, they do one of two things: they either give you a concoction of herbs or special mantras that will actually reduce the inflammation by reciting the mantras.

There's a whole world of practices, advanced practices. The gaze matters. How you look matters. Usually in doing concentration, you look with the eyelids about 70 percent closed and the angle of the eyeballs is [angled down] about 45 degrees, looking at nothing in front of you about the distance of an arm's length. That's the usual procedure. If you are doing Lion's Gaze for awakening, then you typically turn the awareness back on itself, and the gaze is straightforward and straight, and that's a whole different world. If you're doing the visions, you look at what we call Iron Mountain Gate, gaze turned up.

So, there's a whole world with each gaze that dials up a different level of cosmic reality. So, the gaze is an advanced level practice matter. So, this idea that you meditate with your eyes closed is primitive, from that perspective.

Student 2

Yeah, it happens during Lion's Gaze.

Dan

Yeah, it happens during Lion's Gaze because you have your eyes wide open.

Student 2

Yeah, that's the only time it dries up.

Dan

Blink, and go right back to what you're doing.

Student 2

Okay. Thank you.

Dan

After a while, you keep opening up that pathway; you don't need the gaze. All you need is the intention to look, and you shift your basis to awakening—you don't need the gaze as a prop, if you will. It just comes naturally. It's a learned pathway, and you've got to keep opening it up.

Student 3

I'm a psychotherapist, and I studied recently a lot of the emotionally focused therapies—Sue Johnson, Diana Fosha. So, in the consulting room, it's really delving into those emotions so that they'll resolve. And lately, from my own practice, I'm wondering about—and perhaps this is just a shot of metacognitive awareness that I need—how do we know when we've truly emptied and resolved some emotion, versus just repressing it?

Dan

Oh, that's a good question.

Student 3

I was really hoping you would say that! Thank you. [Laughter]

Dan

That doesn't mean I'm going to answer it! It's a good question! [More laughter]

The difficulty with answering your question is, we have two different models of the mind here. And in Buddhism and Bon traditions, these are awareness-based traditions. So, there's no concept of an unconscious. Freud doesn't exist in those cultures. There's no concept of psychological defenses, or self-deception. If you have a strong conflictual emotion—what they call *nyermang*, or they call "afflictive emotions"—if you have a strong emotional state, the presumption in Buddhist practice is that you are aware of that emotion.

So, if you have anger, you're aware of your anger, immediately aware of it. If there's an underlying feeling that goes with that anger, like, say, hurt; you would be aware of that. But, in contrast in the West, that's not the case at all. We have a great tradition of studying self-deception. One of the seminal works in psychoanalysis was John Gado and Arnold Goldberg's book, *Models of the Mind*, which came out of the Chicago Analytic Institute, and they look at the different models that Freud had—five different models for the mind at different points in his discoveries. And they say the whole thing comes down to one central point—the problem of disavowal—that the whole psychoanalytic enterprise is about disavowal, that we compartmentalize or disavow certain aspects of our experience, for one reason or another, that are uncomfortable. We're not aware of it. And that's completely alien to the Buddhist tradition.

Now, in that sense, I think the Western psychotherapy tradition adds something that's missing in Buddhism, because if you did patience practice, what Buddhists say is that aggression-related states cause deterioration of all positive states. So, when you're aware of your aggression, you move beyond it. You just don't go there, because it never goes anywhere good. It causes deterioration of all positive states. It's not hard to understand where Buddhism comes in with that. You can think about it in terms of performance, both in the West or the East. Aggression causes deterioration of performance. That's well documented in martial arts. If you piss off your opponent, you're going to win, because they're off their game, and that has been thoroughly exploited in modern American sports. We call it "trash talk." If you piss off your opponents enough, their performance deteriorates.

The best example of that here in Boston was a game two or three years ago, when Kevin Garnett played for the Boston Celtics basketball team, and they were in New York playing against their rivals, the Knicks; and their superstar was Kevin Carmelo Anthony, who at the time was the second-best shooter in basketball. And Kevin Garnett had a reputation of trash talking, and he relentlessly trash talked Carmelo Anthony for the first half of the game, and in the second half of the game, he [Carmelo] missed sixteen shots in a row. In fact, he didn't sink a single basket. This is the second-best shooter in basketball, and he couldn't sink a shot. So obviously, the anger got to him. He was so enraged; he paced up and down in rage after the game was over, waiting to confront Kevin Garnett, who stood inside in the window and just laughed at him for being so caught up in his state, and he got to him.

So, in Western performance, or in Eastern martial arts, anger causes the deterioration of our performance, what we do. In the meditation tradition, anger is said to cause the deterioration of all positive gains of meditation. So, no matter how far along with your meditation experience and your realizations, if you get angry, the whole thing goes down the tubes and you have to start over again. Because once you're angry, you've lost it.

That's why there's that famous passage from the Dalai Lama when a reporter said, "Do you ever get angry at the Chinese?" He said, "Well they invaded my country fifty years ago; our people are scattered all over the world; Tibetans are the dwindling minority in our own country, only 13 percent of the people who live there are Tibetans anymore and most of them don't have land and work permits; most of the resources of the country have been destroyed; and we'll never go back. Do I ever get angry at the Chinese? Why would I give them my mind, too?" That's a statement of patience practice. You move beyond it.

But, in the West we wouldn't presume that. Because the starting point [in Buddhism] is that the meditator knows that he's angry and he practices patience; but in the West we would say, "What about all the people who don't know that they're angry? What do they practice?" They practice bringing it into their awareness first. They have to overcome the problem of disavowal, like in *Annie Hall.* He calls her and she breaks up with him over the telephone. So immediately after this abrupt break up with her, he gets in his car, backs his car angrily into another car, moves forward and smashes into the car in front of him, and backs into another car in back of him, and then the cop comes along; he's babbling senselessly to the cop while the cop's asking him for his driver's license. And while he's babbling, he's defiantly ripping up his driver's license in front of the cop, but he's "not angry!" [Laughter] It's a pretty good portrayal of this—that in the West we have this great tradition of self-deception. We can be angry or we can feel other things and not know that we feel them.

Now, you mention … I don't know Susan Johnson's work enough, but Diana Fosha's work I know reasonably well. And what I find interesting about her work in Western psychotherapy is that it is something that she personally evolved, but it really covers both traditions. It's genuinely integrative because there are three levels to working with affect. When she sits with a patient, she tries to be a good attachment figure. She provides them with a safe haven and is trying to be completely attuned and present to them. And what she does in the way that a good parent would do is she tracks what William James once called the vitality affects. Moment by moment tracking of the shifts in state, being that carefully attuned—which most people don't get.

So, if you're that carefully attuned, then that first level, which is all the defensiveness … if you're in the dyadic relationship, if you're that tuned as the therapist, the people start to get beyond their own self-deception. You start noticing the shifts in their state and you give voice to what you think the affect is and label it, and they start looking at it and they start labeling it. And at some point, if you do that enough, they move beyond all that self-deception and there's a transitional phase where they can actually sense something shifting.

And then they go to the second level, which gets to the core affective state. And it may be different from the first affective state which is more defensive. And then you get to the full experience of that affect; and if, in the therapy relationship you continue to attune and get them to explore good attachment ways and explore their own state and look into it more carefully, at some point there's a second shift to a third level. And that's really interesting because in her model, all emotional states at their core, at that third level, are deeply positive. There's no negative affects anymore.

Now that starts with self-deception and uses the relationship and the careful attunement and the attachment relationship as a vehicle to get beyond self-deception so you can get to the full affective experience; and if you explore and look into that, get the patient to look into that thoroughly, eventually it becomes positive.

Now compare that practice to something like what the Buddhist would do with emptiness of an emotion. So, let's say we have fear. You'd roam around with high-speed awareness. And the more you roamed around looking for the solidness of that, it keeps slipping away. And at some point, there's nothing solid about that emotion left, and there's no reactivity or grab left to it. And what's left is what we call the liveliness of awareness manifesting as the pure energy of manifestation of that emotion. It's deeply positive. So, without using the same language, what Diana Fosha is accomplishing in her three steps—using the awareness of the attachment relationship—ends up to be dangerously close to an emptiness meditation on emotion in Buddhism.

There's a difference, and it's a rather interesting difference. The stages are the same. You end up in this positive place—there's no negative emotions left. The difference is that in the Buddhist tradition you use your high-speed awareness to search through the field until the emotion is empty and you affirm the pure energy of manifestation of that as lively awareness, whereas in therapy, you're using the therapist's careful attunement, their awareness, to search in the context of a dyadic relationship.

Student 3

Almost "pointing out the way."

Dan

Yeah, it's like a pointing out style. But you see the only difference is who the agent of the awareness is; and in that case, she's using the attachment relationship to remind the person how to search their own field of experience. And it's very much like an emptiness meditation.

Student 3

So, no duality?

Dan

No, ultimately there's no duality in either of the systems. I don't think Diana would use that language but that's what she does. I know that for sure because I had her come up to Boston on two or three different occasions and teach to my network, and we had fun once. We did a … I suppose you could call it the "Psychotherapy Battle of the Bands." Right after she taught here a couple of times I said, "Here's what we're going to do. You're going to offer your ADAPT model and all the steps of that in one day in a three-day workshop. I'm going to do my Ideal Parent Figure Attachment Representation model the second day. And I'm going to send you a patient, and we both get two hours to interview that patient on videotape and then we're going to present how the patient responded to both models. And then, after we finish, we're going to get a neutral party to interview the patient about what they thought about both models." Remember the old film, *Gloria*? They had Albert Ellis and Fritz Perls and …

Student 3

Karl Rogers.

Dan

Karl Rogers interviews the same patient. Then they talk with the patient about what they thought about. We did something like that. We did a retake of *Gloria* from an attachment point of view. It was fun! So, I know her work in that sense. It has some similarities you can see.

Student 3

That's helpful. Thank you. Very helpful.

Dan

Mm-hmm [affirmative]. That was a good question. You see, if you push that to its limit, in Sanskrit and therefore Indian Mahāyāna Buddhism, the ultimate state of enlightenment is called buddhahood; and the root Sanskrit word *budh* means realized one. But when those traditions made their way north to Tibet, that's not how the Tibetans translated buddha. The ultimate state, they translated with the Tibetan word *sangye*, and it's a compound term. *Sangwa* means purification, and *gyewa* means flourishing.

And what they're really talking about here is that one of the things that happens as you go along this path is you eradicate all negative states till there's none left. And because they clouded over the positive states, which are the eighty positive states of a buddha mind, all of those come out at once; they flourish. So, if you stabilize awakening and you have this view of the groundless ground of being—the vast expanse of empty awareness space which is the unbounded wholeness of everything there is—within that expanse, everything that arises within that groundless ground arises in an unconditioned way as the lively expression of awakened awareness. It's all the show of awakened awareness.

If you hold that view—what we call "the inseparable pair" of the vast expanse, the space-like vast expanse of awareness and the liveliness of what arises within it—you hold those two views simultaneously and you hold them in such a way that whatever arises within that groundless ground goes completely in its own way; and you don't engage any of it because engaging stuff is what cases karmic impressions to form. Every time we engage anything in our mind, we form a new karmic memory trace. And the billions of memory traces get put in the storehouse mind.

So, if you set up that view and you hold it just right, and you do it all the time, 24/7, you stop forming new karmic memory traces. And it forces the mind to rapidly release all of the previous storehouse of karmic impressions at a rapidly accelerating rate so everything just races through the mind and nothing sticks. We say, like writing on water. And that defines the process of meditation that we call *dharmadhātu* exhaustion. Exhaustion here doesn't mean tired. Exhaustion means you exhaust the bin. You clean it out.

So, if you do that practice all the time, 24/7, on average in about six years, there's nothing left. And you will directly understand that there's no negative experiences left. And all of the positivity of the mind just flourishes. And that becomes your ongoing state.

Many years ago, Jack Engler and I gave Rorschach ink blots to people at various stages along the path.[18] And with those who could do that, it was very interesting because they didn't look like anything we've seen before. They were absent of any negative states, particularly aggression states, and everything was deeply positive; and they were by far the most loving, connected people we had ever encountered in our lives. So, it's possible to fundamentally transform the content of your mind so there's no negative content left whatsoever, and you manifest all the positive states. So, it's not like just these momentary core affects that Diana Fosha talks about. It's a permanent way of being.

That goes far beyond anything we have in the West, of course. But if you follow the path, that's where it goes. And the Tibetans were careful to use a new vocabulary because they wanted to get beyond this first turning of the wheel where everything is about suffering. And they decided, no, it's more about positivity. It's not just getting rid of the negative. It's causing the flourishing of everything positive that's possible. That's a better state to be in for the rest of your life. Now as a therapist, consider the implications of that for mental health. It's not just the absence of illness or psychiatric condition or the absence of negative states.

The goal of mental health from a Buddhist perspective would be the flourishing of everything good. We don't think about that in Western terms in psychotherapy unless it's the small group of people doing positive psychotherapy, which is a relatively new movement. We don't really think that our role as

---

18 They did this research in Burma with members of a Buddhist community—both beginners and advanced—practicing in the lineage of Mahāsī Sayādaw.

therapists is to induce, cultivate, and develop the whole range of positive qualities as an aspect of daily living. But the quality of your living is far better if that's where you're coming from. So why wouldn't that be a legitimate goal? Probably because the insurance industry wouldn't pay for it. [Dan snorts humorously] "I want to be happy." "Well, you get three sessions for that. [Laughter] Right, then you get a happy pill."

Okay. That's a good question. There's a lot to it. But what I like about Diana's work is that it comes really close to the ultimate vision of the mind which is that it's deeply positive. That's not usually a Western psychotherapy view.

Student 3

One more pathology-centered.

Dan

Yeah.

I mean the strongest proponent of that was really Wilfred Bion, the British psychoanalyst. I remember him coming to the US to give a series of teachings; and he was blunt, and he said, "Yeah, it's all crap." That's not a good view of the mind or even a correct one. Now compare that "it's all crap" to the name of the primordial Buddha Kuntuzangpo, which literally means "everything good." So, from that perspective, crap is an illusion. And ultimately if you transform the mind, you return to its original purity and everything is good. That's a better state of mental health, I think.

It's worth developing that more as a goal in the West. See we don't stop as therapists. We just take what's out there. We don't stop and think about where we want people to end up. That's why models like, say, Ken Wilber's Spectrum Model, matters. You clean up the emotional stuff and then you go on to the spiritual stuff. There's an evolution here. You can put the whole thing across one big path, but it doesn't end with psychotherapy. That just cleans up some of the emotional stuff. It's good.

February 10, 2016

Themes: A Healthy Sense of Self Is Important; Emptiness Is Not Nihilistic

Dan

Welcome everyone. You have a question?

Student 1

I've been wondering about the distinctions between working with people to help them develop or improve self-esteem and an internalized locus of self-esteem regulation, and pride from a Buddhist perspective, and …

Dan

Oh, what an interesting question.

Student 1

And what the distinctions are.

Dan

Wow, good question. So, I've got to give you a Western and an Eastern answer to that. Let's start with the West. The psychological sense of self is something that develops over time. Infants don't come into the world with a sense of self that's developed. And as Western self-psychologists tell us, the psychological sense of self develops at around eighteen months. And that corresponds to the development of representational thinking. If you can represent, you can represent self. So, representational thinking as a level of cognitive maturation develops from twelve to twenty months.

So, if you develop the psychological sense of self of what defines "me"—Dan-ness, in my case—there are several experiential consequences to having a sense of self. It serves as a central organizing principle. Once I develop a sense of self, I organize daily experience around Dan-ness.

Second, it's related to the overall level of organization or what we call coherence of mind. So, if I organize my life around Dan-ness, my internal experience is not scattered and chaotic, it's organized around that sense of self. So, the internal world feels more together. You can see that expressed in colloquial language, like "I have it all together," or "I don't really have it together today." That's a statement about organization of mind, and organization of mind is a consequence of having a self-representation.

And thirdly, it provides you with continuity across time, space, and state. So, if I have a sense of self, it has continuity over time; so that was emphasized in Erik Erikson's work. With identity formation in adolescence, it provides a sense of sameness throughout all the changes in one's life cycle.

So, I have had many different developmental ages, and phases of my development for the last sixty-seven years. And, with all the different experiences I've had, I still feel like the same person throughout all that, with all the differences aside. If I travel to different places and I have different roles, I feel like the same person. So, that sameness across time, space, and state is one of the consequences of having a psychological sense of self. We call that object- or self-constancy, in this case. And developing that psychological sense of self would be the first step.

We take that for granted if we have a sense of self, but there are people out there who don't form a psychological sense of self, and that's a problem. Most psychotic individuals don't have a developed sense of self. And there's a story that sometimes you hear me tell about how I once saw a young woman who was a genius; she had 165 IQ, and she read everything, but she also heard voices and she had delusions and passive influence phenomena. She was a young schizophrenic, and she didn't have a sense of self; and she would come in and review in great precision twelve different theories of literary criticism. And then I would find myself saying to her, "That's all well and good, but what's your view?" And she couldn't answer the question because there was no central self, central organizing principle that could say, "This is what I think." So, I'd ask questions like that frequently to get her to develop some metacognitive capacity to shape that sense of self, as a central organizing principle. So, that's the first step.

Once we develop, or children develop a sense of self, as a core sense of themselves, the next step is what's called self-agency. Self-agency is the internal representation of yourself as an effective agent in the world and the world of others. It starts with physical agency. I remember when my kids were young, I would patiently build up some blocks; and they would wait for me to build up the blocks and then they would smash them apart. And they developed a sense of agency, of having the effect of smashing them all down. We'd do that endlessly. [Dan chuckles] Six months later, they would be building them up and developing a more complex sense of agency from constructing something rather than destroying something. But still, what they're doing is they're representing, in the mind, having an effect on the physical world.

Later, particularly with the acquisition of language, kids develop a sense of agency in relationship. They can verbally and nonverbally communicate their needs, and in a good enough attachment relationship, they have a sense of directly affecting the parent. We think that it's one-sided, that the parents affect the child's internal world by careful attunement and responsiveness. But it works the other way, too. Tiffany Fields once coined the term "infant eliciting behavior." Infants shape their parent's behavior, and smart kids know how to do that contingency shaping. They can actually get their parents to respond the way that they want. And from that, they develop a healthy sense of agency, that they actually have an impact on others.

There's a whole class of people out there who never develop agency. They have a sense of self, but they never develop agency. So, they feel like the world of relationships happens to them, rather than making it happen, because what's missing is the agency. Usually, the agency comes in two stages. First is the effect on the physical environment and second the effect on others, in relationships.

And then thirdly, once you develop agency, the next step developmentally is self-esteem. And I like the definition that developed at the Hampstead Clinic in London: "Self-esteem is the developmental linkage of positive emotional states to the self-representation." That's a developmental outcome. You learn to coalesce around that sense of self, of positive emotional states. You link them together.

So, what that means is that if you have healthy esteem and you've developed that linkage as an older child or an adult, when you conjure up your sense of self in daily life—if I conjure up Dan-ness—I evoke it against the backdrop of positive feeling. That's what self-esteem means experientially. But there are people out there who, when they evoke their sense of self, haven't developed that; they haven't achieved that developmental task. So, when they evoke their sense of self, they have a strong sense of self, but they just evoke it against no feelings.

So, they might be high functioning, but they feel like there's something fundamentally missing in their life, and they can never pin down what that is. Or they evoke the sense of self, and they evoke it against the backdrop of mostly negative feelings, in which case they're depression-vulnerable. But what they can't do is evoke it against the backdrop of positive feeling. In Western terms we call them narcissistically vulnerable, which basically means chronic self-esteem failure.

So, you can think of three stages in self-development in Western terms: the development of the sense of self as a representation; the development of agency, particularly inter-personal agency; and thirdly esteem, feeling good about yourself. And that you can have a developmental arrest at any one of those levels. Some people don't have a sense of self, and if they don't have the sense of self, they don't have agency or esteem. They just don't know who they are. That's mostly in the psychotic range. Some people have a sense of self, but they don't have agency. We call them personality disordered. Some people have a sense of self and they have agency, but they don't have esteem; we call them narcissistically vulnerable.

It's one thing to know who you are, it's another thing to know what you're about and the impact you make on the world and the world of others. And it's yet another thing to feel good about yourself. Those are three successive developmental achievements.

And the outcome of that in Western terms is what we would call the structurization of the self. You develop the self as a solid internal structure in mind. So that means that, in Western terms, there's a number of people out there who don't complete those stages in the way that we would normally expect. We would say that they have significant self-pathology, and it happens on one of three levels. Either they don't have any sense of self, or they have a sense of self but they don't have agency, or they have a sense of agency but they don't have esteem, at which point they use the agency and over compensate with the agency to compensate for the lack of self-esteem, which is why narcissistically vulnerable people are often very accomplished and very successful, because they never feel good about themselves so they're always driven to do more and more. And then you can't get off that cycle, so you become a Republican presidential candidate. [Dan and others laugh.] Sorry, I couldn't resist that. But that's what I would say in Western terms.

So, what's the issue? Not knowing who you are, not knowing what you're about, or not feeling good about yourself? And in Western terms, we always work from the bottom up developmentally. So, if they have good agency, then you work at self-esteem issues and developing that. If they have a sense of self, but they have no agency and no esteem, then you work at the agency issue. If they have no agency and no esteem, then work on the sense of developing the self. And you have to develop that first, because when you look at self from a Buddhist perspective as empty, you're trying to see it as just a representation. Those practices of emptiness of self—and particularly the earlier practice of a more nihilistic version of no self in the earlier turning of the wheel—are problematic.

In the 1970s, Jack Engler and I wrote somewhat extensively about that in our *Transformations of Consciousness* with Ken Wilber. And what we found is that when Burmese mindfulness retreats were just getting popular in the West, there was a significant number of people who would go for the first time on a three-month retreat, which is a long time. There were a number of those young kids in their twenties who did have very poor self-development. They never really developed a strong sense of self. So, they would go on these retreats, silent retreats for a month, get more depersonalized, the sense of self would get more vague, they would get more panicky about it because they would lose their sense of self, and yet they would somehow use the language of early Buddhism, like the language of no self, as if somehow that validated their experiences—"finally somebody understands me." So, they'd gravitate to the retreat for the wrong reason, as if somehow Buddhism seemed to understand or talk this language of no self, so that finally they were understood, and they would get better. And they did all the wrong things, like isolate themselves from relationships completely in the silent retreat and think that somehow that's going to make the self better. It doesn't.

I remember one guy who was actually a TM'er. He did a long round in TM, starting when he was nineteen. He did TM all day long for ten years. He was a serious concentrator, until ten years later he had a psychotic depression, and was hospitalized. And then quite poignantly he said, "Look I just wasted ten years. I used meditation in the service of escape, and I never dealt with the issue of not having a clear sense of self. Now it's much worse, and I've wasted a decade." And unfortunately, what he said was right. So, it took some degree of repair to sort of build the self in the right way for the first time. So, in Western terms, you have to develop the sense of self as a prerequisite to working with emptiness of self. Or as Jack Engler once said, "You have to be somebody before you can become nobody."

The people who have a weak sense of self do these practices for the wrong reason and they get all messed up with them. So much so that in the early days we recommended that these retreats pull people from the retreat and then send them to therapy instead. Because that's what they really needed: a good, self-psychologically orientated treatment that would repair the esteem issues.

But here's the problem. In Western terms, the methods that we use to work with self-esteem are at best primitive because we have blind spots in our knowledge. And here's what Buddhists' *Abhidharma* psychology says, which I agree with, which is, "The techniques used to develop and work with negative states of mind and the techniques working with positive states of mind complement each other, but they're not reducible to each other."

So, if you want to—if you introduce methods to reduce negative states and they're effective, you should expect the relative reduction or maybe the absence of negative states. But the absence of a negative is not a positive. It's just the absence of a negative. So, you see the problem here. Almost all of our Western psychology is around working with negative states.

The psychoanalytic tradition works with inter-psychic conflict, a negative state. The cognitive behavioral tradition works with limiting beliefs, maladaptive schemas, negative self-talk, maladaptive behavior. Developmentally informed therapy works with developmental deficits. Every great tradition of Western psychotherapy is designed to work with negative states—the one exception being the most recent movements in positive psychology, which are young.

So, you can't repair a self-esteem problem if you take the definition that I gave you: that the problem with self-esteem is the failure to develop and then link positive emotions of the self-representation. How was working with negative states ever going to help with that? Because it misses the point. Their methods are too indirect. You need to develop positive emotions directly related to the self.

The classic example of that was a paper by Heinz Kohut, the grandfather of self-psychology. He wrote a paper called "The Two Analyses of Mr. Z." And, in that classic paper, written in the early '70s, the story was of a patient who came to Kohut with a lot of work-related issues and inhibited himself a lot—in meeting his potential at work and all the competition issues—and also had very poor esteem. And as the story goes in that paper, Kohut saw him for a number of years with a classic analysis and saw all that competition stuff and low esteem was basically oedipal issues. And the guy never got better. Then, he came back to Kohut after some interruption of the analysis, and he explained all the things that were missing in the analysis, and that he needed to focus on the self-esteem issues and do it completely differently. And Kohut had the presence of mind to say, "Let's approach it completely differently." And he developed a self-psychological approach. That was the first seminal paper.

Then the development was that we needed to focus with more careful attunement to our narcissistically vulnerable patients since classic analysis makes them worse. One of the things that Kohut said in that paper is if you focus on negative states with people who are narcissistically vulnerable and you do the classic thing, which is interpret defenses, what happens to the narcissist? They hear the interpretation as making them feel worse about themselves, so it actually erodes the self-esteem, which is a problem in the first place, and they get worse, which was the legacy of Mr. Z.

We now know that there's no Mr. Z. Mr. Z was Kohut, himself. I know that because he was one of my supervisors, so I know the story firsthand. He was really writing about his own experience about why a classical psychoanalysis couldn't possibly work with somebody who was narcissistically vulnerable. And he, towards the end of his life, began to focus on positive states because he thought that was important in people who are narcissistically vulnerable.

I'll tell you a story about that. It's sort of a funny story, but many years ago, in the mid-1970s, we gave Rorschachs to people at various stages of meditation. And we found that at the beginning of this, they would look at the Rorschach inkblots and they would see bats and butterflies and people. But when they got really deeply concentrated and all thought activity stopped, they would see ink. And they would spend just as long looking at the shape of the ink, but they wouldn't make it into anything because the thought elaboration had stopped.

And then when they go to the very subtle level of mind that we call Ocean and Waves, they would have infinite creativity, and the content would change all the time. Then when it got to the stage of first awakening, the Rorschachs looked like ordinary Rorschachs, except there was no defensiveness. The reactivity of the mind dropped off. Then we looked at the people who had *dharmadhātu* exhaustion. They were like nothing we'd ever seen before. They had no negative states left, completely cleaned up of all negative states. So, the Rorschachs changed dramatically at different levels of practice.

My mentor at the time was Erika Fromm—who was at the Chicago Analytic Institute—because I did my training at University of Chicago, and that's where I worked with Kohut at Michael Reese Hospital. Erika said, "Why don't you come down and present this meditation research at a brown-bag lunch to the analysts?" So, I was young in my career, and I presented this to the analysts, and they destroyed it. They were not subtle. They just thought this is all isolation of affect and defensiveness. And they just completely decimated everything I just presented.

Kohut sat there very calmly munching his sandwich. He didn't say anything, but he had the last word. At the end of the talk he said, "Look, you guys can't talk with each other. He's trying to tell you that this is very unusual data, and you're reducing it to classic psychoanalytic terms because that's all you know. And he's trying to tell you it's different from this, and you can't hear it. So, here's the way I look at it. Ask yourself the question: what kind of people come out of this meditation? Are they kind? Are they altruistic? Are they sensitive to others? And if the answer to that is yes, then he's got something here you can't explain away." That was his last comment. Nobody said anything after that. He died three weeks later. That was his last gift to me.

He had something he had discovered through his own misdirection in psychoanalysis that there needed to be a different approach to self-esteem. And that if you take people who are narcissistically vulnerable, who generally mostly feel bad about themselves, and you try and have them feel good about themselves, then that works better than interpreting things because the interpretation is they end up feeling worse about themselves. They feel shamed by interpretation, even if the interpretations are correct. See the difference?

So, because I was interested in the short-term work and visualizations, we, in the '80s, developed a protocol that worked very well for people who are narcissistically vulnerable. And, as a visualization, I'll do that with all of you tonight if you want. It's based on the work of Sander, who said basically, "Self-esteem is the developmental linkage of positive feelings to the self-representation." So what if, we thought, you simply had a person imagine a situation in their life where they felt really good about themselves, and generate that scene and feel their way back into the emotion? And you're getting them to directly generate positive feelings about the self and link it to the self. And what if you kept doing that over and over again? We found that it worked.

Imagine a scene where you feel really good about yourself—especially good about yourself, where you really liked yourself. Even the most narcissistically vulnerable person you're ever going to meet in your life can always relate that to situations. So, the first part of the protocol is situationally based self-esteem, feeling good about yourself in certain situations. The trouble with a narcissist is they can feel good about themselves in certain situations, but they can't sustain it because it's limited to doing well in that situation, usually through agency. Are you following me? Now, if you do that and you generate the effect, and you amplify the effect, and keep doing it over and over again, they get to the point that they can, like any other kind of learning, they can generate that good feeling associated with the self pretty much at will.

Then, the next part of the protocol is to imagine good feelings about yourself in relation to others. That's harder.

The third is what we call skill development and includes a number of steps. See how quickly you can generate this good feeling about yourself—immediacy. See how long you can sustain it—duration. See if you can bring it into some other situation you don't normally feel it in—transferring the state of mind. What you do is you introduce into the therapy the task of doing it more immediately, holding it longer and longer, and eventually bringing it outside of this visualization to everyday life. And then as the last part of the skill development, we actually give them assignments. They practice the visualization at home, and they have to keep a journal in terms of how long they can sustain it in daily life. The actual expectation is for them to extend the good feeling about themselves for longer and longer duration, and they have to come in and report to you. They need the structure to see how long they're actually sustaining it. And at some point, what happens is they're holding a good feeling about themselves more of the day than not, and everything starts to shift.

The next phase is called "challenge." They generate a good feeling about themselves, and we make a list of all the situations they don't feel good about themselves. And you have to have them; with visualization, hold a good feeling about themselves in exactly the situations that are hardest. Then you give the homework assignment to go out and evoke that good feeling and hold it in the most difficult situations. So, even then, they can hold it.

And the last phase of the protocol is what we call the transition from doing to being. Now, they can hold a good feeling. They don't have to do anything to get it; it's just a matter of who they are in their being. And when they can do that, there's no relapse—average time, six months to two years. Not bad given that most self-psychological analyses are ten years, because they focus on exactly what the problem is. What's missing is generating good feelings about the self.

What causes that problem, from an attachment point of view? One of the necessary ingredients of healthy attachment of a parent to a child is what I call expressed delight. Healthy parents are effusive about, show the joy about everything the child does, and they're not subtle about expressing it. There's the positive affect. The parents are constantly effusive about everything their child does, and that's so infectious that the child will internalize that during the phase when they're developing representational thinking. But the reason why we have an epidemic of narcissism in this culture is because that's what's missing out of all the other things that we do in terms of healthy attachment—because parents are too busy.

So, parents are really good with the job of attachment. They're not very good with the joy of attachment. They don't enjoy their kids. They're too busy to enjoy their kids. But kids who are raised with healthy esteem, their parents are effusive and expressive all the time about everything the child does. It's a source of delight for them. The child knows that they're the central thing in this parent's life. And their whole life, their whole parent's life, revolves around everything this child does.

But more importantly—and this is the issue—the child perceives that their being matters. The parent is delighted in the child's being. Narcissists never get that, so they always have to *do* things in order to ever feel good about themselves because they can't just be and feel good about themselves. That's what's missing. We don't live in a culture where we have that kind of joy in our kids, and that's why we have so many people out there who are narcissistically vulnerable. They're always having to prove themselves.

The heart of this is a rather simple principle: generate the self, link positive emotion to it, keep adding on more positive emotion, sustain the duration of that until, after a while, it tips the whole balance and they hold that good feeling as an evocative memory most of the time. So, they walk around with a backdrop of good feeling—exactly what they didn't have before.

And you can see, here's the problem with a blind spot in Western therapy. Nobody does that because we're always interpreting meaning, and, you know, all that stuff just makes them feel worse about themselves because it doesn't get to the heart of what's wrong. So, our bias, what we think we do in therapy, is just not well-matched to what narcissistically vulnerable people need. So, that needs to be developed. And then, in Western terms, "you have to be somebody before you can be nobody."

In Eastern terms, the issue of self depends on what stage of Buddhism we're talking about. In the early Buddhism, one of the three signs of what you got out of your practice was what's called *anatta*. During deep concentration meditation, your sense of self would drop away, and there would be awareness doing the meditation, rather than, in my case, Dan. Just this thought gets deconstructed. Self-representation gets deconstructed.

That led into a 500-year debate. And what came out is something very different. And that was the theory of emptiness of self. And emptiness means "just a construction." In other words, Mahayāna Buddhist thinking on emptiness of self is not very different from Western constructivist psychology. The psychological sense of self is a representation; it's a construction. In relative reality, that's useful. But here's the difference. Ultimately, it's just a representation, and where emptiness comes in, in terms of Mahayāna Buddhist practice, is the problem of what they call *nozhyin* in Tibetan, which means taking it as too real. I actually think that Dan exists as an independently existing thing. I actually think I was born with Dan-ness, and I take Dan way too seriously. I forget that it's just a representation.

By reifying, by taking it as too real in Buddhist terms, that has two consequences. One is "grab." The self has a lot of grab to it. If you don't like what I'm saying, and you disagree with me, I'll get reactive to that, and I can experience grab. If you like what I'm saying, and you praise what I'm saying, then I'll get reactive to that and I'll experience grab. We can perceive grab. In Mahayāna Buddhism, the origin of suffering is all the grab of daily life organized around self. The other problem is *mūmpa*—the self becomes so solid it clouds over the real nature of an awakened mind. And as long as I'm operating out of self, I'm not operating out of the awakened nature, which is always right here. In fact, if I try and take the self and have Dan grasp after awakening, as if it's a state I could grasp after, that doesn't get me very far, does it? Where Buddhism comes in, it says, "Yes, the self is a representation that develops from certain causes and conditions." And in relative reality, that's useful because it's a central organizing principle. But don't take it too seriously because, ultimately, it's just a representation and if you make it too solid, there are consequences of that. Your experience has grab, and that causes suffering, and then it clouds over your true nature.

In the theory of emptiness, there's a lot of work to try and correct for what was called the problem of nihilism. You don't get rid of the self. That's nihilism. You don't get rid of the self. You get rid of its capacity to obscure. So, insight meditation, the word in Tibetan, doesn't mean insight. It means *lhag-tong*. *Tongwa* means seeing, and *lak* means beyond, so you're seeing beyond the seeming solidness of the self into the deeper nature of the mind's awareness. That's what it means to have insight. That's useful.

So, there's nothing incompatible about Western theories of constructing a self in relative reality, and then on the level of ultimate reality [in Buddhism], seeing that it's just merely a construction. In fact, they fit together rather well. You have to develop the sense of self because that helps you in relative reality, and people who have a stronger sense of self do better in everyday life; but then you can move beyond that by seeing that it's just a relative construction of mind so it doesn't cause suffering and it doesn't get in the way of things, so you can come closer to your true nature. So, these two kinds of practices go together pretty well. And if you like, we'll do the self-agency and self-esteem protocol in Western terms, see what it's like to develop that sense of self. And then, we'll switch gears and do the emptiness of self.

If you do emptiness of self, you don't lose the self. You just go beyond it. It's still there. You shift your basis of operation. Another way of saying this is that that's not where you're coming from anymore. You're operating out of a field of awareness that's cleaned up of self. It still exists; you just don't get rid of it. As many of you heard the story, I'll say it for the people who haven't been before, but it reminds me of my first clinical placement at Michael Reese, where Kohut was the head of my department; and in the 1970s, it was Roy Grinker. He was old enough to tell me the story of his personal analysis with Sigmund Freud. And Freud pushed people. Most of his analyses were two months long, three months, never ten years or twenty years like Woody Allen.

He told me this story that Freud was really pushing him, and he was changing so rapidly, he was afraid that he wouldn't know himself anymore. Freud sensed that, and Freud leaned over and said, "Roy, when you finish your analysis, your friends will probably still recognize you." [Laughter] Likewise, if you do emptiness of self correctly from a Mahayāna perspective, your friends will probably still recognize you. You don't lose it. You just see beyond it.

But for people in the West who are narcissistically vulnerable, they hear the language, or mishear the language, of no self as if it gives them a validation for significant self-pathology. They don't need to go off and do long silent retreats where they have no interaction with people. What they need to do instead is to be pulled out of the retreats and go into a good relational-based therapy where the focus is on building the sense of self or self-agency or self-esteem. And if they don't do that then it just gets worse, like the guy I told you about who spent ten years in a psychotic depression. Does that get to your question, pretty much?

Student 1

I guess, pride is one of the poisons, or …

Dan

Sure. Well, let's look at pride in Western terms and then we'll look at it in Buddhist terms, okay? Because that was the second part of your question. Thanks for reminding me.

Pride has to do with self-reference, calling attention to yourself. And in Western terms, people who are narcissistically vulnerable, we would say are "proud" because they never feel good about themselves; they are always calling attention to themselves. And no matter how much they call attention to themselves, no matter what they do, they never can feel good about themselves. So, the calling attention to themselves gets inexhaustible. But they need to do that, otherwise they can never feel good about themselves.

Unfortunately, in the diagnostic literature, when people define narcissistic personality, they say that the person was grandiose—they've got an inflated self-esteem. But anybody who's ever worked with narcissistically vulnerable people knows that the flip side of that is equally true. People can either have a grandiose and too high a sense of self, or they can have the opposite, which is a degraded sense of themselves. And those two things are a pair that always go together.

What they can't find is a middle path. They either are calling attention to themselves and get more and more grandiose, so they get filled with themselves and more out of control. Look at Donald Trump when he talks. No, I'm not trying to say that facetiously. What worries me about him is that the more he gets media attention, the more grandiose he gets, and the more insensitive he gets, and he gets more and more filled with himself, that's scary. That's how Hitler started.

But, you see, the problem there is that when people have an underlying felt sense of insecurity, and they can't feel good about themselves, they're constantly trying to find ways of calling attention to themselves. And in certain contexts, they will get more self-inflated and grandiose, and it escalates. But the opposite of that is also true for the same person. They can get really down on themselves at times. It all depends on context.

My first Root Lama had an interesting way of talking about that. He talked about the pride of lowliness, meaning that people who always put themselves down, he said that was just as much pride as the people who were always elevating themselves. It's an interesting way of looking at it, because it is the same issue. It's just the valence is different, whether it's elevated or whether it's degraded. Still, it's pride. It's about perpetual inexhaustible self-reference, or what Ḥāfeẓ, the Sufi poet, calls "the tiresome project of maintaining the self." Isn't that a nice one?

Yeah. So, you see, there's the problem. Whether it's elevated or whether it's degraded, the problem is still that they don't have that sense of self that's just clean. They don't need to do that self-reference anymore, they just feel okay about themselves; they don't feel strong in themselves. So, that's a kind of pride, but the pride can either be the pride of elevation or the pride of lowliness. And both are the same kind of pride.

Now, in Buddhist terms, it's a little different, because, yes, they talk about two kinds of pride. And one kind of pride is pride of ordinary beings. It would include being elevated or degraded, and that's no different, East and West. But in Buddhism and in some other spiritual practices, or some of the early Desert Fathers, too, you get a different issue, and that's spiritual pride.

John Cassian, who was one of the early scholars of the Desert Fathers of the church talked about that. And he reserved that for people who've actually gotten somewhere in their practice, their spiritual practice; and it's the belief that you actually got somewhere. [Dan chuckles] And what Cassian said about it, which I think is worth noting, is that the further along in your spiritual practice, the more advanced you are, the more spiritual pride is a problem, not the less. So, it's not an issue for ordinary people—it's reserved for people who actually get somewhere with their practice. And the more you get somewhere with your practice, the more you have to watch out for spiritual pride, because it can very easily shade off into something rather mundane, which is that of self-importance.

And how many spiritual teachers have we seen from the East come to the West and get bitten with the rich-and-famous bug, or the sexual misconduct bug? And they come over here; I mean, probably the worst of that is if you think about somebody like Sogyal Rinpoche, who wrote a bestseller, *The Tibetan Book of Living and Dying*. So far, so good, it's a crystal-clear book; it was on the bestselling list for over a year. But following that, he collected about twelve Lamborghinis and Ferraris and fifty sexual misconduct allegations. So, something went wrong. So, he didn't do a good job with handling all that pride that comes out of becoming that important in the West and producing a bestseller—for a year, or over a year. It's a problem. And the conduct is abominable.

And how many stories have we heard like that? That's one of the worst ones, but throughout East and West monastic traditions where people get somewhere in their spiritual practice, and they get involved in the self-importance as teachers, or their self-importance in accumulating money or a center and all that kind of stuff. And it leads to pride.

We're particularly vulnerable to that here in the West, particularly with self-realized people. And there can be very legitimate realizations, but if they come on their own, there's no checks and balances. That's the difference between doing it in a lineage tradition, because with them there are always checks and balances.

So, you work on the pride. I remember going to my teacher, Menri Trizin, because he sort of looks right into you, and he can read minds. And I found that pretty useful in retreats because all I would have to do is show up in his room, and he said, "Now do this." And I didn't have to explain my meditation. Useful.

I remember going to him once, and he said, "You're doing a lot of teaching around the world." He says, "Watch for the pride." I said, "Busted. Thank you." And I find that helpful, because I never go that far, because he'll bust me. [Dan chuckles] And I look forward to that. He'll find a way of busting me one way or the other. But he'll do it with kindness, and some great humor.

So, the pride thing is problematic, spiritual pride. And it's a big problem in the West when you have people teaching who might have legitimate realizations, but they don't come out of lineage traditions. They come out of self-discoveries. I mean, there are teachers who … I remember teaching at a center once, and there was somebody else teaching there at the same time. I mean, we worked our butts off; we teach morning, afternoon and night. You don't sit there silently. Every retreat is—every class is different. You're always moving along with this thing. It's a lot of work to do these retreats.

And there was another teacher there, not from a lineage. I had taught at this center for two or three times, and it was a nice center in some ways. And then I show up about an hour before we're going to teach and we've got a … they have a nice faculty residence place overlooking the mountains, and they say, "Well, that's not where you're staying."

I said, "What happened?"

"Oh, this other teacher is taking it for her attendants."

And I said, "Who is this person?" It's a Western person and their entire spiritual path became going to the Ganges River, looking in somebody's eyes, and saying, "I got it." That's it.

I worked for forty-five years. And I said, "You're taking me, who's been a part of a lineage tradition for forty-five years, and [accompanied by] a Zen master, and you're bumping us for her attendants, as a Westerner?" I said, "How disrespectful is that?" I said, "Let's look into the teaching."

Turned out her teaching involved putting on videotapes all day and showing up for one hour a night. Now that's pride. I said, "If you guys can't see the difference in the quality of the teaching here, I have absolutely nothing to teach here." As for the center, she had written a book, so they wanted to market it, so it's all about money-making. I said, "That's not the place to teach. If you can't see the preciousness of these teachings, bye. You won't see me again." The Zen master said the same thing.

So, we have to watch out for Western bullshit. Because what you get is people who are, they might have something, but it doesn't get refined because it's never part of a lineage tradition. And it represents, ultimately, the self that never got dealt with enough in the emptiness of self meditations. So, it's all about spiritual pride and thinking that you're important as a teacher. That's a problem.

Another person I know is a very good teacher, except the problem—where I disagree with him is that it all came from his own realizations, and when he teaches, all he does is talk about his own realizations. He never shows you what to do. So what good is that? If he calls attention to the self that much, there's something fundamentally wrong with it.

If you can't see that with your own intelligence, then maybe you deserve that teacher. Because the way I look at all this Western crap about all the messes that we've made with spiritual teachers is that both the teacher and the student are responsible for that. The teacher is responsible for exploiting the situation—that's a serious karma. The student's responsible for not using good judgment. Nobody asked you to park your intelligence outside the door when you walk into the meditation hall. You have to use your best metacognitive intelligence to see what you're getting and see accurately what you're getting. If it doesn't feel right, don't do it.

My first Root Lama was Mongolian. He wasn't even Tibetan. He was a horse trader, and he said, "Don't buy just any horse. Check out the hooves, check out the teeth, make sure you're getting a good horse. Do the same thing with your teacher. Don't just buy the teacher. Check out the teacher's hooves." Good advice.

So, you can see that we've made a mess of that in the West. And it's all around this issue of narcissism, because why do we keep messing it up in the West? Because we have a narcissistically vulnerable culture, where the great majority of people don't feel good about themselves. So, what do you do if you don't feel good about yourself? You idealize. And where there's idealization, the higher you idealize somebody, the bigger the fall. Idealization is followed always by disillusionment, and both sides contribute to that. But it's a cycle that you can easily see and avoid, and it's not necessary. It's a stupid cycle; it is always damaging.

So, beware of people who are too self-important, because if you learn anything in spiritual practice, there's no place for spiritual pride. Or, I like to say, "If you learn one thing in spiritual practice, it's that self-importance isn't terribly important." Or somebody once sent me a cartoon, and the cartoon said, "I finally looked at the bigger picture in life. I wasn't in it." It's a good cartoon.

That's what I would have to say about it. Does that answer your question about the pride?

Student 1

Mm-hmm (affirmative).

Dan

The further along, the more you have to watch for it.

In the Christian early Desert Fathers, one thing that's unique is the work of Saint Simeon. The Desert Fathers were at the formation of Christianity. [At that time] there were a number of [Christian] yogis. It started with Saint Anthony who went off to the desert and did serious practices. They evolved the practice called Prayer of Quiet, and then they refined that. The movement started in about the year 150 A.D. and peaked at about 250 A.D. and then died out by about 400 A.D. It was very popular, so popular that some people were leaving the church and running off to study with the Desert Fathers. It became very popular, so much so that the church got threatened by it and they sent out several great scholars to debunk it, and they didn't do a very good job of debunking it. They gave it a very positive billing.

Anthony was the first, and then there are others who are the greats of that tradition. They didn't write anything down. All we have left is student notes. And some of the greats were Evagrius and Macarius the Egyptian. And one guy who was pretty interesting in that group was Saint Simeon, because he wrote and he defined spiritual practice in terms of levels of humility. So, the greater the refinement of your spiritual practice, the more humility you developed. It's a nice model, something I think that we should use for modern Western athletes. [Laughter]

So, they left some good things behind, but not a lot. And then, it mostly died out because the church made active attempts to suppress it, because what they were saying was something that threatened the fundamental theology of the church because the church evolved as a power-based organization around the historical life of Jesus and believing in Jesus. And that's not what Saint Anthony said. Saint Anthony said if you did these practices you'll become Jesus. And everybody has Jesus nature. It's sort of like buddha nature. You can see why the church wouldn't want these practices that anyone could do and evolve themselves. So that's why it was doomed at some point not to exist.

May 4, 2016

Themes: Constructions of Mind; Grab; Emptiness Practice

Dan

Welcome everyone. You have a question?

Student 1

It's been occurring to me lately that I mentioned to you, Dan, that I've been getting into snorkeling lately. And that wonderful experience of being in the water, feeling at one with the water, moving with the currents with no resistance, and seeing so much. Doing exactly that, moving with the currents without resistance, and being in this, quote, other element of water.

Dan

If you stop seeing things out there in the water, you'd be in a natural state so easily.

Student 1

Well, that's, that's exactly it, I think. It occurs to me that—you know, I just sobbed about it my whole flight home the other night from the Keys. And it was about—you know, in the past what I was sobbing about would have been recognized by me as pain and grief, and so forth. And it wasn't like that at all. The topics were, in a sense. But the line that came up in my mind is like, "it appears that we are all petals of the same flower." And it occurs to me that in the water there's that experience, and out of the water there's that experience. And there is no in and there is no out, and what's in is out, and what's out is in. So, I'd love you to comment on that.

Dan

You've already got your visualization, so what's to comment on?

Student 1

And there's some aspect of this related to the body. You know, like, that's a thing that's been shifting, too, is I think I even experienced my own body as something, in a sense, that, like, with some kind of separation from me. And there's, like, that seems to be an element, like, too. And yet not nothing.

Dan

Well, so this is maybe a good metaphor to understand the conditions in which it's easier to realize the natural state of the mind, *nelu*.

Student 1

In the Caribbean? [Laughter]

Dan

So, all we have to do is to go to the Florida Keys. [Laughter]

So, there are too many conditions of the ordinary mind that cloud over the mind. So, it's very difficult to directly realize awakened nature. But in the Essence traditions, as you know, the metaphor to understand the real nature of the mind's awakened nature is the metaphor of the sun and the clouds. So, if it's raining, and at some point the rain and the clouds clear, we say, "The sun just came out." But that's not correct. The sun's always out. The sun inexhaustibly shines day and night. But from the perspective of being under the cloud, we can't see what's already shining until we remove the clouds, and we'll have cracks in the clouds that the sun shines through. A more accurate statement would be, "Now I can see the sun has always been shining."

And it's like that with the ordinary mind and the awakened mind. Always right here is an infinitely vast ocean of awakened awareness-love. That is your true nature, your buddha nature. But you don't recognize it because the ordinary mind has layers and layers of clouds. And until you clear away the clouds, you can't see the radiance of the awakened mind that's clouded over by all the seemingly substantial solid structures of the mind.

So that's where emptiness practice comes in. A good synonym for emptiness is "merely a construction of mind." Or another good synonym for emptiness is insubstantial. The structures of the mind are not independently existing. They're not solid. They're just constructions. They still exist. But they exist only on a level of relative reality, because there are certain causes and conditions that make them exist that way. We have thought. Thought's not going to go away. Thought comes and goes because the mind, by nature, generates conceptualization. The ordinary mind isn't going to stop generating conceptualization. You're never going to stop thinking, except for short periods of time. You can suppress thinking, but you can't stop it.

But the trouble is not that we have thought. The trouble is that we reify thought. We make it a reality in itself. We forget to see that it's just the stuff of the mind, because the mind does that thing. Sense of self, personal identity, Dan-ness, is another construction of mind. Humans don't come into the world with a developed psychological sense of self. It develops slowly over time. It forms, roughly peaking at around eighteen months, roughly concurrent with the capacity for representational thinking. When you can represent, you can represent self.

And that's useful. Having a sense of self serves a central organizing principle of daily life in relative reality. It's useful to have a sense of self. But once we develop a sense of self, we forget that it's just a construction of mind. We reify it, we make it too real. We take the self as independently self-existing. We think, I think, that Dan always existed—that I was born with it. And I take Dan way too seriously.

So, the trouble is the mind constructs, that's what it does. It makes the sense of self. And in relative reality, it's useful to use that sense of self as a central organizing principle in daily life. And where Buddhists come in is that there are two problems that come from reifying the self, from reifying thought, if we take it as too real and independently existing. It has grab, *dzin-pa* in Tibetan. So, I can go around my daily life and I can observe the grab of thought. I'm attached to certain thoughts. I've put a lot of investment into them. I can go about my daily life and observe the grab of self. If you don't love what I'm saying and you criticize it, I can notice the grab. If you like what I'm saying and you praise it, I can notice the grab. If I'm disagreeing with somebody and getting defensive, there's a lot of grab in that. And self-grab becomes your main source of suffering in Mahayāna Buddhism. There are lots of variations on the theme of self-grab. You can go about the day observing all the instances of grab in your daily life. And then you'll see how that contributes to the suffering of your daily life.

But the second thing is that once we reify or make too real some seemingly solid structure of mind, it has the capacity to cloud over our true nature. We lose that true nature. So that's what emptiness practice is about. Emptiness means you see it for what it really is. You stop forgetting that it's really a construction. You see that in my case, Dan-ness, personal identity, is just an empty construction of mind. And it exists in relative reality because the mind constructs representations. So, once you see that it is just a construction of mind, you see beyond it. The Tibetan word for insight, which is often translated as that, is *lhag-thong*. But insight is not what it means. *Tongwa* means to see; *lak* means beyond.

So, if you look into the seemingly solid, independently existing structures of mind and you really see them for what they are, they're insubstantial. They're not independently existing. They exist in relative reality as simply constructions of mind, but they don't ultimately exist. There's no cosmic Dan out there in the universe. There's no thoughts that come from somewhere else and appear to me. The mind generates all that stuff.

Another big structure of mind is time. There's no cosmic time clock out there, the kind that exists in Greenwich. It's just a construction. It takes about eight years for a child to develop the structures of time. In an everyday reality, a relative reality, having a developed sense of time is useful. It's how we meet deadlines and get to places on time. Time, like self, becomes one of those central organizing principles. But we make the mistake of reifying it. I think that time is an independently existing structure in the world. I locate it in out there, in Greenwich. Because I reify time, it has a lot of grab. As soon as I'm running late, as I'm trying to meet a deadline, or get someplace on time, or I'm stuck in traffic, I find it has a lot of grab. But more, it has the capacity to obscure the real nature of the mind, which is beyond time. It's timeless.

So, when we look into the nature of things and see them as not independently existing, as insubstantial, the more we search into them, we can't find that substance. But you have to look into it. You have to roam around in awareness and look into it to see that it's really insubstantial. The more you look into it, the solidness of that structure of mind slips away. That's why the Dalai Lama says the essence of emptiness as a meditation is *nirme*, unfindability. The more you look for the substance, the more it keeps slipping away.

So, what happens is you look into the nature of these structures of mind, search into them with high-speed awareness, and the solidness keeps slipping away and it's unfindable. And when you see that shift occurring, that experiential shift of unfindability, you look into what's left. And what you learn is something new about awareness.

You know that that whole path is captured in the Heart Sutra mantra. *Gate gate pāragate pārasamgate bodhi svāhā.* Gone, gone, gone beyond, gone way beyond, ooh, what a realization.

The first structure of mind that's too solid that we get way caught up in is conceptual thought. But if you calm the mind through concentration meditation, you move beyond thought. You don't get rid of it. You see beyond it. And what you open up is a level of awareness cleaned up of thought. We think that thought and awareness are the same thing. We mix them up. But if you calm thought enough so there are long periods of stillness in your concentration meditation—if there's no thought—what are you operating out of? What knows? What you discover is you're operating out of the field of awareness. Awareness has a property called *gongpa*, intention. And that intention works at lightning speed. It's much quicker than thought. So, you learn to go beyond thought, separate out thought from that pure field of awareness. That's the first gate. Awareness gone beyond thought. And that's where you, that's where you're operating out of. We say that's your "basis of operation."

But then if you do emptiness of self, and you see beyond the structures of self as simply empty structures of mind, you go beyond self. That's the second gate, awareness itself gone beyond personal identity. Now you've separated out pure awareness from its being mixed up with self. So, if I go back to the meditation at that point, it's not Dan doing the meditation anymore. It's pure awareness doing the meditation. Probably awareness will do a better job with it than Dan does. Because it has inherent intelligence, more than Dan had.

But then awareness still fluctuates in this structure of ordinary time. It comes and goes. But if I do emptiness of time, I find the level of awareness is absolutely timeless and changeless. It's always right here. It doesn't get affected by the convention of time. And since time and space are related, if I open up that level of awareness in my basis of operation, it's not only changeless and timeless, it's boundless. So, we call that ocean-like, changeless, boundless. That's a big shift. That's why it's linguistically marked in *parāgate*: gone beyond the convention of time to affirming ocean-like and changeless, boundless awareness as your basis of operation.

But, at that point, even though that's a much bigger shift, I'm still reifying the operations of my information processing system; I'm still locating my consciousness somewhere, localizing it. And with the right instructions, called "crossing-over instructions," I can step out of that moment-by-moment thing that my information processing system does, and the localization of consciousness. And I become that ocean-like, unbounded wholeness of awakened awareness-love. That's a much bigger shift; that's why it's linguistically marked *pārasaṃgate*: gone way beyond the operations of your information processing system, and your individual localized consciousness, to being the unbounded wholeness. And when you recognize that shift, that's a much greater shift, so that's why it's linguistically marked *bodhi svāhā*, oooh, what a realization. But you have to recognize it.

So, the Heart Sutra mantra is very popular because there's your whole path. Every step clears away some seemingly solid and substantial structure of mind, not to get rid of it, but to see beyond it. So, you shift your basis of operation and clean up awareness for whatever that structure of mind is that's clouding the whole. You separate the clouds from the radiance of the mind, or if you want a good Tibetan metaphor, you separate the pure milk awareness from the curds—the solid curds.

Now, when you practice emptiness, and clear away these structures of the mind, at a certain point, thought doesn't get in the way anymore, because that's not where you're coming from; you're not operating out of thought. You're operating out of that field of pure awareness, and you start to notice more and more that that awareness has intention, which has lightning speed to it. So that when things arise in your mind, you can notice them much more quickly.

When you do emptiness of time, you open up a level of awareness that we call ocean-like, changeless, boundless awareness. And then you ease up and you can let all the ordinary content of the ordinary mind come back. You can let thoughts occur, and emotions and sights and sounds and body sensations and all that stuff, but the issue is where you're looking from.

You're looking at all that stuff and it arises within an ocean-like field of changeless, boundless awareness, from the perspective of that ocean-like awareness. Stuff still comes up, but you're not looking at that from operating out of thought, you're not looking at that from operating out of self, you're looking at it from being that ocean-like, changeless, boundless awareness—"like an ocean, viewing its own waves."

And just as an ocean isn't affected by its own waves, whatever comes up comes up without any grab. Once you stabilize that ocean-like changeless boundless awareness, you open up what we call "the path of spacious freedom." Because whatever comes up, comes up in that vast, infinite, awareness space, and it has no grab whatsoever. And here's your first taste of spacious freedom. When it not only loses grab but later down the path it loses forming any new karmic impressions, and you release all habitual karmic memory traces. We call that "the path of infinite freedom," one more level up.

But when you get to that point of ocean-like, changeless, boundless awareness, viewing whatever comes up like another wave, whatever comes up is another expression of emptiness. It's all starting to be seen as just a lively expression of awareness. It has no substance to it anymore; nothing has much substance to it. It's all illusory, like a dream.

When you're in that range, because you're operating out of a pure field of awareness, it's not hard to look more quickly with that lightning speed, and you can catch things at the head, every moment, by moment, by moment. It's sort of like catching a wave as it begins to form rather than after it's already formed and begun to break. And you can look with that kind of lightning speed at every moment, by moment, by moment, and then a funny thing happens: everything comes up automatically expressed as emptiness. And you move into what we call "automatic emptiness."

Now, that's a very important state of mind. Because, you see, the problem with what clouds over awakening from the ordinary mind perspective—the thing that clouds it over most is trying to conceptualize about it. But let's say you have a strong foundation in automatic emptiness. Every time you have any slight tendency to conceptualize about state or outcome and grasp after that outcome, but you don't yet know what awakening is—every time there's any tendency to grasp after what the state or outcome is, it's immediately expressed as empty. So, it doesn't go anywhere.

So, automatic emptiness is like a clearing agent for all conceptualizations. It's the only time in practice when you can get completely clear of the grab of thought in such a way that thought can no longer interfere with the direct realization of the awakened mind and any tendency to do anything. As soon as you try and do something, you want to make something happen, you try to change the surround, you try to strive for an outcome, all of those things that will get in the way of awakening, all those tendencies to do anything are immediately expressed as empty upon arising so they don't get in the way even if they happen.

So, "the mind returns to its natural simplicity and freshness," we say. So, when you have automatic emptiness, the mind has simplicity, which means all doing is expressed as empty, so there's no interference by any type of doing. When you have what we call a natural state of freshness, it means that all conceptualization settles out of the mind, so whatever you perceive is immediately fresh without an overlay of conceptualization about it. And the result of clearing and stripping the mind of that outer layer of conceptualization, which is a bad habit, the result of that is that something about this field of awareness would seem much more obviously lucid and bright.

Now, if you keep looking into this field of awareness, and if you look into the surrounding space—right now, look at the space. And mix your awareness into that space. And the space into your awareness, so it's one field of awareness-space saturating everything. And now look at it so that field of empty awareness space includes all the objects in it and is part of that awareness. And now, fold the knowing of those objects into it. So, with the empty awareness space that saturates everything, the objects in that space, the sights, the sounds, the thoughts, the emotions, and the knowing of those objects is one single nondual, unified field. And when you add that ingredient, now you have what's called "the natural state."

You have a vast, ocean-like field of awareness. It's all awareness. And whatever arises within that field is automatically expressed as empty every moment. So, nothing has any substance to it. Nothing can distract from holding that completely undistracted view of that field of ocean-like, changeless, boundless awareness. And any tendency to do anything that would interrupt that state is immediately expressed as empty so that state stays simple. And any tendency to conceptualize about whatever's happening will be immediately expressed as empty so the state stays fresh. And there's a bright field of awareness that saturates everything. And it's a completely nondual field, so there's no grasping after things out there.

And when you have that, you have the natural state of the mind. That is the prerequisite state of the special crossing-over instructions that will lead to awakening. If you do not have that state, and you try using the crossing-over instructions, you're going to think your way through it, and it can't happen. The thoughts will preclude awakening. If you don't have that state, then the self will try to grasp at something it thinks is called awakening, but the self can't become awakened. Dan doesn't get awakened. When Dan gets out of the way, awakening happens to itself, by itself. Dan doesn't teach you anything. All the teachings come spontaneously from the state. Dan gets out of the way.

So, when you set up those conditions just right, that's when you can hear the instructions in a way that might work. We call those, in general, crossing-over instructions. In Mahāmudrā, they call them non-meditation meditation instructions. In Dzogchen Great Completion meditation, they're called *trekchö*, thoroughly cutting through, because you cut through all the residual conceptualization of the ordinary mind, right down to the bone of the awakened mind.

But even if you set up the view, just correctly, it's not enough—you have to recognize awakening, as you mentioned. And that's where having the precious human birth matters. Because in Buddhism, we say that all creatures down to the smallest insects have awakened nature, but only humans have the metacognitive capacity to recognize awakening. You have to use your metacognitive awareness and step back and say, "Hey, this is what's happening here."

And there are two pathways of recognition. One is what we call the lucidity pathway, where the other is called the nonlocalization pathway. If you're holding the view of a vast, ocean-like expanse, and you turn that awareness back on itself so you're not looking at anything particular, but looking at the entirety of the unbounded wholeness of awareness every moment by moment—"like a child looking at a temple," taking in everything all at once, and nothing in particular—if you hold that view and step out of the particularizing, at some point you may notice, just by holding that view, that you no longer operate out of the constraints of individual consciousness, or your information processing system. Something has shifted into being the unbounded wholeness. You have to recognize that shift.

Or there's the pathway through lucidity. At some point when you're holding that view, you come to see there is something about awakened awareness that's different from ordinary awareness. It has *danpa*, brightness; it has *hrige*, awakeness; it has *gnar*, intensity; it has *dongpa*, sacredness; it has *bole*, softness; it has *trule*, sparkling immediacy. These are what we call "yogi terms."

There are certain descriptors, because it becomes obvious at some point that awakened awareness is different from the ordinary dull awareness that we walk around in our stuporous daily life with. Either one of these pathways of recognition can open up awakening. Only humans have that capacity to recognize it. And once you recognize it, you've shifted your basis to that ocean-like, unbounded wholeness of awakened awareness-love and that's where you're operating from; and we call that shifting your basis of operation.

Now the foundation for setting up the view that opens up awakening is the natural state of the mind. If you do not have the natural state, any tendency to conceptualize will throw this whole thing off. Any tendency to do anything will throw this off. That's why I like Mahāmudrā, because it step by step builds to this natural state. Dzogchen, the term, means great completion. And in Dzogchen the teachings tend to be more advanced—as the name implies, it completes the path to buddhahood, and it presumes you already know how to do this stuff.

So, they only give you a very abbreviated version of it. They'll say, "Relax the mind." Well, that doesn't mean anything because as soon as you relax, that's a doing, that's a strategy. That can't possibly open up awakening. "Settle the mind in the natural state;" you see, all of those *trekchö* instructions, thoroughly cutting through instructions, are too brief. You need a more detailed unpacking of how you set up, step by step, this natural state. And once you set it up just right, and you have just the right conditions, awakening is simple at that point.

So, let's suppose you're floating under the water. It's a nice metaphor. When you're snorkeling, the fact that you're in this vast ocean-like expanse of space, the body seems somewhat insubstantial in that state. The only activity is the breathing, and it sort of becomes the same as the water. So, nothing seems quite real when you're under the water, and it's a whole reality in itself that's like a dream. So, it has automatic emptiness built into it. It has emptiness of body built into it. And you're focused so carefully on whatever you're looking at that you're not likely to spend a lot of time thinking. You're just seeing. So, conceptualization drops away, for the most part.

And other than floating around looking at the wonder of the magical display of everything, there's not a lot of doing taking place. So, the only thing that screws up making that snorkeling experience the natural analog to the natural state of the mind, is there's still the tendency to see things out there and to grasp at them because they're out there. So, you have to do a little bit of practice with that nonduality thing. View the surrounding empty awareness space, all the objects in that space under water, and the knowing of those objects as one single unified field, with no inside and no outside.

And if you take that view, just like I'm saying, and you see it that way, then you can use snorkeling as an analogy that will help you to quickly appreciate the natural state. And then, you can be awake in the water. [Laughter] Or then some random fish will come along and bite you. [Laughter]

But it's no different. If you look at Dzogchen for example, there are several props that are used. A common one is sky-gazing. It's not hard to do that on Tibetan mountains. If you're at 14,000 to 15,000 feet, then there are no clouds in the middle of the day. And you look out from the mountain as we once did from Rahob's ashram; and all you see is this vast expanse of space. It naturally pulls you out of looking at anything in particular but taking the unbounded wholeness as the object. The same way in Lion's Gaze, you turn the awareness back on the unbounded wholeness of awareness. And in the unbounded wholeness, nothing in particular becomes the ongoing moment by moment object of your focus. So, you see, if you stand on a mountain without clouds and you look out into that space, it's a natural prop that's an analog to that state of mind that we're trying to create in the view of Lion's Gaze, which is one of the crossing-over instructions. You can use it. That's why it's so popular.

Another one, later on, when you're developing the visions of the mind, you gaze not at the sun, but you gaze in certain angles of the sun, not directly in your eyes, but if you look at the visions on the surface of the fluid Eye Lamps, they dance. If you close your eyes when you go to the beach and you try to sleep while you're lying on the sand, it's hard because when your eyes close, the sun's coming down, it's pretty light in there. There's lots of dancing energy. There's your *tögal* visions, there's your bypassing visions. That's what the eyes do in sunlight, the energy drops dance. They come alive and you can view all that stuff.

These are sort of like nature's analogs to certain kinds of practices that one can do. Of course, they didn't develop the snorkeling analog because they don't snorkel in Tibet because there's no ocean—it's landlocked! [Laughter] There isn't any reason why that doesn't apply in the West. You can use it the same way.

The natural state has five ingredients:

1. **Automatic emptiness** arising in a field of absolutely
2. **nondual perception** so that everything that arises, any kind of doing, any tendency to do anything is immediately expressed as empty upon rising. This way the mind returns to its natural state of

3. **simplicity**, and every tendency to conceptualize is immediately empty upon arising and the mind returns to its natural state of
4. **freshness** every moment; and because it's stripped of that outer layer of conceptualization that clouds over everything, there's a kind of obvious or
5. **transparent lucidity** to the field of awareness.

It mirrors all prerequisite conditions in just the right state so that the crossing over instruction for setting up the view of Lion's Gaze will work, so there's a great probability you could recognize awakening from that point. Not more complicated than that—straightforward.

If you want to practice your view while you're snorkeling, take a buddy along, don't practice alone. I once had a mentor, early in my career, who was a little self-destructive, and he went snorkeling by himself and they never found him, never found his body. He just disappeared. Don't practice alone. Have somebody spot you when you do.

Student 1

I always have, always will.

Dan

It's a good question. The whole foundation of these teachings is to set the mind in the natural state, but you can't just say, "Relax into the natural state." That makes no sense whatsoever—the doing-ness involved in that cancels out the natural state. The path to get to the natural state is always and necessarily the path of emptiness. The emptiness clears away all the seeming structures, so when everything is empty, what's left is the natural state. You don't get rid of anything, just see beyond all these structures. Emptiness is the path. Good question. Yes.

Student 2

I want to ask about this experience of feeling like you're trapped in a *bardo* state. I've noticed when I go to sleep and dream, I feel like I'm just trapped in more delusion and …

Dan

You are.

Student 2

I just want to ask about that.

Dan

Okay. There are six *bardo* states, and *bardo* means intermediate. There's your ordinary waking existence, that's a *bardo* state. There's your dream state. There are the states that develop through advanced concentration. Then there are three *bardos* in the dying process. So, there are six in all. When they say *bardo* states, they don't just mean that in the more narrow restricted terms of an after death state. We're talking as well about what happens during normal sleep and dreams, just to clarify. That's fair to say what you're asking for?

Student 2

Yeah. When I dream lately, I tend to feel like I'm trapped in some sort of delusional realm. I guess that's what dreaming is.

Dan

You are—that's what dreaming is. You see, in order to understand this, you have to understand how dreams are explained in Indo-Tibetan theory of mind. It has to do with the larger view of karma theory. Karma theory is Tibetan learning theory, like our Western learning theory in psychology. What karma theory says is that every action you engage in, not just behaviors, but also mental actions, every action that you engage in results in the formation of a karmic memory trace, *bagchag* in Tibetan, *samskara* in Sanskrit. There are millions and millions of karmic memory traces that are placed in the storehouse mind, like a giant reservoir. Some of those karmic memory traces have greater weight than others, so if you engage something incidentally, it still stores a karmic memory trace, but it's not likely you're going to activate it. If you did some strong behavior, if you worked out for a long period of time, positive or negative, it would have a much stronger weight to it, or force. All karmic memory traces are placed within that storehouse mind for lifetimes. That's the signature of all of who you are, the accumulation of all those karmic memory traces.

Under certain conditions they *minwa*, which means to ripen, they develop. Certain karmic memory traces get activated and when they get activated, they ripen to full maturity and they first appear as spontaneously emerging states of mind; so all the content of your mind is the result of karmic memory traces. Second, if they have much strength, they appear in the background, influencing your behavior indirectly, or if they have great strength, they appear and they influence your behavior directly. Thirdly, if the karmic memory traces have great strength they influence the unfolding of events in your life. The fact that we're all here listening to the teachings is because we have fortunate karma. We have karmic connections to the teachings.

Where dreams come in is that in our diurnal rhythms, our daily sleep and wake cycles, dream states are when karmic memory traces are most active in the ripening of karmic memory traces. That's the Tibetan theory explaining what dreams are. Dreams are the laboratory, if you will, where you can observe the ripening of karmic memory traces. What traces, with the billions of traces that we have in our storehouse mind, what traces get activated? It's an interaction between which ones have the greatest weight and which ones get triggered during the day, so that you can have some remote memory trace getting activated by some experience you had today and you don't know exactly what that connection was, but it's there.

It's very much like what Sigmund Freud said in his theory of dreams about day residues. What gets activated has to do with some weird experience you had during the day that activates this memory over that memory. It's similar. The very first thing that happens when you wake up in the morning is you have a residue of all the karmic memory traces that were activated during the dream state. If you get the average of seven hours of sleep a night, then you'll probably (in terms of sleep lab studies) have four to five dream periods a night, each lasting about twenty to thirty minutes. When you wake up in the morning with that heaviness, the last thing that you do before you wake up is you have a dream. That heaviness upon awakening is the cumulative effect of that ripening of karmic impressions. Usually, we ignore it and go about our daily life. It still has a kind of influence in the background of awareness on our daily life.

There's a certain level of practice, advanced practice, where you can allow everything to come up in that ocean-like awareness and not engage anything.

Just let it come and pass through. It's a very specific achievement and has to be done exactly right. If you don't engage anything that comes up in that vast, ocean-like expanse and just let it go its own way, it immediately disappears, leaving no trace. Every moment is like writing on water; whatever comes up immediately dissipates and you watch everything dissipate, and the process gets automatic. They call that *dharmadhātu* exhaustion. Because you're not forming any new karmic memory traces it forces the mind to release all of its storehouse at a rapidly accelerated rate. So, if you practice all the time, automatically, 24/7, on average, in six years you'll clean out all the karmic memory traces and there will be none left. You'll have no more negative states of mind for the rest of your life. Since those negative states mask all the positive states—there are eighty positive states to a buddha mind—and all those come out at once and flourish.

If you want to accelerate that process so it's quicker than six years, what you do is you do session-based practice. You do it at certain times of the day; and some are more strategic to that practice than others. The first thing you do when you wake up in the morning is you do this practice of self-arising self-liberating, once you know how to do that practice. It immediately will release any residual influence from all the dream states of your previous night. They're just all gone. The day will be much more clean and fresh. Just before you go to sleep, you do another short version of that to clear out all the karmic memory traces that built up from all the actions that day, so you're accelerating that process of *dharmadhātu* exhaustion, cleaning out all the karmic memory traces.

If you don't do that, if you don't practice at all, then when you get caught up in the dreams they are like delusionary states. You're caught up in what you take to be a "too substantial" reality, much like we take this as a substantial reality. Since most of those karmic memory traces tend to be more negative than positive; then, more times than not, you're really caught up in a nightmare.

You have to come to see all that as an insubstantial dream, and that's where emptiness practice comes in. The best practice, the foundational practice, is to see dreams as empty, insubstantial, so you reduce the grab, just like you do any other meditation practice on emptiness with thought or emotions. The superior practice would be to look at those dreams from an awakened state of mind with no engagement so that all the likely karmic impressions would just release themselves with no grab whatsoever. Then you're free.

There are two levels of practice. One is from the level of the ordinary mind doing emptiness practice and the other from the level of relatively continuous awakened mind, which is *dharmadhātu* exhaustion. Then you don't get caught up in one of those states. In fact, after a while you don't even have them. You've reduced your overall dream time the longer you go with this.

Student 2

I sometimes get the impression that I dream without really sleeping, without resting; it's just almost like a hallucination as opposed to sleeping.

Dan

Well, Tibetans don't make a big distinction between waking reality and dream reality; it's all hallucinations.

Student 2

Yeah.

Dan

The object is to do the emptiness practice on external reality strong enough so it's all like a dream. So, there's no difference between the waking dream and the dreaming dream. It's all one state. That's true.

But there's a popularity in the West of lucid dreaming, training yourself to be awake during dreaming, or aware-dreaming. That's very different from what the Tibetans talk about. The difference is that in lucid dreaming in the West, it's ordinary awareness of the dream, whereas the Tibetans are very specific that if you're practicing dream yoga, it has to be awakened awareness, not just ordinary awareness. That's a huge difference because then the dream doesn't have any grab to it.

May 11, 2016

Themes: The Vast Expanse; Visions; Considerateness

Dan

Welcome everyone. You have a question?

Student 1

This is a practice question. Last week you made reference to sky gazing and sun gazing, and you referred to the sky as a prop. So that made me think of this question. So, I'm curious about your opinion about using props, or using modern technology as support for practice. So, you might be familiar with binaural beats—some people use those to enter into meditation states; more specifically, the one that I'm interested in is folks are using SAD lights for vision practice. Yeah, those lamps, but they're using them to do, essentially, indoor sun gazing. So, I'm curious …

Dan

Interesting. I've never heard of that before.

Student 1

And apparently to some effect. So, I'm curious what your opinion is about that.

Dan

Okay. So, we have to set a larger context for what the question is about. Specifically in Dzogchen, or Great Completion meditation, you have to take certain views. The view that you take is the most important thing; it's how you look at things—we say, "The view is the meditation." The trouble is if you try and look at the mind from the perspective of thought, you're not really looking at the mind, you're just thinking. If you look at the mind from the perspective of self, it's the self, thinking about the mind. If you go beyond thought, you go beyond self; still, what you're looking at in terms of the field of awareness can be very narrow. And it will fluctuate in time.

But if you do emptiness of time, you'll open up a vantage point of awareness that's changeless and timeless, that doesn't come and go, it's always right here. And since time and space are related, that awareness is vast. You can set up a view of ocean-like, changeless, boundless awareness and let everything arise within that field of ocean-like, changeless, boundless awareness, and just look at it without doing anything to it so it loses its reactivity and grab.

Now, if you let everything arise within that, everything that arises loses the sense of solidness and substantiality. It still occurs, but you don't see it as independently existing, you don't see it as substantial. And after a while, when you get very quick at looking at everything, you get to a point in your practice of automatic emptiness where everything arises of its own momentum already expressed as empty upon arising. The process sort of goes by itself.

Then you can refine that to what we call the natural state. Any tendency to do anything at that point is immediately empty upon arising, so no kind of doing, trying to make something happen, trying to strive after an outcome, all those things, they don't get in the way anymore. Any tendency to conceptualize about your state or outcome, as soon as it arises is expressed as empty, so you move beyond all conceptualization, and that doesn't get in the way anymore.

Then, when have a strong foundation for what we call the natural state of the mind, you can set up your view towards awakening. And the view that you take has to be, we say, the vast expanse. It has to be a panoramic view in all directions, and it has to be limitless. It can't be narrow. It has to be inclusive of what we call the unbounded wholeness of awareness. The view is of that scope. Now you can set up that view and it if gets narrow, there are little things you can do with that. If you think this awareness has some boundary, move right into that boundary with your awareness and move beyond it into the awareness beyond it. And keep doing that until all the boundaries collapse. Then you have a vast scope to this awareness. You can do that just with your mind.

But think of going to the top of a mountain. And looking off the mountain when there are no clouds in the sky. And looking from that perspective, it naturally pulls the mind out towards this vast expanse. That's what sky gazing is. If you have a hard time setting up that view of the vast expanse, the mind naturally goes out to the vast expanse when you're looking off a mountain and there is nothing obscuring the view, like clouds.

So that's what I mean by using a prop. It helps you; it naturally helps you to take that view. If you can do that view without having to climb up a mountain, it's much more convenient. [Dan chuckles] So we say that the people of best capacity can just take that view, and they figure it out. But some people of lesser capacity need more help with it, and they need the props; and they can figure it out with the prop and it makes it easier for them, and then once they figure it out, they don't need the prop anymore. So, sky gazing is sort of like training wheels on a bicycle. It allows you to set up external conditions for which the mind naturally is pulled out to a panoramic view in all directions. So, it grasps the unbounded wholeness and limitlessness of this empty awareness space.

Now, if you're working with bypassing, where you are training the mind to use what's called the fluid Eye Lamps to see the visions, the main reason for not seeing the visions is because you haven't purified the mind. And the impurities of the mind obscure seeing the visions which are already here. So generally, you don't do bypassing practice and train the visions until you've done *dharmadhātu* exhaustion, until you let the karmic memory traces release themselves so the mind gets more pure, clean, or stainless, whatever you want to call that thing.

So, there's a natural progression if you do *dharmadhātu* exhaustion. You set up a view of that vast expanse, so that whatever arises within it, you don't engage, you just see it; you don't do anything to it, you don't act on it. It's that engagement that causes you to form karmic memory traces. If you set up the view just right and you're not engaging anything, it immediately arises without any mental engagement, so it immediately releases itself. And you watch everything release itself. And since you're not forming any new karmic traces, it forces the mind to release all the storehouse of previous karmic traces at a rapidly accelerated rate.

And if you do that all of the time, on average in about six years, you'll have no negative states left in your mindstream. It cleans out the bin; that's why we call it *dharmadhātu* exhaustion. You won't have anything left. No negative states. Sometimes that's called *drime*, stainless mind. I like to call it squeaky clean mind. The field of awareness gets squeaky clean.

So, if you have that degree of clean mind, stainless mind, then nothing obscures the visions, so you don't need the props. They just come up naturally. So, there's a natural progression to this. But, if you don't, and you try and do the visions more prematurely, there's a tendency to force them and grasp after them and then you see the visions out there, and as soon as you see them out there, game over, it stops. The visions are very much like a psychedelic experience, but the danger there, similarly, is if you see them as "out there," it messes it up. It's all part of a nondual unified field.

However, there are other things you can do as aids that will help you get the visions started if you don't have that process of *dharmadhātu* exhaustion. Think about a time that you went to the beach in the summer, and you lay down on the sand and you closed your eyes, and you maybe drifted off and got sleepy. What are you seeing with your eyes closed? Is the field dark? No. You can see all this dancing, lively energy because the sun is beating down on your eyelids, and there's a whole internal field of all that dancing, lively energy—there're your visions.

And sun gazing is like that. You sit only at certain times of the day. Usually, you sit when the sun gets moderately developed, not right away in the morning. So, if the sun comes up at six o'clock, you'd go from about 7:00 a.m. to about 10:30 a.m. Not in the strong sun. And then you can go back to it again at about maybe 3:35 p.m. to 5:00 p.m., where the sun is moderately strong but not too strong. You *do not* look into the sun. You put the sun behind you. When you set up the Lamps, if you look up, you can see what we call the fence—the fence of the eyebrows. You can see there is a boundary there.

You look just below the boundary, and you look at the surface of that. And the surface of the eye is like a movie screen. It has a film on it. You look at that film and if you have the sun behind you, you'll watch all this energy start dancing on that film. And you'll get energy drops moving and coming together and scattering; and filaments, splashes of light, and sometimes spheres that look like cells under the microscope, floating in space; and the whole thing is very alive and energetic. So, at the beginning you use the sunlight as a way of making the visions dance.

There are four levels of visions. The first are just energy and light. Colors. Not very well organized, except that the patterns sometimes come together and they scatter, and they come together and get organized. Things agglutinate and then they come apart again. At the second level, they start to suggest shapes, simple shapes and more elaborate shapes. The third level of visions is quite remarkably different. It's when you open up all the buddha realms. You get entire celestial realms with the palaces and the deities and the *dakinīs*, and it's quite a psychedelic show. As soon as you see it "out there," you screw it up. You have to see it as what we call "self-arising."

Then the fourth level, when those visions come to their full fruition, they start to wind down and they actually stop. At some point, just like you did with the exhaustion of karmic memory traces, you exhaust the visions. We say *tsema*, meaning they reach full measure, and they stop. They just disappear, and you don't have any more visions after that.

And what happens is all of the boundaries between different realms of time and space collapse and you end up with all-at-once-ness. You end up with a huge, limitless awareness that contains all realms and times within it, all periods in history, all realms simultaneously. And all of the creatures within all those realms are all connected by loving threads of *bodhicitta*. It's one organic reality, and you are that structure of reality. You *are* that living, ultimate reality. Then it's "game over," it's the end of it.

So, bypassing is, we say, "a quick path to enlightenment." It helps you to stop and not have to make a lot of stops along the way. It's like if you were driving through Boston and you took street after street, there'd be a lot of stop lights and it'd take you a long time. But if you go via the Big Dig[19] and you just go right through it and bypass all of the stop signs and traffic lights, bypassing is like that. It bypasses all of the places you usually stop and you just go right to the end point quickly, through these four levels of visions. It takes a little to set them up, and the sun gazing is seen as a prop that helps you get the visions to start dancing. Once you know what to look for, you don't need the prop anymore.

---

19 The Big Dig was a megaproject in Boston that rerouted the then elevated Central Artery of Interstate 93.

But it's best to do them with the right guidance. Lopön Tenzin Namdak put out an oral rendering of a book by Shardza Tashi Gyaltsen called *Heartdrops of Dharmakāya*, and it has a brief description of the sun gazing, sky gazing, and visions in it. And some idiot took the book and thought sky gazing meant you looked into the sun, so he stared at the sun for hours and fried his corneas, and then he sued the Lopön for practicing on his own, which he never should have done in the first place because he damaged himself by trying to do something stupid like that.

In the West, we sue everybody, right? In the words of South Park, "We way sue everybody. We're gonna way sue you." [Dan chuckles] So, like that, you don't look at the sun. You should do it with guidance.

If you trust in the natural unfolding of this, you don't need any of the props. It's not necessary.

Student 2

Recently, I was with my family for a family event, so there was a lot of extended family there. It's so interesting that whenever I'm with my family, it seems as though if there's one unfortunate word, it has to do with … I don't know if other people experience this, about how judgmental people are about each other, other people in the family, and so on ...

Dan

You mean your family's not perfect?

Student 2

I was hoping for a perfect family…

Student 3

They're right here! [Laughter]

Student 2

Thank you. So, when I was thinking about that, it seems to me as though what I've noticed in myself and in others has to do with people having a strong sense of self and clinging to that, not understanding that, and also not having awareness in knowing the interconnectedness of all beings.

Dan

The important issue here is: how do you practice? The simplest practice is you open up Ocean and Waves as a level of practice, where, from the vantage point of ocean-like, changeless, boundless awareness, you can more easily directly perceive that everybody is interconnected within that field of ocean-like awareness. You can't sustain the selfishness of the single-minded point of view on yourself. It's hard to.

The refinement of that practice is in the *Six Perfections* under the teachings on the ethics of considerateness. When you practice the ethics of considerateness, you go about your daily life holding the view of ocean-like, changeless, boundless awareness so everybody that you interact with is part of that field of awareness. You intentionally cultivate the view that everybody is part of the same field and we all influence each other. You bring into that view some perception, discernment of what the other person's needs and motivation are, what the state of mind is. As you go about your daily life, rather than being oblivious to everybody around you, you bring them into your field of awareness and you notice what they need. And you practice balancing your own needs against the needs of everybody's interpersonal field whether you know them or not. So, it just makes you more basically considerate in or outside the family when you get out of that more self-absorbed perspective.

It's a very powerful practice. And there's some common ground between the Buddhist practice of the ethics of considerateness and what we know is the best of what happens in families around attachment themes. The best attachment, with the most secure attachment, is with parents who are interested, continuously interested, in their kids' state of mind. They're always trying to give their best estimate of what the child is feeling and what motivates their behavior, what they're thinking, and how they put together their world. The child feels seen and known. Secure attachment and self-development blossom within that interpersonal field where somebody is aware and genuinely interested in what your state of mind is.

The human organism is programmed to flourish in that context of that kind of genuine interest. And that's similar in the ethics of considerateness. You intentionally practice taking everybody else that you would normally not notice and be oblivious to into your interpersonal field. And try to think what they need, so you don't go about your world with your own selfish preoccupations.

What's the opposite of the ethics of considerateness? Cell phone behavior. You have twenty people in this small space and somebody's talking loudly on their phone, and whether those twenty people like it or not, they have to hear that conversation because the person's clueless. When you have the ethics of considerateness, you notice people and what they need.

We were just teaching in Amsterdam and we went to see an old friend in Belgium; we had to go from one train track to another, and I had like five-minutes exactly to make the connection between them. We had all of our suitcases for all the meditation stuff. And I lug all this stuff, and there's no possible way I'm going to be able to lug all this stuff and get it up the escalator. And somebody saw me struggling with it and said, "Here, I'll help you. I'll take one and you take the other one." That was considerate. We just made the train connection because somebody helped. I didn't ask for it; they just saw that that was what the situation needed. And some people cultivate that kind of awareness.

Imagine if you did it all of the time. Then you're not operating out of some state of self-absorption. You're always aware of everybody around you and what they might need and responding to that in a considerate way. But we move further and further away from that as a culture and as a practice in the technology realm that we live in. Because it's all about selfies and people are sitting there in the middle of the sidewalk doing this, this, and this, and nobody can walk by them because they're blocking the sidewalk, and they're completely clueless as they do what they're doing. I mean, how many times a day do we see this? We're seeing more and more of that self-absorption in that little electronic machine, and no consideration for anyone around you. It's stunning to me.

My wife and I went to New York last summer for our anniversary, and we went to a very romantic hotel, with the panoramic views of all of New York. And there was a couple in their twenties sitting next to us, with this beautiful view of all of New York and the wonderful food, and they spent the entire time looking at their individual cell phones, and they said not one word to each other, and they never looked out the window. Why would you go to a restaurant like this? It made no sense. There was not one interaction, unless they were doing it on the cell phone, back and forth texting each other, [Dan chuckles] which is a little inconceivable. But there's something fundamentally self-absorbed, and we're getting more self-absorbed. You can't even take in your partner, never mind take in the rest of the people, or the environment, or anybody else around you? I find that markedly disturbing.

But maybe the ethics of considerateness are coming to the West at this particular time because we're not going to survive without it. We won't. It's all about selfishness. Right now, 1.5 percent of the population owns 95 percent of the wealth. Some months ago, there was a conference on fiduciary responsibility in Wall Street. And do you know what the prevailing view was? "We have no fiduciary responsibility for our clients; we use their money to make money for ourselves." That's the runaway train. It's not going to work like this. We won't survive. And the whole culture supports it. Is there any sense of responsibility for each other?

So, whether it's inside the family or outside the family, it's the same issue. Either you practice considerateness as a view, or you don't. And you can refine that practice and it's very profound.

Towards the end of his life, I asked my first Root Lama—it was one of the last things I asked him before he died—and I said, "Of all the practices you've done in your lifetime, what was the one that was the most difficult?" And he immediately answered, and he said, "Treating everybody equally. That was the hardest thing to do."

So, it's a good question.

We have time for a short one. Anything else? Yeah?

Student 3

I raised my children with the Hasidic Jewish tradition, so there's so much talk about the mystical experience, but no one teaches us how to have it. But there's so much thinking about it. Anyway, the point is one of my daughters—she's my youngest and she's twenty-six—and she grew up without any trauma. Maybe it's inherited trauma in having me as a mother [Dan laughs] because I come from Holocaust parents and all that craziness, but she had a lot of love and she was very normal, she never had any problems. The thing is though, now, like in the last—I don't know how many years … so, she takes psychedelics. Like, lately she's taken ayahuasca, she's done mushrooms—no cocaine, no addictive stuff like that—and she's opened up an art, like she does amazing … She went and she got accepted to art school; she was never an artist as a kid, she never had that inclination.

So, I'm just wondering, as a mother, is that okay? Do I have to guide her some way? I don't know if it's good or not good because I know I'd be really scared to do it, because I'd probably go into a mental hospital if I did that. But I'm just wondering, could it be okay, because there isn't a real path. Like in Judaism, I think because of the Holocaust, maybe it was lost. I don't know. But there are no real kind of spiritual teachers like the way you're talking here, where you go level by level and you have guidance. And could it be some kind of … Because she experiences the oneness, and she's really happy, and she has lots of friends, and she's very fulfilled in a lot of ways, so I'm just wondering about that.

Dan

That's a good question. I actually can give you an informed answer, because I'm left over from the '60s. [Laughter] One of my patients once said, "If you remember the '60s, you weren't part of it." I actually worked on the last human subjects project on LSD in 1970 and '71, before they stopped all the research in this country. We were giving it to terminal cancer patients to give them an experience, so they wouldn't be so terrified of death. They would open up to see that death was just a phase in the transition of things.

I think—I mean, the name, psychedelic, literally means "mind manifesting." Certainly, at that age for me, it opened up an entire world that I didn't know existed, which was quite profound. That's the positive part. The negative part is that, from what we do in the meditation stuff here, you tend to get attached to states and experiences. And particularly since the ayahuasca tends to be a recurrent thing that people do, you tend to look for more and more weird and wonderful states. And you get further and further away from the game plan, which is to see all that as lively awareness. You forget that it's awareness and you make it into a thing. So, it's the opposite of emptiness practice.

We certainly have, over the years, a number of younger people who've taken these retreats and who've been on the ayahuasca circuit. And over time, even though we offer to follow students after the retreats, rarely do those people work out—because they can't get out of still looking at everything for more weird and wonderful states.

So, it has the positive value of opening up and seeing what the potential is, of the mind is, which is awesome. Breathtaking. But you tend to get attached to states. So, if it's a useful phase, and if it opens you up and you go on to some other more stabilizing way of doing it, then that can be a very important, positive experience.

The thing that the kids on the street don't know about, particularly with the phenethylamines—the street name would be Ecstasy, something like that—phenethylamines cause extensive vitamin B-1 exhaustion, which can result in something like Korsakoff's or hippocampal damage. It can be reversible. So, basically, it's a rather simple thing. But the kids never do this. If you want to do something like that, including ayahuasca, then when you're coming down, take a good B-complex vitamin. And there's no negative effects if you do that, but it's not part of the street culture that people know to do that. It's rather easy to correct. So, there are both pluses and minuses to it.

It's a phase. These were all once sacred plants and they had a very special use, and in that sense, they command respect. They're not always misused. A lot of people use them because they're searching for something; and they go through a phase when they're searching for something, and they get more settled with it and then they go on from there, so it's not like all drugs are the same. It's not like taking other drugs.

June 1, 2016

Themes: Our Culture of Greed and Selfishness; Be Honest in Your Practice

Dan

Welcome everyone. You have a question?

Student 1

I'm going to state the obvious. From a Buddhist perspective, what do we do if someone becomes president? [Laughter] You can pass on that question if you want, but I have a feeling you don't want to, so …

Dan

You mean, it's really a decision of which country we're moving to, right?

Student 1

Well, I mean, Tibet was taken over.

Dan

Well, it's a difficult question. Because it's not about the nature of the candidate and his substantial limitations and flaws; it's about all the people who would find that okay. So, it really is more a statement of a culture in decline, and when you get a culture in decline, we need to put it in a larger context. When you have a culture in decline, then people have much greater security fears and are much more vulnerable to rigid beliefs and extreme forms of nationalism and irrationalism and all sorts of other things. But that's the way I see it. It's a culture in decline.

We have a history of enjoying a pretty comfortable lifestyle in the country. But if you look at the larger issue, we sold this country, somehow, over the last twenty or twenty-five years. It's been the case that it's happening all around the world but mostly we're leading the way in this country. 1.5 percent of the population owns 95 percent of the wealth. 70 percent of all the wealth in the world is owned by sixty-two families. So, we have evolved a world oligarchy. So, that's a significant trend in our lifetime alone. We've given a small group of people everything.

And the other significant trend that's in this country, if you look at the Supreme Court's decisions, we sort of sold out individualism, individualists, to corporations. You know. If you own a small business in this country, you pay about—between state and local taxes, you pay about 48 percent of all your earnings in taxes. Google, Facebook, Microsoft, and Apple paid no taxes whatsoever in any country for twenty years. Do the math. If you calculate the amount of money that those four companies alone owed in back taxes, there's your entire national debt right there. So, why are individual middle class people having to bear the full burden of that?

The whole financial structure of this country was sold. And we're all suffering that. But the solutions are like grasping at straws. Nobody wants to look at the reality of what it really means to unpack the financial cancer in this country and the enormity of the task that we as a generation let get away from us. We let our precious democracy slip away. And we're all responsible for that. For me, that's more the issue than a particular candidate that's just a symptom of a larger structural issue.

And it all comes down to simple things: selfishness and greed. And we have established an entire culture of selfishness and greed in the financial industry in this country, which is out of control. About eight months ago, there was a debate in Wall Street about fiduciary responsibility. And the overwhelming consensus was that financial advisors saw themselves as not having any fiduciary responsibility to the clients. The generally pervasive attitude was that they used their clients' money to make money for themselves. There's something fundamentally wrong with that attitude. It's a runaway train. And if everybody does it, how do you change that culture? So, it's not so simple.

So, I don't know, I don't know what the solution to that is except that at least in Buddhism, realization is measured in terms of conduct towards the welfare of all sentient beings. So, the more you practice, the more you have the duty to serve the purpose of others. So, that means squarely taking on these issues and doing whatever you can within your capacities to address them. That's important. And to work on your own negative states in the course of doing that.

That means using your practice to work with your own reactivity and your own discouragement and to find some way of, with a kind of positive determinedness, working with it in the face of the overwhelming odds of what we have to do to change this country. I mean, I'm of the belief that we have had this precious democracy here, and we've pissed it away. And that's worth fighting for. And I think that became more important to me after having children because, as parents, I think we have a duty to provide a better world to our kids and we all failed. Most of our kids can't buy houses. And their kids' kids won't be able to afford houses. So, how did we let the world become like that?

The leaders of a culture are what we call in psychology, generative people. Highly generative people. Generative people think in terms of what they pass on to others and what they pass down the generations. About a quarter of the people are generative people in the culture. And it's worthy to study that, because these highly generative people are concerned with what we're passing on. The rest of it is just about taking more for ourselves, living in the moment, and doing whatever we can to sort of grubble to get the best that we can out of the immediacy of the situation, with no long-term planning of what it takes to make a stable world down the generations.

I remember, years ago, I used to work for the World Bank; it was in the early 1980s. I was a cross-cultural consultant for the bank. So, when big businesspeople got together over a table, the business deals didn't fail because they couldn't deal with the cultural issues involved in making the deal. I remember the CEO from a very well-to-do Swiss company having a complete tantrum at the American CEOs—and this was the early 1980s—and he was very prophetic, and what he said was, "You guys lost the whole point." He says, "You're obsessed with quarterly reports, and most of it's garbage figures anyway. And you've lost sight of the main fundamental principle of good business. Good business is building long-term relationships with people." How prophetic was that? We don't care about people. We don't care about quality of life.

We like to think we have a good life here. All you have to do is go to a nice restaurant in Europe and you book the table for the night and it's quiet and you're supposed to savor and enjoy every moment of it because they're proud of what they've created for you. You book a high-end restaurant in the U.S. and they only have three tables a night, and they're going to push you in, push you out. It's going to be so noisy you're going to have to shout at people and you can't hear anybody. Because it's all about making money. And getting more in and getting more out. It's not about the quality of the food or quality of the enjoyment of the evening. Right there, you can see the differences in the culture. It's like the obsession with the quarterly report. It's all quick immediate gains based on selfishness.

So, what drives all of this is selfishness? If people are wealthy and use it to invest more in wealth, does that make them any happier? It's an obsession; it's an addiction. And rather than getting more accumulation of stuff for the self, what gets lost in that process is the larger vision we all share as an interconnected humanity here. And either we make it as an interconnected humanity, or we go down over it. And it is that serious.

So, the real issue, from a Buddhist perspective, is how do we overcome selfishness and self-grasping? It's a central issue, because self-grasping and self-importance is the fundamental explanation of all suffering. If you take too much, it's always at the expense of others. And we have wonderful ways of defending ourselves about thinking about that. So, we never have to think of the consequences, of how many people get exploited in the process of what we accumulate. So, from my perspective, those are the more important issues. And how do you change that? One person at a time?

So, maybe somebody takes a meditation retreat, and they see the emptiness of self, and they move beyond self-grasping. Maybe they open the heart and start making a vision of life that takes in the greater social good. That's useful, even if it's one person at a time. But the practice has to be authentic.

Years ago, Trungpa had talked about "spiritual materialism." We haven't moved far away from that, quite frankly. Look how popular mindfulness is. Mindfulness is everywhere. And there's lots of self-important mindfulness people out there. And what's the motivation behind it? Become more self-important as a mindfulness teacher? What good is that? It misses the entire point of the practice. If you learned anything from any kind of spiritual practice in any tradition, the single most important lesson is: self-importance isn't terribly important. Even the spiritual traditions can easily be misconstrued as other means to support self-importance.

It requires that you balance your practice with a kind of metacognitive honesty about what you're doing. Then there's a path and a set of methods that work to move you past self-grasping if you use that path well. And in the process, you begin to think about the greater social good, the welfare of others more naturally as an outcome of your realizations. And if you stabilize that, and you start living your life that way, maybe that makes just a little bit of difference. Or maybe it means one less selfish person to have to worry about on this planet, because there's plenty of others to worry about. But does it do something? Absolutely. Because things aren't always the way they appear to be. So, I'm not as discouraged as all that, quite frankly.

Each special state of mind is associated with one of the three poisons. If you get attached to bliss, you get attachment. If you get attached to clarity, you get hatred. If you get attached to nonconceptual stillness, you get ignorance. Think of the implications of that: attachment to clarity leads to hatred. You want a clear example of that in everyday interactions? Think about a couple that's fighting and disagreeing about something and one or both say, "I'm right." There's your attachment to clarity. And what does it lead to? More aggression, more hatred. Attachment to clarity leads to hatred. You can see that in Trump. He, more and more, thinks he's got the truth and that he's right. And the more he develops that attachment to what he believes to be clarity, the more the hatred spews out. And that's worrisome. Attachment to clarity leads to hatred.

Self-righteousness is an ugly poison. Because when you're self-righteous, the view of the self is that it's so right that it's not open to any other points of view or diversity. It becomes a close-minded system. And the more the self-righteousness, and the seeming elusive clarity of that, the more it's accompanied by aggression and hatred. We've destroyed entire cultures under self-righteousness. We call it missionary behavior. We actually developed the idea that our beliefs are the only important ones, and the only right ones, and everybody else is primitive. And think of the destruction we've wreaked upon the world with that one. Still paying for it, from centuries ago. It's the same story. It's just another version of how self-righteousness leads to hatred—and the seeming illusory clarity that comes from that. For me, the world is more complex. I don't live within these cookie cutter polarities the way that Trump does. It means having compassion for a large segment of our own population that's really deluded. That's painful. Because we might go down over it.

It was really interesting when I was recently in the Netherlands and Belgium; and the Europeans tend to think more about politics than we do—in everyday conversations, not just every four years. And the overwhelming consensus is they weren't so much concerned about Trump, he was just the symptom. They were concerned about the American population who would allow that to happen. And what they saw and what is happening in this country is very similar to what they saw in the rise of Mussolini and fascism. It's not so different. It's based on simple cookie cutter answers that everybody grapples with and says, "Wow!" But it's all sound bites. It's all based on hatred. That's never going to go anywhere good.

And the real problem is that everybody is so fearful and insecure because the world is falling apart and everybody is grasping at something to put it back together again. And the one who purports to have the simplest and strongest way of doing that, however illusory it may be, wins the toys, rather than doing the hard work it's going to take to get us out of this mess that we've made.

But all we can do is, one person at a time, try to make them deal with their own issues of selfishness and hatred and the poisons, and evolve their consciousness, and move beyond self-grasping, and open up their hearts, and develop a more authentic sensitivity to other people. And maybe that goes somewhere useful, maybe it doesn't. But I couldn't do anything other than try. I don't have any grandiose illusions here. I'm not going to promise you the things that Trump promises here. [Laughs] All I can do is try.

I appreciate you bringing it up because it's in the air with everybody. It's a concern. It's a big concern.

Student 2

The over-arching concern is how people could allow themselves to be that deluded. Looking at those simple answers.

Dan

Right. Doesn't have to be right, just has to be what people want to hear when they're so insecure.

Some years ago—it was in the 1990s—in an interesting experience at UMass Boston, there was a three-day invited think tank on political psychology. The theme was around suggestive influences in politics, and I think I got invited because of my hypnosis and suggestive influences research. It wasn't my field at all. But what was interesting about this three-day think tank was they had the people who had organized the presidential elections for the twenty years previous to that, like Carville and all those people. They were all in the same room, Republicans and Democrats alike.

What the Republicans did was they brought in these researchers, they spent millions of dollars on—starting after Eisenhower, over twenty years of research on suggestive influence in politics. And it was all around the issue of security fears; and what they realized is that most people don't have a very long memory, so you have to play the stuff out about three weeks before a national election because if it's too far before, they won't remember it.

So, three weeks before the national election, you blitz people with it, the whole country, with advertisements. And you shape the idea that the opposing candidate is going to cause you to be insecure around national and international relationships, and around national security and economic freedom. And that your guy is going to do the opposite. So, your guy is going to make the economy perfect. We're going to have good international relationships with everybody, and the streets are going to be safe. And the other guy is going to do the opposite.

If you play all of the themes of those advertisements, however inaccurate or untruthful they may be, if you play them out in the right way at the right time, they calculate it empirically and they tested this with replications, showing that you can capture up to twelve percentage points of the vote. That's usually enough to win. And they were very proud of this research.

It's like apples and oranges. The Democrats were saying, "Well, don't the issues matter?" And the Republicans say, "No, the only thing that matters is that you win." And they couldn't talk with each other because the Democrats were sort of nervously impatient with the suggestive influence thing and they weren't willing to entertain the idea—which was naïve—that it influences every aspect of our life. You know, from advertising, to spin in the courtroom, American courtrooms, to political advertisements. It affects everything.

We're all the victims of suggestive influence. Most of our beliefs are shaped by suggestive influence, and we don't stop, step back, and say, "Hey, wait a minute. What's going on here?" So, the whole thing is, that way, pretty much scripted. You saw the most successful example of that, which was absolutely scripted, which was Willie Horton and Michael Dukakis. All they had to do was create the fear that he was going to let murderers run out in the streets. It was clearly orchestrated. And they won the election over that, because that's what the research suggested. And they were good at using this research.

And that's pretty much the structure of American courts. You know, juries are shaped by suggestive influence. It's not about what's true, it's about who has the best spin. When I worked on the International War Crimes Tribunal, the tribunal tended to see the American lawyers as a joke, because they [the Tribunal] just wanted facts. They were completely impatient with any of that kind of stuff that we do here in the courts all the time. It's just not allowed in international courts. It's uniquely American. We live in a culture of spin. That's become the entire culture.

It's even influenced science. We don't report scientific facts. We have spin. We see that in terms of the tension with all the drug outcomes studies. And the tension is where they put a certain spin on it and minimize the side effects. You saw that when there was some drug; I think it was a cardiac drug, and it caused heart failure. It slipped by, even with the flaws in the study and the number of people that died; it slipped by the *New England Journal of Medicine*, which is pretty prestigious. And the way it slipped by was it said, well, there's another study that we're doing that's going to report some of the negative findings, and that will be in a future study. And the peer reviewers let it go by. But they never intended to make a future study of that. That was a way of masking the clear knowledge they had of the death effects from this drug. They just put a positive spin on it, minimized the risks. Welcome to *samsāra*. Everything is dishonest. And we support that kind of culture.

But we're not stupid. I mean, how many times do you see people on TV talking and you know what they're saying is complete bullshit? But we allow it to happen because that's what the culture does. We have better capacity than that to discern what's true. It's disrespectful to assume otherwise. It's insulting that that's the kind of spin that's on everything, every message that comes across, at every level of this society. It's all bullshit.

So, how did we allow the culture to become that dishonest? You could never do that kind of stuff in the '50s. But then again, we did away with all kinds of regulations because they were considered a bad thing. Well, maybe they're not such a bad thing.

When you practice meditation, you have to use your metacognition. You have to look honestly at what you're doing. So, that kind of metacognitive honesty starts in your practice. You have to retain that metacognitive part of the brain, which is the right dorsolateral prefrontal cortex—part of the frontal executive system. It has nothing to do with the association cortices that have to do with thought. It's just seeing with awareness, clearly and honestly what it is. What your state of mind is. Without bullshit, without all that overlay of conceptual rationalizations of why everything's okay, but it's really not okay. So, if you want to retrain the mind and that kind of honesty, it starts with your meditation practice on the pillow, really seeing clearly what you're doing in the meditation and what you're not doing in the meditation. So that you're not thinking your way into states that you don't really have, because it's just all thought fabrication.

Sitting isn't good enough. You have to sit with a kind of metacognitive honesty. You have to monitor your state so you're always trying to improve and do better with it. You've heard me repeat that little Sufi saying: "A log sits on a wood pile very quietly for years. But logs never realize God." So don't sit like a log, sit intelligently.

There are studies on concentration meditation that show that the difference between beginning and advanced concentrators isn't the degree of concentration, it's whether you bring metacognition to it—you're always improving the quality of your concentration. You're looking more quickly at when things get distracted. You're staying on track. So, that kind of honesty and bringing it back into the culture starts with looking at your own mind honestly.

Human beings have a remarkable capacity for self deception. We're unique in the animal kingdom for that. Only humans have the capacity to lie to themselves. So we deceive ourselves, and through all of the suggestive influence, which is steeped in our culture now—and we influence and lie to everybody else—where's that going to get us?

But there's a way out. And the practice provides you with a way out of *samsāra*. Personally, I like being in *samsāra*. [Dan laughs.] This is the place to practice, the best place to practice. As Zorba the Greek says in the film, "the full catastrophe." Where else would you practice? It's not a time for caves. If you're going to make your practice work, you have to make it work here in the midst of all the crap. That's good practice. And in the midst of all that, if you can, preserve some positive outlook and some light heartedness. It helps. Then, the rest of it is—well, when my youngest kid was sixteen, he said, "Dad, it's just all stuff." It's just all stuff. And maybe the stuff doesn't bother you so much. You just try harder to move beyond it. That's your duty—each of you—to bring to this an honesty, to train your own mind, to consider the welfare of other beings.

In that sense, the practice is simple. If you can do that, that's profound, in the midst of it all.

Good question, thank you. It's relevant. You're speaking to what we all feel but are not addressing. So that, in itself, cuts through. It's a kind of honesty, you see. It's good.

Now you're going to go out and vote for Trump. [Laughter]

Anything else? Yes?

Student 3

It's a very different kind of question about off the pillow practice, and so I wonder if you could comment on this: it seems that resting in a state of naked open awareness, it is possible to watch the operations of the cognitive mind; and what that appears to be like is that the mind moves towards something and kind of latches on to it and it feels like a hardening. And, the question is, and then there's something that shifts in the experience of that open awareness where the operations of the cognitive mind take more of a front seat in terms of the foreground of the experience. The question is that it feels like—in my experience, when the cognitive mind is functioning in the ways that I feel like I need the cognitive mind to function because it's, you know, I need to strategize about something or I need to write something or whatever, that sort of basic experience of resting in awareness sort of recedes to … it's almost like a diminished window on a computer screen. I don't know how else to say it.

Dan

No, that's a good way of saying it.

Student 3

It's like in the background and it's not the cognitive mind, it's not that the cognitive mind functions are obscuring it, but it's like the experience shifts so that the cognitive function feels like it's more in the foreground. I'm just wondering if you would comment on that.

Dan

Okay. The larger question that you're raising here is what in Buddhist and Bon studies is called the pathway of deludedness, *trulwa*, delusion. Always right here, like the sun that never stops shining, is the radiance of an awakened mind. But either you recognize that awakened awareness as your true nature or you fail to recognize it. Either there's *rigpa*, recognition of it, or *marigpa* (no recognition). So, all delusions start with any instant that you fail to recognize your true nature—like awakened awareness that shines forth all the time, like the sun that never stops shining. In the instant that you fail to recognize awakening, you're creating the conditions for dualistic thinking. Now we have something observing something out there.

So, the next step in that process of the pathway of deludedness is dualistic grasping. Now we have an inside and an outside. And we're looking at events and grasping at them. And the first thing that we do in that grasping, once we have *marigpa*, is the mind starts reaching in lightning speed, milliseconds; it goes towards something, and the outcome is to make it a something. We call that *yila jepa*, particularizing—the tendency of the mind towards something. The outcome is to make it something particular. The next step is that you see something particular. In Western psychology we would call that stimulus perception.

Now you have a specific event out there based on duality, and you're perceiving that particular stimulus event. Once you perceive a particular stimulus event, the next step is engaging it. That's called *langdor* in Tibetan. Either you reach out towards it to make more of it and to process it further—that's *langwa*, sometimes translated as "accepting the experience and going further with it," processing it further—or *dorwa*—you act on it in such a way as to stop processing it, and erasing it so you can go on to something else.

Accepting and rejecting it are two forms of what we would call mental engagement. And that's what forms habitual karmic memory traces. Every time an event comes up in the field of experience, as soon as you do anything to it, you form a new karmic memory trace. Those karmic memory traces are stored in the storehouse and eventually they get activated and they ripen. And they influence the unfolding states of mind, they influence your behavior and they influence how events come forth.

The next step is that after you engage an event at very high speeds, still in terms of milliseconds, you categorize that event in terms of pleasant, unpleasant and neutral. That happens very quickly. We do that with people perception. Within three seconds we decide whether we like them or not, or whether we feel neutral about them. So, we act upon a stimulus to classify it as pleasant, unpleasant, or neutral before we even know very much about what it is. It's that quick. In Western psychology, we call that hedonic tone—simple high-speed categorization of pleasant, unpleasant, and neutral. If you follow the aggregate model, the first is stimulus perception of form in Buddhism. The second is hedonic tone: pleasant, unpleasant, and neutral.

The third thing that we do is we develop perceptual categories. So, we say this [picking up a singing bowl] is round, it has metallic quality. So, now I've gone beyond this simple perception to develop, not thought, but certain perceptual categories about it. Stimulus features, we might call them in Western psychology. It's the third aggregate, perceptual categorizing—*dushe* in Tibetan.

Then, we start bringing conceptual thought into the picture and we appraise that event. And we compare it to our database and we assign meaning to it. That's the fourth aggregate: *duje*, the formative aggregate. Once we assign meaning to it, it's not simple color and form anymore. If I was just looking at this with the eye consciousness, this would be color and form. But, if I integrate the eye consciousness with the mind consciousness, now I call it a bowl.

The summation of all those stages of information processing is the fifth aggregate, which is the conscious perception of that experience. That's the five-aggregate model. If I add that to other models of information processing that came later in Buddhism, like the eight-consciousness model, there are additional things we have to add to that. Now, we have to add self-grasping and the personal meaning of that object for the self. So, this is just a pillow, and it doesn't have any personal meaning for me. I don't know it. But, this pillow, it's "mine" and I've sat on it before. So, it has a special meaning.

And that's the seventh in the eight-consciousness model: the integration of that perceptual event with the self-system. And the eighth is memory. Now, I compare that experience to memory. I can think of all the times that I was meditating with this pillow and the different places. It brings back a whole network of memories. This other one doesn't do that because I don't have any memory associated with it. So, you see, it gets more and more layered.

If we go through the steps of that again, the moment you fail to recognize that everything is the liveliness of awakened awareness manifesting itself to itself without any duality, that moment of failed recognition is the start of the pathway to delusion. The next step is that the mind starts reaching and defines stuff and defines duality, *yila jepa*, particularizing. The next step is you have a specific particular stimulus event now out there. The next step is to engage that event. I either process it further and keep chasing after it to make more of it or engage it enough to stop processing it. The next step after chasing after it is to divide it into pleasant, unpleasant, and neutral—to categorize it. The next step is I make simple perceptual categories. The next step is I compare it. I can have all sorts of complex conceptual categories for that event. Now, I assign meaning to it. Then it becomes associated with the self-system and it becomes associated with a memory system. Then, it gets more and more complex.

And the outcome of all of that is I'm not even seeing the object anymore; I'm mostly seeing it through the lens of all this mass of conceptual thoughts about it and memories about it that I don't even know what's out there anymore. I've gone way beyond the information given. And I'm living mostly in conceptual thought. We don't see things apart from our conceptual thought. If I say to you outside, "look at the tree," you don't look at the tree. You look at the idea of tree in your mind. But you don't look at the raw sensory experience that we call tree. And that's such a habit—that we just look at the ideas that we have in our mind rather than the raw sensory experience.

We do the same thing with people. You don't look at the person; you don't really see the person. You see all the fabric of ideas you have about that person. Most of which have nothing to do with the person. That's what Jean-Paul Sartre's novel *Nausea* was about. The protagonist in the story, Roquentin, looks at a tree and rather than seeing the idea of tree, he actually sees the raw data. And he's so unused to doing it, he gets sick, because it stunned him. We do it so infrequently.

So then, the final outcome of all that conceptualization and self-grasping and memory, the last stage of that is the development of the five poisons.

Now this perceptual event is associated with attachment, or hatred, or ignorance, or jealousy, or pride. And, it all has to do with all the memories associated with it. So, I can take my precious little meditation pillow now and I can see how the poisons interplay with that. I can see that I'm attached to a certain kind of pillow or other pillows, which is the poison of attachment. I can see that if I meditate with the wrong pillow, I don't like it, I get uncomfortable. That's the hatred. Or I get so preoccupied with the pillow that I forget about meditation, and there is the ignorance. If I have a good meditation session, I think I'm the best meditator in the entire world, so there's the pride. Or I notice that somebody else has a different pillow or a different seat than I do and it looks better than mine, and there's the jealousy. We've all done this, right? And the outcome of that is *trulwa*, a deluded mind of *samsāra*. Okay?

But here's the issue. Unlike Western psychology that describes how we process information about the world out there, Buddhism was never intended to be an information processing system or, for that matter, a science. It's a system of liberation. So, the only purpose of describing the stages of information processing is to show you the way out of that mess, the way out of the pathway of delusion. Or the way home, if you want.

And it's rather simple. All those steps that we just went through, as a meditation, you go through them in reverse. Some of you have done this with me before. It's a very powerful meditation. In fact, it's stunningly powerful. Okay?

So, you start with the poisons, and you strip them off of this. Then, you strip off the memory and get back to the pure perception. And you strip off the self-grab and you strip off the conceptualizations, and you strip off the chasing after anything, and you strip off the categorizing. You get back to the pure perception nakedly, free of all conceptualization. Then, you strip off the simple categories like neutral, pleasant, or unpleasant. Then, you hold the larger field of awareness within which that event is occurring, and you look more at the field than the event. And, as you look more at the field than the event, you strip off the mental engagement.

And, as you're just holding one nondual field, you strip off the duality. And, as you hold that field, you start looking at the totality of the field and nothing particular in it. And you strip off the particularizing. And, when you finish stripping all that stuff out, you end up with awakened awareness. Simple.

So, the purpose of describing these various models—like the five-aggregate model, or the eight-consciousness model in Buddhism—they weren't little laundry lists of information processing models; they're supposed to be live practice—you use them as a way to find your way back to your true nature and directly experience that awakening. If you don't use them for that, they are just dry, boring models. [Long pause] And return to the true nature of things, just the way they are. So, questions about this model?

Student 3

So, understanding that the functioning of cognitive mind is lively awakened awareness, is it possible to engage cognitive thought without in any way obscuring?

Dan

Yes. If you were to take the nature of thought at the beginning of practice, thought is a remarkable cloud, like layers and layers of clouds that obscure the radiance of the sun that's always shining. So, thought has become such a deluded habit of mind that it has the function of obscuring … one of the things that it does is to make you think thought and awareness are the same thing. So, when you concentrate, you separate out thought from awareness and when you concentrate enough, you get long periods of stillness. Where is the mind operating if there is no thought going on? So, just the concentration alone forces the issue, and you start operating out of awareness mode rather than thought mode (thinking that thought mode is not only the "default option," but the only option.) "Awareness gone beyond thought."

So, if you have that experience, then you can start looking at the fact that thought is insubstantial, it's empty. When a thought arises, where does it really come from? Can you find anything substantial about where it comes from? If it stays for a while, where does it stay? Is there anything substantial that stays? When it goes away, where does it go? Is there anything substantial about where it goes?

Or the metaphor approach to that from Padmasambhava: "Clouds move through empty space. They don't come from anywhere. They don't go anywhere. And when they stay and move, they have no substance. Yet they move and have direction. Look into your own mind and see if thought is like the clouds." So, if you do that practice of emptiness of thought, thought loses substantiality; it loses the capacity to obscure. It still occurs, it has directionality, but it's not so solid anymore, and you don't get lost in it so much anymore.

But if you have stable awakening, then a funny thing happens. You begin to view thought as the lively expression of awakened awareness like the rays of the sun viewed from the perspective of being the sun. In that case, thought doesn't obscure any more. It becomes the vehicle by which awakened awareness expresses itself. And if you purify thought to its absolute state, it becomes one of the five wisdom energies, discriminating wisdom. In that case, thought is no longer something that gets in the way. It's a most useful tool of a buddha-mind. Buddhas use discriminating wisdom to determine what thousands of beings need. That's how a Menri can read minds. All you have to do is put the lightning speed of awareness directed towards a being and you can see exactly what they need, exactly how to respond. Discriminating wisdom.

So, on the pathway of delusion, thought becomes this huge cloud that we get caught up in. It's our biggest cloud. But along the pathway of awakening, thought becomes the best tool of a buddha to serve the purposes of many, many, many beings. So, thought isn't the enemy. It's how you experience thought that's the issue.

So, there's no problem here. If you're operating out of awakened awareness, you're not going to get clouded by thought. It's useful. So, if I write a book, I hope that the thoughts are clear. I'm still directing it, but it doesn't have all that crap in it when the mind gets clear; it's just clear. It's just much more lucid because the thought serves the matter of true nature. When people are clear and they talk, you can tell right away; this is clear, this is the way it is. You can tell right away. And you can tell when it's not, when it's muddled. That's a function of realization. So, clear teachers are clear because their realizations are clear—they don't waste a lot of words. "This is it. Just like this." Thought is useful. The problem isn't thought, it's the perspective from which you see thought, and whether thought serves the pathway of deludedness, or serves the pathway of awakening. Nothing wrong with thought. Good.

June 8, 2016

Themes: Processing Different Kinds of Grief; the Indestructible Essence

Dan

Welcome everyone.

I'm happy to say that we're in collaboration with Judd Brewer, who's the head of the Neuroimaging Lab at UMass Medical School, who did key studies on the neuroimaging of mindfulness meditation. Judd's taken this course [Dan's Level 1 course]. Now, in collaboration and with a grant from the Fetzer Foundation, we got a grant to study the neuroimaging of awakening. So, we're just going to start that in the next couple of months.

We're going to scan students in Ocean and Waves, the natural state, setting up the Lion's Gaze view, and then awakening. And also, do it when they're not in the awakening state and then see what the contrast is. And I think we have enough local students who can have stable awakening part of the time, but not all of the time, so that we can get a contrast between when they're awakened and when they're not. So, we're working on the neurocircuitry of awakening. It should have been done years ago.

So, [a student] just helped me make the five-minute instructions—exactly five minutes each for emptiness of time, Ocean and Waves, automatic emptiness in the natural state, Lion's Gaze, and then five minutes of stabilized awakening. They'll listen to the instructions and then hopefully they can do what we ask them to do. If they don't, we'll punish them. [Dan chuckles]

So, open for questions either about your practice or about spirituality in everyday life and then we'll frame it into a meditation.

Yes.

Student 1

So, it has to do with grief and loss in the sense of … because I haven't done a retreat yet, which I plan to do, so I'm not grounded in practice. You know, I just started coming to these classes. And I came because my husband passed away and then I had built a career in New York, which I walked away from. So, he passed away in November. I walked away from that in January and then my best friend was diagnosed with terminal cancer in the end of January.

So, there's been a lot of loss. And I found this class to be so—in terms of grieving, it was so overwhelming, but I actually found it to be almost a way in for me. But now I feel like, I mean I think my question … or to talk about … I feel attached to the loss in a way. What I mean by that …

Dan

What does that mean?

Student 1

Because it's been sort of such a profound experience of everything being gone—from identity of career, to partner, to my mother who also is now dying. So, it's from best friend to … so, it feels like all of those things that I identified my life, myself with is they—it's actually somehow helped me.

But then I feel like I am … that feeling of grief is so much more real to me than some of sort of, you know, all the things that I've been doing for the last twelve years in terms of achievement and career, that I'm recognizing it's almost like, "Well am I using the grief in a way that I'm actually attaching to it?" Because I'm thinking about—I'm also having more joy in little things. Like literally growing peonies, which is, so everything seems like, not that it's a cliché, but I hear all the cliches like in the simple things.

But I am feeling that the … I don't want to walk away—I guess I don't know really how to talk about it even. Because it's not like you walk away from the loss, but I'm sort of—I don't want to attach to the loss. Do you know what I mean? I don't want to create the loss as another identifier.

Dan

Well, okay, let's talk about that. We'll talk about it from a Western perspective. And we'll talk about it from a Buddhist perspective, both. When you lose somebody close there's a natural process of grieving. And there are stages to that grieving process. First, with grief, if a loss comes suddenly, the first thing that the mind tries to do is make sense of it. Why did this happen? Why did it happen now? Why did it happen like this?

And then there's a tendency to, because the feelings are overwhelmingly strong, to minimize the impact, emotionally and cognitively. But after a while the memories and feelings of the deceased slip into awareness, intrude into awareness. So, you alternate between being in denial and having intrusive imagery around the feelings about the loss. And that process has a natural progression to it. And eventually you process the loss and bring it to some integration and closure, and the symptoms of grief go away.

There is a good deal of research showing that there's a difference between what we call simple and complicated bereavement. In simple bereavement, you get grief reactions. You deal with it, and within a reasonable amount of time it goes away. And then it's mostly ended. With complicated bereavement, it doesn't end so simply. The symptoms of grief persist.

The original article on grief was by good old Sigmund Freud called "Mourning and Melancholia." And he noticed that the symptoms of grief very much parallel what we see in chronic depression or what he called "melancholia" in those days. And complicated bereavement, the reason why the symptoms persist is either that the person can't accept the circumstances of the death and/or the relationship was complicated. And in many cases of complicated bereavement, there was some conflict in the relationship. Ironically, if we're close to somebody and the relationship is a good relationship, it's easier to mourn, as counterintuitive as that seems. But if the relationship had complications in it, those conflicts retard the natural grieving process.

But whether it be simple or complicated bereavement, all of the models in the West of bereavement center around the theme of what we would call disrupted information processing. The loss suddenly disrupts the relationship, and we don't process it well. We tend to put it out of our mind and as was once said,

"Resistance guarantees persistence." The more we don't process it, the more the symptoms persist. And if you provide somebody who's bereaved with the right conditions, so that you encourage them to process the memories and the feelings about it and they integrate that into consciousness; then in most cases, except when there's extreme conflict, the symptoms stop persisting. And providing the right context so that people can process the memories and feelings about the loss is the heart of all grief work in the West.

Now that involves a number of things. First, it involves making sense or meaning making. And that's somewhat dependent on how the person died. If they die in a slow, chronic illness and of natural causes as a result of that illness, then it's not hard to make sense of that because you experience it over time. If a person dies suddenly, say, from a heart attack or something like that, the suddenness makes it more difficult to make sense out of it.

And in some situations, the person might die, and we don't know how they died. For example, I remember seeing a mother whose only child died when he was sixteen in a car accident driving in the country when he smashed his car into a tree. And basically, the car lit on fire and he burned to a crisp. That's hard to make sense out of. Because what happened that led to the crash? We're not there to observe it. All we have is the end results, which are gruesome.

So in those cases, the issue of meaning making is much more salient because we can't make sense out of what doesn't make sense. And the mind is constantly grasping for different scenarios to try and figure out which one fits. How long does that go on? Until you make sense out of it, even if the making sense out of it is not entirely accurate. At some point you have to settle with it. So, in those situations, it's more difficult, you see. So, making sense out of what happened is part of the process of grieving.

Another important part of the grieving is somehow integrating the meaning of that relationship. And, of course, if it was a positive relationship, the loss is hard but it's clean. And that's easier in an ironic sense. But if the relationship had conflict and complications in it, the more the complications, the more the likelihood that the grieving is going to be complicated. You have to identify and unhook the conflict. And until that happens, the grieving tends to persist sometimes for months and years. So, the nature of the way the person dies, the nature of the relationship, all of those things matter and that's a part of the loss. Assessing and integrating the nature of the relationship—the good, the bad, and the ugly.

And then there's a third part which you're mentioning—which is the strong part for you—that when we lose somebody that's close to us, we lose more than the person. We lose roles. We lose our role as an intimate partner, which we've been involved with for a long time, and all that goes into that. And there are benefits you get out of that role as an intimate partner. You get to be a caregiver. Where's the location for that role after you lose your partner, all those things that you do that are positive things? There's no location for them anymore. And in your case, the loss of role isn't just about losing the role as a partner, you're losing your job. That's a loss of role. It's a significant identity in the nature of the work that you did, and you let go of that after the loss.

So now you're dealing with, in some ways, a double loss because it's the loss of your partner and whatever is involved in that, but there's loss of a whole life, which means your role at work, and where you're going in life; and you've lost your bearings in more than one respect. And that makes it more complicated, you see. So, when you process what's not processed, it means making sense of the loss, making sense of the relationship, and making sense of your wider life that has also been lost. That's a lot.

So, all grieving in the Western sense comes down to a rather simple point. The grief counselor provides the right relational conditions for you to begin and invites you to process that loss at your own pace in a way that you can tolerate. At the beginning that means making sense of what happened. In the middle stage it means coming to grips with the relationship and settling with that. And then moving on, and losing and mourning old roles, and deciding what new roles are best fit for this stage of life for you. Those are the essential processes of grieving, in Western terms.

There's lots written on loss and grieving. The best work that I know, in the Western terms, is a little protocol. It was developed in the late 1980s in Australia by a guy named Manthorpe. And it reports sixty-three cases of complicated—not simple, but complicated—bereavement all of which were resolved with a maximum of one to three sessions. And that raised my eyebrows. But as many outcome studies done in those days, it just reported broad strokes of what the protocol did and not a lot of detail.

In order to make sense of what he was doing that seemed so remarkably effective, we took the protocol, modified it, tried to develop more careful wording for it. And, like Manthorpe found, we found that it worked wonders. And I don't recall very many times where I ever went over three sessions even with the most complicated bereavement. So, it clearly works and is proven. It's about providing the conditions to make sense of the loss, to work through whatever conflicts occurred in the relationship, and to say goodbye all in one fell swoop. It's a remarkably simple protocol and I was impressed over the years about its effectiveness. So, we've used it a lot in over two hundred cases of grief.

What you do, basically, is take advantage of part of the common observation of people who are grieving. In the early stages of the grieving process—if you lose somebody, if you think of them, it feels like they're a live presence in the room with you, like a visitation. Almost everybody does that. So, you simply ask the person to close their eyes and bring to mind the person who has been deceased as if you could imagine your relationship with them so vividly you could actually feel their presence in the room. It doesn't take long, and most people can do that.

This whole model of grieving is based on two things: one, processing what's not been processed, and two, resolving conflict.

So, the first part of the protocol is to process what's not been processed. So, what you do is you ask the person to imagine that they're there with the person who died, who's a live presence, and you can feel their presence. We call that revivification. And having done that, you ask the person to talk out loud to the person who died as if they could hear you, understand you. And if they weren't very good listeners in your lifetime, you imagine that they could really listen and take in everything you want to say in their current state.

And you ask the person who's bereaved in a heartfelt way to give voice to whatever, what feels most emotionally unfinished, and to keep doing that. So, at the beginning it's about making sense of what happened. Then it becomes more about whatever was left unsaid about the relationship, whatever you never got to say. And you keep doing that and keep doing it until it feels finished. That's processing. That allows a context for you to process the unfinished feelings and memories. And you keep doing that in a heartfelt way. You get right to the heart of the matter until it feels settled. That handles the meaning-making part of grief.

The next part of the protocol is sort of brilliant. And what you do is you say to imagine that that person, the dead person, has things that they want to say to you. They can see how you've struggled with this. And in terms of how they know you, there are certain things they want you to know and leave you with. And when you do that from the other talking to the bereaved person, whatever the underlying conflict is gets exposed and worked through.

It's remarkably simple. As if the other person already knows that, and through the metaphor of the deceased other, they identify the conflict, address it, and put it on the table for the both of you. And that person keeps saying what they want to be first, whatever feels unfinished in the relationship for them; they see that, and they put it out there. And eventually, whatever it takes, whatever they see about how you need to get on with your life, they put that out there too. So, they leave you with a reminder, and somehow, they know about how you're about how to get on with your life and move on.

The last part of the protocol is leave-taking. You have to say goodbye. What you get to keep are memories and feelings. What you don't get to keep is the relationship. And you separate those things out. Now, it's time for each of you to take leave of each other and go your separate ways, keeping the memories and feelings you have that are so special about the relationship, but otherwise, saying goodbye. So, you force the issue of making a clean ending, but you get to keep the memories and the feelings. You don't get to keep the relationship. If you don't do that, the person constantly goes back to clinging and holding onto the relationship.

Sometimes that leave-taking part is assisted by rituals and objects. There are things that help us to keep a link to that very close relationship with the deceased. We call those linking objects. So, for example, I saw a woman who was a victim of child sexual abuse with an Irish Catholic alcoholic father. There were three girls and one boy. She was a twin with the boy. All three girls were sexually abused repeatedly by the father. And the twin brother died, and she had a hard time with the bereavement because he died of a heroin overdose. This is a guy who was a state star in sport. A very promising life. Got into heroin and went down the tubes and died.

When we did the first part of the protocol, the emotional press was to make sense out of how he died. And she remembered vividly the last time she saw him. He had come to some family gathering and she could tell right away from his eyes that he was high; and the last interchange she had with him was being angry that he would come to the party high. And she was left with not making any sense out of why shortly thereafter he died of an overdose.

As she reviewed and reviewed it in her mind, she remembered all the times that he would jump in and take on the father when he would come home drunk, and pick a fight with the father so that the father would deflect his rage at him in order that the girls not get sacrificed. And she needed to tell him what was unfinished about that—that she knew that he had sacrificed himself and his life to protect her. She wanted to thank him for that. That was what was emotionally unfinished. That was the conflict in the relationship. But it didn't settle it.

First was making sense of what happened. Then the next part was finishing the unfinished business within her; what she was conflicted about it is that she felt guilty that he had sacrificed himself so many times and she got to go on with her life. She was the only one in the family that made it. She had a successful career. She had a healthy marriage and two young kids. She was a good attachment mom. So, she had done it completely differently.

But then we said, "He has some things from his current state of mind; he sees things and he has some things that he wants to tell you." And this is what he said. He said, "Stop feeling guilty for my death." He said, "You didn't understand. I didn't just overdose. I did it intentionally." And she said, "Why?" He said, "Because from the needles I had AIDS, and I was going to die anyway, and I was sparing everybody." And she said, "So you did it again, you protected us." But she could appreciate it, because now it made sense. So, now she had made sense of the meaning of why he died. She was able to talk about her appreciation for all that he had sacrificed.

But the one piece of unfinished conflict was she felt that he never had a chance, because he died, to see how her life went and the fact that she had a happy family life with two healthy kids. That's where rituals come in. And what she did is, they just moved into a big new house and they had a playroom, and in the playroom, she set up an altar with his picture so that he would always watch over her kids playing. And he could see what he never got to see: the fruition of his self-sacrifice. Powerful. Total time, three sessions.

It's how you approach it that matters, you see. Meaning making, resolution of conflict, processing the unfinished feelings and emotions, that's the heart of the protocol.

I had a woman come to a workshop that I was doing many years ago. It was a three-day workshop and in the middle of the workshop, she disappeared and didn't come back. I didn't know why. Then she called me three days later saying that she was suicidal. And what had happened is in the middle of the workshop, she had one son, a sixteen-year-old, and his car crashed, and he was burnt to an unrecognizable point. And since it was very hard for her to conceive, and that was her only child, she thought her life was over.

I saw her on an emergency basis. The first part of the protocol was to make sense of what happened. And when she was reviewing how this was a country, windy road, she first thought, "Well, maybe he reached down to put a CD in and he wasn't paying attention to the road." But then she remembered what she didn't want to remember: that in the months before this accident, he had increased his drinking quite a bit. And the sense that she made out of it was that the likelihood was very high that he was drinking too much. And both of them were in denial about that. And probably, he was drinking and that's what caused him to crash into the tree. Since his body was burnt so badly there was no blood alcohol level that could be taken. But she made sense out of it. It made sense to her.

Then in a heartfelt way, she processed both the loss and that this was her whole life. She had spent so many years trying to become pregnant. They worked really hard at it. This was her only shot. But that didn't unhook the conflict. So, at some point, I turned it around and said, "He has some things he wants to say to you. In his current state, he sees your grief. He sees your suicidality. He knows how deeply distressed you are. But there are things about the relationship that he wants you to know about." And what do you think he said? Remember, this is her mind, her imagination.

He said, "Ma, get a life." He said, "You were always in my face. You controlled everything that I did." And he said, "Now, you want to die and control it again. Let me go on my own way now, finally, and get your own life." You know I wouldn't have thought of that in a million years. But the fact is, it comes from her because on some of the deepest level of mind she knew that. That unhooked the conflict. And she got a life. And she and her husband went to a fertility clinic, and within a year they had twins.

Some many years later, about ten or fifteen years later, I met her at a conference, and she said, "I'll be back." She brought the twins to meet me, and I got to see what happened with the successful resolution of this. And she was much less over-involved and much more relaxed about being a parent; and even though she raised twins, which is a hard thing to do, basically it resolved. It took two sessions. It's not what you do, it's how you do it that matters.

I hope that those examples give you some feeling for the power of how this works. Beyond resolving the grief, you may do additional sessions to sort of think about how a person renews their life, and that's where the other part of what you're talking about comes in, loss of role. How do you move on, how do you develop a new life without that person as a central reference point in your life?

But as the Taoist Master Zhuang Zhou once said, "Crisis is opportunity." And if you look at it that way, after you do most of the grieving and the grieving winds down, you're free of that. And there is a remarkable opportunity there to discover and explore new ways. And if anything, the loss impresses upon [us] our own mortality and how preciously short this life is. And if you really understand that, then maybe you move on and lead a better life in the precious time you still have to do that. That's a good lesson to learn. Some people call that benefit-finding. You take a loss, and you find some benefit in it. It's an opportunity to do it differently, to do what you want.

On the other hand, from a Western point of view, I have to introduce a caveat. And as much successful grief work as we've done over the years, I have to say in all honesty that I think that if a parent loses a child, that's a different magnitude of loss, and you rarely fully overcome that. It doesn't really fully ever resolve the way that relationships with others, family members, or significant others are. To lose a child, because safety and protection is built into the evolution of attachment—it's not easy to get over. So, in that specific situation, it's more humbling, more difficult.

From a Buddhist point of view, there are two things. One is emptiness practice. Grief would be under the domain of emptiness of emotion, and how you see the emotion as something that doesn't have grab and something that is isn't substantial. You take your high-speed awareness and you roam around in grief and find "grief-ness." Where do you locate grief? And if you think you've located a specific point, roam around in that part of the body that you think you've located it in; and the more you keep roaming around in that, the thing that you seek as solid keeps slipping away as unfindable; and you keep doing that until there is nothing solid left of it. Grief becomes the liveliness of awareness, but you clean it up of the labels, you clean it up of the grab, and it doesn't have that grab anymore even though it may still come back.

Now, comparing the East and West model, quite frankly, I like the grief model in the West better for working with grief. And normally with people, even my meditation students, I would start with that. And often if I'm doing a week-long retreat and I have somebody at the course who is stuck in noncomplicated bereavement, I'll try and find an hour in the break to do the Western protocol for that. After they've processed the grief, then the emptiness of grief adds another dimension to that to clean it up. So, they really leave it behind.

But I think there is a problem if you don't do the Western grief protocol, and you just start with emptiness of grief. Then it easily shades off into nihilism like we're trying to get rid of the grief reactions, and that just leads to the Buddhist version of suppression or repression, not necessarily the right way to be going with it. So, using emptiness of grief to deal with grief is a slippery slope unless you're really honest with yourself. You're using Buddhist meditation practice in the service of defense, and that doesn't resolve it. But from a spectrum point of view, you do the Western grief work first and then you can complement it with emptiness of grief. That's not a bad combination.

In terms of moving on, the best meditation for that is to appreciate the preciousness of life, which is called *daljor*, precious opportunity. You imagine all sorts of unfortunate circumstances of others and imagine them as if that were your life, and then you contrast it with what you have right now; and each time you develop another scene of somebody with unfortunate circumstances and then you come back to what you have, it hammers home the preciousness of what you've got. So, then you don't want to waste the seemingly precious short life that you have. And if you do that practice as a daily practice, you'll cut out all the extraneous stuff that you do in your life and spend your time making priorities about what matters. So, we'll do a visualization on those things after the break. That's a good question.

It's a little bit different with grief when the person dies suddenly rather than if a person dies of a slow debilitating illness; like say they had cancer or ALS or AIDS or something like that, and they died over a couple of years, or Alzheimer's. Because when you imagine at the beginning the person as a live presence, you have to modify the protocol and imagine the time before they had their ailment—when they had all their faculties if they had Alzheimer's, or when they were healthy in their body if it's something like ALS or AIDS or something like that.

You have to imagine them in a time that they had both the body and mind intact before they deteriorated. And remember them like that because if you want them to communicate to you about how they see you—of course, if they have Alzheimer's, that's not going to work. But if you have them imagine a time before they contracted that, then it works better, you see. So, you have to modify the approach depending on whether it's slow deterioration or sudden onset. And it's a relevant topic, more as we get older. Someone once said you know your age when you start reading the obituaries and see your friends there. It's true. So, no guarantees anymore. Life becomes very precious. It's important.

Okay? We have time for something else before we take a break. That's a good question. Thank you. Anybody else?

Yeah.

Student 2

I had two questions. One relates to … why do some people get a lot of luminosity, and other people don't? And my second question is totally different. It's more of a metaphysical question. My friend just wrote a thesis about why the soul should be included in psychology. And in there, she talked about, I think she incorrectly said that in Buddhism the goal was to transcend the regular mind to merge with the mother mind. And I said I didn't think that was accurate. This is what I told her I thought because the paper is about transcendence and transmutation. So, I just wanted to tell you what I told her and just get your reaction to it.

I saw in Buddhism that transcendence is a big part of it, but it's more about transcending the traps of the mind so that we can transmute to be a higher person and to bring more eminence or divinity to make reality better—may all beings find the way, you know, make a better world. Anyways, I just want to get your reaction to those two questions.

Dan

Complicated.

Is there a soul in Buddhism? The middle path position is between the extremes of nihilism and eternalism. The standard Mādhyamaka approach would be that the concept of the soul is empty. It doesn't exist other than being a construction of mind.

However, that got a little complicated because in the literature on the dying process in Tibetan Buddhism at least—not Indian Mahāyāna Buddhism so much, but more in Tibetan Buddhism—there's clearly this notion of an indestructible essence. And that indestructible essence is lodged in the heart at conception and fixed in position by four chakra knots. And that indestructible essence is like a computer chip. It contains the memory imprints of all your previous lifetimes.

So, when you die, that indestructible essence … during the dying process the chakra knots around it loosen. It's freed up, is retained in the central channel for up to three days—not necessarily three days, but up to three days—and then is released through one of the orifices of the body. And then it basically recycles itself.

It's a little complicated because from a Buddhist perspective, we would say that indestructible essence doesn't have substantiality. It's a computer chip of awareness. In that sense, it's not like a soul which is more substantial. On the other hand, it has continuity across lifetimes. So, in that sense, it's like a soul.

Now, it gets more complicated in the Bon tradition which is originally shamanic because what they say is there's a *la*, there's a soul that's different from the indestructible essence. It can leave the body in certain states and certain sicknesses, and you've got to track it down and retrieve it like any good shaman does. Chongtul, who is the Bon lama and one of the Bon lamas I teach with in New York, has a two-year course in soul retrieval. From an indigenous Bon tradition, they have a thing like a soul: it persists, it survives human death. So, I'm not sure it's that clear, that much different, except from a Buddhist perspective it's less substantial.

There's an interesting scientific Western argument about this that I once heard, which I found compelling. The study of human survival of bodily death has been anathema to modern science, but it was popular in the late 1890s, and the person who made it popular was the great American psychologist William James; his best friend, FWH Myers, wrote a rather large textbook: *Human Personality and Its Survival of Bodily Death*. It was a very hot topic. William James was very interested in it. And with the rise of behaviorism in the 1920s, it died completely out, never to be addressed again in science.

Something seems to survive, and that's why Tibetans make a distinction between physical death, which is the point that you stop breathing and your brain shortly thereafter dies, and spiritual death. Because after the brain dies and the body is dead, the indestructible essence is released into the central channel, and it stays up to three days. You're still not spiritually dead, which is why the Tibetans say, "Don't move the body until the indestructible essence leaves."

How do you know when it leaves? It's not subtle. At the point it leaves, blood congeals at the mouth or the nose, and the body emits the smell of death. Before that it doesn't. You can tell when it's left.

With lamas who have some capacity for rainbow body, you can tell not just that it left. You can tell when it's leaving because rainbow lights will appear in the sky around the body.

It's a good question. There's a lot to it.

Now this whole thing of transcendence, what it means is if you directly experience awakening, and stabilize that awakening, in some way it will occur to you that that awakening isn't limited to the physical location of your brain or your mind. It certainly isn't limited to your body. And at some point, you'll understand that dying is just a change in phase, in state. "There's no dying to be done," as Milarepa said in one of his songs. Not possible.

But great lamas, great yogis, not only master the dying process, but they can voluntarily control how they want to come back, in any form. That's part of the *phowa*, or consciousness transference. In that sense, they've truly transcended death. You can choose to come back in any plane of reality you want to help serve the welfare of sentient beings, or you can choose to repopulate yourself in awakened *dharmakāya* space, and, as a fully enlightened buddha in awakened *dharmakāya* space, you can stay there as long as you want in the dormant state or you can intend to come back and repopulate in any form you want any time in the future. That's what's called a *tulku* or an emanation. So, you gain complete voluntary control over the dying process and how you want to return if you so choose.

Ultimately, through the dying process, not even the body dies if you have rainbow body. The body turns into rainbow light. There's a similar system in the Taoist system. It's a secret system called Shen practice. It's a special energy channel system that's not normally used. If you do the Shen system and perfect it, the body disappears and turns to pure energy, stored in the form of a star. Stars are conscious in the Taoist system. Stars are previous beings who have been enlightened. And they store themselves, their star energy, until they decide to return. In that perspective, the universe is conscious, not physical. But there are almost no surviving texts on the practice of the Shen system. Very little. Very few practicing places in Taoist system in China anymore.

But it's an interesting time. I got to talk with His Holiness Menri Trizin, the head of the Bon, this last weekend. He began the talk by saying that all the ancient teachings that people thought were lost are all going to come back to the West now. So, none of these things were lost. It simply appears that way. God knows we need it—our attitudes about death are so screwed up.

Student 2

But would you agree—the last part of my question was that this transcendence that we're doing, going to awakened awareness, is helping us transmute, be better people, which is going to make the world a better place. You're hypothesizing it that …

Dan

Spiritual realization is always necessarily the test of conduct.

Student 2

Right.

Dan

It's how you lead your life, not what you think about your realization.

Student 2

Right, it's an enabler though, right?

Dan

If you have realizations, the spontaneous manifestation of that is conduct serving the welfare of all beings. And if you have full enlightenment, then it becomes *trinlé*, enlightened activity, inexhaustibly serving all beings across many planes of reality simultaneously. It's the ultimate in multitasking. So?

Student 2

And my first question: why do people get more luminosity than others?

Dan

There are three special states that you can get attached to: luminosity, bliss, or non-conceptual stillness. Most people in deeper states of concentration will show glimpses of all of those. When you're doing Ocean and Waves practice and extraordinary emptiness practice, they come up again more strongly. If you have stable awakening, they come up as accompaniments to awakening.

There are three points in the path where these three states, the special states, come up. One of them will predominate over the other two, and that depends on your everyday ordinary mind. If you're the kind of person that's over ideational, then nonconceptual stillness will be your state of attachment. The opposite is if you think too much, you'll get attached to not thinking. If you're visually predominant, and the information processing system is dominated by visual forms, then you get luminosity as your special state of choice. If you happen to be more body-oriented or more feeling-oriented, then bliss will be your attachment special state.

So, the answer is it depends on what your everyday life experience is and what's predominant. That determines which special state will be the one that would be most problematic for you. Choose your poison.

Student 2

I must be more thinking than visual because those are the two that come up, and I'm trying to learn to be more, get more bliss because that's the part I don't have yet. I'm expanding my question.

Dan

Look for the ones that are missing, right?

Student 2

Yeah. You've already answered a lot of my questions …

Dan

Well, it's hard to look for that. If you want bliss and you don't normally have bliss, then the best practice is inner fire practice. That will super charge the bliss.

Student 2

I don't know that one yet. Could try it sometime here maybe.

Dan

We're doing a course on it in early September. The whole course is about central channel practice.

Student 2

Okay. What level is that? It's a Level 3 something?

Dan

I don't know. Whatever it is. We've lost track.

Student 2

Thanks.

Dan

You'll get bliss.

Student 2

Thank you.

Dan

There are eight levels of bliss. You have to have all eight of them.

July 13, 2016

Themes: Mixing Practice; Asanga's Nine Stages of Staying

Dan

Welcome everyone. You have a question?

Student 1

This took me a while to formulate, so bear with me if I get a little bit lost, because I've had some difficulty conceptualizing it. I feel as if with my practice, I've had a fairly good development of my own internal skills. Those skills being able to turn off conceptualization and turn off what you refer to as the information processing that goes with everyday thought.

My difficulty has been not in everyday interactions. I can get off the cushion and keep that at a level that I'm comfortable with and I feel like my awareness, my skill is decent at keeping that awareness. But when I'm involved in more detailed, more complex relationships with other people, they require that I turn that information processing back on and be dealing with them at a level that requires a lot more in the way of understanding their conceptualization using language.

I find that I get clouded over really easily. I sometimes become very, very reactive and very sensitized to relationship issues that I don't feel like I have the skill to handle. And I don't know what to do with that, how to bridge that, between my practice when I'm by myself or in relationships, or in social situations that are less loaded in contrast to interactions that are very highly emotional or have a lot more meaning to them.

Dan

What you're describing is that when you're in such situations, awakened awareness is out to lunch.

Student 1

Okay.

Dan

The issue is that if you shift your basis to awakened awareness, because of the force of habits of the ordinary mind, you lose that view and you shift back to operating out of the ordinary mind. And there are certain situations where you're much more likely to shift your basis back to ordinary mind from awakened mind. So, you're asking, how do I sustain the awakening as the basis during difficult life situations, especially those that I can't maintain it in.

Student 1

Particularly ones that require that—I think the way I've heard you phrase it in the past is that having the self is very useful in day-to-day interactions with other people, but you shouldn't be reifying the self. So, the question is: how do you shift back into using the self without losing awakened awareness? How do you project that when you need to?

Dan

If you're operating out of the unbounded wholeness of awakened awareness, that's not exclusive of operating out of self or even operating out of conceptual thought. Self and conceptual thought can arise within the vast expanse of awakened awareness in such a way that it doesn't preclude or obscure awakening. It's part of the field. But you're not operating out of that narrow thing that we call the self-representation, where you get lost in thought. The thought just occurs like a wave in the ocean from the vantage point of being the ocean. So, it's quite possible to sustain awakening while you're thinking.

Technically speaking, what you're talking about from a practice point of view is what is called *drewa*, mixing practice. Typically, if you had some taste of awakening, and you've had some stability with that, then what you want to do is stabilize the awakening on the pillow more. So, once you've had a taste of awakening, then your task is to set up the same view that opens up awakening, frequently. So, you can open up awakening on the meditation pillow more frequently, for longer duration. See how long you can sustain it before you shift back to ordinary mind. And open it up more immediately; that is, just by the intention of looking, you shift your basis to awakening. So frequency, duration, immediacy, on the pillow, and you keep doing that.

In addition, when it shifts back to ordinary mind, and you know that you're shifting out of awakened mind back to ordinary mind, you get lost in ordinary mind of thought, or self, or time, or out-there-ness, or whatever else. Then you have to look at the patterns using your cognitive intelligence. What is it that's causing you to shift back to ordinary mind?

Or, like one of my students says, "What are your favorite clouds?" Find out what you get caught up in the most. You'll see there are patterns there. By identifying those patterns, you can start doing more carefully refined emptiness practice around what those patterns are. So, if you get caught up in conceptual thought, you do emptiness of thought. If you get caught up in emotions in general or specific emotions, you do emptiness of emotions.

And through those practices of setting up the view repeatedly, looking at how it clouds over, and doing a dedicated emptiness practice in terms of where it mostly clouds over, over time you can sustain awakened awareness on the pillow more frequently, for longer duration, and more immediately.

Then the question becomes, having developed some skill in sustaining, stabilizing awakening on the pillow, at what point do you start taking it off the pillow? There are different answers to that. The answer that I typically adhere to is when you have awakening most of the time on the pillow, number one, and number two, when just by putting the intention of looking, it shifts to awakening. You don't have to do all that work setting up the view, the emptiness of time, Ocean and Waves, automatic emptiness, refining the automatic emptiness into the natural state, setting up the view of the Lion's Gaze, and recognizing the shift to awakening. You don't have to do all that stuff. Just the intention of looking shifts your basis to awakening. That's the point when you can start taking it off the pillow.

Now, in mixing practice, generally speaking, you develop a hierarchy of situations from easiest, to more difficult, to much more difficult to sustain awakening in. For example, many people who have shifted their basis to awakening on the pillow, if they were to get off the pillow while they're in the awakened state and walk around in nature, there's a pretty good likelihood that they could sustain it in a quiet place of nature for some period of time before they shift back to ordinary mind again. That would be something low on the hierarchy.

It may be that walking around in a more busy environment, like a city environment, where there are lots of people around, even though you're not interacting with them, would be a more challenging place to sustain awakening. It would be higher on the hierarchy. It may be engaging in complex interactions with people like what you do at work when you're working with patients, and you have to figure things out and you have to interact with them at the same time, be compassionate towards them, understand what's going on with them. It's a lot to do there. It may mean that that requires so much busyness of the ordinary mind that you find yourself easily shifting out of awakening and back to ordinary mind again.

So, if you made your own hierarchy of situations from more easy to more difficult, you wouldn't start with that. But you would start with taking it off the pillow and going out to nature or taking it off the pillow and then being around people, but not necessarily talking with them. And then see how long you could sustain the awakening and then recognize more with your metacognitive awareness when you shift out of awakened back to ordinary mind.

And a funny thing starts to happen. You sharpen your ability to recognize when you shift out of awakening and back to ordinary mind. And each time you shift back to ordinary mind, and then you set up the conditions for you to shift your basis back to awakening again, you're engaging in a process that in the Bon Akhrid system of Dzogchen is called *chikba*, dismantling the residuals of the ordinary mind. You start taking apart the ordinary mind and its residual habits that are sometimes called the *nyigpa*, the dregs of the ordinary mind. And after a while they just don't come up. So, the propensity to cloud over doesn't come up as much.

And when you get that point at the mid-range of your hierarchy [where] you can shift back to awakening and that tendency to cloud over doesn't happen so much, then you can take on the most difficult things in your hierarchy. Go on the pillow, set up your view of Lion's Gaze, hold it until you shift your basis to awakening, stabilize the awakening, shift the view into continuous liveliness, and really stabilize the awakening. And once it's really strong, then put yourself in that situation, like interacting and complex cognitive tasks with patients, and see how long you can sustain the awakening before you lose it. You'll find that you'll sustain it each time a little bit longer. And when you lose it, go back to your view. Establish awakening and come back at it again. Go back to another interaction with a patient and see if you can sustain it there. And over time, you learn to sustain awakening in the most difficult of life circumstances.

Now, when you're engaged in that complex task, a funny thing happens. You're still operating out of the unbounded wholeness, the vast, infinite ocean of awakened awareness space, but the self exists within that ocean. Conceptual thought exists within that ocean. So, it's not like the return of the self and the thinking self that all interferes with that awakening. You don't shift back to ordinary mind again. The actions that you engage in come spontaneously from awakened *dharmakāya* space, so they're much cleaner. They're not filtered through all that cognitive stuff of the ordinary self. There's much less grab, so you would end up doing exactly what's needed in the situation that's the best fit. It comes spontaneously from awakened *dharmakāya* space. You don't have to work so hard at it. Everything arises spontaneously with the best fit for the situation at hand.

So, you see, even in those situations it becomes possible to sustain awakening. When I was working on mixing practice with His Holiness, Menri Trizin, the hardest things for me were to sustain awakening when I was talking with other people or translating, thinking. So, I spent an entire month with him, off the pillow, doing nothing but conversing with all the people who would wait outside his room to talk with him, to have an audience with him. My task was to maintain awakening while I was talking with all his guests or working on the computer and translating while I maintained awakening. And if I lost it shifting back to the ordinary mind, I'd go back to the pillow, set up Lion's Gaze, wait until I shifted my basis back to awakening, and go back to my computer again.

It's just like any other kind of learning task. You get better at it over time. Then at some point you sustain awakening, mix it into most life situations easily. At that point, awakening doesn't go away, even if, in whatever situation, it clouds over, it's like a thin veil. It would seem perfectly ridiculous to you that you could ever lose it. You attain what's called *dengwa*, confidence. You can't ever lose it.

Once you're firm, or clear about that, you won't ever lose it. But you've got to develop it in these steps. The Tibetan word is *chungwa*, which means to cultivate it. It also means to nurture. You've got to take care of it; you've got to develop it. It's a precious thing. You've got to nurture it. Then you'll have it all the time.

Ultimately, when you get very advanced with it, you can do what's called heroic *samādhi*. And there you don't need favorable circumstances to sustain the awakening. You intentionally put yourself in the most difficult of life circumstances as a test of your awakening—the worst of whatever—and then see if you sustain the awakening. If you can sustain it and even develop it and enhance it in the worst of life circumstances, then you'll see you're beyond any effect on the awakening by favorable or unfavorable life circumstances. Nothing can cause it to fade.

That process of working first with favorable and unfavorable circumstances is sort of like awakening relapse prevention therapy. After a while, even in the most difficult of life circumstances, you don't shy away from those situations. They become your best opportunities to deepen your realization. So, you'll welcome them.

Like the Milarepa song:

When it comes out just a hodge-podge, even better still.

When the bully's getting worse and worse, even better still.

Whatever the negative circumstances—the best moments for practice.

For me, professionally, my best move is to practice this on the stand in the abuse trial while being cross examined by opposing attorneys. That's where I do my best practice. And that's when I'm clearest.

These days practicing primary care medicine is like a cross examination—so it's not so different [Dan laughs]—with the average time now per visit being twelve minutes.

Good question. Develop it skillfully, but don't judge yourself when you lose it. Every time you fall out of the view, and then you shift back to awakening again, you're dismantling more and more of those residuals of ordinary consciousness. At some point, you won't fall out of the view anymore.

Student 2

Working on patients is the next step then …

Dan

Reactivity is just another wave of the ocean. It's all liveliness. Doubt is liveliness. Fear of losing it is liveliness. Reactivity is liveliness. You hold the view; can't possibly leave it.

Student 2

Thank you.

Dan

It's good? Yes?

Student 3

I wondered if you could talk a little bit about the five faults and the eight antidotes and how they are used. Are they only used in the beginning of the practice or are they used throughout the journey?

Dan

You're talking about … is this is from the Elephant Path?

Student 3

I think so. I'm testing my memory here. I'm going to see if I can remember here. I'm reading this book, *Walking Through Walls*, and he …

Dan

That's the Elephant Path, yeah.

Student 3

While reading them, it seems like they could be used throughout the whole journey. I'm trying to figure out how.

Dan

Okay. If only I could remember these. I don't use that system so much. Do you have the book with you?

Student 3

Yeah.

Dan

Go get it. Good. And please do me a favor. Go into my office and get my glasses so I can see the book. [Laughter] Getting old sucks.

Student 4

Just liveliness.

Dan

Just liveliness. [Laughter] Okay.

Student 3

Sorry about this. I guess it's more simple.

Dan

What do we have here? Oh, those five faults, all right! [Laughter] Alright, so, you want me to give a commentary on this? Is that what you want?

Student 3

Yeah, I guess so.

Dan

Let me say something about the context of where this comes from. Asanga wrote the main work on concentration practice. It's called *The Semnegu*, or *Nine Stages of Staying*—literally that's [what] the title is. He wrote that book. It's from a larger work called the *Nyensung*, or "*The Ground of Hearers*," and that text was downloaded to him when he was deep in *samādhi* in his cave. And the future buddha, Maitreya, came to him and downloaded lots of teachings to him, and he said he just got up from his meditation and wrote it all down. So allegedly, these teachings on concentration come directly from Maitreya.

There was a time, I think it was in the 1980s, when Jeffrey Hopkins was developing his program at the University of Virginia Doctoral Studies of Tibetan. He invited this lama from Germany to come over—who was a Gelugpa lama—and do a series of lectures in the summer on concentration training, using *The Semnegu*. So, the lama came over and did a remarkable synthesis of all the teachings on the Elephant Path, as we call it.

The trouble with the Elephant Path is that since he wrote it, when Asanga wrote *The Yensung*, there's been no commentary on it—no one has ever written an official commentary to that book. So, there's not a lot of writing about the Elephant Path, other than the original work itself. There's somewhat of a commentary by Tsongkapa, the guy who founded the Gelugpa, the Dalai Lama's sect. And there's some other small pieces of work. And in some of that material, like the Gelugpa material, there's an elaboration of what are called the five faults of concentration and the antidotes, or remedies for those faults. And that's what our student here is referring to. He wanted to know how you would use that, basically, when it comes up.

I should say a couple more things about that book [*Walking Through Walls*]. If you buy that book, there's a second part of it that's just a *sopche*, an outline. Because he was supposed to come back the second summer and give the course on the stages of emptiness meditation. But in the interim, he died, so it was the second part of the book that never got finished. But they decided to publish the book anyway because it was a remarkable synthesis on the stages of concentration meditation that any Tibetan would involve themselves with.

The trouble is when they published the first edition of this book, which is what you have, they titled it *Walking Through Walls* because if you develop strong concentration abilities, you've got some supernormal capacities and you could walk through walls. So, they published the book and nobody bought it because when they gave it a weird title like that, nobody knew what it was. So then on the second edition, they changed the title to *Calm Abiding and Special Insight* because that's a less esoteric title, more about what's in the book, and so it sold much better. We have the original version called *Walking through Walls*—the first edition.

When you concentrate say on the rising and falling of the breath, there are things that will get in the way of deepening your concentration. And those are called the five faults.

The first is *lelo*, laziness. It means that you don't organize or prioritize your life to do concentration enough. So, the positive opposite of laziness would be *sindru*, which is often translated as enthusiastic perseverance, or often diligence. Sometimes we refer to it as "the work horse of diligence." So, laziness is the problem that you see mostly in the monasteries where the monks have a variety of things they do to take care of the monks. They may have a bunch of chores, and they have a comfortable lifestyle. They keep putting off their meditation and not really doing anything. So, it's largely a motivation issue.

If you take a meditation retreat, if you take the Level 1 retreat and you get all of this exciting new stuff and then you go home and you don't do anything with it—I mean, I've had people who've taken the course, even got a taste of awakening, and then I talk to them a year later and I say, "Well, what'd you do with it?" "Nothing." They don't have a daily practice. They threw the whole thing away.

So, it's a problem with motivating yourself to organize and prioritize your life so that you have a daily practice, discipline. So, diligence or enthusiastic perseverance is one in the West that we say—in particular in the National Football Club—that's called good work ethic. It means you show up to practice on time. You're well prepared. In the off-season you work out at a gym every day. You know, you don't come into the spring training out of shape. You've kept yourself in good shape. You're always working at your practice twenty-four hours a day, 365 days a year. Well, yogis even have a good work ethic—or they don't. It's no different. Some people organize their lives around doing practice and some people don't. So, those who never really quite get around to prioritizing daily practice would be called "lazy."

But in the West, we have a different version of laziness. One time I was teaching in the West—the Elephant Path—with Denma Locho Rinpoche. So many years ago. He was the abbot of the Dalai Lama's monastery at McCleod Ganj at the time. And one of the Western students said "Well, how do I deal with laziness?" And he immediately said "No! Laziness is for the monks at the monastery. For you Westerners, your version of laziness is busyness. That's your laziness. You preoccupy yourself with all these things to keep you busy and you never get around to practice." So, busy-ness is our laziness. It's Western laziness. We have so many other things to do, but we never get around to practice.

There are a number of antidotes or remedies—there are four of them. The first is dapa, or faith. I like to translate it as trust. You have to trust in your own intelligence and your own resourcefulness that you can actually do this practice. So, one of the reasons that people don't put in the daily practice in doing the work of the meditation is that they don't think it's going to get them anywhere. They have too much doubt. So, one of the antidotes, they're saying, is that if you have strong trust in your own ability and your own resourcefulness, you're more likely to exercise that trust by diligently practicing and overcoming laziness or busyness that way.

The second is aspiration, *monlam*. And aspiration means you think, "Well, why am I doing this? I'm doing this to better the condition of the world. I'm doing it to help serve the welfare of others." So, if you have strong aspirations that these practices improve the world around you and help people, then it's a way of getting out of yourself. Whatever your preoccupations are, you can more easily put them aside. And then you practice better.

The thing I learned the most from being a parent was that it's a unique life experience. It teaches you how to get out of yourself in a way that other life experiences don't quite do. I remember a time when I was teaching in California and my oldest was about eight, and we were teaching at Esalen. And the kids would go with us there a couple of times a year, and they were used to picking up whatever organic food they wanted from the garden and just eating it. So, we were walking along in Monterey, in the city, and my oldest saw what he thought was a potato plant on the side of the road and he immediately picked it up and started eating it. Not a good thing to do. And I said, "You can't do that." So, he got very, very sick. Sort of like a night with the exorcist—projectile vomiting all night long. I think we completely destroyed a hotel room.

Student 3

Wow.

Dan

It was bad. Really bad. So, after the sixth or seventh time he woke me up, I was just so dog tired that my immediate response was, "I just want to go back to sleep." But you'd never allow it to yourself as a parent. No matter what it takes, you just get up and you deal with it. And there's no other life experience that helps you get out of yourself in quite that way. You have no choice about it. You just do it. And there's something peculiarly freeing about it.

So, when you think about doing this practice, not for your own gains but because it's helpful to others, you get out of yourself. It's like being a parent for the world. And that's why aspiration is an important antidote to laziness and busyness.

The third is effort. You have to work at it. Whatever it takes. If you put more effort into it, one of the things that comes, the cumulative effect of that effort, is the mind is more alert.

You know, I started this in my late teens. I remember when I was living with my first Root Lama in my twenties, and I tried to meditate, I would get a lot of struggle with sleepiness. I remember going to him once and saying, "What do I do around sleepiness?" and he said, "Effort." So, I went back and I tried a little harder and that didn't seem to do very much—I had little comprehension of what he was saying. So, I thought about it for about six months since it was not working and thought that I would ask him again in a different context. So, I asked him again with a different context and he said "Effort." [Laughter] So, I plugged away at what I thought he was trying to get at, which I had no idea what he really meant.

Another year elapsed, and I was still struggling with it. I even sat on the edge of the pillow once, thinking I couldn't possibly fall off, because I was afraid to fall off. It kept me better. [Laughter] I got more and more alert. But it was difficult, so finally I decided if I sort of just have a normal—just chat with him, small talk—I would find a way of bringing this question … [Laughter] and he wouldn't know the question I was asking and I'd get a different answer—finally. But then I got the same answer: "Effort." So then, I said "Look, I just don't understand what you're asking me to do." So, he explained it in more detail.

So, if you keep putting in more and more vigorous effort, it does make the mind more alert. And you'll overcome the dullness. But I had to see how that worked, and that's what they're talking about here.

And the fourth is pliancy, *shinchong* in Tibetan. It's a kind of resultant skill from all your efforts. Sometimes it's referred to as pliancy or flexibility of life. There are two kinds of pliancy: physical pliancy and mental pliancy. If you sit for long periods of time and hold the posture, you develop *tak*, signs of progress. And the first sign of progress is that the body starts to generate a lot of heat when you get concentrated. It's a side effect of the concentration. Then the body gets light and buoyant, like you're bouncing on a balloon. And then thirdly it gets more pleasurable. There's a diffuse pleasure throughout your body. And then fourthly, this bliss is in raptures and it's quite pleasant. Then you don't want to stop sitting, you want to keep going. So, at some point the pliancy overrides all that discomfort that builds up in the body, so it's easier to sit.

And then, in the mental pliancy, there are different kinds. One is the capacity to shift from one meditation object to another. So, if you work with the breath and then you work with the body using two meditation objects, you can flexibly shift quickly between one and the other. That's a kind of pliancy, similar to what we call generalization of learning in the West.

Another kind of pliancy is the ability to track the meditation object through all of your shifts of state. Whatever your state of mind is, you track the object and keep tracking. Another kind of pliancy is the ability to shift levels of mind, so you can start at the coarse level of mind and its content, and you can shift to the subtle level of mind, which is all mind moments and not elaborated content. Although there is no elaborated content, the very subtle level of mind is where everything is interconnected and ocean-like, changeless, boundless awareness. Or shift to nondual awareness or shift to awakened awareness. Just with the intention of mind you can shift, like shifting gears in a car.

So, people who have developed strong pliancy can make these state shifts in a matter of seconds. We were doing the work with a tachistoscope, a high-speed electronic board, testing the speed of the mind in our lamas; the Dalai Lama gave us his best concentrated meditators. What we found was the average time it caught—that it took for them to shift state—was about one to two seconds to stabilize it. That's pliancy.

And the last kind of pliancy is to operate not out of conceptual thought, but the lightning speed and directionality of the intention of awareness—the ninth stage of the Elephant Path. So, whatever you intend with lightning speed, the mind's awareness goes just to that, only that, and it does only that, with nothing interfering with it. So, whatever you put the mind on, it does just what you want it to do—including thinking. You have full control over the mind now. We call that making the mind serviceable.

Now, those are all different kinds of what we call mental pliancy. So, what they're saying in those four antidotes, the best antidote is mental pliancy. If you're lazy, or busy, and you don't do your practice, simply putting the intention of your mind on doing it, it does it. Nothing gets in the way of it anymore. Then you've got no more problem with laziness or busyness. Just intend to do it, you do it, get it done; done, like that.

So that's the first, and it's not an accident because this commentary on the five faults and the eight antidotes was written in a monastic setting. It was basically developed by Tsongkapa, head of the Gelugpa tradition, which is the Dalai Lama's tradition. And, of course the biggest problem within the monasteries is the monks get lazy, with a cushy lifestyle.

Our biggest problem is busyness—it's different. So, because this was written in a monastic context, we get four antidotes for laziness, because they see that as the biggest pernicious problem with developing concentration meditation. Monks don't work at it. And most monasteries are not necessarily the best places to practice. The real practice has always been the culture of the cave yogis, for the hermitage yogis, which is, unfortunately, dying out.

Okay. The second of the faults is forgetfulness, *trende*. It's one of the fifty-one mental factors from the *Abhidharma*. And mindfulness is defined as not losing track of the task at hand. Mindlessness means losing track of the task at hand. So, if you're counting your breaths and you're counting twenty-one breaths and you get to six breaths and you say, "Whoops, I just lost track, what was I doing?" Like that, that's losing track of the task at hand. So, the trouble when you're beginning to meditate is you keep forgetting to stay on the concentration object.

An interesting thought comes along. It's so compelling, you're chasing after the thought; you're chasing after one thing after another because it's interesting. And you say, "Whoops, I just lost track of the task at hand"—that's forgetfulness. And the opposite of that is what's called sustaining the rope of mindfulness. You guide yourself along by holding onto the rope of mindfulness so you're always tying the object onto this awareness. You're always being aware of the concentration object. Not cutting the rope. So, you have to train yourself to sustain that more and more over time. And after a while you get less forgetful, and you tend to stay on track there.

The third is, it's done in a pair: *gyurpa*, which means agitation, and *chengwa*, which means drowsiness. So, when you get better at staying on the concentration object, you enter a phase where there's not a lot of thought activity getting in the way anymore. But what gets in the way is that there are times the mind is too excited or agitated. It bounces around so you can't stay on the object. Or you get dull and you're facing staying awake during the meditation.

I'm going to suggest to you that agitation and drowsiness are two sides of the same coin. The common factor is that they are the extremes of your energy level or arousal level; the consequence of both being the same—the mind won't stay on the object.

You can think about it like this: this time of year, if you went sailing and you came in to dock but it was rough and the boat was bouncing around when you tried to tie the rope onto the cleat [on the dock], so you can't secure the rope onto the cleat. Like that, if the energy level of the mind is too high, the mind's bouncing around too much so that you can't keep the mind on the meditation object—the energy level, the activation of it is too high. You have to calm the mind down to be able to stay on the object.

On the other hand, you might have been out sailing and there's no wind; so you came back and there's no current [or breeze] at all when you tie the boat up, so you put the rope too loosely on the cleat, and even the smallest of currents keeps pulling that rope looser from the cleat. So, when your energy level is too low, it keeps slipping the rope of mindfulness, keeps slipping off the object. You can't sustain it.

They're saying that the antidote for that is metacognitive awareness; and with your awareness, you have to be aware of the fact that you're in an agitated state, not be oblivious to it. You have to be aware of when you're getting drowsy, not just fall asleep. You have to catch yourself in this state, and then there are various antidotes to shake it off, depending on whether it's agitation or drowsiness. It's different in each case. But the first thing you have to do is you have to catch yourself doing it.

Metacognitive awareness is terribly important in meditation. So, you also have to catch yourself when you're chasing after thought. You have to see that you're doing that. Otherwise, you just get lost in the thought. But metacognitive awareness isn't thinking about what you're doing, it's just seeing what's happened, the pure awareness.

We often, as Westerners, because we're so dominated by conceptual thought, we think that metacognitive awareness is a kind of thinking what we're doing, about our state of mind. It's not about thinking. The metacognitive center of the brain, the neurocircuitry, is the right dorsolateral prefrontal cortex that is the executive control system. That area of the brain gets activated in concentrated meditators who are skilled because not only are they holding the mind on the concentration object, they're constantly monitoring with their awareness what they're doing. So, they stay on the object, and they quickly catch themselves going off and bring it back. Unskilled meditators are still concentrated, but they don't use the dorsolateral prefrontal cortex. They don't use their metacognition. So, they can work for years and years and never improve their staying. So, with the development of metacognitive awareness, *shezhi* in Tibetan, is how you monitor your progress so you're always improving it and making it better and better.

Okay, the fourth fault is non-application, and the fifth fault is over-application. What does that mean? It has to do with this factor called "intensifying." If I say look at this lineage poster for Rahob Tulku, and you just direct your mind to that, that's called *sentong*, directing the mind, like a steering wheel in a car. Now, *really* look at it, and you *really* look at it—you've done something else. You can't just say that you directed your mind to it because you already did that. So, what are you doing in addition to directing your mind? And the Tibetan word for that is *chugpa*. *Chugpa* means to intensify. It requires more effort, but it's not just an output of effort. It's the effort that leads to staying more closely engaged with all the subtle details of the object. Okay? So, when people are concentrating, if they just have the capacity to direct their attention to the object, and they never intensify, concentration is going to bottom out. They're not going to look close enough at the object, and they're probably only going to get to the first and second stage of the nine stages of the Elephant Path.

All the rest of the stages open up through intensifying. You've got to burn with your concentration. You've got to look so closely, see that there's a whole world in there, in what you're looking at. So, what we're saying here is that one of the faults is that people never learn to intensify and that's called under application. And the antidote for that is intensifying.

On the other hand, there are people who try too hard in the intensifying; just looking closer at the object, it just becomes an output of energy. And they're constantly being reactive to this state, like it's not developing quick enough, and they get really impatient. And that's the fault of over application. They're just trying too hard. It's like pure wasted energy. Because really, if you're intensifying correctly, it means you're staying more closely engaged in all of the subtle details of the object. It's not just putting out effort. It's close engagement. So, for people who try too hard and just put out more effort, the antidote is equanimity, nonreactivity of the mind.

So, this was a system that Tsongkapa developed in order to address the common problems for people at the beginning and intermediate stages of concentration practice with the Elephant Path for the nine stages of staying. And each one of these is a common problem that beginners make mistakes with; and each one of these, as you can see, has a very specific antidote. And it was meant as a kind of a guideline by itself so you could do your own self-assessment in terms of what's missing here.

And if you learn the Elephant Path, if you learn to set your motivation at the beginning, in the pre-meditation routine, and you learn to direct the mind and then intensify correctly, and you learn to apply the antidote when you get agitated or sleepy—basic tools of concentration—then these problems just won't come up. I think that these problems are a function of how it's taught. If it's taught well, you won't get the problems very much. It's where you're not given adequate or detailed instructions, and you try and figure it out on your own. That's when these problems are likely to come up, frequently.

But remember, this is part of a monastic tradition, when meditation was being done in very large numbers—you know, big monasteries, like three to five thousand people at a pop. So, when you're trying to manage that many people, this is where you get writings about all the problems that come up because if not, if people are not followed closely, not being taught carefully, it becomes more like a management problem. So that's the context out of which this writing comes.

July 20, 2016

Themes: Awareness Beyond Concepts; Nonduality Is Not Awakening; Ultimate Compassion

Dan

Welcome everyone. You have a question?

Student 1

So, I have two questions, Dan; actually, one is to do with my meditative practice.

Dan

Okay.

Student 1

And it is to do with … there are times when I'm sitting and I'm searching for that emptiness, and breathing, and focused, and concentrating, and then there are other times when it's not the business of my mind like, "Oh, what am I gonna do next, I gotta do this, the car, the laundry, this and that." It's not that, it's almost as though there's a streaming of information that comes forth.

And well, I'm going to count on—one day you said you kind of anticipate what people are asking. I feel like I babble at you, and you sort of …

Dan

This is not one of those times. [Laughter]

Student 1

Oh man. And you kind of ferret out the question. Okay. So, the question …

Dan

I have no idea where you're going with this.

Student 1

Oh good. All right. Is there such a thing then as information that's not thinking?

Dan

Of course.

Student 1

Okay. Can you talk to me about that so I can make the distinction?

Dan

Yeah, it's a very good question actually.

The Buddhist logicians Dinaga, Chandrakirti … people like that laid out a rather careful infrastructure showing that there are two modes of knowing that humans engage in. One is conceptual knowing—we frame the world in terms of our ideas and knowledge about it. And the other is nonconceptual. It's knowing directly through immediate awareness. And awareness, direct perception, is in Buddhism, a legitimate way of accessing knowledge. In fact, all knowing that occurs in meditation, which results in the realizations that you have, is based on direct knowing; it's not based on conceptualization.

That's difficult for us as Westerners to understand because if you look at the stages of knowing in the West, like say Piaget's stages of intelligence, they're all based on conceptualization. And if you look at the extension of Piaget's work to what's called postformal stages of development, or stages of intelligence beyond formal operational thinking—the best that you get to in Piaget is formal operational thinking, which means thinking in terms of possibilities, infinite possibilities, which is the kind of thinking that occurs in adolescence. All adolescents are existentialists. They think in terms of "the infinitude of possibilities" as the existentialists say. You can do hypotheticals. You can think of possible outcomes. And in that worldview, all knowledge is relative. All knowledge bases are relative. But some people, post-Piaget, have tried to extend that knowledge and say, "Look, if you take Piaget's model, which is very child-focused, and we draw the conclusions from that, one of the implications is that human understanding stops with adolescence." That's not a very good model. Are we to believe that there's no knowledge or levels of knowledge that develop beyond adolescence? In that case, as a society we're in big trouble.

Student 1

The brain hasn't even finished.

Dan

Right. So, some people have tried to define what are called the levels of mature adult postformal cognitive development, levels beyond adolescence. And if you simplify that literature, it all comes down to taking larger and larger perspectives. So formal operation means you can think in terms of everything being relative to everything else.

But the next level beyond that would be to see beyond the information that's obvious, beyond the information given, and to go deeply into the nature of whatever's at hand, much more deeply into it, like you do in emptiness practice. The next level beyond that is to see that there's some whole holistic knowledge that is beyond all the relative. It's not all just infinitive knowledge systems that are relative to each other. There's something that integrates all of that—like you get in Ocean and Waves practice in meditation. That's a different stage.

Then there's a level beyond that, where not only is all knowledge holistic rather than partial and relative, it's also not represented. In other words, there's direct awareness knowing of things. That's where most postformal development in the West stops. It's not that Westerners don't do that, it's just that they don't have the tools to open those levels of awareness up, so they're not very advanced. Susan Cook-Greuter, who's looked at those stages of postformal development, says, "Well they exist in humans, but they exist in less than three percent of the general population," so it's hard to study them. But in Dzogchen, for example, we have entire procedures to open up those levels of development. So, it's not hard, from a Dzogchen perspective in meditation, to say the higher you go with your meditation practice, the less you're operating out of the conceptual mind and the more you're operating out of direct seeing and direct awareness. This is not something that Westerners easily accede to, because we are so biased in thinking that all knowledge is conceptual; but it's not the case.

In fact, when you get out of conceptualization, that's when you really see things. And that's what all direct meditation experience is about. It's using awareness, not conceptualization, to directly see things the way they are. In fact, the further you go along the path in Dzogchen or Great Completion meditation, the more you leave behind what are called the "residuals of conceptualization," and purify the mind, and operate out of a mode of knowing that's purely based on awakened awareness. Awakened awareness is a better knowledge vehicle than conceptual thought.

Student 1

Are the residuals what you've talked about with regard to attachment and the push and the pull?

Dan

Just the residuals to conceptualize. One of the ways that comes up in advanced practice is what's called *jeshe*. It's hard to translate. It literally means afterthought or after knowledge. It means you have a direct experience of awakening, you see something about the nature of reality with awakening, and then, by force of habit, thought comes back and you start thinking about it. At which point you drop out of awakening, you're back in ordinary mind, and you're thinking about it rather than directly experiencing it. That's a residual. Not uncommon. Because at that point you've had the direct experience of awakening, but it's not stable yet. So, you go back to the default option which is conceptual thinking.

Student 1

Trying to make sense out of it.

Dan

Yeah, which doesn't really work very well.

Student 1

Diminishes it.

Dan

Yeah, well it makes you drop out of it, is basically what happens. So, it's an important question you're asking. What we're talking about here is a direct knowing through awareness. Awareness does a better job with knowing ultimate reality than conceptual thought because conceptual thought can't know ultimate reality, because it's always partialized. A great Dzogchen scholar, Mipham, once said, "The function of conceptual thought is to delineate. When it's this, it's not that." Whereas awakened awareness is always based on the unbounded wholeness. It's never partialized. It can't be partialized. So, it's a completely different way of knowing in the world.

Student 1

That's my second question. Can I?

Dan

Sure.

Student 1

I'm no great scholar, but it seems no matter what the …

Dan

It's probably to your advantage. [Laughter]

Student 1

No matter what language, whether it be religious or biblical, or Buddhist or philosophical, it seems as though—and you've talked about an ultimate reality—then there's this human experience. And it seems like the trick, or the task, is to live in this human experience fully but from a ground of being that knows about this ultimate reality that includes all of what goes on in the world and in my life—and there I'm babbling at you again.

Dan

It's probably not a bad way of saying it. A slightly different way of saying it is that you're being ultimate reality, and ordinary relative reality is just a part of that, that you're being. So, you never lose the experience of operating out of ultimate reality and everything you do in everyday life.

Student 1

I look forward to that.

Dan

Then, you see, there's no contradiction. That's why we say relative reality is the best vehicle to express awakening. You use all the stuff of everyday reality. And the most advanced practice is called "the *samādhi* of the heroes"—*surangama* in Sanskrit, or *senpapa* in Tibetan. The *samādhi* of the heroes is you don't need favorable conditions to deepen your realizations. You intentionally put yourself in the most difficult life circumstances because that's the best place to deepen your realizations. You welcome all the crap of everyday life. That's where you get your deepest realizations. Then you're a hero.

Student 1

That's the dilemma I've been experiencing. This idea that I should care about the problems that come up in the world whether that be human trafficking, or Trump, or whatever and yet … It's unavoidable, isn't it? [Laughter]

Dan

It's unavoidable, it is. [Laughter]

Student 1

It just feels like a dilemma that I want to stay detached from, or not involved with—the grab or the resistance to things—and at the same time, there's this notion that I should care about so many things that are in the world that need to be cared about.

Dan

Why?

Student 1

Why?

Dan

That's where conduct comes in. You immerse yourself in all of the thickness of *samsāra* as the best place to do your work, as spiritual practice. That's where you get your deepest realizations and where you develop your strongest compassion, in the thick of it. That's best practice. It's not easy to do, but that's when you practice as a hero. You put yourself in the worst of it. And having a spiritual vision is necessary, particularly in terms of what's happening now.

Having compassion is necessary particularly in terms of what's happening now. You mentioned Trump. How do we have compassion for someone who fosters the idealization of power and hatred? But you can, because it's not about Trump. It's about a proud nation that's on the decline. When a proud nation is on the decline, what you see is rigid nationalism on the rise, like what's happening in this country and what's happening with Brexit in Great Britain. The British Empire is finally falling down. There's a lot of people who want to preserve what they've got.

Student 1

Doesn't work.

Dan

No, but that's what it's about. It's all about this kind of rigid nationalism that develops when countries fail. We're a failing nation. It's not about Republicans and Democrats. We sold this country to corporations twenty years ago. Now we're paying the consequences of that. And everybody knows it's on the decline and nobody wants to admit that, so they're looking for quick simple solutions, because everybody's terrified. That's worthy of compassion.

Irrespective of Trump, he's just a player. He's just the voice of that rigid nationalism that can be very destructive. But it's something we have to watch for. It's the same thing that happened in Nazi Germany, the same thing that happened in Italy with Mussolini. It's not Trump that's the problem, it's all of the people who think he's great, preaching an ideology of rigidness and hatred. That's about half the country. So, we're deeply in trouble. That's worthy of compassion. People wouldn't think that rigidly unless they were scared. They have reason to be scared. It's a culture on decline. Until we address that, it's just going to get worse.

Student 1

How?

Dan

Well, I had some hope in Bernie Sanders, although he might not have been the right medium for that. But my candidate has always been Elizabeth Warren because she's got the strength to take on the financial industry.

I once calculated that Apple, Google, Facebook, and Microsoft paid almost no taxes in twenty years, in this country or any other country. If we collected those twenty years of taxes from those four companies alone, we'd have no national debt. So why should I, having a small business, pay 48 percent in taxes when the major corporations pay almost nothing? Mitt Romney, when he ran for president, paid 13 percent with twenty-six billion dollars of assets. Doesn't that seem fundamentally wrong? We're not telling the truth here.

We've developed a country where a small number of people own everything, and we've developed a privilege to let that happen. And until we face the truth of that, we don't have a country anymore. We sold it. Now we're leading that way, but all the other countries have become the same way. 1.5 percent of the population in this country owns 95 percent of the wealth. Sixty-three families in the world own 95 percent of the wealth. That's not going to go anywhere good. And that's where spiritual practice comes in—any spiritual practice, whether it be Buddhist, or Hindu, or Christian, or Jewish, or Muslim.

All spiritual practices come down to the same thing. And I don't equate that with religious institutions. As the great American psychologist Williams James has said, "Religious institutions are the biggest impediment to spirituality." But if we're talking about genuine spirituality across all religions, it comes down to one simple point—self-importance is not terribly important. And that's why spirituality is so necessary right now: because we won't survive without it, because it's that selfish preoccupation that we're getting more and more. It's basically killed this planet. Until we fix that, we're not going to go anywhere good. That's the main lesson. And the only way we're going to see that is through direct seeing, not through conceptualization.

All you have to do is turn on the TV and watch the Republican National Convention. And what do you see? It's massive conceptual bullshit. Many Republicans who are disaffected by Trump, they go up there and talk nicey-nicey and they have all these ways to rationalize it; it's all using concepts to say what's not true. Everybody knows that. But people do it anyway. It's remarkable what we can give voice to that's not true. And we all know it. So why even bother?

And that's the way conceptualizations work. It's not a good vehicle to trust truth with … conceptualization.

We kill people with our ideas. We take things away from other people with our ideas. There's no basis to trust conceptualization. But direct knowledge, awareness and awakened awareness, you can trust that. It will never lead you astray, because what's built in is good conduct. You can't act badly if you're realized, it's not possible. You're not afforded that luxury—it's just not possible. And there's the safeguard that will keep this planet going. You've got to develop that.

It's important. It's a good question. We're the only species, the human species, that kills people based on ideas. And we actually think that's a good thing. You can shoot up an entire population of people in the name of God. Cause massive destruction everywhere and actually think that's a good idea. And that's wacked. So, you see, in that sense one could argue that conceptualization is a basis of knowledge that's substantially flawed, not something to trust well.

And people have the idea that you can behead someone on TV in front of millions of people, and that it's a good thing to do. There's something fundamentally wrong with our ideas. And that's where religion becomes an impediment to spirituality. The irony here is that the very thing that starts out good can turn really bad unless you keep it on track right. Killing people in the name of religion is a bad idea. It's contrary to everything that's the heart of spirituality.

No religion has been innocent. I'm not a strong fan of ISIS. And I'm also not a strong fan of Christian fundamentalists who destroyed many cultures around the world with their missionary behavior. That is as violent as ISIS. But we don't look at that because we're involved in that.

I remember once when I was living in Chicago, where I went to the University of Chicago for graduate school. I loved the natural history museum. They had a funny exhibit once. It was about how third world countries viewed colonialism. And the best exhibit came from the Cameroons, where there was this very overweight British bureaucrat governor who had taken over the country. And there were six very small Cameroonian Black people carrying him on a sedan, and he was fanning himself. But if you look at the way that they set up this thing, it looks like they were serving him, but that wasn't the case at all. They were making fun of him; they were making fun of his self-importance. And you could see it in how they sculpted this thing. It was really clever. And he didn't get the humor. They thought this thing was a remarkable joke the

Western culture did on themselves. There's a lesson in that. Self-importance is not terribly important.

Good question. Anything else?

Student 2

At least from that conceptual, I've been doing more the unheroic path lately, I think, because what I've been working on is accepting the limits in my energy and age and resources, seeing less clients, pulling back from projects that had to do with suffering. And as I've gotten more gentle or compassionate with myself, it's been easier to have the clarity …

Dan

That's not the wimpy path. We're talking about two different things.

Student 2

Yeah.

Dan

One is intentionally putting yourself in difficult life circumstances for the sake of developing a practice. The other is pulling back on the preoccupations of everyday life, for the sake of doing better practice, establishing better conditions. That's different—nothing to belittle about that.

Student 2

I certainly find that it is helping, and the more that I can accept that everything that I perceive and think and feel are just momentary arrangements, then it's easier to see compassion and experience it, not really as something that I have or to give, but more of just a quality of how things are. And I wonder if you could talk about the way that compassion and the insight, those sides of the coin, feed each other.

Dan

Well, it's hard to develop compassion towards others unless you first develop compassion towards yourself. What you're doing by being more conserving of your resources is being compassionate to yourself.

I remember once teaching with Denma Locho Rinpoche, who's the abbot of Namgyal, the Dalai Lama's monastery. And we had taught together for a number of years. Unfortunately, he died last year. But we taught together for fifteen years. One time we were teaching—this was years ago—and one of the Western students said, "In my daily practice I get lazy; what do I do with that?" And he said, "No, laziness is for the monks in the monastery. You Westerners, your laziness is busyness." Busyness is your laziness. I always thought that was very astute.

So, you see, if in your professional practice and your personal life you're too preoccupied, then there isn't really the occasion to make a presence for your spiritual practice. So, what you're really saying—and hopefully not judging yourself in doing it as a bad thing, because it's a smart thing to do—is as you're being more conserving of your energies and pulling back on your clients and pulling back on other things that you preoccupy yourself with, you make the space for spiritual practice. That's actually smart. Don't judge it. The action is smart. The judgment is not. It shows good intelligence in what you need for yourself. Just do it. No problem here.

Anybody else?

Student 3

So, before this started, we were talking about just this question … the thing it brought up for me in a sort of … hidden inside of the sort of thoughts going around for me is sort of reflecting … I'd love to hear you talk about the role for effort and Frank Sinatra's "dubee dubee du," and how that fits into all this.

Dan

"Dubee dubee du?" I just know "I Did it My Way." [Laughter] That's exactly what we were talking about earlier. It's the wrong approach. What's the "dubee dubee du?" You have to translate this for me.

Student 3

So, there's always this thing of … it started with when you were talking about the tsunami and people getting hooked on people suffering, and also just—I always had this feeling like I want to be doing more to help the world. And you said something about feeling sort of guilt about it or something like that; I have this feeling that there's so much out there that needs fixing. And yet, at the same time I know that if I go get off center and start engaging in that way, that it's just going to ruin everything. So anyways, that's … there's a question in there somewhere.

Dan

Yeah. The question is about the difference between relative compassion and ultimate compassion. Relative compassion is compassion that you do that comes from the self. I think that I have to act more compassionately towards all the suffering in the world. Such compassion is always partialized. Such compassion always entails a self that's being reactive to what it's doing compassionately or not doing compassionately. So, the danger there is that you serve the needs of the self rather than to genuinely be compassionate. You think you're being compassionate but you're really not helping other people. And you're really helping yourself being with this idea that you're being compassionate.

A good example of that kind of compassion is missionary behavior. We've destroyed entire cultures with missionary behavior, but we think we're doing a good thing because we replaced their so called "primitive religious beliefs" with our superior religious beliefs. Some people will call that imperialism, but we call it doing a good thing in the eyes of God. That's the problem. Because all of that stuff, if you're really honest about it, serves the self. It's not really selfless; it's not really compassionate. But if you do emptiness of self, then when you operate out of compassion, it doesn't come from self. It comes from some place deeper within yourself, hopefully awakened awareness. So, the compassion spontaneously arises as the best fit to what's needed in the situation—maybe not in ways that you would think of doing, because it doesn't come from thought. We just act according to what's needed. You don't make a big deal out of it; you just do it because that's what's needed in the situation.

That kind of compassion is inexhaustible. We say that ultimate compassion is like being the sun. The sun doesn't decide who to shine on, it doesn't shine on some people and not on others; it shines on everybody impartially and inexhaustibly. And the sun has infinite energy; it never gets compassion fatigue, because it doesn't come from self.

So, the best way of practicing compassion is ultimate compassion, cleaned up of self. Then you don't get into this overwhelming sense of, "I have to do what I've got to do here, but what am I going to do there?" You just respond to the immediacy of the situation, spontaneously. You don't think about it. That's the whole point. You just do it. The response is not a choice. It just is.

I remember once, years ago, with my first wife—we went to a movie theater in Cambridge, and some guy reached under the seat behind us and tried to steal her pocketbook. And we saw it happening, so we called out, and this big guy just ran away. They turned the lights on in the theater. And then he ran away. We got a good look at him. Sure enough, six months later we're in the same movie theater, and we watched the same guy come in, because that's where he did his thing, and he walked in front of us about six or seven rows and he walked right behind this couple and reached under and tried to grab their pocketbook. And just as he tried to grab it, the husband saw it happen. And he jumps up and says, "This guy is stealing my [wife's] pocketbook." The light goes on and this guy is caught red-handed in front of everybody. He's about six-six. And he runs out. And the only two people that chased him were the husband and myself. Two hundred people were in the theater. And the security guard walks out of the way, letting him by. And lets us chase him.

So, we chase him—this was in Cambridge in Harvard Square, so we chased him up to a building where we got on our cell phones and we called the police. And they surrounded the building, and they caught him. And, I'm thinking, "Who's the criminal here?" We have a petty thief, that's his only living. He goes to the same movie theater, he rips it off every day, and the movie theater knows that. But they don't want to do anything about it because if they do anything about it, they get bad publicity and they lose business. So, they shut up about it. So, who's the thief?

And the security guard who's hired to keep order, steps out of the way because he doesn't want to get involved, but he is taking his pay. So, who's the thief here? They're all thieves. And all the people who stand by and watch this thing when the guy is standing in front of two hundred people and no one does anything. They're thieves, too.

Student 3

It's really interesting; it sort of circles back and around.

Dan

It's pathetic. But you see, the idea here is that if you operate out of some sort of spiritual practice, you don't think about whether you're going to be involved. There's no choice involved. You just do it. Because it's the right thing to do. You don't think about the risk, you don't think about the danger, you just do it because it's the right thing to do.

Years ago, there was all this research on altruism, after World War II, where people interviewed the people who risked their lives to save Jews and hide them during the Nazi occupation in Europe. And every one of them said the same story, "Why are you interviewing me, I'm not a special person. I just did it because that's what you do." It's the same answer. Because it doesn't come from ideas. And it certainly doesn't come from self. You just do it. Important. Go ahead.

Student 4

Hi, Dan. My question is about recognizing nonduality in sitting practice.

Dan

Okay.

Student 4

I'm just having trouble with that part of my practice.

Dan

Open your eyes. Look at the surrounding empty space. Right now. Mix your awareness into the empty space and the empty space into your awareness so it's one field of empty awareness space. It's all empty awareness space that saturates everything. You got that?

Student 4

Yes.

Dan

Now come to see that all the objects in that field—the thoughts, the emotions, the sights, the sounds, the taste, the body, body sensations, and the knowing of those objects—are all one single unified, nondual field. The field itself saturates everything. The field of empty awareness space, all the objects in that field, and the knowing of those objects is one single, unified field without inside or without outside. One field. Got that?

Student 4

Yeah.

Dan

That's it. Simple as that.

Student 5

So, if I … I still feel like I have a central location.

Dan

That's different, okay? That's different.

Student 5

Okay.

Dan

If you have nonduality, there's still localization of individual consciousness. That drops away in the next step. That's awakening. Okay?

Student 5

Okay.

Dan

You've got an idea in your mind. That's the problem. Nonduality is not the same as awakening. With nonduality, inside/outside, and the fact that you're looking at something from somewhere else, that drops away. Okay? But localization doesn't drop away. When you're in awakening, the localization drops away and then you're being that unbounded wholeness. Learn to discriminate the markers of ocean-like, changeless, boundless awareness, nondual awareness, and awakened awareness. They're all different. You have this idea in your mind that localization should drop away, so you're missing nondual awareness. Which, as you can see, you easily opened up. It wasn't hard. You did it immediately. Okay? You got that part down. Now you have to work on the localization. To do that you have to set up your view of Lion's Gaze. Understood?

Student 5

Yes, Thank you.

Dan

Okay. Yeah.

Student 6

That's a perfect entry. I also had a nondual question. I think I was in the situation where I was meditating better than I ever had and I had a moment where the actual localization dropped, and I just was the field and it was really intense. And I immediately was like, whoa, that's too intense. Anyway, that was just …

Dan

As soon as you hit that, that's *jeshe*, that's after knowledge. As soon as you had the taste of awakening, you immediately started to think about it and you fell back into ordinary mind again.

Student 6

So, but that's … it was showing me that's where …

Dan

Once you open up, it opens up easier next time.

Student 6

And it was kind of like also … when I was having this experience I was noticing … if I just looked at the field of awareness, and just kind of said, "This is me, this is me," you know?

Dan

Set a better foundation in automatic emptiness so that every tendency to conceptualize as soon as it arises is immediately empty upon arising.

Student 6

Okay.

Dan

When you're strong with that, when the after knowledge comes up, it's immediately empty, and you won't go there, and you won't fall out of the view.

Student 6

So, more sealing, better sealing.

Dan

Yeah.

Student 6

Okay. Alright. Thanks.

Dan

It's good. Anything else?

Student 7

I don't know if it'd be appropriate in this setting, but could you talk at all about the weeklong thing that you're going to be doing at the beginning of September?

Dan

The energy course?

Student 7

Yeah.

Dan

Sure. At some point, when you get more advanced in your practice, it's probably necessary to learn how to work with the body as a vehicle for practice. So, the course is designed as a primer on the body. So, we'll do how you work with breathing exercises, like the nine-round breath, in some detail. We'll focus on the three main channel practices—central and the two side channels, and basic inner fire practice with that. How you visualize the three channels, how you do vase breathing. And we'll do some work with vase breathing. We'll talk about the different channel system. We'll work with the five main winds, which is what you do in *rushen* practice. Most people know the *rushen* practice, but they don't know it in much detail. Each one of those five winds has twenty different features to it. We're going to go through it in that detail and unpack how each one of those winds work. It's a much more detailed, refined version of that.

Then we'll do a number of other wind-related practices so you can see how there are many winds; there are 225 winds. We'll work with the primordial wisdom winds so you can see what it means to open up primordial wisdom through those winds. Then we'll go on to working with energy drops and we'll do a version of mind-only practice where you take all of external reality and you translate it into energy drops so that the entire world is filled with energy drops. There are only energy drops. It's very powerful to see the insubstantiality of external reality by transforming the whole thing into energy drops.

Then we'll work with seed syllables, different sites in the chakras. Then we'll probably do some inner fire practice to see if you can open up some of the blisses. And then the last part of it is on the elements. We'll work with how you diagnose imbalances of elements in the body. We'll work with how you use the *dākinī* of the elements to extract certain elements from the vital essence directly from the universe so you can balance the elements in the body. They're very powerful visualizations.

Then we'll work with how you strengthen your concentration in your Dzogchen practice through using the elements to enhance the meditation practice. Then we'll work with how you dissolve the elements so that you can transform everything to vital energy and understand clear light body. So, it's mostly stuff that nobody's heard before. It's a complete primer on the energy body. That's what I'm going to try and do. It's the first time we've done it, so it's a little bit of an experiment here. But I thought that we needed to open this up because it's a strong foundation for what we call the third map practices to buddhahood, and ultimately, to the experience of clear light body and what's called youthful vase body. So, we're trying to open some of that stuff up. It's another piece of the third map and we're trying to open that up. My hope is that in the next two years, we can give you a complete set of all the third map teachings. You'll have everything you need when I finish what I can do here. So, I'm trying to give you a complete set of the teachings.

Student 8

So, you have no prerequisites?

Dan

You have to have taken at least the level 1 and the 3A. You have to have some taste of awakening to do this and have to have it approved by a teacher. But most people here have done that, so they meet those requirements. A lot of people have. So, we're going to open it up.

Student 8

Where does that practice originate from?

Dan

It's the cave and hermitage yogi practices. There is a cave yogi culture, and they all trade the same practices irrespective of lineage or school. The practices that I tend to operate out of are mostly Bon Dzogchen practices because that's what I've been translating for the last couple of years. And they're very, very rich and detailed. The more popular version of those practices would be what you'd find in, say, the Six Yogas of Naropa, but the Bon version is infinitely more detailed than the Six Yogas. The Six Yogas are like a skeleton structure of it. This is far more detailed. But it's basically Six Yogas stuff. There are six yogas. There's four yogas. There's twelve yogas. There's ten yogas. They all share these things and put them together in different orders, but amongst the cave and hermitage yogi teachings, there's a common set of practices, and we're trying to extract out some of the foundational practices for that and make them available to people. So that's what the course is about.

You'll be supercharged. [Laughter] So, it's good.

August 10, 2016

Themes: Postformal Cognitive Development; Interconnectedness

Dan

Welcome everyone. You have a question?

Student 1

I've been thinking about the interconnectedness of all beings. And this is one of the things that I've noticed, and this is, for me, sort of a rather simplistic way of looking at it. But one of the things that I've noticed is that—and I don't know if other people have the same experience, but at work we've had a lot of things going on where a lot of nurses are leaving, and we've had some patients who have died as well. But some people have … it seems as though the administration isn't seeing some of why people are unhappy, and what I notice is that I wonder if people can fail to see how things are interconnected just in a simple way in that has a way of sort of permeating the whole environment, even when people aren't talking about it. It almost seems to be happening like at an energetic level. And so, to me that was an example of beings being interconnected.

Dan

But not knowing it, is that what you mean?

Student 1

Perhaps not knowing—well, I shouldn't say not knowing it. They're sensing it, but they can't really put a voice to it.

Dan

It's another good question. See, I think of interconnectedness, in Western terms, as a mature level of cognitive development. If you think of Piaget's model for intelligence, with the sensory motor intelligence of a young child, everything is through doing, preoperational intelligence, which is more immediate and action oriented. Then at about seven or eight you get concrete operational thinking where the child develops an internal world. Then, at about sixteen or seventeen, you get formal operational thinking, where adolescents can think in terms of possibilities, or the infinity of possibilities, as the existentialists would say. All adolescents are existentialists because that's the level of cognitive maturation that develops.

There are infinite ways of looking at things, and in terms of world views, that's the world view of relativism. All knowledge bases are relative. The trouble with that view—and where some of the critics of Piaget have come in—is that, according to Piaget's model, because he spent his life observing children and adolescents, cognitive maturation stops with adolescence. If cognitive maturation stopped with adolescence, we're deeply in trouble. So, some people in the West began to focus on stages that are beyond formal operational thinking, or what's called postformal thinking.

The trouble is, when you get into those higher levels of mature adult cognitive development, there aren't a lot of subjects who demonstrate that they live in that realm. Suzanne Cook-Greuter used the Loevinger questionnaires and tried to study subjects who had a more mature view of the world, but she had a hard time finding subjects. And by her estimates, people who manifest these postformal stages of development are less than 3 percent of the general population. So, they're hard to study because we don't have a technology or even a system of knowledge about how we open up these postformal stages of development in the West. But you can open them up in meditation practice. Ken Wilber tried to do that in his work. He likens that there are twelve stages of cognitive development. Piaget has the first five. There are seven postformal levels of cognitive development.

But Ken doesn't know the meditations that open those up, so he developed a list from a synthetic system, which is Aurobindo's ideas. And it's not bad except that it's a synthesis of different spiritual traditions and they're not really practice oriented. Whereas in Dzogchen, you can develop methods to open up every one of these levels, and many of you know these levels. And it comes down to a rather simple point, and the simple point is that in each level of postformal development, you take a wider perspective and an even wider perspective and an even wider perspective.

The first postformal operation is to go beyond relative and to look deeper into things. As Jerry [Jerome] Bruner once said, "you go beyond the information given, and you keep looking deeper into the nature of the mind." There's more there to see that goes beyond whatever knowledge base you have. There are deeper structures of the mind. So, if you analyze everything as empty, and you look deeper into that kind of analysis, that would be an example of that.

The second postformal stage, or the seventh stage in this model, beyond all systems of relativism, is a whole. There's a whole beyond the partial views, and you start shifting your perspective out of some relative knowledge base to seeing the whole and operating out of that whole, so you're operating out of the whole field rather than parts of the field.

You know that as Ocean and Waves practice, where there's a wholeness to the field of awareness; it's huge and vast, and everything is contained within that. That's the stage in which you can appreciate interconnectedness, whereas you can't appreciate interconnectedness from a partialized point of view. You have to grasp the whole ocean of awareness and see how everything is contained within it, and all knowledge bases are within that. They're all relative, but they're all also interconnected. Each relative knowledge base is an approximation, but we can never quite get at that whole. And the reason why no knowledge system can get at the whole is all knowledge bases are based on conceptual knowing or representational knowing.

And this requires us to acknowledge that there's a level of knowing that's nonconceptual but is known through direct awareness, because awareness isn't partialized the way concepts are. When you shift to that seventh level or the second postformal level, you're operating out of a pure, whole field of awareness that directly knows everything, and everything is contained within in. You appreciate the relativism, but you're operating out of wholeness.

Still, there's a sense of knowledge knowing something particular, so it has duality to it. So, at the eighth stage, it's one field. The events and the content of that field and the knowing of those events is the same field. In addition to interconnectedness, that total field is now a nondual field.

The next level would be similar to awakening. You drop the individual localization within any field, and you're operating out of a much larger field that supersedes all fields. With that comes "the path of infinite freedom."

The next shift beyond that is a much larger super-field, or super-system, which is all-at-once-ness, where all realms and times are all connected within a much larger field. And you open up the buddha bodies.

The next level is becoming ultimate reality. It's even a larger field, full enlightenment. But still, you exist within the body. In the last stage of that knowledge, the body becomes part of the field too; it's all light—rainbow body.

So, we can open up meditation practices for each one of those levels. When you get glimpses into those, they're not stable. We call those "states," but if you practice them long enough, they become stable states of mind or traits. And that's where you live, out of that field of. So, you can mature along these lines. I'm trying to contextualize for you where interconnectedness fits. You have to step out of the dominant view of the West, which is relativism, to see that there's a larger whole, so you're operating out of that larger whole, that larger system, rather any parts of the system. Then everything is genuinely interconnected from the perspective of that whole.

Now if you operate out of that, that has profound implications for mental health because whatever comes up in the vast spaciousness of you operating out of that whole has no grab to it whatsoever. In that experience, as you let everything arise, viewed from the vantage point of ocean-like, changeless, timeless awareness as you know, nothing has any grab, and you get a first taste of what's called "spacious freedom." Nothing has any grab within that spaciousness. But that has profound implications for mental health, because grab is the root of all suffering. And if you drop out the grab in a stable way, you don't suffer in the same way.

But it also has profound implications socially if you operate out of that interconnectedness, the second postformal level, the ocean-like awareness. Because when you operate out of that total field, everybody's contained; all their needs are contained within that same present awareness and you can't exist selfishly. You can't say, "This is what I need, and this is what I'm going to do," because you have the awareness at all times of the totality of the field and how we're all interconnected and we all influence each other within that field. That has profound social implications.

I'll tell you a story about that because mostly in the 1970s and '80s, in the early days, I participated in the Mind and Life conferences. The Dalai Lama was interested in science, and we had a number of conferences around certain scientific topics; public dialogues with His Holiness the Dalai Lama for two or three days, sometimes a week. And it's hard to engage in genuine dialogue; you don't just get up and give a talk. You arrange what you're saying so that the Tibetans can respond to it, and then you have a dialogue back and forth.

When my Root Lama, Geshe Wangyal, died in 1980, the first thing I did was I went to see the Dalai Lama because my Root Lama, the Dalai Lama, and Denma Locho (who's the head of the Dalai Lama's monastery), the three of them were the main students of Ling Rinpoche, in the Gelugpa tradition. My teacher was much older, so he died. So, when he died, I went to see the Dalai Lama (this was in 1980). In those days it was easy to call him up, or talk to him, or email and go over there—it was easy to have access to him. Now he's a movie star, and I never see him anymore. But in those days, we had a lot of time together.

So, I wanted to get his advice in terms of what he wanted me to do after my teacher died. I went to talk with him on a number of occasions; and meanwhile, Denma Locho and I were teaching Elephant Path concentration and basic emptiness together to Westerners, which we did for about ten or fifteen years.

And I remember every time I would go to Dharamsala in the '80s, there were waves and waves of new refugees escaping from China because the climate wasn't very good for Tibetans in those years. So Dharamsala and the surrounding area was getting more and more overcrowded and there was increasing tension between the local Indians, which was a smaller population.

You see, basically when Tibet got overtaken and all these refugees poured into India, Nehru took Dharamsala—which was a ski resort for the Brits, so it wasn't very populated with Indians—and said, "You can have this land because it's not very populated." And that's where he put all the Tibetan refugees originally. But there was an increased tension between the Indians and Tibetans because it was all getting overcrowded, and I thought that it might be a hot spot and some violent outbreaks between the Tibetans the Indians might happen the way that that had happened in the history of this with the Hindus and the Muslims around the time of Indian independence. I thought we might go through another round of that kind of thing in a way that would be really bad.

And the last conference I went to, which was in 1990, for a week dialogue on Tibetan medicine and Western medicine—and these are fairly high-level dialogues—we all had dinner and went to a Tibetan *tsam*, one of these stylized dances that they do with all of the costumes. So, I was sitting at dinner and next to me there was an Indian man with a turban, and he's very stately, so I just made talk with him, and it turns out he was the magistrate of HP [Himachal Pradesh] there, where the Dalai Lama's place is in that province. And I said, "You know, it's very different this time." I said that there's increasing tension because of all the overcrowding, and this time it's noticeably absent, and I was curious to know what his perspective on this was as a government official. And this is what he said.

He said, "Oh, maybe I had a little bit to do with that." He said, "You see, the way I see it, I tell the Indian shopkeepers, 'You need the Tibetans. Without all these Tibetans, nobody shops in your shops. You can't exist without the Tibetans. You need them', and I tell the Tibetans, I said, 'Without the Indians, you have no infrastructure, you have no roads, you have no plumbing, you have no electricity. You need the Indians.' So, you see, the way I look at it is everybody is interconnected and everybody needs each other, and I have to educate them about this. That's my duty as governor."

And I thought to myself, "This is the right man in the right position," because he had matured his level of cognitive development; and because he operated out of seeing the larger picture, and seeing everybody is interconnected, he could implement policy that actually did that in a way that had a huge effect in the entire population. He was a good leader because he had matured his own mind to see that vision of the larger view of interconnectedness of everything, and to educate everyone else to do that.

You can get glimpses of that, but what's missing at your work is that kind of leadership—to have that vision that we are all interconnected and we all influence each other and we all need each other. Then we don't have to build walls to keep people out. We don't have to denigrate and devalue ethnic differences. We don't have to see people as something foreign or other.

You all know what I'm talking about because it's very present to all of us. Genuine leadership requires a maturity of mind. And that is something that is a duty of a leader. Whatever you do or do not like about Hillary [Clinton], at least in her speech about how it takes a village [to raise a child], she operates out of seeing that there's a larger interconnected world that's far more complex than the other candidate will ever acknowledge because most of Trump's thinking is at a pre-operational level, to be honest, and that's scary.

We need leaders like that magistrate, whether it be at a smaller level like at your work site, or on the national stage. It requires you to see and operate out of the bigger picture. Rarely do we see that. I mean, how many truly great world leaders do we have who can see that larger vision? Like Gandhi, Mandela, maybe Gorbachev, at least in his view of *perestroika*. But it's rare to find that. The trouble is, when people have that vision, they probably don't want the job, [Dan laughs] but they're probably the ones that, out of compassion, might take it.

I remember a funny cartoon when Obama first got elected, not this last time but eight years ago. I had to vote absentee because I was in Israel, teaching at the time. So, we watched the election results from Tel Aviv and the next day they had a cartoon in the Tel Aviv Times that said, "Trust the Americans to give a Black man the job nobody else wanted." It's hilarious because if you really think about it, who would want this job? The ones who most don't want it are probably the ones who are best equipped to do it, and they have to get beyond that to look at the larger vision of what they're capable of doing.

But, you see, if you do your meditation practice and you stay at even the level of Ocean and Waves or nonduality, and you do that a lot so it starts to spontaneously affect your daily life, so you operate out of Ocean and Waves more than not off the pillow—maybe most of the time off the pillow—then it's no longer a state, it becomes a stable structure of mind or a trait. Then you are stably manifesting that level of mature cognitive development, and how you experience and see the world. That's different. Most people notice that difference right way. That's why when Suzanne Cook-Greuter was analyzing these responses to the Loevinger questions; you can tell right away who's in a more mature level of cognitive development. They just don't think like most people do. They really think in a wider perspective out of the box, and it's deeply effective.

I remember earlier this year, during the shootings in South Carolina in the church, and the Black couple who had lost their family members got up and they came on national TV, and there they are on national TV—I don't know if any of you saw this, it was quite extraordinary—and in the background was the shooter in his orange uniform, in handcuffs, and they pleaded on national TV that we shouldn't hate this man because to hate him makes you like him. That's such a mature view, to just have lost family members who were gunned down in a senseless way, by this crazed violent hatred, and to be able to step out of that and say, "Have compassion for this limited being and don't respond with hatred." That's profound. And such a lesson for all of us.

I remember once, Bob Thurman wrote a book on why the Dalai Lama is important politically, several years ago. And then Debbie Solomon, when she was working for the New York Times, interviewed him about his book. And he's very funny and had some interesting things to say. At one point she asked him if he was enlightened and he said, "Anybody who would say yes to that clearly is not." But the answer to the question she asked him that was hilarious was, "How do you do compassion meditation?" and he said, "I imagine that I'm a young mother and I have a young baby Dick Cheney at my breast suckling it." And it's sort of hilarious, but he wasn't joking, he meant that. You have to have compassion for the Dick Cheneys of the world and the Donald Trumps of the world, as hard as that is. That's profound.

You have to step back and see that all that self-importance and hatred comes out of a profound insecurity. It can wreck a nation, but it's not hard to see where that's coming from. And when you see into the nature of that, it will open your heart. You'll soften, but you won't vote for him. [Dan laughs] I had to say that. You know what I mean, it softens it.

So, you have to get to that larger common humanity, which is part of what naturally arises if you hold the view with everybody interconnected. It's not hard to do. You just have to take that larger perspective. You have to know it exists, and take a larger perspective on that, just nonduality and a larger perspective on that, which is being the unbounded wholeness, which is awakening. And a larger perspective on that, and everything is here, all realms and times, all at once, and a larger perspective on that, which is the structure of ultimate reality. You are "that." Enlightenment. Game over at that point. No more larger perspectives.

The trouble is that we don't have the technology in the West to open up those larger perspectives because we don't observe them enough; because we don't practice the methods that will open those up. In Dzogchen, they're quite readily spelled out in great detail. Even Ken Wilber, when he tried to open up the seven postformal levels, he couldn't find enough evidence to describe them in any detail, so he smushed them all together and called the whole thing the "integral level." That's not good enough. You've got to develop them. And there's enough of a knowledge base out there in terms of how you actually open these things up, and it's worth looking into. We have that knowledge. We just have to open it up. Better that you become it.

Thank you, good question.

Student 2

So, when you mentioned Bob Thurman's answer to the compassion question, I just kind of let my mind go with that—picturing Donald Trump as a little baby and nursing him—and it's interesting because …

Dan

Some babies are more difficult than others. [Laughter]

Student 2

I mean, the thought that came up was, "Well, someone's got to do it." [Laughter]

Dan

That's called being begrudgingly compassionate.

Student 2

Right, I'm admitting that was the first thing that came up …

Dan

The necessity of compassion.

Student 2

Like, "Someone's gotta do it," and I'm seeing this orange head, you know, but what happened…

Dan

I almost got in trouble the other day because when I went to testify against this expert; it was so funny because I walked into the court room and he was there on the stand ready to testify, and I look at him and he looks just like Donald Trump, that same blotchy face and the same hair thing and the same … so I turn to the prosecutor and I said, "I gotta testify against Donald Trump?!" and she started laughing, and we both couldn't stop laughing in front of the judge. I thought we were going to get kicked out of the court room. [Dan laughs]

Student 2

But it was interesting, just in the few moments this experience happened inside of, yes, recognizing the little bit of the Republican Convention that I watched. One of the things that was interesting was there were no stories of who Donald Trump was. There are no stories really of where he's come from and so that image of him never having been nursed, metaphorically, never having been … you know, talking about attachment disruptions and problems.

Dan

He wasn't part of that village.

Student 2

That's right. And individuals are damaged as a result of that and they damage others as a result of that, and so it was … because what shifted inside of me was not, "Oh, poor Donald, I'll vote for him," but what shifted inside of me was some clarity about who he is; and the other thing that shifted is suddenly nursing all of the people who are rabid fans of him …

Dan

Yeah, there's a vulnerability there.

Student 2

Absolutely, and recognizing that there's a similarity there …

Dan

At the times when people are afraid, what you see is this kind of rigid nationalism. Whether it be what's happening with the people voting for Trump, and this kind of "kick everybody else out" nationalism, or you know, we were teaching in London during the Brexit vote and there was no difference. The same mentality. And what you're seeing is the fall of an empire. The British empire's waning so that they vote for Brexit. The American dream is fading, there's no middle class anymore, so everybody's scared, and when you get that kind of decline in the culture, you get rigid nationalism, which is something we have to watch for. We've seen what happens in the past with this kind of stuff; this never goes in a good direction. It's scary. You have to be compassionate to people's fears.

Student 2

Right.

Dan

This culture is in decline.

Student 2

Right.

Dan

We sold this country to special interest groups, and everybody knows that. And it's on the decline, and everybody's paying for that. It's sad. The irony of that is that what's destroyed this country is selling it to special interest groups, so the solution is to elect an oligarch? It's bizarre. It just makes it worse.

Student 2

And so, I'm curious about, you know, just in the few moments where I was imagining this meditation, noticing the shift into genuine compassion, the shift into clarity, and the shift into genuine compassion for the people who are voting for him and so forth, and then the compassion there and the clarity there. So, there's that level to work on, but I'm just curious about what would it be like doing some sort of meditation like this and what the effect is on the matrix of the world. You know, what can we do? I was thinking of offering, in my community, a pre-meditation weekly kind of thing. No mention of the election, but knowing that, from my heart, that's what it's about. So, I'm just curious about that.

Dan

Well, that's an interesting question. And that is that if you understand that larger view of interconnectedness, if we all influence everybody else, and everybody practices interconnectedness, does that change the nature of the field? The TM people once made that claim. They claimed that if enough people on the planet meditated at the same time, in the same way, that it had a kind of influence. So that … in areas where there was a concentration of people working on their mind through meditation, they collected statistics, expecting that the crime rates would go down, that there would be more positive things happening in those environments. And they took that very seriously and they collected a lot of statistics about that. I got asked to be one of the independent reviewers of all that stuff, so I had to review all that stuff.

The statistics were complicated, but I couldn't see anything wrong with how they went about it. There was something to what they were saying. Don't think they claimed it the best way and I wasn't always convinced about their science, but there was something to what they were trying to get at that I thought it was worth studying. I didn't think they did it in the best way. But I couldn't say that this is junk, because it wasn't. So, I gave it a fairly favorable review. I thought it needed to be studied more carefully. It raises an interesting question of field effects from a Western point of view. If a number of people get together and they're all doing something similar, it's positive. Does that have a positive effect on the surrounding environment? Personally, I think there's something that we need to understand there more.

I'll tell you another story. The first time I went to India, I went to visit His Holiness, and this was in 1970-something. But the first thing I did before I did that was—I wanted to go to Varanasi, the City of Light, and see the all the pilgrims who went to the *ghats*, and see the burning of the bodies at the *ghats*. I mean, if you want to understand India, you have to go experience the life, death, and disease in Varanasi. So, I arrived in Varanasi, and I didn't know—it was sort of by the luck of the draw, it was during a solar eclipse. So, I went down to the Ganges just around the time of the solar eclipse, and I wasn't prepared for what I was about to experience. Imagine walking up the stairs of a building to get a view, a panoramic view of the *ghats*, the steps that go into the Ganges River, the sacred, the holy river. And I'm hearing all this noise, and I finally see what it's all about …

Here are three million people all praying and chanting at the same time! I've never seen anything like that. It had a deep impact on me, even today, as it's coming, an image comes right up. Imagine three million people all meditating and praying and chanting at the same time. The field effect of that is enormous. So, that impacted on me that there's something to this, even in the smallest ways.

There's an old Zen story that says, "If you take the smallest pebble and you drop it into the nearby stream, it changes the course of that stream, and that changes the course of the river downstream. And that changes the course of the bigger river downstream, and that bigger river enters into the mighty ocean. And that changes the course of the ocean beyond the stream." From a perspective of interconnectedness, everything that we do is like dropping a pebble. It affects everybody else in the field.

The real question becomes, first, are you aware of the effect of that pebble because you are operating out of the larger field of being the ocean? But the other question is what kind of pebbles do we want to drop? That makes a difference. What are you putting out? Are you kind? Are you compassionate? Are you concerned for the genuine welfare of others? Are you operating out of the positive qualities of mind? Or are you putting out selfish greed, taking for yourself—getting more and more? Because we have an entire culture that's based on greed and taking more. That's what's destroying this planet: smaller numbers of individuals who own everything and they just want more. The entire culture of Wall Street and the banking industry that supports that, it's like a runaway train.

There was an actual discussion about six months ago on Wall Street about fiduciary responsibility. And the overwhelming consensus was: "We don't have any fiduciary responsibility to our clients. We take our client's money to make money for ourselves." That's the entire culture. That's about as far away from interconnectedness as possible. That's why this planet doesn't work anymore.

I was talking to a cousin of mine this last week because our aunt died and we'd come up to scatter the ashes, and I was talking with him. And he was a well-to-do banker. So, we were just updating ourselves and he stopped being a banker. He and his wife were bankers together. I say, "Why did you quit?" He says, "Because the entire culture of banking now is how to rip off the customer with all these fees. So, we got out of it, went into Credit Unions because they support honest people working." I said, "How far this has gone!"

There's no sense of interconnectedness. It's all a runaway train about getting more from others and being on the take. That's the entire infrastructure we've set up. We're in trouble.

So, the practice of interconnectedness and getting out of selfish greed may be the necessary ingredient to keep this planet going. Whether we have enough time to do that, who knows? We still have to try.

August 17, 2016

Themes: Dying, *Phowa*; Capacity; Mindfulness vs. Awareness Practice

Dan

Welcome everyone. You have a question?

Student 1

So, my question is about permanence, Dan, and whether or not there is, in fact, an essential—well, any word falls short. I mean, there's no essential personality, there is no essential being. Who reincarnates? Who is left when absolute reality is seen and awareness is achieved? Who's there? We must stay as some form of identity that is … all the words fall short; if I use the word personal, it's not correct. I'm babbling at you. I hope you can ferret out the question.

Dan

I understand.

Student 1

Okay.

Dan

In the Tibetan system, what they say is left over is a little bit of energy, an essence, or *dütsi*, a vital essence that is an "indestructible essence." And at the point of conception, that essence enters this field. And as the embryo develops it's tied into the heart with a series of energy knots. Something like a computer chip. It's a little essence, a seed, an energy drop, and packed into that energy drop is an imprint of all the information of all of your lifetimes. It's like a fingerprint of the mind; it has a signature of its own uniqueness. Nobody's indestructible essence is like anybody else's indestructible essence. So, in the Tibetan system, that indestructible essence is packaged in your heart space and is tied by four energy knots.

Now, in the dying process, as the elements of the body dissolve, and one by one the physiological systems shut off, amongst other things that happen is that those four energy knots loosen. And that energy drop, that indestructible essence, is released from the heart space. It flows along the golden tube channel and enters the upper part of the central channel and remains in the central channel. That indestructible essence has a very subtle consciousness to it. It's not the normal consciousness that we usually operate out of, but in the dying process, you shut off all conceptual thought. We shut off all perception, and shut off all memory, but there's a very subtle consciousness that survives.

When the body physically dies, when you take your last breath and the brain dies, there is still a very subtle consciousness residing in that indestructible essence in your central channel. And that stays in the central channel for either an instant, in the short run, or up to three days maximally, in the long run. And, at some point, that indestructible essence leaves through one of the orifices. If it comes out the crown, then you're likely to be born as a human. If it comes out your butt, you're more likely to be born in the hell realms. Depending on what orifice it leaves from, it determines which of the six realms of *samsāric* beings you're going to become again.

So, there's a distinction in Tibet between physical death and spiritual death. When the breath stops (the coarse level breath) and the brain dies, you're not dead. You're physically dead, but you're not spiritually dead as long as the indestructible essence resides in the body for up to three days. This is why they don't remove the body for a couple of days. Now, you know when that indestructible essence leaves because there are *tak*, or signs of that. And the signs are that there will be blood congealing at either the corners of the mouth or the nose dried blood, and/or the body will give a distinct smell of death. You'll know when the body is starting to smell like death. But before that, it stays fresh. At that point, that tells you that the indestructible essence has left the body.

And it's like a computer chip and it has all the karmic imprints of lifetimes. And it recycles itself. What form it takes as it leaves the body and enters the universe again is some form of energy, because energy can transform from one type of energy to another. And eventually, usually within a cycle of forty-nine days, it recycles itself; it takes on a different form, whatever form of rebirth you're going to come back into. And then it's packaged in that body and you don't remember the previous life, usually. But if you're a realized being, you could remember that because if you have all-at-once-ness, then you remember across time and space. You could, but most people don't. But it recycles itself.

So, from that perspective we can say that there is something that survives and something that recycles itself. But it doesn't mean like the Western stuff that says, "Gee, I was the pharaoh of Egypt three lifetimes ago." That's crap. That's all mental constructions and imagination calling attention to the self. It doesn't work like that. But is there something that you can say that is left over beyond physical death that is more like lively energy awareness? And does that transform itself and take on a different form and eventually recycle itself? That's a more palatable argument that seems quite reasonable from a Western point of view.

Student 1

So is that, that essential self … the question I'm having, is if that's the motivation, beside the question of what remains after death in current life, it seems as though there's always been a motivation to find out what there is that's "more." What more is there, and here I am now in this life.

Dan

Well, from a Tibetan point of view, dying is an opportunity. Because, while the best opportunity of course is to do your practice in this lifetime and to awaken and to stabilize the awakening and to bring it up to full enlightenment—that's what you want to do in this lifetime—the backup plan if you don't fully do that is you have a second, you have a backup plan. And the backup plan is that during the process of dying, you can become enlightened because despite yourself, when you're dying, all conceptualization drops away. All perception drops away, all the residual impurities of the mind drop away. And all that's left is the pure essence of the mind, which, if you recognize it correctly, is called "the clear light of dying." And if you recognize the clear light of dying, it's that lucid field of bright awakened awareness, it is awakened awareness. And, if you understand that, game over. You don't go through the recycling process.

Now, in Dzogchen's Great Completion teachings, there's two schools of thought about this. Some schools of thought, which is probably the minority position, say you don't teach the dying practices because they want to give a strong message that we want to become buddhas in this lifetime. And, if you teach them the backup plan, then you're conveying the message that, "I don't really think, I'm not confident you can do this." Do you what see I'm saying? It's not the right message. Some teachers will not teach you the backup practices, to put the emphasis on developing them fully in this lifetime.

The other school of thought, which is the majority position of Tibet, is that most people aren't going to become buddhas in this lifetime, so teach the backup plan. And the backup plan is *phowa*, or what they call "consciousness transference." Traditionally, if you do your hundred thousand preliminary practices and you finish them, the next thing you're doing at the end of the preliminary practice is you're given *phowa* practices. And basically, what *phowa* is about is that in the energy body, you have three main channels. There's a central channel that is about the size of an index finger, blue in color. It runs from four fingers below the navel right up to the crown. Then there are two side channels—one on the right which is white, and one on the left that is red—that go through the nostrils, loop back, run parallel down the central channel, and they all loop at the bottom with loops coming around what we call the juncture, four fingers below the navel. That's the main channel system.

In *phowa* practice, or consciousness transference practice as it's normally taught, what you do is you take an energy drop, a *thigle*—it's a rather big one [since] most energy drops you start with are about the size of a pea, but this one is about the size of a quarter. Sometimes you use the size of a pea, but the bigger ones are better; and you visualize that energy drop typically starting at the navel, or you can start at the juncture.

Then what you do is you utter a sound and simultaneous to uttering the sound, you visualize that energy drop being pushed up by the sound and up the central channel. You go, "Hic, hic, hic, hic, hic, hic, hic, hic." [Dan pronounces these as high-pitched, short sounds.] And as I'm doing that, step by step [or hic by hic] I'm visualizing moving that energy drop up the central channel. Then I inhale and start again and move it up a little further, and then start again.

That energy drop is like a roto rooter. What it does is it expands the size of that upper central channel, and you move up by steps. Up to the navel and up to the heart, and then past the heart; and particularly you want to spend some time and care working it from the heart up to the throat, and then from the throat up to the crown.

Now, when you get to the crown, what you want to do is you want to force that energy drop out through the skull. The skull is made of plates, so when you get to the crown, if you keep forcing the energy drop against the bony plate, it starts to move away the plates, and it can move away the plates quite a bit. If you move away the plates and you keep forcing it against the crown fontanelle and the bony plate, you start pushing them apart.

The *tak*, the sign, that you're doing that correctly is it will start leaking fluid, and you'll get a swelling and edema right at the top—like there's an egg on the top of your head, like somebody hit you and you got a goose egg—and it gets very tender and somewhat inflamed. If you keep doing that, then you'll actually push the plates apart. There's a hole there. So, the test is, the lama will then take a straw, like from a broom, and put it right through the hole, and it will stick up because you've made a hole in your head. What you've done is you've widened that central channel permanently.

Here's the rub. You can't just open that [by yourself]. You've got to do this under supervision, and the lama has to test that you're doing it right because the most important thing is that after you open it, you've got to plug it up, and you plug it up with a seed syllable. You visualize a seed syllable, and you just plug the hole like a stopper. You've got to do the visualization. You have to have enough concentration to be able to stop it correctly because if you don't, you can prematurely die.

Now, that's normal *phowa* practice. The average time it takes to do this under supervision is about two weeks. It's not a hard thing to do, and it's sort of like building an ejection seat in a jet plane. When you're in the process of dying and the body's crashing and burning, all you have to do is use the "hic" and eject your indestructible essence right out of the crown at the very beginning of the dying process. Then you don't have to go through all these stages of the *bardos*, and the after-death states, and the rebirthing. You eject right out of the crown, and you immediately become fully enlightened. You become a buddha, and the mind then resides in its own place in awakened *dharmakāya* space. You're now a fully enlightened buddha.

The *phowa* is thus a pretty good backup plan because when the body crashes and burns, and all conceptual thought and all perception and all that stuff of the ordinary mind stops, if you push the ejection button at the right time and come out the crown, it immediately leads to full enlightenment. You become a buddha. You don't have to go through the process of rebirth. You've gotten full mastery over that.

Now, what happens from there is interesting because this indestructible essence, which is now merged with awakened *dharmakāya* space and the vast expanse, still has intention and still has signature. You can intend to take any form you want in the future. You have voluntary control over the dying process. If you want to come back in some plane of reality to help beings, all you have to do is use what's called *gongpa*, enlightened intention, to come back in any form that you want, in any realm that you want; or you can take many forms simultaneously and serve the benefit of others.

Usually, *phowa* is taught as a way of giving you voluntary control over the dying process so you can come back intentionally, emanating in any form that you want. If you have that capacity to emanate, we call that a *tulku*, an enlightened form body that emanates. For example, Rahob Rinpoche, who's an emanation of Padmasambhava, his name is Rahob Tulku. He's decided to emanate in a certain area of Tibet over a number of generations in order to convey certain teachings for a certain amount of time, then he'll stop. That's what *tulkus* do.

Now we're having *tulkus* in the West. They'll come here and teach for a while, and then when they finish what they're doing, they stop emanating, and they do something else. You don't just rest in awakened *dharmakāya* space. You can emanate in any form you want at that point. There's no dying to be done. Only the physical body dies, and at that point you have voluntary control of the dying process. What I've described here is called internal *phowa*—the teaching on how you transfer yourself at the time of dying.

What's more rare is what's called external *phowa*, or external consciousness transference, and Rahob's monastery is one of the few places that teaches it. External consciousness transference can be where if a person dies, and if they die of unfavorable circumstances like they died of some big crash and they had a lot of fear suddenly, or they died because they killed themselves, a lama can intervene if they know the external *phowa* practices, which are only taught in certain lineages. With those practices, the lama can use sound when the indestructible essence of that person leaves the body, usually under untimely circumstances. You can use sound, the "hic" sound, to grab that indestructible essence out of the universe, like grabbing a cell phone number. They'll bring it down using the "hic, hic, hic, hic, hic, hic," [Dan gestures as if it's coming into the palm of his hand], and they'll comfort it with "shew, shew, shew," and clean it of all the terror and all the confusion that happened, comforting it, then "phat!" [Dan sounds the sharp phat syllable], they'll compel it into awakened *dharmakāya* space.

Now, that's a great gift because the lama's kindness is intervening directly in the karmic cycle, which is especially important to do if somebody suicides. Because you can set them free out of the lama's kindness if external *phowa* is a practice that's known; and it's sometimes done in certain lineages, but it's not very common.

The third is secret *phowa*. There's external, internal, and then secret. In secret consciousness transference, there are two types. One is what we already mentioned, when you get the capacity to emanate through enlightened intention to any form that you want, and the other is to do rainbow body, which is called "great consciousness transference," where at the point of dying, if you've mastered what are called "bypassing great completion practices," in which you transform everything into light, the last thing to go is the physical body. At the point of dying, you can transfer the physical body and transform it into light. A great lama will do that at the point that they know they're going to die, because they can read the signs when they're going to die.

You can tell when a person's dying. All you have to do is follow what's happening to the breath. You can track it right down to the hour just by following the changes in the breath. There are some texts in *The Tibetan Book of the Dead* cycle that actually point out what we call the external signs, how to read when a person's dying, so you know when they're going to die.

If a lama knows when he's going to die, he'll just tell everybody, "Put me in the cave," or, "Zip me up in my tent, and don't disturb me for three days." And then if they're working on their great consciousness transference, they'll do the residual transformation of the body into light. At the end of three days, there will be a rainbow light that will appear in the sky, and then, poof. Disappeared. If you open up the tent, all that's left is the hair and nails, all the inanimates of the body; but the physical body, the live parts of the body, are all transformed into light and disappeared.

Now, it's very rare. I saw that once, but it's not very common. But sometimes when people are working on rainbow body practices, they can, while they're still alive but towards the end of their life, they can transform into rainbow light and then back into a physical body again. I saw one guy do that. They had that capacity also. That's considered changing the body into physical light and is considered the highest attainment, as far as you can go beyond enlightenment. It's the last attainment. In Dzogchen Great Completion practices, rainbow body is the marker of the highest degree of enlightenment.

But there are texts that teach how to do rainbow body. Apparently, it's not limited to the Buddhist Dzogchen tradition. I suppose we could say Christ achieved rainbow body. He disappeared in three days, too. That's not so different. It's the same practice.

There are stages of transformation. The first is clear light body. That's when everything turns to light. The body feels like an empty glass bottle filled with light, and then the second is what's called "youthful vase body" where you reverse the aging process. While you're still alive, the gray hair turns to your old color again. The skin gets bright and shiny again. All the aging spots disappear. Obviously, I haven't done youthful vase body. [Dan chuckles] Then the final transformation is rainbow body. This is all spelled out. There's a whole set of advanced teachings for each one of these things. The rainbow body and becoming a *tulku*, emanating any way you want and getting voluntary control, are what are called secret *phowa* practice. There's external, internal, and secret.

You have an entire cultural system here that maps out in a very sophisticated way the survival of whatever there is after physical death, something that we don't even entertain much in the West. There's a lot out there about how you do this, and it's rather detailed and sophisticated.

But *phowa* is not hard to learn. *Phowa* is pretty easy to learn. I'm from the other school of thought. I'd rather have you work towards awakening and develop your awakening and set your intention on developing it in this lifetime, so that's why I don't emphasize the *phowa*. I don't want to undermine the message that the purpose of these teachings coming to the West is so you can bring your full measure of practice to those teachings in this lifetime.

Student 2

About the English word "signature" that you've used just a moment ago. You were talking about enlightened intent. Sorry, a few moments ago you said that when spiritual death occurs, that enlightened intent and a signature remained, and you said *gongpa* is enlightened intent. I'm wondering if there's a Tibetan word that corresponds directly to "signature."

Dan

Dakni—dak means self, and *ni* is an intensifier, like selfness, but it doesn't mean self in the ordinary sense. It means the very essence of your identity. *Dakni* means the very essence of your identity. That's why buddhas are all different. That's why we have many methods of teaching because different people need different skillful means. There are 84,000 means for 84,000 types of people. That's a lot. Most of this is untranslated. There's a vast treasure house of this knowledge out there. I know this much. [Dan makes a hand gesture indicating "just a pinch."]

Student 2

It occurs to me to ask if this essence has an intent to expand itself, to, in whatever way, whether it be meditation or otherwise, with some mistaken choices I'm sure, but that we want to develop ourselves. And I'm wondering if that's so for all beings.

Dan

Yeah. There's a really important technical term called *gongpa*. It's not so easy to translate. I like to translate it as "enlightened intention." And non-ordinary beings, those who dwell not on this level of reality, but in *dharmakāya* space or *sambhogakāya* space, have enlightened intention.

If we think of Kuntuzangpo as the primordial state of buddhahood, Kuntuzangpo has intention, enlightened intention. The intention of Kuntuzangpo's mind is to show the path to itself for the sake of its own realization and to make the world appear in this way for the sake of training our own compassion. The whole magical display, however we construe it, is designed with its own intelligence and intention. The whole purpose of this whole show is for you to come to the realizations, to set it up, and to keep showing the way it is for you to bring about your own realizations, and to train your own compassionate mind. That's why the show is this way. If you complete the path, ultimately what you discover, when you have full stable enlightenment, is that your mind is enlightened intention—the same as Kuntuzangpo's, because you are Kuntuzangpo. Everybody enters that state.

I was recently retranslating *Heart Drops of Dharmakāya* because I discovered that it wasn't really a full translation. Lopon Tenzin Namdak, the great Bon Lama, gave a series of teachings on this, and the students took notes, and they wrote down what he was saying, but it wasn't an exact translation of the text. So, I thought it would be better for our students for me to go back and translate it line for line.

One of the things that I found curious is that the title of the book in Tibetan is not *Heart Drops of Dharmakāya*. The exact title of the book is *Heart Drops of Kuntuzangpo*. That's far more meaningful because what it means is if you do these advanced Great Completion bypassing practices, and you refine them to the stage of full enlightenment, you realize that the intention that guided you and showed you everything along the way is Kuntuzangpo. You are Kuntuzangpo. We're all Kuntuzangpo, and that's our buddha nature that's planted in our mindstream. It's part of the programming. It's rather profound.

The path is programmed to show itself to itself, for the sake of its own realization and for the sake of developing its own compassion. That's intention. It's profound. The further you clear away conceptual thought and the residuals—what we call the *nyigma*, the dregs of the ordinary mind—the more pure the visions get. The more the path shows itself to itself with its own intelligence. So, at some point, all the teachings come to you because they're all right here. You may be guided at that point in practice. It always just shows itself to itself because it's part of the programming. The path has its own intelligence. It has the intention, enlightened intention, to show itself to itself, by itself, for the sake of its own realization and to make the world appear this way for the sake of developing our compassion. There is no *samsāra*, it just appears that way. You've got to get the lesson. It's like a massive video game; and you've got to figure it out.

Just think that Donald Trump is only an illusion. [Laughs] Some illusions cause more harm than others; that's the problem. At least from our perspective it appears that way.

Student 3

To build on it, can you say a word about the nature of consciousness, what is doing the thinking?

Dan

Well, it's not like that in the Tibetan system. First of all, they don't use the word consciousness like we do. Consciousness in the West is sort of an overall; it's much like the Tibetans use awareness. The word consciousness in Tibet is restricted to sense consciousness. So, if we look at something, that's called eye consciousness. If we smell something, that's called smell consciousness. If we hear something, that's called sound consciousness or hearing consciousness. That's how the word consciousness is used. And the mind that interprets that is called the mind consciousness.

And none of that has to do with awareness. In fact, it interferes with awareness. The overall concept in the Tibetan system is awareness. And there's ordinary awareness, *trenpa*, and there's awakened awareness, and they're very different. And that's important to appreciate. So, the whole part of this video game that we're figuring out is how to directly recognize the nature of awakened awareness as distinct from our ordinary level of awareness, which is usually mixed up with conceptual thought.

Conceptual thought is not important in this system; it's considered an interference. So, the Buddhist logicians say there are two ways of knowing: there's this conceptual knowing, and there's direct knowing through awareness. And the only valid system to directly realize awakened nature is through direct knowing through awareness. You can't think your way into awakening. All thoughts partialize. So, you can't grasp an awakened mind through partialization mode. So, thoughts can't be used as a way of awakening; they just get in the way. So, it's after you see beyond thought and there's no longer an interference and it no longer creates grab, that's when you have more likelihood of directly recognizing awakened nature.

Thoughts are like clouds. You can't see the radiance of the sun when the clouds are covering everything. But when the clouds clear, the radiance of the sun has always been shining, is always right here. Your awakened nature always is shining radiantly, but you don't see it because there are too many clouds. So, emptiness practice sort of removes the clouds, gives you a glimpse of that awakening. You don't have to get rid of anything. You just have to see beyond it. Then, once you see the awakening, the clouds come and go, but they don't obscure the radiance of the sunlight. Once you get a taste of awakening, even if thoughts come and go, they don't obscure that. But generally, thoughts get in the way for most of us, and they're not considered the way of knowing in great completion practice. So, it's not consciousness. We're talking about the nature of awakened awareness. The key ingredient here is awakened awareness.

But just being aware isn't awakened awareness, and that's my criticism of the popularity of the practice of mindfulness, because mindfulness is ordinary awareness. And you might be less reactive, and you might have more continuous awareness, but very rarely do the mindfulness teachers ever talk about awakening. So, why are we doing this thing? You're training yourself to harden ordinary awareness, and that's not going to lead you anywhere useful.

So, know what you're getting. You spend all this work making it harder to achieve awakening and you think you're meditating. Does that make it a little clearer? It's all about the nature of awakened awareness. And the reason why in great completion, one of the paths is called *trekchö*, or thoroughly cutting through; what it means is you get instructions that cut through all the seeming solidity of the ordinary mind and its conceptualization and its perception. And you move beyond that to awakened awareness.

Anything else?

Student 4

Yeah. I had a question that was kind of stimulated last week when you were talking about Ken Wilber, and I was kind of wondering if in Ken's model he has what he has called "lines of development," which just means different intelligences. And one way that he does an analysis is he'll look at different lines of intelligence like analytical thought or athleticism and he'll put a whole bunch of them together, call it a "psychograph" and show how people are doing on [each of] them. And what I was wondering is if you had ever thought … what are the different lines that are needed to be good at the *Pointing Out The Great Way* meditation practices? Like maybe staying could be seen as a line of intelligence, or mental pliancy, or metacognition. And I was just wondering if you ever thought about it in that way, and if so, what would the lines be?

Dan

It's a good question. The traditional way in Buddhism is the notion of the three capacities: best, middling and lesser capacity. So, best capacity students, when they hear the teachings, they figure it out rather quickly; they don't need a lot of meditation practice. They just get the realizations; just by hearing the teachings, they wake up.

Middling capacity, which is most people in this room including myself, have to work at it. You hear the teachings, they make some sense to you ,but you've got to sit down and put them into meditation practice, and over time the meditation practice leads to *nyam*, or different kinds of meditation experiences. And the *nyam* leads to *tokpa*, which is realizations. And then the realizations lead to further meditation experiences, which lead to further *tokpa* realizations. And it goes on like that all the way up the path to full enlightenment. So, it comes in stages, gradually.

Then there are those of lesser capacity, and the people who are lesser capacity gravitate towards the teaching, but they don't really know how to either intellectually understand it and grasp the depth of it, and/or they don't know how to put it into meditation practice. But they understand the preciousness of it. So, those practitioners tend to be more devotional, but they don't meditate very much, and they don't really get the realizations in meditation experiences. But they can be very deeply devoted to the practice.

I remember teaching a retreat and there was a Western nun that came to it, in a different country, and she had no capacity whatsoever to do concentration. Her mind was so jumping around; she had a wild elephant mind. She couldn't get more than 5 percent of the session, staying on the concentration object after working on it for three days. Didn't understand this notion of emptiness at all and ended up after three days giving up anything that we were teaching and going back to what she was familiar with, which was doing compassion visualizations with the rest of the course, and she'll do that for the rest of her life. Nothing we tried to show her was she open to learning or seeing to do differently. That's a good example of that capacity level.

On the other hand, we had another Western nun come where we were teaching. This was in Australia where we rented a space from a Catholic center. There's this Tibetan Western nun who's walking around the center. And I said, "What are you doing here?" She says, "Well I'm here doing a private retreat." So, I said, "You can come to this course if you want." She got it right away, had a good awakening, stayed for the second week, did the advanced teaching, stabilized awakening, and in two weeks she had pretty much stable awakening. That's best capacity. Did the whole thing in two weeks. See the difference? So, the model in Tibet is best, middling, or lesser capacity. It's a legitimate way of approaching this.

You're talking about something quite different, and I like it. And you're talking about whether we could isolate out some concepts from Tibetan Buddhism that would mark progress like stability of concentration, like the degree to which you have mental pliancy. And as a teacher, of course, we do that kind of thing. We may not articulate it as much as that, but you're getting me wondering about this. But certainly, what I look for is the speed of realization with pliancy. How flexible and pliant the mind is so that whatever you intend to focus on, it just does that and only that, and nothing else gets in the way.

So, that kind of un-interfered-with pliancy is an important part of metacognitive capacity. We always look for the range of metacognitive capacities that students have, to recognize the different states that they're in. So, those become, pretty much, markers of what we see. The students who have good metacognitive ability, the students who have good pliancy, usually do much better. That's true.

Around awakening, the students who are able to step out of particularizing and don't talk about their realizations in particularizing terms, that's a more clear marker that they know how to do that. So, these are some of the things we've learned along the way, but certainly there's a lot more that we could learn over time about that. I'm still a work in progress at trying to figure those things out.

Student 4

I mean it seems like you certainly, when you answer the questions, you're often targeting something very specific like, "Oh, I can tell this is metacognition in the class." So, it feels like you're certainly … Yeah, I was thinking it could be really useful to have like those out as an assessment tool. Then we could self-assess or you can mark it.

Dan

Well, as the *dharma* gets more fully seated in the West, maybe we'll develop those tools as Western tools, and I think that's a good idea. Right now, my motivation is simpler than that. I'm trying to translate all three maps. The first map goes from the beginning to awakening, but it's not stable. The second map is stabilizing awakening on and off the pillow, so you have it all the time in all situations. And the third map is the practices that bring up full buddhahood, which means the path of *dharmadhātu* exhaustion, the path of the exhaustion of the bypassing visions, the transformation of clear light body, and things like that. We're trying to translate all of those things, and then put them in a form that works for Westerners, and find a way of wording them that Westerners can make sense of. Once we finish that, then these are other things that I'll get to at some point, if I live that long. But right now, I estimate it's going to take us two more years to finish the full set of teachings on this.

Student 4

I might take a stab at something else and I'll send it to you; you can let me know what you think.

Dan

I appreciate that. We did try and work up the stages of adult mature cognitive development in these terms from Ken's model and fill it out more with actual meditation practices. That part we worked on.

Student 4

Cool, thanks.

Dan

Anything else?

Student 5

Could you comment on the basic mind training of the Elephant Path, as just the preparation for insight meditation, so you could hold the view because you've got the concentration?

Dan

No, not like that. In the beginning of practice there are two broad types of meditations. Okay. We say that the ordinary mind is like a wild elephant; it jumps around and goes everywhere. So, you have to tame the wild elephant mind. So, there are two ways of taming elephants.

First you can tie a chain around the elephant's neck and put a stake in the ground and tie the chain onto the other end of the stake. So, every time the elephant wanders off, it feels the pull of the chain and gets pulled back, wanders off, gets pulled back, wanders off, pulled back. If it does that hundreds and hundreds of time, and if it's a smart elephant, it sort of figures out that it's not going to go very far because it's tied up. So, it settles down.

And that's a metaphor for concentration meditation. You tie the rope of concentration onto a specific object, be it the rising and falling of the breath or a recited sound like a mantra, or anything, a candle flame. And every time the mind goes somewhere else. you pull it back. You keep pulling it back over and over again and, over time like the elephant, the mind learns that it's not going to go very far, so it stops chasing after thought and chasing after sense experience, and stays.

So, the development of concentration is two things. First, *nepā*, staying more continuously on the object. And the second is *shiwa*, all that background noise of thought calms down and it gets rather still and quiet so you have long periods of stillness, absent of thought activity.

That's concentration. You tie the rope of concentration onto a single object. In neural imaging terms, that's the ACC, the anterior cingulate cortex. You effortlessly focus on one thing; everything else you tune out. So, when you concentrate, you activate the ACC. It's the same area of the brain that gets activated when you have competing attentional demands and you effortfully focus out one thing, and focusing just on the other thing.

The other way of training the elephant is not tie it up, but you track the elephant with your eyes, and no matter where the elephant wanders off, you never take your eyes off the elephant. You just track it, continuously. And that's the metaphor for awareness meditations. And the goal is different from concentration. The goal of concentration is staying and calming thought. The goal of awareness meditation is to have continuous awareness and free up the continuous awareness from what normally happens which is that there are chunks missing of awareness. In our ordinary mind, awareness is discontinuous. We have lots of lapses in awareness and periods of forgetfulness.

So, when you're practicing what's called awareness meditations or mindfulness meditations, the goal is very different. Awareness meditation is continuous, uninterrupted awareness of whatever comes into consciousness. You don't tie the mind up to anything. Okay, so whatever comes up is the next object. So, it's the continuous tracking that's the issue, like never taking your eyes off wherever the elephant goes. And that is a very different skill. The examples of that would be Krishnamurti's choiceless awareness, and Shikantaza, just sitting style of Zen. Those are the main examples of that—pure awareness meditations. And what happens with that in terms of neurocircuitry is with the other end of the cingulate cortex—the posterior cingulate cortex—gets deactivated.

The PCC is what gets activated when we categorize and judge experiences—this is good, this is bad, this is hot, this is cold, this is pleasant, this is unpleasant. When you cultivate continuous nonjudgmental awareness, you're taking that judgmental part of the mind offline. So, in studies of Burmese mindfulness, or "non-meditation" meditation in the Tibetan system, you're taking the PCC off-line. It's a completely different neurocircuitry and a different skill.

Now here's where it gets complicated. The Burmese mindfulness that became popular in this country is a hybrid. When most practices had deteriorated into folk prayers and local rituals, and meditation wasn't popular about a hundred years ago in South Asia in the Theravādin tradition, Mahāsī Sayādaw took the great stages of meditation in the Theravāda system's *Visudhimagga: The Path of Purification*, stripped it down, simplified it, and made it into a practical application called "Burmese Mindfulness." He made it available, and it became so popular that there were over two hundred centers throughout South Asia and over two hundred thousand people took it in the first forty years. Then it made its way to the West.

But it's a hybrid system. He felt, quite correctly, that if you say "be aware of everything," most people can't do that. So, he starts with some concentration on the breath to still thoughts enough; that's the first modification. Second modification is, after you concentrate for a while, you use categories to approximate continuous awareness. When a thought comes, "thinking." You don't think about the content of that thought, just at that moment, thinking is occurring—and [then] hearing, seeing, feeling, sensing; he used the categories to approximate continuous nonjudgmental awareness, or "mindfulness." You follow me?

That's the kind of mindfulness that became popular over here. It's neither a pure awareness meditation nor a pure concentration meditation. It's a bit of both. So, in that sense, it's a beginning meditation and somewhat popular. And there's nothing wrong with that. The trouble is a lot of the tools to deepen concentration were stripped out of it when Mahāsī Sayādaw made it available to Westerners and in his own country first.

Furthermore, some of the important teachings in the Visuddhimagga got left out, like the whole problem of who's doing the meditation—the problem of self. In that Theravādin tradition, you work through that with what's called "aggregate practice" and the five aggregates. That got completely stripped away from the simplified version of Burmese mindfulness. So, there's no tool to work with the problem of self. And it's interesting that that's the version of meditation that became the most popular in the West. So, you can be very mindful and very filled with yourself because there is no tool to work with it. These practices aren't designed for self-importance, but that method doesn't give ways to work with that issue adequately, in my opinion.

And second of all, what got lost in that system is where it ultimately takes you. When was the last time you went to a mindfulness class and heard the teacher talk about awakening, or enlightenment? So, mindfulness in the West as it became secularized became an end in itself. You can have continuous, or relatively continuous awareness that's nonjudgmental. Does it have benefits for mental health? Absolutely. But the trouble with that from a Tibetan perspective is what you're really training is you're training yourself to harden ordinary awareness. And that actually makes it harder to awaken because right from the get-go, you're just training ordinary awareness, and that clouds over the awakened mind more thoroughly.

Student 5

And is there an element of particularizing then, also with mindfulness, because you follow everything?

Dan

Yes, because you're following everything. It creates subtle bad habits in the mind that are problematic here. But because everybody thinks they're meditating, and developing an identity around this, it's hard to convince them that maybe this is not the best thing to do here. That's a problem. Just because it's popular doesn't necessarily mean it's the best thing and, unfortunately, it has lost the heart of this whole tradition.

Student 5

I'm thinking of Marsha Linehan with DBT [dialectical behavior therapy] and her mindfulness practice as being an example of what you're talking about where it becomes the end in itself and works to stay focused, and not get judgmental, and to some extent get rid of reactivity, but it doesn't make you aware.

Dan

Well, I'll answer that from a Western point of view. Because of her personal interest in mindfulness, all borderlines get mindfulness, so you learn to be aware of your internal state. But there is more sophisticated research coming out of the Rome Institute for Cognitive Therapy that says there are different metacognitive skills needed for different patients. What they found is that borderlines were very good at being aware of their internal states, but very poor at being aware in a way that regulated those states, where narcissists were the exact opposite. Narcissists are completely unaware of their own and other peoples' state of mind, but they're very good at regulating it. So, what do you want to do here? What you really need to do is train metacognitive regulation for borderlines. But because of her own interest in mindfulness, she got it wrong, we know now, because there is nothing there teaching metacognitive regulation.

So, this is [an example of] where we popularize things without really thinking through what we're really doing. Now we know better. But try to get any DBT person to change what they're doing, because they're attached to their system, even though it doesn't work. There are no outcome studies that show that borderlines get better from it. But if you look at some of the mentalization-based treatments, about 70 percent of them get better in two years. That's a remarkably different database. So, you have to read between the lines here. Simply because something is popular, that doesn't mean they're the best things out there.

We found in our very different attachment work—our book came out last week[20]—that we got very good outcome data because it works. We got a treatment effect size of 6.2. It doesn't get much better than that.

---

20 *Attachment Disturbance in Adults: Treatment for Comprehensive Repair*, Daniel P. Brown & David S. Elliot, 2016, W. W. Norton, New York.

Student 5

That book is now available through Amazon?

Dan

It's the "featured work" this week at Amazon.

Student 5

Really?

Dan

Yes.

Student 5

Thank you, Dan. That's very clear. That's very helpful.

Dan

It's a huge book—almost eight hundred pages—and I'm really happy to say they gave it a fair price. It's not that expensive. I like Norton. It's my second book with Norton. What I like about them is that they're the only publisher that's owned by the employees. It's not a corporation. They're all very proud of what they're doing because they all have a vested stake in it. They do a good job with things.

Student 5

Can that generalize to other diagnoses other than borderline?

Dan

What do you mean?

Student 5

Well, you said treating attachment, so I assume that shows up with what diagnosis …

Dan

What I'm saying is that what we've learned, particularly from the Rome group on metacognition, is that there are different cognitive skills, and that certain diagnostic groups are missing certain of those skills, so you can't just do metacognitive work. You have to match the skill to what's needed by that patient. That's true in the Rome group and that's also true in our research group—you have to match the metacognition right.

But metacognition is key to this path both in awareness and in concentration meditations. Metacognition is the right dorsolateral prefrontal cortex. There's nothing about thought. It's seeing clearly your own state of mind and self-correcting it if you're doing a meditation practice. There's a famous Sufi tale that says, "A log sits on a wood pile for years very quietly, but logs never realize God. So, don't sit like a log, sit intelligently." Use your metacognition.

And there is one study showing that the difference between advanced and beginning concentrators had nothing to do with how many years they concentrated. It was whether they used metacognition to constantly move it along to improve it. Not to do the same old same old and make the same mistakes over and over again. It's true in concentration meditation, it's true in mindfulness meditation, awareness meditation, and it's true in learning to drive a car. Some people use metacognition to learn from their mistakes and they learn very quickly, and some people keep making the same old same old mistakes over and over again, and they don't learn it so quickly.

The key is what you were saying earlier—the key to one of these skills, to see who advances in meditation, is how much they develop their metacognitive intelligence so they can actually see what they are doing and self-correct mistakes, bring out the positive qualities more clearly, constantly moving the path forward, so they don't just sit quietly like a log.

August 31, 2016

Themes: Preparing to Die; *Phowa*; Stages of Change; Cognitive Dissonance

Dan

Welcome everyone. You have a question?

Student 1

[Asks about a Level 1 retreat that Dan led recently in Gloucester, MA.]

Dan

It was a good retreat, I thought. Yeah, it's my neighborhood. It was a thrill, with Gretchen and myself to teach the *dharma* to our neighbors. It was a different group, economically. I mean, most people who come to these retreats have to be professionals to be able to afford to take a week off from work and come to the retreats.

A lot of the people were working class, and they had to have scholarships, so financially it was sort of a bitter disaster. But it was such a fun group to teach; it sort of offset that just fine, because we just loved the group. They were very sincere and appreciative of what they were getting, and very, very hard working, and devotional. So, it was a wonderful group. I'm happy with it.

Student 2

Since the last meditation group, last week I believe it was, when we did the dissolution meditation.

Dan

Okay.

Student 2

Some thoughts have been marinating in my mind, and among them are—you mentioned about having an auspicious exit, or through an orifice that would be auspicious.

Dan

Don't come out your butt. [Dan laughs]

Student 2

Exactly. I didn't want to say that. The thought came to my mind, what is the emphasis placed on, because there are so many people who pass, and they're medicated. They're either on morphine, because they're in extreme pain, so their exit isn't under their control. How much emphasis, or gravity, is given to the life well lived?

Dan

Well, those are two separate questions. But, let me answer both of them.

Student 2

Okay. Thank you.

Dan

The issue of being snowed with morphine, or some other drug, from a Tibetan point of view, is a problem. We don't make much of a distinction in this country between palliative care and hospice care. Most hospice care is really not hospice care, where you prepare people for the dying process; it's really palliative care. And as the name palliative care implies, the fundamental belief system in palliative care is that we should make people as comfortable as possible when they die.

In Western terms, that means giving them drugs. Then we can think that we're actually helping them because they're going to be in less pain and discomfort when they die. But first of all, that assumption may not be correct, in terms of understanding the dying process. And second of all, it's driven by our socialization by the pharmaceutical industry that if people are uncomfortable, you give them drugs. So, much of medicine has uncritically accepted that point of view.

I'll tell you a personal story about that.

I remember once when I was much younger, and I was playing father and son karate with my kid and kicked a little too hard and tore my knee up. So, I had to go for knee surgery. And in the knee surgery, they did an epidural so that you don't lose your consciousness—it's not a general [anesthetic] but you can't feel anything from the neck downwards, which is sort of weird. You still have a brain and your mind is working, but it takes a while for the feeling to come back into the legs, then work up the body, and then you get your feeling back. It takes a couple of hours. And I remember having gone through the surgery being quite curious about what they were doing with my knee, because they had it on their video camera so I could watch the whole thing, and I was just really quite absorbed in it. I didn't feel any discomfort. Then I went to post-op, and in the post-op there were six people all from post-op in the same room from surgeries, not all knee surgeries.

And there was this woman next to me who was absolutely in a panic state about her level of pain. It was pathetic, because every five minutes a nurse would come by and she would demand to get more medication, and they would say, "Well, we've given you the max. We can't give you anymore. We don't have any orders to give you anymore." So, they stood by with their little clipboards and could do nothing for this woman, because their fundamental assumption was you give them meds, but the meds clearly weren't controlling the pain, so she was working herself up into more and more a sense of a panic, and they had absolutely no idea what to do with her.

So, I watched that go on for about forty-five minutes, in a sort of weird, disembodied state, but having once run a pain clinic, and knowing something about the mind, I said, when the nurses went away, I said, "I don't want to be intrusive here, but maybe I can help you." And I had her do some simple breathing exercises, and then taught her some ways of focusing her mind in a way that she could actually master the pain experience. And within about twenty minutes, she settled down just fine and took no more medications, and she was fine.

It struck me that absolutely none of the people in post-op, where you'd think they would know about this, had any sense of how to deal with pain experience outside of giving them a pill. That's what our socialization in medicine has become. And the idea of working with the mind to control that was completely alien to anybody in that room. But it worked. Then when the nurses were there in the background saying, "What is he doing with her?" I had the good fortune of having somebody on the nursing team who knew me, and he said, "Let him do what he's doing." It didn't take that long to help her use her mind to master the mind that was out of control with both panic, fear, on the one hand, and unbearable pain on the other hand.

You see, that's a story about what medicine has uncritically accepted. [If] people are in distress, you pop a pill. We are all socialized into that view, and all you have to do is look at the profits of the pharmaceutical industry. It was when Bill Clinton was in office, and in the first month, Hillary took on the question that she got slapped down for; and Hillary and Bill said way back when, "What kind of company in this country can boast 25 percent in profits or more, every single quarter for over a decade? It needs to be regulated." Have we regulated it? No, we've done the opposite.

Now it has become an exploitation of the elderly and the poor, and we've thoroughly socialized medicine into believing "if you're in pain, pop a pill." So, how do we cut through that attitude towards the dying process? Because in the whole enterprise of end-of-life care, the word palliative care means "ease their discomfort." As if that's the main goal. Well maybe that's not the main goal. Maybe the main goal is preparing them to die.

Student 2

It's often not of the volition of the patient …

Dan

Yeah, okay. So, here, you have to talk with the patient about their beliefs and attitudes about dying, honestly and openly, and find out what they want. Some people might want palliative care, and some people might not. Some people might want to be given alternatives, and the laws around informed consent in this country include the fact that we [should] always bring up alternative approaches to what we're giving them. We don't often do that, we say, "This is what you get."

From a Tibetan point of view, if you snow a person with medication, it clouds the mind. It might help soften the fear through the dying process. I suppose we could argue that would be a good thing, but it softens the fear by creating a more … what the Tibetans would call *trulwa*, a deluded mind. And a deluded mind can't see the nature of the transitions that the dying process involves. Almost every lama that I've talked with says that worse than the fact that we sort of put the bodies away right away, before spiritual death occurs, a worse problem is the use of drugs, because it snows the mind.

And we do that for our own beliefs about what's necessary, rather than asking the patient, in an informed consent way, about what they really want. Maybe they want to prepare for dying. Maybe they want an alternative to some medication that would snow them. Maybe they want a medication that would help them prepare for dying; that's an alternative we haven't even considered.

In the '60s, or in the early '70s, there was a good deal of research with terminal cancer patients in this country on using hallucinogens to prepare people to die. A well-known person who did that on himself was the famous author Aldous Huxley. When he was in the final stages of dying, he took, I think, mescaline or psilocybin. What his wife told me were his final words were, he smiled and said, "I thought so." [Dan chuckles] So, you see there are lots of alternatives, even with medications, that would make people more conscious in the dying process rather than snowed during the dying process, but we don't offer those. We don't offer them to prepare people for dying.

That's a problem, that's a big problem from a Tibetan point of view. From a Tibetan point of view, dying becomes an opportunity, and here's why. When the body crashes and burns, and it's in what we call "the jaws of death," the dying process itself, as each physiological system in the body systematically shuts down, with every one of those systems shutting down, first of all, all your action plans, your residual plans about what you want to do in your life, that all goes down the tubes. Then all conceptual thought, which is the biggest cloud to awakening, goes down the tubes. And then one by one, each of your perceptual systems goes down the tubes. Touch—you can't feel things, so even if somebody, or your loved one holds you during the dying process, at a certain point, you don't feel that anymore. Your loved one thinks they're doing something helpful for you, but you don't feel that. Then you can't hear them; they may still talk to you, but you lose hearing. Then you lose taste, then you lose smell, and ultimately you lose being able to see anything.

Now, if there's no conceptual thought left, none, and there's no activity of the five sense systems, what's left is your residual, what we call very subtle consciousness. At the point of physical death—Tibetans make a distinction between physical death and spiritual death—physical death you can track as each of the elements of the body disappears, the final element to go is the wind element that dissolves into the space element, and at that point you give up your final breath.

If you want to know when that's coming, the exhalation gets much longer than the inhalation. At the end of the exhalation there's a gap, and the gaps get longer and longer, and sometimes there's a funny sound that we call the death rattle. If you want to know when a person's going to physically die, count the gaps, just like we count contractions with somebody coming into life with birthing. Count the gaps in the dying process. They get farther apart the closer you get to the dying process. That way you can get a pretty good estimate of when the person is going to physically die.

I did that with my dad, and when he was dying, we were able to estimate within a four-hour time window when he was going to physically die. That happened to be in the middle of the night, so I told my mother to get over there, so she was with him when he died.

Student 2

He was on no medication?

Dan

He was off medication by default. They had snowed him with morphine, and he had a paranoid reaction to the heavy morphine load, so it actually helped him.

See, if you go through the process naturally, what the Tibetans say is that when all conceptual thought stops, and all perception, ordinary perception stops, when we say that the earth element dissolves into the water element, and the water element dissolves into the fire element, and the fire element dissolves into the wind element, and finally the wind element dissolves into the space element, that's the point of physical death.

Breathing, external breathing as we observe it, stops; and shortly thereafter, the heart stops; and the brain stops its coarse level activity. That's just physical death. At the point that all that stops, there is an indestructible essence of consciousness in the heart that gets loosened up—the energy knots that tie it up get loosened up—and then it gets released into the central channel. It stays there for up to three days, not three days, up to three days. It can be gone in a minute, or it can stay for up to three days.

How do you know when it's at some point in that three-day period? It leaves through one of the orifices. The preference, of course, is it leaves through the crown, because that guarantees a recycling with a better rebirth. Okay? Now, in that window of opportunity up to three days, that indestructible essence, which is your very subtle consciousness, it's still alive, and that resides in the central channel of your now physically dead body. What's the consciousness like? It's absolutely vast, limitless, clear, bright awareness with no content. We call that the clear light of death, or the clear light of dying. It's no different from in your lifetime recognizing awakened awareness as that lucid brightness, using your metacognitive awareness to recognize that. If you recognize that at that point in the dying process, game over. You don't go through the other after-death states.

There are three after-death states. Okay? The first one is the process of dying itself [the moment of death, or *chikhai bardo*]. Okay? The second is what's called the after-death state, or the *bardo of dharmātā*, the *chonyi bardo*. That's sort of like what I like to call the sound and light show. And then the third one has content. It's the *sidpa bardo*, which is the *bardo* of rebirth, and depending on what content comes up, it determines where you're going to be reborn.

Now, from a Tibetan point of view, you can be reborn in any one of the six realms. You can be born in the hell realm; you can be born in the hungry ghost realm or the animal realm—those are the three lower realms; or you can go to the demigod realm, the god realm, or the human realm [the three higher realms]. What determines what realm you get born in is the karmic ripening of which of what we call the five poisons is predominant in this lifetime. If your predominant poison is hatred, you get born in the hell realm—you don't get to "pass go," you don't "collect $200";[21] you go straight to the hell realm jail, okay? If your predominant emotion is desire, you go to the hungry ghost realm. If your predominant emotion is ignorance, you go to the animal realm. If your predominant emotion is envy and jealousy, you go to the demigod realm and you're always fighting each other for power. If your predominant emotion is pride, you go to the god realm, okay? Those are the five predominant emotions.

If you've had somewhat of a virtuous life, and you're not overwhelmed by negative karmic ripening, then you have a shot at being born in the human realm. The reason why that's important is, from a Tibetan point of view, they say, "All creatures, even the smallest insects, have buddha nature but only humans have the metacognitive capacity to recognize that nature." An animal can't recognize. An animal can't become awakened. Only humans can become awakened. So that's why getting a human birth first, getting a human birth at a time in history when, and in a geographic location where there are teachings available, so you get a chance to be reminded of this stuff and keep working at it, is very precious. Okay?

But, if you recognize the clear light of dying, at that point, game over. You become awake and you have a good chance to become enlightened, not just awake. And you become a buddha. You don't go through the rest of cycling existence. You don't get reborn. You get relocated and awaken in awakened *dharmakāya* space. And as a non-ordinary, fully enlightened being you can intend to emanate in any form you want. You're no longer in cyclic existence. You can come back and work in any way you want to help beings, but you don't have to. You're operating out of what we call *gongpa*, enlightened intention, at that point.

So, from a Tibetan point of view, given the fact that recognizing the clear light of dying is the most important task at hand, dying becomes an opportunity. As the body crashes and burns, conceptual thought and all perception naturally is destroyed, and there's a clear light there; and if you recognize it for what it is, game over. So, dying becomes a remarkable opportunity for awakening.

But the best preparation for that is practice in daily life. Not just meditating but recognizing awakening. If you have the pith instructions, the precious instructions, the pointing-out instructions that allow you to practice and

---

21 From the card in the Monopoly game, "Pass go, collect $200."

recognize the true nature of the mind and awaken to that, and you put them into practice and you awaken, that's the best preparation for dying because even though conceptual thought crashes and burns and stops, and perception stops, that seed of metacognitive awareness never stops during the dying process; and since you know the learned pathway already about how to recognize awakening in your lifetime, the odds are much higher that you can recognize awakening during the dying process. That's your best preparation.

So, if you look at the famous cycle of teachings that's called *The Tibetan Book of the Dead*, which was written probably in the eighth century by Padmasambhava and his consort Yeshe Tsogyal, they wrote it for the future at a time that they foresaw that people would get weirded out about death, so that people would discover these secret treasure texts and then use them because they were necessary for that time in history. And if you look at the structure of that cycle of teachings, there's the famous fourth chapter. And what it is basically is a pointing-out instruction of how to awaken to the true nature of the mind. It's been taken out of *The Tibetan Book of the Dead* and used as a pointing-out instruction in Dzogchen. And it's a very precious instruction in the Nyingma tradition. Because that's the teaching.

If you get that instruction in your daily life and you can recognize the awakened awareness during your daily life, then that's the best preparation for dying you could do. But I suppose, going back to what we originally talked about, we have a lot of good yogis here. I suppose you could be a good yogi, practice to the point that you can recognize and get some stability of your awakened awareness in your daily life, and then when you get towards dying, get snowed by medications and forget everything and have everything cloud over that you ever learned about your practice, about setting up your basis of operation as awakening. So that's a problem. Which means you ought to be carefully considerate about what you want to make as a will, as a living will, about how you want people to approach the whole process of dying with you.

Student 2

I should probably admit that this question is born of experience. My mother passed six years ago and was in extreme pain. She infarcted her bowel. It was an emergent situation and she was screaming in pain, and this was prior to my exposure to any Tibetan teachings. Because I was the physician in the family, they looked at me to make the decisions about what should be done with her, and obviously she was in extreme pain and I didn't want her to be in extreme pain, so this question …

Dan

And you did what you learned. Hmm?

Student 2

Well, I didn't want her to be …

Dan

Right.

Student 2

You know, screaming and … But then I think about her mind that wasn't in a state where she could, you know, do what you're describing.

Dan

Yeah, because we don't have a society where we prepare people. So, with your patients now, you can learn it differently. The most important thing from a Western point of view is to talk with people about their attitudes about dying. Find out what their beliefs are and how they want to approach it. You have to ask them. And, you might still in some cases use the pain medications because that's some people's belief system and that's what they want. But I think our duty as health care providers is to provide a variety of options to people. That's the spirit of informed consent, and some of those options ought to include something different than just palliative care—depending on the person's beliefs and what they want.

And you have to be alert to the fact that they may change their mind about that. Some people, when they get close to death, get scared and want palliative care. Some people, when they get close to dying and they know they're dying, want the opposite—they want to prepare. And you can't always say that what they tell you in advance is what's going to happen when they actually face what we call "the jaws of death"—it changes. But it's not something as a culture that we deal with a lot, and I think that's very unfortunate.

I used to do a lot of continuing education things for people in the mental health field. And I tried some years ago, maybe ten years ago, to offer something. So, I developed two new courses that I was excited about. One was all the research on aging and how to help people age optimally, and the other was all the research on preparing people to die East and West. I think I had three people that signed up for the aging course and five people signed up for the dying course, and that was a clear message that people don't want to deal with this stuff in this society. [Dan chuckles] So, I never did it again because people didn't want to hear it. So, we don't want to do what's necessary here, which is weird. Hmm? I don't know. You do the best you can with it. That's all I can say.

But sometimes it might be preparing them for the actual process, where they can use the dying process as a remarkable opportunity; and that's the way the Tibetans look at it. But, even better is to take one's lifetime as an opportunity. About two years ago we, Asonam and I, from the Bon Great Completion system, translated the Akhrid system, which is a—it's a remarkable system of meditation. It started in the eighth century as a step-by-step, fifty-session lesson plan. You do one and then the next and then the next. Over time they cut it down to fourteen sessions that you do for about a week each that go from the very beginning up to full buddhahood. It's sort of like the managed care version of enlightenment. So, it's quite interesting what they decided to put in those fourteen sessions. You know? So, we translated that and the commentaries to it, and it's coming out probably late this fall. It's mostly done.[22]

And for the final Akhrid session, among the people who developed this system, there was a disagreement. There were two schools of thought because there was a fifteenth session, a session on *phowa*—consciousness transference for dying—and one school of thought said, "We're not going to include this because we want to give a strong message that if you do Dzogchen Great Completion practice and you get the right pith instructions, and they're clear enough, then you can not only become awakened in this lifetime, you can become a fully enlightened buddha in this lifetime." That was the message that they wanted to give. Other people had the view that [said], "Well, give them a

---

22 *The Pith Instructions for the Stages of the Practice Sessions of the A-Tri (Akhrid) System of Bon Dzogchen Meditation*—available on Amazon.

backup plan. If they don't make it in this lifetime, then they can use the dying process as a second shot." And the former group said, "Well, but you're giving a double message here. If you tell people, 'You can become a buddha in this lifetime, but you probably won't because we're going to give you this other thing as a backup plan,' you're undermining their confidence about what they can really get done in this lifetime." The first group won out, so the fifteenth session, which is the backup plan, wasn't included in the text. It was published somewhere else, but not included as part of the original teachings. We dug it out at some point and translated it, but it's an interesting point.

What message do we really want to give people about their practice? If we're saying that you have buddha nature, then you have to practice in such a way that you have the confidence that you can bring this practice not only to a taste of awakening, but to full enlightenment in this lifetime. You become a buddha. And to give people anything less than that is to undermine your belief in their buddha nature, in their intelligence and resourcefulness to practice. I tend to favor that first view.[23]

The backup view is, "Well, not everybody can do that, so teach them consciousness transference, what's called *phowa*." And what you do with *phowa* practice basically is: the best exit route when your body's crashing and burning and you're dying, is to come out the crown. Okay? So, that pretty much guarantees a human rebirth. So, what you can teach people in this lifetime is to take an energy drop about the size of a quarter, place it in the navel on top of the navel chakra; and then, simultaneously make a sound repeatedly [Dan makes a high-pitched sound, something like a small bird call], "hik!" What you do is you have the person visualize taking that energy drop and raising it more and more up the upper central channel until you can get it to the place that the energy drop actually strikes the inside of the [top of the] skull. Then you have them imagine pushing that energy drop right through the skull.

It takes about two weeks to practice this. So you focus on the energy drop and you go, [Dan repeats the syllable with eyes closed] "hik!, hik!, hik!, hik!, hik!, hik!, hik!, hik!, hik!, hik!, hik!, hik! *Gya*." You bring the energy drop back down, you bring it up more, you bring it back down, you bring it up more, and when it hits the inside of the surface of the skull you keep pushing it up and

23 Even so, the decision was made to include Session Fifteen in Dan and Geshe Sonam's translation of the text.

at some point the [skull] plates actually move. And the *tak*, the signs of that are there's an edema, a swelling, so you get like a little bump like a rhinoceros here [Dan points to the very top of his head], and then there's a fluid leakage, it leaks a little bit because it gets inflamed, and the plates actually move a bit.

So, it takes exactly two weeks to do this if you do it right. Sometimes it takes people who don't quite get it longer, sometimes they can never do it, but sometimes people take longer than that. The average student takes about two weeks of daily practice to do this. They don't do it all day long. They do it a number of times during the day. And then you take a straw from like a broom and you can put it right through the skull and stick up. And that's the test that you've actually opened that skull plate.

Now here's the point, if you open it, you've got to close it. So, you close it with a seed syllable. You take a seed syllable and you stuff the seed syllable right into the thing, like a cork, like a plug. And you stuff it tight. If you don't seal it, if you try and practice on your own and you don't know that, if you get a strong hit like a whiplash in a car, the indestructible essence in your heart will suddenly leave, and you'll die. You'll just leave your body prematurely.

So, you've got to do this correctly or with the right supervision. You don't want to do it on your own. Okay? But, it's sort of like a Roto-rooter for the upper central channel. The size of the energy drop is such that it inflates the upper central channel and makes it bigger and bigger and once you open it up, and rout it out, it stays that size. It stays open for the rest of your life, with a plug on top. So, when the body is crashing and burning, it's sort of like a jet that's crashing. You just push the ejection seat and you come out of the jet and you parachute out.

Student 2

You've already made the path.

Dan

You've already made the path. Right. So, when you get to the early stage of the dying process and you're taught to recognize that, you just eject yourself out. The death is immediate, and you've left the crown, and you've already recycled yourself in some favorable birth in human rebirth somewhere. So, you have, through *phowa*, essentially voluntary control over the dying process, which we don't have a concept for in the West. Of course, we have no concept of recycling either. The Tibetans are into recycling. So, you can control how you come back.

Now, if you become a buddha, rather than just ejecting to another rebirth, which is a superior practice either in this lifetime or recognizing the clear light of dying in the dying process, under either of those conditions if you become a buddha, then you can just intentionally emanate in any form you want, any place you want, any time you want. That's why they're called *tulku*. *Truwa* means to emanate. So, a *tulku* is an enlightened form who is emanating to come teach or to help people in certain geographic areas of certain times in history. You have full control or voluntary control over the dying process that way. That's the superior path. So great teachers and enlightened beings come back. They come back for a certain time in history in a certain geographic location and they keep doing what they're doing. So, that's the best practice.

So, there's a lot. There's a whole world in what you're saying here.

Student 2

Thank you.

Dan

Sure.

Student 3

So how do you help someone who believes that where they go after death is nothing? And that they're, right now the person is ill, doesn't believe they're in the dying process and may or may not be, but is experiencing a lot of fear around the current illness.

Dan

That's a good question. I would handle that clinically. There's a principle in physics. Remember high school physics where we all study momentum? Every action has an equal and opposite reaction. That applies to limiting beliefs. In other words, the more polarized and rigid a certain belief is that a person holds, the [greater the] likelihood is there's another part of them that feels the opposite of that. So, you talk the language of parts.

There's a part of you, maybe the dominant part that believes absolutely that there's nothing after death. It's a done deal for you—it's a shut case. But I wonder if there isn't another part of you that, even if it's a small part, somehow doubts that, and probably remains open to this question, but it's not as completely shut as you think it is. And sometimes when you make it that shut it's because you're actually admitting that doubt. So, let's look at the other side of that.

And you talk the language of hypotheticals: if you were to hold that other belief, what would that look like for you? Okay? And if you keep exploring that, and the only way that you're going to explore that is to identify the adaptive function of that rigid part. "You have to shut this down because…" And the way you get at that is to say, "You have this completely fixed belief that there's nothing after. This is not something that you humans can know about easily. We don't know. But for you it's a shut case. Because it's so cut and dry for you, what does it do for you to believe it that thoroughly? What do you get out of that belief?"

And you have to identify the adaptive function of that. It sounds like a strange question but it always works. "What do you get out of holding that belief? What does it do for you to hold this belief that there's absolutely no life after death or there's nothing, just nothingness. What purpose does that serve for you?" And ultimately the answer to that question is always some variation of the theme of protection. It protects them from the fear. Otherwise, they'd just be too terrified.

And you can empathize with that. "I can see how this works for you. If you were to open that up you would be so terrified that it's better to shut the whole thing down and say I'm done with that—not gonna open it up. And that does work to protect you. But, there's another part of you that might have some questions about that that aren't so settled as that part thinks." Then you have what we call cognitive dissonance.

We have seventy years of research on cognitive dissonance that works, and as clinicians, we never use it. So, what you do there is you say, "There's a fundamental conflict within you about the part that thinks there's absolutely nothing, and the other parts that think there might be something. That's a deep conflict within you. It's not as settled as you think." You hold the dissonance to them.

Don't let them minimize it. And what we know about cognitive dissonance is if you can amplify the dissonance, it shifts the position.

So, let's go back to the roots. Cognitive dissonance was something that was developed by Leon Festinger starting in 1944 at MIT. And here's what he did [in a later study]. He had postwar college students, bright college students at a well-to-do university, rate their political beliefs. Zero was the midpoint. [Dan holds up his hand pointing first to one side and then the other when describing the range of numbers from low to high.] It went from zero to ten in this direction for more liberal beliefs, and zero to ten in this direction of more conservative beliefs. And right after the war, most of the students stood more on the liberal side. Let's say a student rated his political beliefs at about a six or a seven, the liberal side of the equation; then they were given what was called a "counter attitudinal task."

For the next month, the people who rated themselves as quite liberal had to go around the college campus and recruit people for the young Republicans. And what do you think happened at the end of that month? If they re-rated their ideological position, it shifted to the neutral position or somewhat slightly over to the conservative position. They had to argue in favor of the very thing that they resisted, and that created huge cognitive dissonance by developing a counter-attitudinal position. And the only way they could reduce that remarkable internal cognitive dissonance or discomfort was to shift their ideological position.

So, cognitive dissonance works. The more extremely polarized the belief is, the [greater the] likelihood there's another side that doesn't quite believe it, precisely because the extreme is that, the belief is that extreme, and there's your dissonance. You've got a lot of dissonance in the system. The more extreme the belief, the greater the dissonance. If you know how to use it, without ever taking a position, you can get them to shift that to something far less extreme. In this case, a shift from being absolutely cut and dry, from it's a shut case that there's nothing out there, to being open to it, and you can talk. Because what you have there is somebody who's open and vulnerable now. Then you can talk with them in a more honest way about what they might want and what the options really are. But you've got to start with that.

As a clinician, there's a straightforward way and we know how to deal with that, and it's true for any extreme beliefs. Whatever the belief or the behavior, if it's that extreme, you can use dissonance as the intervention. But we don't do that.

Let's say we have somebody with a substance problem or an alcohol problem. We're a physician. And we say, "These drugs or this alcohol is really harming your health." What do we do? We say, "You've got to stop." And they say, "I know, doc." And you get into a power struggle with them. And what you've done wrong at that point is that you've created the polarization between that part, the one who doesn't want to stop, and you. But, if you did something slightly but profoundly different, if you said, "There's a part of you that really doesn't want to stop, and there's something you get out of it. In the best sense, despite all the ways that it's harmful, in the best sense, what does it do for you?" And name the adaptive function of it.

If you keep leveraging, as we call it, and saying, "You know, there's something you really get out of this, no matter all the harm. There's something you get out of it." And what's going to happen? If you take that side of the dissonance, what are they going to say? They'll naturally take the other side. You keep saying, "But you keep going back because there's something you get out of it." They say, "But, I got to stop, doc." You say, "But you keep going back to it." They say, "I got to stop, doc." And where does that go? You can script it in a way that will actually get them to actually take the position that they have to stop and act on it.

But, as soon as we say, "You have to stop," if I'm being the mental health professional, I've diffused the dissonance. I've taken the dissonance out of the system and I've made it a power struggle between myself and my patient. Is that ever going to go where it's useful? But, we do it all the time because nobody knows how to use the dissonance.

It's no different. We could do that not just about drinking or about drugging. We could do that about spiritual practice. "I really have got to practice, but I find I can never organize my daily life about it." Well, then talk with the part of the mind that doesn't want to practice, for whatever reason, and find out what that does for them, what's adaptive about it, and then talk with the part of the mind that knows they have to practice but doesn't. There's your dissonance. In other words, it's a simple rule of thumb here: the more extreme the belief or the behavior, the more polarity, the greater the dissonance. All you have to do is ask for it. There's your leveraging right there.

A lot of people are going to be that rigid, but you see it's not good enough as a health provider to say, "Well, I asked them about their belief. They're too rigid. I'm not going to go there." That's easy for us because we don't have the time to do anything anyways, but if we spend time with our patients and we worked with it in this way, you're going to open up a whole world of vulnerability in there, and then you're really talking.

Student 3

Thank you.

Student 4

Dan, I've been brewing on a question about addictions and behavioral changes, and that points right at it, that I'll just be very personally revealed. There's discipline, but discipline intervenes on a behavior, but it doesn't eliminate the fear that that behavior will then win and take over again. So how does a person exercise two things? I'd love you to teach a class on dissonance and how to use it because I have a seventeen-year-old, and also so that I can learn how to exercise that dissonant conversation with myself. Do I make sense?

Dan

I'm not sure what the question is here.

Student 4

The question is, you know, I've been addicted in a number of ways, whether it was drugs and food. How do I intervene without, I mean I can discipline myself to behave in a correct way. "I got to stop, doc. I got to stop, doc." I can talk to myself that way.

Dan

Well, I'll answer it in two ways. I'll answer it in terms of your question about addictive behaviors, which are rampant in this culture, and I'll answer it in terms of motivation for spiritual practice because it's the same answer.

In the West, in the clinical field, there's been a lot of research on this. Prochaska and DiClemente out of Rhode Island did this in the 1980s, and they came up with what was called "stages of change" model. They first described four stages of change: pre-contemplative, contemplative, action, and maintenance.

They first discovered that what contemplative means is that you're thinking, you're contemplating the fact that you have a problem, and you're contemplating on doing something about it. Most people enter psychotherapy or any kind of healthcare when they're in the contemplative stage, and if they are effective in that therapy, they'll go through a change that they directly experience as rapidly changing. Some people have argued that at that point, there's a whole other set of interventions that are necessary, not the ones that got them to that change process, but in order to stabilize that change process. That's called the action phase.

And then, once they get better and they leave treatment or are about to leave treatment, then there's a number of risk factors towards relapse. So, there are a number of other techniques that are necessary to maintain the changes after they leave treatment—contemplation, action, maintenance. But then, it was discovered that there are a number of people who come to psychotherapy who are not in the contemplative stage of motivation. They're what we call pre-contemplative. They still come to treatment and it never works. And they do one of two things. Either they're not ready to change, or they don't acknowledge that they have a problem, though other people might see they have a problem.

It was first discovered in a smoking intervention in the late '70s and early '80s. A pre-contemplative would come to you and say, "I got to stop smoking, doc," but they don't see smoking as a problem. They have no intention to stop smoking, and they're being pressured to stop smoking by family members or their doctor. They're pre-contemplative. They can't see that they have a problem, or they see that they have a problem, but they're not ready to do anything about it. And then it was discovered that there's a big chunk of people in the addictions field out there who are pre-contemplative. Either they don't know they have a problem, or if they do, they still don't want to do anything about it. Everybody else might think they have a problem but they're not ready to do anything about it.

And then it was discovered that it wasn't just people who have addictions, but that it's true for a lot of people who come to psychotherapy. So, if they're pre-contemplative and they come to therapy, they go through the motions of it. And a lot of times, they're doing it because they think they should do it, or because somebody is pressuring them to do it, but they don't really want to do it. They don't really want to change. And it hardly ever works.

And in the '80s and '90s, there was a good deal of research on how you identify people who are pre-contemplative, and then what you would do to help them with it. So, how do you move people from being pre-contemplative to contemplative? How do you motivate them to organize their life around fundamentally changing something they don't want to change?

There were different answers to that. One answer was it was observed that people don't change until they have some sort of crisis point in their life. When they have a crisis point, that puts the fear of God into them and then they really want to change. I remember seeing somebody who was in the field and had been in two long-term psychoanalyses over twenty years accumulated analytic time on the couch, and didn't change at all and got absolutely nothing out of it. He wanted to use hypnosis to see if that would make any difference. And it took two years, and it wasn't making a dent in him until a funny thing happened.

He got one of these funny new viruses around. He got Guillain-Barré syndrome, which causes you to be paralyzed. And he was paralyzed for about three months and then slowly he got his limbs back, and he was fully recovered. That put the fear of God into him. He came back a completely different person. It took another year to consolidate everything he didn't gain previously, that he sort of learned but never put together because he was ready for change at that point, because his life was threatened.

So, sometimes that's one of the things that happens to people. They face a crisis in their life or somebody close to them dies and then they suddenly change and they're motivated. Sometimes people change because of family pressure. The addiction field is specialized in that. We call them interventions. You get everybody together in a loving, nontoxic but firmly confrontational way to get the person to see that the way they're going about their life is not only detrimental to themselves but to everybody around them. You're trying to do that in a caring, firm and loving way to get them into treatment. If the interventions are done right, then that can be very powerful. That doesn't work very well for people who are not in intact families. Some people, whose addictions have gone so long, they've destroyed all those connections.

So, what's the other way of leveraging it with people that we use instead? Twelve-step groups. You put a person in a group with like-minded individuals, all who have the same addiction, and they call each other out on all the games and all the rationalizations in a way that nobody else can because they're the only ones that know it. It's very powerful. But the key there is the homogeneity of the group. You've got to put people in who have the same problem. You can't just do mixed groups. It doesn't work. Then they call each other out in a caring way.

Now, if you're working individually with people and you don't have the leverage of groups and families, then the best and strongest intervention is what I just talked about, which is the cognitive dissonance intervention. It leverages people to change.

In the last twenty-five years there's been a huge amount of sophisticated work in the Western psychotherapy field about how to motivate people to fundamentally change in therapy rather than just going through the motions of it and not being in it. And that's mostly pretty effective if it's done right.

Now take that same set of comments and apply it to spiritual practice, because that's what the Tibetans deal with. How do you motivate people to give up all the busyness and distractions in their everyday life to take spiritual practice seriously? Many people say they want to do that, but they're not really ready to spend a couple of hours a day practicing and go to retreats and all that kind of stuff.

It's the same problem, isn't it? Because we could say that there's a lot of people out there, in Western terms, who, about their spiritual practice are pre-contemplative. They're not ready to change, and they don't see it as a priority. They think about it. They give lip service to it, but they're never really going to put in the time it takes to do this thing. We've had people take the course, get really excited by the Level 1 course, even get a taste of awakening, and then never practice after that. That's like nuts. The issue here is that it's a stage of change issue. Even that realization hasn't motivated them to organize their daily lives differently.

The Tibetans have their own answers for that. And there are three methods to motivate you to do spiritual practice. The first is like what we did last time. The first is you meditate on impermanence and dying. You look squarely at the issue of impermanence and you rehearse your own aging and dying process. For many people, that'll do it.

The second answer to that question is you have an encounter with a non-ordinary being. You find a genuine spiritual teacher. In the *Pointing Out the Great Way* book, the Mahāmudrā book that I wrote years ago, I read a text where the entire text was on how people get motivated for spiritual practice after encountering a teacher. The whole text was about that. It was a really important text, I thought. And what it said is you go through essentially five stages. The first is *dunpa*, interest. The second is *merpa*, admiration. The third is *gerpa*, respect. The fourth is *depa*, trust, and the fifth is *chundrul*, diligence. It's a natural progression.

If you encounter somebody who has got a genuine spiritual practice—not because they hang out their name and say, "I'm a spiritual teacher," a lot of them don't have genuine practice. But if you find somebody who's real with that, there's something quite different about that and you can recognize that right away. So, you keep coming back. And if they're genuine, over time you begin to see their positive qualities as uniquely different from most other people. That's called *merpa*, admiration. At first, you keep going back. That's called interest. You get curious about this weird person. And you keep going back for more. And then you start to see that there are some qualities here that most people don't have. There's an accumulation of positive qualities that's not what ordinary people have. And as you start to appreciate that, that's called *merpa*, admiration. Admiration is always perceptual. Then, if you really find that you develop a relationship with them, then they start to give you something very precious. And mostly what they give you is their interest in your well-being. They want the best for you. And they don't want anything in return. That commands respect. That's the next state, *gerpa*. And you start becoming like them. Not only do you admire those good qualities, but you find yourself manifesting them. And as you manifest those good qualities more and more, and emulate that in your own behavior, you want to be more like them, that's called respect. And then ultimately, that leads to trust.

And there are three levels of trust, or belief. One is the trust that aspires, the belief that aspires; aspires [meaning]—at some point you want to be more like that in your life. But it's still somewhat out there. You see it in the other. The second is trust that believes. At some point you develop a positive belief structure that says you can actually do this thing. You become like that. And the last stage is called trust that's decisive. You actually put it into practice with a sort of decisiveness and conviction that you know how to do this. And that leads to the horse of diligence, applying yourself.

I'll tell you a story about that. When I first met my first Root Lama, Geshe Wangyal, in the early 1970s, I wanted to learn the Tibetan language. And in those days, there weren't a lot of programs around to learn the Tibetan language. So, there was a program at the University of Wisconsin, but Tibetan was so unpopular and the next year up was second-year Tibetan. So rather than wasting two years, I had to find a crash course in the summers to learn first-year Tibetan. And I talked with Bob Thurman, and he said, "Well, I'll introduce you to my teacher, Geshe Wangyal." And I went there, and he told me I could come for the summer, and then I started reading the Tibetan script the first day, and the second day he had me starting to read it. And that was the beginning.

And after about two weeks, this weird old guy; he was just unusual; and I got more and more interested in who he was as a person. And a lot of his qualities were deeply understanding and penetrative and caring, and there's the admiration. And I spent nine years with him, summers, before he died. And I remember, just around when he was dying, one of the last things he said to me, he said, "Dan, when you came here, you wanted me to show you specific meditation techniques, and I never did that. And you're probably disappointed. But that's not what you got. So, here's what you got." He said, "I started studying when I was four years old. And I studied every day until I was fifty-five." He was then eighty-seven. He said, "At fifty-five, I finished the path. So, what you got is an opportunity of seeing what it's like for somebody who is a fully realized being. And if you see that, and you see the preciousness of that, you'll use your own intelligence and your own resourcefulness, and you'll find a way to put it into practice and become the same thing. And if you don't see that, you won't do anything with this. That's what you got. And of course it was enough." Then, what came was wanting to do that, and trusting that I could do it and developing some conviction and then putting it into practice with the horse of diligence. Just like the texts say.

So, that answer is deeply relational about how you move someone along from just being caught up in the busy-ness of *samsāra* to genuinely developing motivation over time.

The third practice is what's incorporated in, but most people don't have the benefit of, that relationship with a teacher. So, the third kind of practice in Tibetan Buddhism is what's called *lözhi*, the four attitudes: precious opportunity, cause and effects of karma, sufferings of *samsāra*, and impermanence. In that order. You don't change anything about your daily life. You do a daily visualization. And it slowly changes your attitude. And all that stuff that's still unimportant, you drop away. And over time you find yourself grasping the preciousness of this opportunity and naturally becoming motivated. It's a nice gentle way of doing this.

APPENDIX 1

Biography of Dan Brown

Daniel P. Brown, PhD
September 11, 1948 - April 4, 2022

The following biography was published as an obituary in the *American Journal of Clinical Hypnosis* [65(1):79-82] by D. Corydon Hammond, PhD (University of Utah)

The beloved educator, researcher, author, translator, hypnotherapist, psychotherapist, and meditation teacher, Daniel P. Brown, PhD, died on Monday, April 4, 2022, at his home in San Francisco, CA. He was 73.

The author of over 15 books, Dr. Brown made significant contributions in many fields of knowledge and clinical practice. He was also well-respected for his courageous work as an expert witness or consultant on high-profile cases involving complex trauma and abuse.

Born on September 11, 1948, in New Bedford, MA, Dr. Brown was the first person in his family to attend college, at the University of Massachusetts, Amherst, where he received his undergraduate degree in molecular biology. He went on to receive his Ph.D. in Religion & Psychological Studies at the University of Chicago, where he also received a Danforth Fellowship, given for promise in teaching excellence, and received specialized training in how to teach.

His first clinical placement was at Michael Reese Hospital in Chicago, and he also commuted part time to The Menninger Foundation in Topeka Kansas to work on the treatment of substance abuse. In the late 1970s he moved back to his home state of Massachusetts where he did a clinical internship at McLean Hospital and a Postdoctoral Fellowship in Clinical Research at Harvard Medical School at The Cambridge Hospital. His research focused on the long-term effects of mindfulness meditation.

In the late 1970s Dr. Brown became interested in the study of trauma and abuse largely through peer collaboration with Sarah Haley, one of the founding members of the International Society for the Study of Traumatic Stress.

In the 1980s Dr. Brown served as Director of Training and then as Chief Psychologist at The Cambridge Hospital. He helped develop a clinical psychology internship and postdoctoral training program to provide the best young talent in psychology the opportunity to work with a disenfranchised inner city chronic mental health population. He also developed and directed the Behavioral Medicine Program, a joint venture between psychiatry and primary care medicine.

In the early 1990s Dr. Brown became interested in the topic of memory for trauma and abuse. His textbook, *Memory, Trauma Treatment and the Law*, co-authored with D. Corydon Hammond, PhD and Alan W. Scheflin, is the recipient of awards from 7 professional societies, including the 1999 Manfred S. Guttmacher Award given jointly by the American Psychiatric Association and the American Academy of Psychiatry and Law for the "outstanding contribution to forensic psychiatry."

Dr. Brown served as an expert witness or consultant on trauma and memory in over two hundred lawsuits, including testimony before the International War Crimes Tribunal for the prosecution of war criminals of the former Yugoslavia. He also worked on behalf of clergy abuse clients in Louisiana for 17 years with Roger Stetter, author of *In Our Own Words: Reflections on Professionalism in the Law*, which the Louisiana Bar Foundation distributed to every lawyer and judge in Louisiana.

Mr. Stetter said, "Dan was a brilliant guy and all of my clients thought the world of him. It became clear from my conversations with people in Newton, where he lived, that everyone there loved him as well. I think it was Dan's combination of brilliance and modesty that made him so special. He almost never talked about himself. His life was about helping others, showing respect and genuine concern for their welfare.

Dr. Brown also served on the Harvard Medical School faculty for nearly four decades, where he co-directed and taught courses on hypnosis, trauma, meditation, peak performance, and attachment. He worked to stay abreast of the latest scientific developments in assessment and treatment, and use these findings to offer clinicians practical, state-of-the-art methods to upgrade their standard of care.

Larry Lifson, director of the Continuing Education Program of the Department of Psychiatry at the Beth Israel Deaconess Medical Center, a major teaching hospital of Harvard Medical School, wrote that "Dan Brown was not only an enormously gifted clinician and highly esteemed teacher, he also was a beloved mentor to so many of his students."

Most of his clinical writing and teaching from the 1980s and 1990s focused on treatment for complex trauma disorders. He co-authored two books on developmental psychopathology—a book on affect development, *Human Feelings*, and a book on self-development from a cross-cultural perspective, *Transformations of Consciousness.*

In the 2000s Dr. Brown began to study adult attachment and received intensive training in the Adult Attachment Interview. His research focused on the relative contribution of early attachment pathology to the development of personality and dissociative disorders in adulthood. He is the senior author, with David Elliot, of a major textbook on the treatment of attachment disorders in adults, *Attachment Disturbances in Adults.*

Dr. Brown taught hypnotherapy for 38 years and wrote several important books on hypnosis, including Hypnotherapy and Hypnoanalysis with Erika Fromm, PhD, a noted hypnoanalyst who served as his primary clinical mentor—a relationship that spanned 35 years.

Dr. Brown's interest in meditation started while at grad school at University of Chicago. During that time, he also studied Tibetan, Sanskrit, and Pali in the Buddhist Studies Program at the University of Wisconsin in Madison. He spent ten years translating meditation texts for his doctoral dissertation on Tibetan Buddhist Mahāmudrā meditation.

Dr. Brown studied many forms of meditation practice over the course of his life, including Patanjali's Yoga Sutras with Mircea Eliade and Dr. Arwind Vasavada, and Burmese mindfulness meditation with Mahāsī Sayādaw and Achaan Cha.

Dr. Brown first learned Indo-Tibetan concentration and insight meditation with his root teacher, the Venerable Geshe Wangyal. He studied meditation practices from the Mahāmudrā, Nyingma Dzogchen, and Bonpo Dzogchen lineages with numerous Tibetan lamas, including H.H. The 14th Dalai Lama and H.H. The 33rd Menri Trizin, the spiritual head of the Tibetan Bon religion.

Dr. Brown also spent 45 plus years translating meditation texts from Tibetan and Sanskrit, and is the author of *Pointing Out the Great Way: The Stages of Meditation in the Mahāmudrā Tradition* (2006, Wisdom Publications) based on his doctoral dissertation of twenty-five years earlier He taught meditation retreats internationally for over 30 years, often in collaboration with Tibetan meditation masters including Denma Locho Rinpoche, Rahob Tulku Rinpoche, Tenzin Wangyal Rinpoche. Dan taught in the spirit of the ecumenical Rime movement, synthesizing the "greatest hits" of meditation instructions from various lineages to develop a comprehensive and precise path from ordinary dualistic consciousness to full enlightenment.

The latter part of his life was devoted to his goal of leaving behind a complete set of instructions to guide Western meditation practitioners along this path.

He was known for his unique integration of contemporary Western research on peak performance and positive psychology with the classical Buddhist meditation lineage traditions.

He spent 10 years conducting outcomes research on beginning and advanced meditators, and led the only scientific study identifying the neurocircuitry of the meditative experience of the awakened mind. He was especially interested in meditations designed to stabilize awakening in everyday life and to bring about the flourishing of positive qualities of mind.

Brown met his wife, Gretchen Nelson, in 2007 at a meditation retreat he was teaching in California. They began teaching meditation retreats together in 2007. They were married in 2010, by Rahob Rinpoche, and besides his wife, he is survived by two sons, Gabriel and Jeremy.

Dr. Brown was held in the highest esteem by his professional colleagues, yet he was perhaps even more deeply loved and appreciated by the many clients and students whose lives he profoundly touched. As prolific as he was, he had a way of making each individual he worked with feel deeply seen and respected for who they were and what they were capable of. His relentless commitment to helping others experience their true potential was unparalleled.

While any single one of Dan's many accomplishments would have made for a life well-lived, Dan never lost touch with his humble roots, and was known for enjoying good food, fishing and football with his friends and family.

Daniel P. Brown, PhD
CURRICULUM VITAE (abbreviated)

Part I. General Information

Date Prepared: July 16, 2024
Date of Birth: September 11, 1948
Place of Birth: New Bedford, MA
Date of Death: April 22, 2022

Education:

1971 B.S. University of Massachusetts, Microbiology
1973 M.A.University of Chicago, Religion & Psychological Studies
1981 Ph.D. University of Chicago, Religion & Psychological Studies

Training:

Internships:

1975-1976 Psycho-diagnostic Clerk and Clinical Extern, Psychosomatic and Psychiatric Institute, Michael Reese Medical Center, Chicago
1976-1977 Clinical Psychology Intern (APA-approved), McLean Hospital, Belmont, MA
1977-1981 Clinical Fellow in Psychology, McLean Hospital, Belmont, MA
Research Fellowships:
1978-1980 Research Fellow in Social-Behavioral Science, Harvard Medical School
Licensure and Board Certification:
1980 Licensed Psychologist, Massachusetts, #2399-PR
1990 Diplomate, American Board of Psychological Hypnosis, #209
Member, Executive Board, ABPH
Other Training & Certification:
2002 Certified Consultant, American Society of Clinical Hypnosis.2006
Successfully completed training in administration & scoring of the Adult Attachment Inventory; passed full 30-case reliability testing at high reliability level. AAI training with Deborah Jacobvitz, Ph.D. Reliability testing with Mary Main & Erik Hesse.

Academic Appointments:

1975-1976 Instructor, Religion and Psychological Studies, The University of Chicago
1980-1990 Adjunct Assistant Professor, The School of Social Work of Simmons College
1990-1991 Adjunct Associate Professor, The School of Social Work of Simmons College

1991-2006 Adjunct Professor, The School of Social Work of Simmons College

Hospital or Affiliated Institution Appointments:

1981-1986 Instructor in Psychology, Harvard Medical School at The Cambridge Hospital

1986-1990 Assistant Professor in Psychology, Harvard Medical School

1993-1997 Lecturer, Dept. of Psychology, Boston University

1990-2006 Assistant Clinical Professor in Psychology, Harvard Medical School

2006-2022 Associate Clinical Professor in Psychology, Harvard Medical School

Other Professional Positions and Visiting Appointments:

1974-1975 CIC Visiting Scholar, Dept. of Asian Studies, University of Wisconsin, Madison, WI

Hospital & Health Care Organization Service Responsibilities:

1977-1978 Staff Psychologist, Department of Mental Health, The Commonwealth of Massachusetts, Westboro State Hospital, Cambridge/Somerville Unit, Special Dual Diagnosis Treatment Team.

1978-1979 Psychology Associate, Highland Counseling Associates, Athol, MA

1980-1986 Supervisor, The Psychotherapy Center, The Cambridge Hospital, Cambridge, MA.

1980-1982 Director of In-Service Training, Department of Psychiatry, Central Hospital, Somerville, MA

1981-1985 Associate Director of Psychology, Department of Psychiatry, The Cambridge Hospital, Cambridge, MA.

1982-1983 Director of Hypnotherapy Service and Training, Department of Psychiatry, The Cambridge Hospital, Cambridge, MA.

1983-1992 Director of Behavioral Medicine Services, The Department of Psychiatry, The Cambridge Hospital, Cambridge, MA.

1985-1987 Director of Psychology Training and Clinical Services, The Department of Psychiatry, The Cambridge Hospital, Cambridge, MA.

1987-1990 Chief Psychologist, Department of Psychiatry, The Cambridge Hospital

1984-2000 Director, Daniel Brown, Ph.D. & Associates, The Center for Integrative Psychotherapy, 75 Cambridge Parkway, Cambridge, MA 02142

2000-2020 Director, Daniel Brown, Ph.D. & Associates, 796 Beacon St. Newton MA 02459

Major Administrative Responsibilities & Committee Assignments:

National/International:

2007 Chairman, Task Force, Division 56 American Psychological Association Liaison to DSM-V on Trauma-Related Disorders

2006 Executive Committee. Division 56 Psychological Trauma. American Psychological Association.

2006 Chairman, Task Force on Hypnosis and Memory, American Society of Clinical Hypnosis.

1998 Consultant, Expert Witness, United Nations, Office of the Prosecutor, International War Crimes Tribunal for the Former Yugoslavia, The Hague, Netherlands. Helped establish standard of evidence for what constitutes reliable memory in victims of severe war atrocities—standard upheld in two appeals

1998-2022 Member, Task Force on Hypnosis and Memory, APA-Division 30 (Psychological Hypnosis)

1998-2002 Executive Board, American Board of Psychological Hypnosis

1986-1990 Director, U.S. Center, Sino-U.S. Qi Gong Health Sciences Development Center, The Cambridge Hospital, Cambridge, MA and The Beijing College of Traditional Chinese Medicine, Beijing, P.R.C. Organized and led a delegation of scientists from HEW and the AIDs U.S. National Commission to China to educate the Chinese on stopping the spread of AIDs in China.

1989-1990 Vice President, World Academic Society of Medical Qi Gong

1987-1991 Association of Psychology Internship Centers (APIC), Post-Doctoral Membership Committee

1989-1991 Chairman, Post-Doctoral Training Site Membership Committee (APIC)

1988-1990 Education Committee, Division 30, APA

1980-1982 Occasional consultant on cross-cultural sensitivity for the Health Services Division, World Bank, Washington D.C.

Hospital:

1983-1990 Education Committee, The Cambridge Hospital, Cambridge, MA

1986-1990 Executive Committee, The Cambridge Hospital, Cambridge, MA

1986-1988 Executive Board, The Erikson Center, Cambridge, MA

Professional Societies:

American Psychological Association—-Divisions 30, 38, 41

American Society of Clinical Hypnosis (Fellow)

Society of Behavioral Medicine

International Society of Traumatic Stress Studies

International Society for Mental Training & Excellence

For a complete version of Dan's CV, please visit www.danielpbrownphd.com

APPENDIX 2

Daniel P. Brown, PhD Bibliography

Books/Monographs:

Wilbur, K., Engler, J. & Brown, D. 1985. T*he Transformation of Consciousness: Conventional and Contemplative Developmental Approaches.* Boston: New Science Library (Shambala/Random House).

Brown, D. & Fromm, E. 1986. *Hypnotherapy & Hypnoanalysis*, with a forward by Ernest R. Hilgard. Hillsdale, New Jersey: Lawrence Erlbaum Associates.

Brown, D. & Fromm, E. 1986. *Hypnosis and Behavioral Medicine*, with a forward by Gary Schwartz. Hillsdale, NJ: Lawrence Erlbaum Associates.

Fass, M. & Brown, D. 1990. *Creative Mastery in Hypnosis and Hypnotherapy*, with a forward by Martin Orne. Hillsdale, NJ: Lawrence Erlbaum Associates.

H.H. The Dalai Lama, Goleman, D., Brenman-Gibson, M., Brown, D., Bolen, J.S., Engler, J., Levine, S., & Macy, J. 1992. *Worlds in Harmony: Dialogues in Compassionate Action.* San Francisco: Parallax Press.

Ablon, S., Brown, D., Khantzian, E. & Mack, J. 1993. *Human Feelings: Explorations in Affect Development and Meaning*, Hillsdale, NJ: The Analytic Press.

Brown, D. & Scheflin, A.W. (Guest Editors). Summer, 1996. Special issue on the false memory controversy. The Journal of Psychiatry and Law, 24, 137-338.

Brown, D., Scheflin, A., & Hammond, C.D. 1997. *Memory, Trauma Treatment and the Law*. New York: Norton.

Goleman, D., (Ed.) with H.H. The Dalai Lama, Brown, D., Davidson, R., Kabat-Zinn, J., Salzberg, S., Valera, F. & Yearley, L. 1997. *Healing Emotions: Conversations with the Dalai Lama on Mindfulness, Emotions, and Health*. Boston: Shambhala.

Brown, D. & Scheflin, A.W. (Guest Editors) Fall-Winter, 1999. Special issue on interrelationship between factitious behavior, dissociative disorders, and the law, The Journal of Psychiatry and Law, 27, 363-706.

Brown, D. 2006. Forward by R. Thurman. *Pointing Out the Great Way; Meditation Stages in the Tibetan Mahāmudrā Tradition*. Boston, MA: Wisdom Publications.

Brown, D. 2009. *The Pointing Out Style of Indo-Tibetan Buddhism; A Guide to Awakening. Volumes 1-3*. Boston, MA. Private, publication manual, restricted access only to previous students and teachers of this style of meditation.

van der Linden, J., Brown, D. 2012. *Dissociation et memoire traumatique*. Dunod: Paris, France.

Brown, D., Elliott, D. et al. 2016 *Treating Attachment Disturbances in Adults; Treatment for Comprehensive Repair*. New York: Norton.

Bru rGyal ba g.Yung drung. 2017. Geshe Sonam Gurang and Brown, D. (Trans.). Translated under the guidance of His Holiness Menri Trizin. Pith Instructions for the A Khrid rDzogs Chen [Bon Great Completion Meditation]. Translated for the Pointing Out the Great Way Foundation.Occidental, CA: Bright Alliance.

Geshe Sonam Gurang and Brown, D. 2019. Translated under the guidance of His Holiness Menri Trizin. *The Three-fold Embodiment of Enlightenment; The Bon Yogi Texts of the Path of Liberation of Shar rDza bra' shis rGyal mtshan*. Occidental, CA: Bright Alliance.

Geshe Sonam Gurang and Brown, D. 2019. Translated under the guidance of His Holiness Menri Trizin. *The Twenty-One Nails, According to the Zhang Zhung Oral Transmission Lineage of Bon Great Completion*, Root text by Taphiritsa and Gyer spungs sNang Bzher Lod Po. Occidental, CA: Bright Alliance.

Geshe Sonam Gurang and Brown, D. 2019. Translated under the guidance of His Holiness Menri Trizin. *The Six Lamps, According to the Zhang Zhung Oral Transmission Lineage of Bon Great Completion*, Root text by Taphiritsa, auto-commentary attributed to Gyer spungs sNang Bzher Lod, Po, three additional commentaries, and Pointing Out the Six Energy Drops, transcribed by gTsang pa Bye Bral. Occidental, CA: Bright Alliance.

Geshe Sonam Gurang and Brown, D. 2019. Translated under the guidance of His Holiness Menri Trizin. *Heart Drops of Kuntu Zangpo*, by Shar rDza bra' shis rGyal mtshan. Occidental, CA: Bright Alliance.

Bissanti, M., Brown, D. & Pasari, J. (2020) *The Elephant Path: Attention Development and Training in Children and Adolescents*. Occidental, CA: Bright Alliance.

Geshe Sonam Gurang and Brown, D. (2021) translated under the guidance of His Holiness Menri Trizin. *The Precious Treasury of the Expanse and Awakened Awareness: The Ornaments of the Definitive Secret*, by Shar rDza bra' shis rGyal mtshan, Occidental, CA: Bright Alliance.

Bru rGyal ba g.Yung drung. (2022) Geshe Sonam Gurang and Brown, D. (Trans.). Translated under the guidance of His Holiness Menri Trizin. *Pith Instructions for the A Khrid rDzogs Chen [Bon Great Completion Meditation]*. Translated and revised for the Pointing Out the Great Way Foundation. Occidental, CA: Bright Alliance.

Chapters in Books and Other Monographs:

Brown, D. (1984) "A model for the levels of concentrative meditation," In D.H. Shapiro & R. Walsh (Eds.) *Meditation: Classic and Contemporary Perspectives,* 281-316, New York: Aldine.

Maliszewski, M., Twemlow, S.W., Brown, D.P. & Engler, J.E. (1981). "A Phenomenological Typology of Intensive Meditation: A Suggested Methodology Using the Questionnaire Approach", Revision, 4: 3-27.

Fromm, E., Boxer, A.M. & Brown, D.P. (1985) "Representations of Self-Hypnosis in Personal Narratives," In D. Waxman, P.C. Misra, M. Gibson & M.A. Basker (Eds.) *Modern Trends in Hypnosis*, pp. 215-222, New York: Plenum Press.

Brown, D. & Engler, J. (1984). "A Rorschach Study of the Stages of Mindfulness Meditation," in D. Shapiro & R. Walsh (Eds.) *Meditation: Classic and Contemporary Perspectives,* pp. 232-262, New York: Aldine.

Brown, D. (1988) "Hypnotic treatment of asthma," Advances, 5: 15-29.

Brown, D. (1990) "Erika Fromm: An intellectual history," In. M.L. Fass & D. Brown (Eds.), *Creative mastery in hypnosis and hypnoanalysis: A festschrift for Erika Fromm*, pp. 1-29, Hillsdale, N.J.: Lawrence Erlbaum and Associates.

Brown, D. (1990) "The variable long-term effects of incest: Hypnoanalytic and adjunctive hypnotherapeutic treatment," In. M.L. Fass & D. Brown (Eds.), *Creative Mastery in Hypnosis and Hypnoanalysis*, pp.199-229, Hillsdale, N.J.: Lawrence Erlbaum and Associates.

Fromm, E. & Brown, D. (1991) "The Hypnoanalytic Treatment of Unconscious Traumatic Memories and Developmental Deficit Caused by Early Incest," In. O. van der Hart (Ed.) *Trauma, dissociatie en hypnose*, pp. 221-248, Amsterdam: Swets & Zeitlinger, Publishers.

Brown, D. (1993). "Clinical hypnosis research in the past five years," In E. Fromm & M. Nash (Eds.). *Contemporary perspectives in hypnosis research.* New York: Guilford.

Brown, D. (1993). "Affective development, psychopathology and adaptation," In S. Ablon, D. Brown, E. Khantzian & J. Mack (Eds.). *Human feelings: Explorations in affect development and meaning.* Hillsdale, NJ: Analytic Press.

Brown, D. (1993). "Stress and emotion: Implications for illness development and wellness," In S. Ablon, D. Brown, E. Khantzian & J. Mack (Eds.). *Human feelings: Explorations in affect development and meaning.* Hillsdale, NJ: Analytic Press.

Brown, D. (1993). "The path of meditation: Affective development and psychological well-being," In S. Ablon, D. Brown, E. Khantzian & J. Mack (Eds.) *Human feelings: Explorations in affect development and meaning.* Hillsdale, NJ: Analytic Press.

Brown, D. (1995). "Types of suggestibility and their applicability to memory distortion in trauma treatment," In J. L. Albert (Ed.), *Delayed Memories of Abuse*, (pp.61-100) Northvale, NJ: Jason Aronson.

Brown, D., Scheflin, A.W., Frischholz, E.J. & Caploe, J. (2002). "Special methodologies in memory retrieval: Chemical, hypnotic, and imagery procedures," In R. I. Simon & D.W. Schuman (Eds.). *Retrospective assessment of mental states in litigation; Predicting the past.* (pp. 369-423) Washington, D.C.:American Psychiatric Association Press.

Brown, D. (2003) "The evolving standard of psychological testing in forensic evaluations," In. R.I. Simon & L.H. Gold (Eds.). *A textbook in forensic psychiatry: Guidelines for assessment.* (pp. 601-635) Washington, D.C.: American Psychiatric Press.

Brown, D. (2009). "Assessment of attachment and abuse history, and adult attachment style," In C. Courtois & J. Ford (Eds.). *Complex traumatic stress disorders: An evidence-based clinician's guide.* (Pp. 124-144) New York: Gulford.

Axelrad, D., Brown, D., Wain, H. (2009; 2016). Hypnosis, In. H.I. Kaplan, A.M. Freeman & B.J. Sadock, (pp. 2804-2832). *Comprehensive textbook of psychiatry.*

Brown, D. (2015). "Body meditation in the Tibetan Buddhist and Bon Traditions," In G. Marlock & H.C. Weise (Eds.) (pp.921-928) *Handbook of body psychotherapy and somatic psychology.* (2nd. ed.).

Brown, D. (2016) "Afterward". In A. Raz & M. Lifshitz (Eds.) (pp. 449-458) *Hypnosis and meditation.*

Steele, H., Brown, D. Sinason, V. (2017). "Bindung und complexes trauma" [Attachment and complex trauma: Essential conditions for treatment of survivors of child abuse]. In K.H. Brisch (Ed.). (pp., 92-112) *Bindungs-traumatisierungen: Wenn bindungspersonen zu tatern warden [Treating attachment disorders—Conference proceedings].* Munich, Germany: Klett-Cotta.

JOURNALS:

Krippner, S. & Brown, D. Field Independence /Dependence and Electrosone 50 Induced Altered States of Consciousness, J. Clin. Psych., 1973, 29: 316-319.

Krippner, S. & Brown, D. Altered States of Consciousness and Mystical-Religious Experience: Methodological Perspectives, Research J. of Phil. & Soc. Sci., 1975, # (1): 39-76.

Brown, D. A Model for the Levels of Concentrative Meditation, Int.J. of Clin. & Exp. Hypnosis, 1977, 25:236-273.

Brown, D. & Fromm, E. Selected Bibliography of Readings in Altered States of Consciousness (ASC) in Normal Individuals, Int. J. of Clin. & Exp. Hypnosis, 1977, 25: 388-391.

Brown, D. & Engler, J. The Stages of Mindfulness Meditation: A Validation Study, J. of Transpersonal Psychology, 1980, 12: 143-192.

Fromm, E., Brown, D., Hurt, D., Oberlander, J., Boxer, A., & Pfeiffer, G. The Phenomena and Characteristics of Self-Hypnosis, Int. J. of Clinic. & Exp. Hypnosis, 1981, 29:189-246.

Shapiro, D., Shapiro, J., Walsh, R. & Brown, D. The Effects of Intensive Meditation on Sex-Role Identification: Implications for a Control Model of Psychological Health, Psychol. Reports, 1982, 51: 44-46.

Brown, D., Forte, M., Rich, P. & Epstein, G. Phenomenological Differences Among Self Hypnosis, Mindfulness Meditation & Imagining, Imagination, Cognition & Personality, 1983, 2: 291-309.

Brown, D.P. & Engler, J.E. An Outcome Study of Intensive Mindfulness Meditation, J. Psychoanalytic Study of Society, 1984, 10: 163-225.

Klagsbrun, J. & Brown, D. Getting the Picture: The Use of Imagery to Clarify Therapeutic Impasses, Psychotherapy: Theory, Research & Practice, 1984, 21: 254-259.

Brown, D.P., Forte, M. & Dysart, M. Visual Sensitivity and Mindfulness Meditation, Perceptual and Motor Skills, 1984, 58: 775-784.

Brown, D., Forte, M. & Dysart, M. Visual Sensitivity Differences Among Mindfulness Meditators and Non-Meditators, Perceptual and Motor Skills, 1984, 58: 727-733.

Brown, D. Hypnosis as an Adjunct to the Psychotherapy of the Severely Disturbed Patient: An Affective Development Approach, Int. J. of Clin. & Exp. Hypnosis, 1985, 33:281-301.

Forte, M., Brown, D.P. & Dysart, M. Through the Looking Glass: Phenomenological Reports of Advanced Meditators at Visual Threshold, Imagination, Cognition & Personality, 1984-1985, 4 (4): 323-338.

Forte, M., Brown, D. & Dysart, M. Differences in Experience Among Mindfulness Meditators, Imagination, Cognition & Personality, 1987-88, 7 (1), 47-60.

Brown, D. Pseudomemories, the Standard of Science and the Standard of Care in Trauma Treatment, American Journal of Clinical Hypnosis, 1995, 37, 1-24.

Scheflin, A.W. & Brown, D. (Summer, 1996). Repressed memory or dissociative amnesia: What the science says. The Journal of Psychiatry and Law, 24, 143-188.

Brown, D., Scheflin, A.W., & Whitfield, C.W. (Spring, 1999). Recovered memories—the current weight of the evidence in science and in the courts, The Journal of Psychiatry and Law, 27, 5-156.

Brown, D. & Scheflin, A.W. (Fall-Winter, 1999). Factitious disorders and trauma-related diagnoses, The Journal of Psychiatry and Law, 27, 373-422.

Brown, D., Frischholz, E.J., & Scheflin, A.W. (Fall-Winter, 1999). Iatrogenic dissociative identity disorder–An evaluation of the scientific evidence, The Journal of Psychiatry and Law, 27, 549-638.

Scheflin, A.W. & Brown, D. (Fall-Winter, 1999). The false litigant syndrome: "Nobody would say that unless it was the truth," The Journal of Psychiatry and Law, 27, 649-705.

Brown, D. (2001). (Mis)representations of the long-term effects of childhood sexual abuse in the courts, Journal of Child Sexual Abuse, 9, 79-107.

Van der Hart, O., Nijenhuis, E., Steele, K. & Brown, D. (2005), Trauma-related dissociation: Conceptual clarity lost and found, Australian & New Zealand Journal of Psychaitry.

Brown, D. (2007). Evidence-based hypnotherapy for asthma: A critical review, Special Edition on Evidence-Based Hypnotherapy. International Journal of Clinical and Experimental Hypnosis, 55(2), 1-30.

Brown, D. (2009). The energy body and its functions: Immuno-surveillance, longevity, and regeneration, New York Academy of Sciences, 1172, 312-337.

Brown, D. (2009). Mastery of the mind East and West; Excellence in being and doing and everyday happiness, New York Academy of Sciences, 1172, 231-251.

Baker, R.L. & Brown, D. (2015). On engagement: Learning to pay attention. Special edition on "Balance in Legal Education Symposium" University of Arkansas Law Review, 36, 337-385.

Schoenberg, P., Ruf, A., Churchill, J., Brown, D. & Brewer, J. (2018). Mapping complex mind states: EEG neural substrates of meditative unified compassionate awareness, Consciousness & Cognition, Jan, Vol 57, pages 41-53.